Emergency Law in Independent Ireland, 1922–1948

Emergency Law in Independent Ireland 1922–1948

Seosamh Ó Longaigh

FOUR COURTS PRESS

Set in 11 on 12.5 Ehrhardt for
FOUR COURTS PRESS LTD
7 Malpas Street, Dublin 8, Ireland
e-mail: info@four-courts-press.ie
http://www.four-courts-press.ie
and in North America
FOUR COURTS PRESS
c/o ISBS, 920 N.E. 58th Avenue, Suite 300, Portland, OR 97213.

ISBN (10 digit) 1–85182–922–9
ISBN (13 digit) 978-1–85182–922–4

Printed in England by
MPG Books, Bodmin, Cornwall

Contents

Preface

Emergency and extraordinary laws were a fact of life in Ireland for hundreds of years before independence. The eighteenth century was notable for statutes that sought to deal with the 'Whiteboys', 'Tumultuous Risings', the United Irishmen and the effects of the 1798 rising.[1] The nineteenth century was marked by a plethora of temporary 'Coercion Acts', and in 1887 the Westminster parliament introduced the permanent Criminal Law and Procedure (Ireland) Act to counter the ever-present difficulties involved in enforcing criminal law in Ireland.[2] During the early twentieth century, the British government also employed the Defence of the Realm Act, 1914 and the Restoration of Order (Ireland) Act, 1920 in Ireland; in late 1920, it introduced martial law to a number of counties in the south of Ireland.[3]

The coming of independence in 1921 did not end the phenomenon of almost permanent public safety legislation. There remained an apparent ambivalence towards the administration of the law among some of the population. More importantly, the Irish Republican Army – the IRA – and its opposition to the independent Irish state repeatedly challenged successive governments to formulate effective measures that would enable the state contend with the organization and its activities. The ordinary criminal law that Ireland inherited from England proved wholly inadequate when employed against the IRA. Between 1922 and 1948, provision for internment was created on seven occasions,[4] and special courts were devised on six.[5] Additionally, special powers of arrest, detention and interrogation were formulated and, on occasion, changes were made to the rules of evidence.

Beginning in 1922, this book considers each public safety bill drafted prior to 1948. It not only examines particular departures from the ordinary law or the special powers devised, but also seeks to understand why and how 29 separate public safety measures were drafted during the state's

1 See G. Hogan and C. Walker, *Political violence and the law in Ireland* (1989), pp 12–14. 2 See generally C. Townshend, *Political violence in Ireland: government and resistance since 1848* (1983); A.V. Dicey, *England's case against home rule* (1886); L. Curtis, *Coercion and conciliation in Ireland, 1880–92* (1963). 3 C. Campbell, *Emergency law in Ireland, 1918–1925* (1994), pp 8–148. 4 In 1922, 1923, 1924, 1926, 1939 (twice), 1940. 5 In 1922, 1927, 1931, 1939, 1940, 1941.

first 26 years of existence; and it further examines how these laws actually worked in practice – the experiences of agencies enforcing these laws and their effects on anti-state organizations. One aim of the book is to understand why it took 17 years to develop the Offences against the State Act, 1939, and why no substantive anti-subversion measure has been introduced since. The book also looks at the Irish state's responses to the two major emergencies that have confronted it – the Civil War and World War II.

Thus, a clear picture is provided of the government's perception of the problems faced, the objectives it sought, and the solutions it proposed. The book is partly an examination of the functioning of government, of how government departments and agencies, particularly the Gardaí, cooperated and were coordinated, how they communicated, and how they formulated legislation. The impact of the Oireachtas (the Dáil – the lower house of parliament; the Seanad – the upper house) and of the courts on legislation is also considered.

I was able to undertake this work by exploiting the vast amount of documents released by government departments for public viewing under the National Archives Acts, 1987 to 1993, particularly by the department of Home Affairs/Justice. These are combined with files from the department of the President of the Executive Council[6]/an Taoiseach.[7] Complementary sources include material from the attorney general's office, as well as files from the departments of Defence, Finance, and Foreign Affairs. I have also relied on a number of private papers. Interestingly, strict government secrecy in the past has ensured that documents were quite explicit: government ministers, civil servants and senior police officers considered problems, articulated views, and proposed solutions with definite frankness.

This book would not have been possible were it not for the assistance of so many different people. I would like to express my gratitude to my publisher, Four Courts Press, and particularly to Martin Fanning and Michael Adams. I would also like to say a special thank you to the staff of the Department of History, UCC, in particular to Professor Dermot Keogh who supervised the original thesis on which this book is based, as well as to Professor Joe Lee and Gabriel Doherty. I would also like to thank Richard Haslam of the Department of Public Administration and Professor David Gwynn Morgan of the Department of Law.

I am indebted to the many archivists who helped me along the way: Tom Quinlan and Catherine Crowe of the National Archives, Bishop Street, Dublin; the staff of the National Library of Ireland, Kildare Street, Dublin; Seamus Helferty of the Archives Department, UCD, Dublin;

6 Until 1937. 7 D/T S. files.

Victor Laing and the late Peter Young of the Military Archives, Cathal Brugha Barracks, Dublin; Fr Ignatius Fennessy, Dún Mhuire, Killiney, Co. Dublin, custodian of some of Éamon de Valera's papers; the late Caoimhghin Ó Beóláin gave me access to some department of Justice documents; and Fr Thomas Davitt gave me access to his father's memoir of his time as judge advocate general of the National Army, 1922-3.

Several other people gave up their time very generously in order to help me fill various gaps in the information I had gathered: Marcus Bourke and Vincent Grogan of the Parliamentary Draftsman's Office; Peter Touhy of Brendan Touhy and Co., Co. Mayo; Michael J. Egan, Castlebar, Co. Mayo; Tomás de Bhulbh, Ruairí Ó Brádaigh, Mick McCarthy, Máirtín Calligan, Muiris Ó Muimhneacháin, Dónal J. Browne, Mr Justice Thomas Finlay, Pauric Dempsey, Royal Irish Academy, and J. Bowyer Bell helped me to track down documents and people or shared their memories of the period 1922-48. I would also like to thank the staff of Enterprise Registry Solutions for their support and encouragement during this project. Finally, I would like to thank Liam Ó Longaigh, Klair O'Brien and Mícheál Ó Mulláin for proof reading and observations.

All omissions and errors remain the responsibility of myself.

To Assiya

1

The Civil War, 1922–1924

The bombardment on the morning of 28 June 1922 of the IRA garrison occupying the Four Courts in Dublin marked the effective birth of the modern Irish state. The provisional government finally calculated that it was both militarily and politically strong enough to enforce the sovereignty of the Irish state and to crush armed elements that stood in defiance of its authority and in opposition to the 'Articles of Agreement for a Treaty between Great Britain and Ireland' – 'the Treaty' – that formally established the new state. Michael Collins, chairman of the provisional government and commander-in-chief of the new state's army, declared, 'the safety of the Nation is the first law and henceforth we shall not rest until we have established the Authority of the people of Ireland in every square mile of its jurisdiction'.[1] Although the British government exerted significant pressure on the provisional government to act, the Irish denied any British involvement in the assault.[2] Its forces, 'the National Army', cleared Dublin's occupied buildings of anti-Treaty forces by 5 July 1922,[3] and quickly moved into the country.

Over six months had passed since the signing of the Treaty – a compromise between British willingness to grant limited autonomy (home rule) under the Government of Ireland Act, 1920[4] and the Irish nationalist demand for full independence.[5] It marked the culmination of over five years of conflict that began with the proclamation of the Irish Republic during the Easter Rising in April 1916. For most of the island of Ireland, it also marked the end of centuries of conflict that had seen English conquest and reconquest, the dispossession of the Irish of their lands, the suppression of their language, laws, religion, customs and, eventually, the decay of Gaelic society. But as the author of *Irish Nationalism*, Seán Cronin, argued, 'The Irish did not recognize that conquest gave any other right than the right of permanent resistance.'[6] English rule could only be

1 *Irish Independent*, 29 June 1922. 2 M. Valiulis, *Portrait of a revolutionary: General Richard Mulcahy and the foundation of the Irish state* (1992), p. 155. 3 M. Hopkinson, *Green against green: the Irish civil war* (1988), pp 123–6. 4 See generally N. Mansergh, *The unresolved question: the Anglo-Irish Settlement and its undoing, 1912–72* (1991); J.J. Lee, *Ireland*, p. 46. 5 See Hopkinson, *Green*, pp 19–33. 6 S. Cronin, *Irish nationalism: a history of its roots and ideology* (1980), p. 8.

maintained by a large army and extraordinary laws – penal laws, test acts, and countless coercion measures.[7] At times, the most extreme forms of repression were employed.

At the heart of the problem were the issues of land ownership and of governing the country. By the early twentieth century, though, the land question had been largely resolved and nationalists had taken control of local government. All that was absent was an independent central government; Seán Cronin wrote: 'the final phase in the independence struggle, from 1916 to 1921, had political, not social or economic goals'.[8] While the nationalist movement established an alternative parliament (the Dáil) and developed an alternative court system, it was the IRA's guerrilla campaign during the War of Independence from 1919 to 1921 that finally forced a settlement of the 'Irish question', though not a defeat of the British army.

The Treaty gave the Irish a central government, but imposed a number of limitations on Irish sovereignty insisted that members of the Oireachtas take an oath to be faithful to the British crown, and provided that a number of ports would remain under British control. It also confirmed the partition of the country into 26 southern and 6 north-eastern counties. By 1921, however, the north-east of Ireland had evolved economically, culturally, socially and politically differently from the rest of the island, and a majority of voters there believed that British rule had been central to the north-east's prosperity and that only continued union with Britain would perpetuate that prosperity. However much nationalists objected to partition, the nationalist movement failed to develop a strong strategy for the northeast of Ireland that would encourage unionists to join the southern state or, failing that, to support the sizeable nationalist minority there.[9]

Nevertheless, the Treaty would be supported by a majority of voters in the south of Ireland (the area which would become the Irish Free State), the Catholic Church, businessmen, large farmers, southern unionists, and most of the press.[10] Support was not unanimous, however. While pragmatists saw the Treaty as a stepping-stone to the republic, 'the freedom to achieve freedom', such was the spectrum of Irish nationalism that many reacted with horror when they heard its terms. The movement that

7 See C. Townshend, *Political violence in Ireland: government and resistance since 1848* (1983), pp 60–3, 88, 131–7; Cronin, *Irish nationalism*, pp 18–20. 8 Cronin, *Irish nationalism*, p. 28. 9 See J.J. Lee, 'The significance of the First Dáil', in B. Farrell (ed.), *The creation of the Dáil* (1994), p. 138 and A. Mitchell, *Revolutionary government in Ireland: Dáil Éireann, 1919–22* (1995), p. 167. 10 Cronin, *Irish nationalism*, pp 137–9; Hopkinson, *Green*, pp 35–7.

emerged after the 1916 Rising collapsed shortly after December 1921. As the historian Michael Hopkinson observed, its 'unity and coherence ... was a very superficial one'.[11] Sinn Féin, which had led the national movement since 1917, was split by the agreement. President of the Dáil, Éamon de Valera, had accepted the need for compromise, but only if the northern question was settled favourably.[12] Some, though, would only be satisfied with a wholly independent 32 county republic. Yet, as Seán Cronin noted, 'No Republican leader attempted to rally the people behind the Republic [proclaimed in 1916] they had sworn to defend.' Indeed, few anti-Treaty leaders clarified their opposition on anything other than legalisms, such as the oath. And certainly, very few believed that partition might be in any way permanent.[13] Michael Collins contended that the Treaty's boundary commission 'would make a political impossibility out of the Northern government'.[14] The Dáil voted 64 votes to 57 in favour of the agreement on 4 January 1922.

The most worrying consequence of the Treaty was its effects on the IRA.[15] While the IRA's General Headquarters (GHQ) supported it, several influential IRA commanders (including Liam Lynch and Ernie O'Malley) dismissed the agreement. Indeed, the most active areas during the War of Independence tended to oppose the Treaty; apparently, only loyalty to Michael Collins and Richard Mulcahy (IRA chief of staff during the War of Independence) prevented greater numbers challenging it.[16] Years later, Mulcahy explained that he believed that rejection of the agreement would force the IRA into renewed war, but, unlike what happened in the War of Independence, it would face an unfettered British army.[17]

In the altered circumstances of January 1922, Mulcahy was appointed minister for Defence, and Eoin O'Duffy succeeded him as chief of staff. Almost immediately, the provisional government set about organizing an army (the 'National Army'), drawing on pro-Treaty IRA, ex-British soldiers and Dublin's unemployed.[18] The British supplied arms.[19]

Tensions within the IRA quickly grew, though the provisional government managed to stave off confrontation for several months. Meanwhile, the possibility of conflict increased as the British army evacuated their posts throughout the country and concentrated in Dublin and

11 Hopkinson, *Green*, p. 4. 12 Ibid., pp 38–40; J. Bowman, *De Valera and the Ulster question, 1917–73* (1982), p. 65. 13 Cronin, *Irish nationalism*, pp 133–6, 148. 14 Quoted by G. Dangerfield, *The damnable question: a study in Anglo-Irish relations* (1976), p. 339. 15 See generally Valiulis, *Mulcahy*, pp 111–39. 16 Hopkinson, *Green*, pp 40–6. 17 Valiulis, *Mulcahy*, p. 115. 18 Hopkinson, *Green*, pp 60–2; Campbell, *Emergency law*, p. 156; T. Garvin, *1922: The birth of Irish democracy* (1996), pp 116–17. 19 R. Fanning, *Independent Ireland* (1983), p. 16.

the Curragh. Local IRA units occupied the abandoned barracks, irrespective of their attitude to the Treaty.[20]

On 26 March 1922, the IRA rejected the Treaty and elected a new executive. In reality, though, the only certainty was the anti-Treaty IRA's disapproval of the Anglo-Irish agreement. More seriously, on 14 April, anti-Treaty forces occupied the Four Courts and other buildings in Dublin, clearly exposing the failure of the provisional government's authority. Although the anti-Treaty forces held the military advantage in the early months of 1922, they failed to take the military initiative against the provisional government or even to develop a coherent strategy. On 18 June, the IRA held another convention and the Co. Cork IRA leader Tom Barry proposed restarting the war against the British army, but was outvoted. Indeed, not only did no coherent anti-Treaty IRA strategy emerge, but the organization split again.[21]

While republicans squabbled over the oath, the British and Irish governments began implementing the Treaty. The British prime minister, David Lloyd George, appointed the Provisional Government of Ireland Committee to oversee the transfer of administrative powers and functions to the Provisional Government. The terms of the transfer were decided by early February 1922 and given legislative effect the following month by the Irish Free State (Agreement) Act, 1922. On 1 April 1922, the departments of the Provisional Government were given legal powers by the Provisional Government (Transfer of Functions) Order, 1922. Matters transferred did not relate to the services proposed by the Government of Ireland Act, 1920, but to 'the functions in connection with the administration of public services in Southern Ireland heretofore performed by existing Government Departments and officers'.[22] Within a week of the Treaty being signed, Hugh Kennedy, the provisional government's law officer and future attorney general, wrote that the 'Provisional Government is for purposes of administration only', adding that, 'the purpose for which it is being set up, viz. administration, will control its operations and … it will not function in the full sense as a Parliament'.[23] In addition to organizing an army, the provisional government needed to set up a new court system and a police force,[24] to draft a constitution and to hold elections to a constitution assembly.

The early months of 1922 had seen several initiatives seeking to bridge the divide between the pro- and anti-Treaty camps. Although the com-

20 Valiulis, *Mulcahy*, pp 127–33. 21 Hopkinson, *Green*, pp 58–73, 115–18; Valiulis, *Mulcahy*, p. 152. 22 The Treaty was ratified in England by this act. See Hopkinson, *Green*, p. 55, Campbell, *Emergency law*, pp 152–3. 23 Hugh Kennedy Papers, UCDAD, P4/301/3,9. 24 See Hopkinson, *Green*, pp 52, 90–2; C. Brady, *Guardians of the peace* (1974), pp 37–88.

mittee established to draft a constitution was racked by disagreement, the final draft delivered represented a genuine attempt to accommodate a large proportion of anti-Treaty sentiment,[25] so much so that David Lloyd George dismissed it as 'a complete evasion' of the Treaty.[26]

Michael Collins had also proposed that both pro- and anti-Treaty candidates jointly contest the forth-coming general election as a Sinn Féin panel, representative of the strength of both blocs in the Dáil at the time. Afterwards a cabinet, consisting of five pro-Treaty and four anti-Treaty TDs would be formed. An increasingly divided Sinn Féin supported the initiative on 21 May 1922. The British government, however, dismissed the pact and ordered major revisions of the draft constitution, which were immediately implemented.[27]

As a result, Collins was forced to repudiate the election pact, having nothing but the Treaty to offer its opponents. On 14 June 1922, he told voters in Cork that they should vote for the candidate of their choice. By early June 1922, therefore, the constitutional limits of the Irish Free State were clearly defined, and the only significant obstacle to the establishment of the Irish Free State was the anti-Treaty IRA. The general election held on 16 June 1922[28] showed that a large majority of voters in the South supported the Treaty.[29] The minister for Home Affairs, Kevin O'Higgins, who guided the constitution through the Dáil in September and October 1922, described the document as 'a strict but fair interpretation of the Treaty'. He conceded, 'we did not drive the British out of the country … If we had been able to do it, the things that are in the Treaty and that are in the Constitution, that many find irksome, would not be there.'[30]

Under article 1 of the constitution, the Irish Free State became 'a co-equal member' of the British Commonwealth. Article 12 created a legislature (the 'Oireachtas'), consisting of the British king and two houses of parliament – 'Dáil Éireann' (the lower house) and 'Seanad Éireann' (the senate). Controversially, article 17 required members of the Oireachtas to take an oath of allegiance to 'the Constitution of the Irish Free State as by law established' and to be 'faithful to H. M. King George V., his heirs and successors' before taking their seats.

25 Hopkinson, *Green*, pp 105–8, D.H. Akenson and J.F. Fallin, 'The Irish Civil War and the drafting of the Free State constitution' (Winter 1970), p. 24. 26 Hopkinson, *Green*, p. 106. 27 Akenson and Fallin, 'The Free State constitution' (Winter 1970), pp 55–9, 63–6. 28 Results announced on 24 June 1922. 29 35 anti-Treaty candidates were elected, pro-Treaty Sinn Féin gained 58 seats and others 35 (also pro-Treaty). The constitution was only finally published on the day of the poll, McEntee Papers, UCDAD, P67/534, 'Departmental Notes on Events', p. 205. 30 Dáil Debates vol. 1 col. 360–1, 18 Sept. 1922.

Additionally, article 6 provided that 'the liberty of the person is inviolable, and no person shall be deprived of his liberty except in accordance with law' and reaffirmed the right to habeas corpus. It also provided, however, 'that nothing in [article 6] shall be invoked to prohibit, control or interfere with any act of the military forces of the Irish Free State during the existence of a state of war or armed rebellion.'

Article 70 provided that 'No one shall be tried save in due course of law, and ... Military Tribunals shall not be extended to or exercised over the civil population save in time of war, or armed rebellion ... Such jurisdiction shall not be exercised in any area in which all civil courts are open or capable of being held, and no person shall be removed from one area to another for the purpose of creating such jurisdiction.' Article 72 declared that 'No person shall be tried on any criminal charge without a jury save in the case of charges in respect of minor offences triable by law before a Court of Summary Jurisdiction and in the case of charges for offences against military law triable by Court Martial or other Military Tribunal.'

In the first weeks of the war, the anti-Treaty IRA (the 'Irregulars', as the provisional government now called it) operating outside of Dublin was capable of effective military action, but despite initially effecting a large number of attacks, successful military operations were rarely, if ever, followed up or exploited. As the National Army moved into the country, it dislodged the IRA from the barracks and towns it had occupied since early 1922. Typically, the IRA withdrew in the face of National Army artillery and armoured cars. The conflict rapidly transformed from one of open conventional warfare to guerrilla warfare.[31]

As the nature of the conflict changed, the provisional government ordered that only persons found in arms should be arrested; other anti-Treatyites would be ignored.[32] On 25 July 1922, Collins suggested that in areas where conventional warfare ended, but attacks and ambushes continued, for example on trains, 'military areas' could be established and special punishments devised for those found carrying arms without proper authority. The provisional government said it would 'support the military authorities in whatever steps they consider necessary to restore order',[33] but W.T. Cosgrave, who assumed the role of chairman of the provisional government while Collins was on military duties, went further, proposing that proclamations be issued warning that 'troops have orders to shoot persons found sniping, ambushing, or in possession of bombs, or interfering with railways or road communications, in areas where military oper-

31 Hopkinson, *Green*, pp 142–71. 32 Campbell, *Emergency law*, pp 159, 179–81, D/T S.1369/3, 16 July 1922, minutes of the provisional government, 17 July 1922. 33 Minutes of provisional government, 25 July 1922, D/T S.1376; Campbell, *Emergency law*, p. 159.

ations have ceased'. Collins was opposed to what was essentially an order to shoot IRA members on sight, even if unarmed; he conceded that the proposal would be defensible when a person 'deliberately shoots a soldier and then throws down his rifle and puts up his hands'.[34]

The National Army quickly extended itself into almost all areas of the state, including the southern counties where the IRA initially appeared to be strongest. By 1 August 1922, it recorded losses of 59 dead and 160 injured, and the capture of 1,986 IRA prisoners. The IRA had evacuated Enniscorthy and Wexford on 8 July 1922 and Limerick on 21 July 1922; the National Army sailed for Cork city on 7 August 1922, which it quickly captured. By early August 1922, only Counties Waterford, Cork, Kerry and Limerick continued to pose definite military problems. The army claimed that a programme of reorganization taking place at that time would see the IRA contained within two weeks.[35]

Collins believed if the problems in the southern counties were resolved, 'Parliament should be summoned, and the questions of Police, Courts, and the necessary punishments for people found guilty of breaking Railways, cutting telegraph wires, looting, carrying arms unauthorisedly, etc., settled.' Once those issues were attended to, he suggested, the army's role could be redefined as one where it co-operated with the police. It was essential, he believed, that the police take up their duties in the south. Doubtless, in many areas, security circumstances would have to improve dramatically before the unarmed police – the Garda Síochána – and the courts could operate effectively.

In the west, Collins wanted to reduce the army's presence to a minimum, though it could not be completely removed because of various dangers faced there. For instance, a column of about 70 men under Frank Carty TD was operating around Tubbercurry and Swinford in Co. Mayo; a column of about 250 men was operating north and south of Sligo town, under the command of James Devins TD and General Liam Pilkington.

In the south of the country, the army was attempting to further establish itself in key areas. Collins hoped this would convince the IRA it had 'lost their grip on the people' and was facing defeat. He was unsure if this could be completed before 12 August 1922, but argued that if the provisional government had to postpone the opening of the new Dáil it would signify how seriously the government wanted to 'clean up this matter definitely', and thus prevent 'the Irregulars in the south feeling that as soon as we came definitely up against them, we hesitated to face them boldly,

34 Cosgrave to Collins 27 July 1922, Collins to Cosgrave 29 July 1922, P7/B/29, quoted in Valiulis, *Mulcahy*, p. 165, C. Campbell, *Emergency law*, p. 159. 35 Campbell, *Emergency law*, p. 156 and D/T S.3361.

and turned aside from the job, and called Parliament'.[36] (The new Dáil assembled on 9 September 1922, though without anti-Treaty TDs.)

In response to its initial military failures, on 19 August 1922 the anti-Treaty IRA reverted to flying columns (Active Service Units – ASU), which it had employed during the War of Independence, relying mainly on guerrilla and sabotage tactics. Despite Collins' optimistic report of 5 August 1922, it seemed that decisive victory over the IRA was some way off. Indeed, army successes during the first two months of the war had, on a number of counts, been superficial. Eoin O'Duffy reported on 22 August 1922, 'Our forces have captured towns, but they have not captured Irregulars and arms on anything like a large scale.'[37] Michael Collins was killed in an ambush that day. After this, W.T. Cosgrave became chairman of the provisional government and Mulcahy commander-in-chief.

Although the conflict appeared to have reached a stalemate, the anti-Treaty IRA's circumstances remained precarious. Its forces were poorly organized, communications between its headquarters, divisions and ASUs were badly managed, and orders often went unheeded. Further, the IRA lacked the vigour that it exhibited during the War of Independence, and the public support and tolerance that had been a feature of the earlier conflict was more often than not absent.[38]

The search for a peaceful resolution continued throughout the autumn of 1922, but a meeting between Richard Mulcahy and Éamon de Valera on 6 September convinced the minister for Defence that there were no grounds for compromise and that extraordinary methods were needed to end the war.[39] Mulcahy reported his meeting to the provisional government the following day, and for the first time it seems that a policy of executions was seriously considered.[40] As Ernest Blythe, the minister for Local Government, explained to the first judge advocate general, Cahir Davitt,[41] later that month, 'drastic action' was needed to end the fighting because 'when any "Irregulars" were cornered they seldom if ever fought it out but usually surrendered tamely, knowing that the worst that could

36 D/T S.3361, Collins to Cosgrave, 5 Aug. 1922. 37 Hopkinson, *Green*, p. 172. 38 Ibid., pp 174–5; Valiulis, *Mulcahy*, pp 166–7. 39 T.P. Coogan, *De Valera: long fellow, long shadow* (1993), pp 333–4, Hopkinson, *Green*, pp 183–5. 40 Minutes of the Provisional Government, 7 Sept. 1922. 41 (1894–1986) son of the Land Leaguer and Fenian, Michael Davitt, called to the Bar in Jan. 1916, he later worked in the Dáil courts during War of Independence. Appointed judge advocate general, 15 Aug. 1922, he was permitted to recommence his practice at the Bar on 16 June 1924, and was appointed temporary assistant judge of the circuit court on 27 Nov. 1926. Gearóid Ó Súilleabháin succeeded him in the office of judge advocate general on 1 Apr. 1927. See Davitt memoir and D/T S.5357A, 7 Apr. 1932. See also P4/258, memorandum by Hugh Kennedy, 7 Aug. 1922.

happen them was a period of internment during which they would be freely supported at the expense of the State. There was … no element of deterrent effect in this.'[42]

But before such a policy could be pursued, a number of issues had to be satisfactorily settled, primarily because the provisional parliament's legislative powers were unclear.[43] Several questions were addressed to Hugh Kennedy. He explained that, in the first instance, laws could only relate to administrative issues, and were restricted in a number of ways.[44] They could be:

1. concerned only with the functions which at the moment under consideration have been actually transferred to the Provisional Government,
2. concerned only with the 26 counties,
3. provisional only, that is to say, concerned only with matters of administration during the period which began on the 6th December 1921 and will end upon the constitution of a Parliament and government of the Irish Free State, or the 6th December 1922, whichever the sooner.

Second, the provisional parliament was restricted from making laws in relation to certain matters:

1. for imposing taxation, or
2. of a permanent character or operating beyond the limit of time already mentioned, or
3. affecting the six North-Eastern counties, or
4. relating to functions or Departments not yet transferred.

Regarding royal assent, which was required before laws would be formally enacted, he wrote:

> I am of the opinion that the office and the functions of the Lord Lieutenant as such have ceased in the twenty-six counties since the passing of the Irish Free State Agreement Act. The time for appointment of a Governor General has not yet arrived. For the purpose of administering the twenty-six counties during the present interval, the

42 Cahir Davitt memoir. 43 The constituent assembly, meeting as the third Dáil, finally assembled on 9 Sept. 1922. See L. Kohn, *The constitution of the Irish Free State* (1932), p. 70. The constitution bill was introduced on 18 Sept. 1922, and received final approval on 25 Oct. 1922. 44 D/T S.1735, 13 Sept. 1922.

> Provisional Government is in my opinion in the position of both these functionaries. But legislation raises the difficult question of assent. By whom is assent to be given? It may well be argued by the British that the King's personal assent is requisite.[45]

The question of royal assent was indeed delicate. Ernest Blythe explained the situation to the Dáil thus:

> There is no power in this Dáil to legislate without Royal Assent; so far as the Free State Agreement goes, that is the only power it has, unless it chooses to exercise the inherent, inalienable and indefeasible power it has to repudiate the Treaty. There is no power unless we choose now to have this Royal Assent given, other that the matter that we laid down in our Constitution, and we are not prepared to do that. And consequently for all practical purposes the Dáil has not the power.[46]

In view of these boundaries, Kennedy proposed 'confining the legislative work of the parliament to resolutions on the subjects within the power of the parliament', and by introducing confirmatory legislation after the enactment of the constitution. Resolutions could be presented thus: 'The Provisional Government with the concurrence of the Provisional Parliament hereby resolve and decree that, etc.'[47]

In possession of this information, Mulcahy returned to the Provisional Government on 15 September 1922 and sought the introduction and use of military courts and committees to the 26 Counties. His proposal was formally accepted and, on 18 September 1922, Hugh Kennedy was instructed to prepare the necessary resolution for submission to the Dáil.[48] The Army (Emergency Powers) Resolution was drafted by 25 September 1922, and approved, subject to certain amendments.

The Army (Emergency Powers) Resolution sanctioned the establishment of military courts and committees to enquire into various offences provided each court or committee included, as a member, at least one person nominated by the minister of Defence and certified by the law officer to be a person of 'legal knowledge and experience'.[49] The military courts and committees could investigate a range of offences, included 'tak-

45 D/T S.1735, 'Supplemental Opinion, Legislative Powers of the Provisional Parliament', Hugh Kennedy to the secretary of the Provisional Government, 15 Sept. 1922. 46 Dáil Debates vol. 2 col. 2040, quoted in Campbell, *Emergency law*, p. 246. 47 D/T S.1735, Hugh Kennedy to the secretary of the provisional government, 15 Sept. 1922. 48 D/T S.1746. 49 Paragraph 1(a).

ing part in or aiding or abetting any attack upon or using force against the National Forces'; looting, arson, destruction, seizure, unlawful possession or removal of or damage to any property; possession without proper authority of explosives, firearms or ammunition; and the breach of any general order or regulation made by the army authorities.[50] Punishment could be death, penal servitude for any period, imprisonment for any period or a fine of any amount either with or without imprisonment. The resolution also permitted the imprisonment 'of all or any person taken prisoner, arrested or detained by the National forces',[51] and the control of firearms[52] by the army authorities.[53]

Introducing the resolution on 27 September 1922, W.T. Cosgrave warned that 'those who persist in ... murderous attacks must learn that they have got to pay the penalty for them.' The minister for External Affairs, Desmond Fitzgerald, added, 'On an occasion like the present there is no opportunity, and there is no justification, for any quibbling about legality or anything else ... the reign of law is going to be enforced, and we are not going to be turned aside by any mawkishness or any other consideration.' W.T. Cosgrave assured TDs that 'A thing that struck the Ministry, and not alone the present Ministry, but the previous one – I mean by the previous one the late President and the late Commander-in-Chief – was, that as soon as an area had been cleared, such as Dublin, of Irregular troops, we would decide to take this action on a given date.' He promised that prisoners would be treated well, but 'we are not going to treat rebels as prisoners of war'.[54] A short period of amnesty would be offered before military tribunals were established.[55] Furthermore, the minister for Home Affairs, Kevin O'Higgins, promised that ordinary civil courts would be established as soon as possible, though they would not deal with the offences covered by the Resolution: 'There will be the ordinary civil jurisdiction for the ordinary offences, and concurrently with it there must be in many places Military Courts also.'[56]

Before the proposed military courts could be established to try civilians, the National Army first had to organize its own legal department to conduct legal matters normally concerning an army. A legal section, headed by a judge advocate general, would be attached to the adjutant-general's office and would conduct courts martial and administer military law gen-

50 Paragraph 1(b)(1)–(4). **51** Paragraph 1(c). **52** Paragraph 1(d). **53** The army council was constituted on 28 Sept. 1922: Richard Mulcahy, commander-in-chief; S. Mac Mathghamhna, chief of staff; Gearóid Ó Súilleabháin, adjutant general; Joseph McGrath, director of intelligence; Diarmaid O'Hegarty, director of organization. **54** Dáil Debates vol. 1 col. 807–8, 809–810, 875, 27 Sept. 1922. **55** P4/542, Kevin O'Shiel, assistant legal adviser, to Cosgrave, 28 Sept. 1922. **56** Dáil Debates vol. 1 col. 918, 28 Sept. 1922.

erally. The former Dáil court judge Cahir Davitt was appointed judge advocate general on 15 August 1922. He later recalled that the position did not initially appeal to him because he envisaged having to undertake a large amount of organizational work and learning. He also appreciated that, eventually, he would become responsible for administering military tribunals against the IRA, similar to those employed by the British during the War of Independence.[57]

At this time, T.C. Kingsmill-Moore (the future supreme court justice) was working, more or less, as a war correspondent for the *Irish Times*. Because he was a barrister of three or four years' experience and had some knowledge of military law and courts martial gained during his time in the British army, he had been asked by General W. Murphy[58] to draw up charge sheets and court martial procedures that would enable officers with no knowledge of military law to conduct trials with some degree of formality. Prior to Davitt's appointment, a number of offences had been disposed of by these courts martial. One case involved the attempted shooting of a superior officer; another involved a civilian charged with the larceny of army property, and though not subject to military law, he was sentenced to three years' penal servitude and twelve strokes of the cat to be administered every three months during the first year of detention. Eoin O'Duffy confirmed the sentence, but the flogging was never inflicted. Another case that occurred after Davitt's appointment involved a civilian member of the adjutant general's office who had been charged with spying. Davitt protested that the man was not subject to military law, but he was nonetheless found guilty and sentenced to death. Only when Davitt pointed out that if the man were shot anybody involved in the case afterwards faced trial for murder was the sentenced reduce to penal servitude for life.[59]

Quickly attending to the new role, Davitt first proposed attaching legal staff to the headquarters of each army command, that is, a barrister or a solicitor assisted by officers with knowledge of court martial procedure, though not necessarily with legal qualifications. All legal staff would be appointed by the judge advocate general in consultation with the adjutant general. Davitt next set about actually finding staff.[60] Legal officers included John O'Donovan who later became assistant secretary of the Electricity Supply Board (ESB), Charlie Casey, a future attorney general and high court judge; and Thomas J. Coyne, future secretary of the

57 Davitt memoir. 58 Later commissioner of the Dublin Metropolitan Police. 59 Davitt memoir. 60 Davitt only recalled some of those involved, but these included J.J. Hearne, Joseph Kenny, Gerald McCarthy, Joseph J. Mooney, Charles Wyse Moore, Joseph Reidy, Eugene Sheehy – all junior barristers – and J.J. Bergin, William Cahill, Trant McCarthy, William T. McManamin, who were solicitors.

department of Justice.[61] All three had fought in World War I and remained at army GHQ during the Civil War. At the army's height, it employed 40 or 50 legal staff. During his time as judge advocate general, Davitt maintained his civilian status, acting in an advisory and supervisory role, while George Pope Hodnett[62] (under Davitt's supervision) was responsible for the direction of the legal staff and the administration of military law in the army.[63] When Davitt confessed his ignorance of military law, Hodnett advised him to buy the *British Army Manual of Military Law*, which he promptly did in Eason's bookshop.

As judge advocate general, the task of drawing up regulations governing the proposed military courts and committees fell to Davitt. He drafted *The General Regulations as to Trial of Civilians by Military Courts*[64] within a few days of the Dáil passing the Army Resolution, and submitted the regulations to the provisional government on 3 October. Practical arrangements were promptly attended to – all legal officers were sent to their assigned posts and GHQ legal officers were given new offices and living quarters in Portobello Barracks, Dublin.

The procedure to be followed by military courts was finally communicated to legal staff in the week ending 4 November 1922. Very often, persons were tried on the orders of the army authorities or the provisional government/executive council,[65] though the regulations placed the responsibility for deciding who was to be tried on the local general officer commanding the command where the offence was alleged to have been committed.[66]

Once a decision to prosecute was made, the general officer commanding had to convene the court and affix a time and a place of sitting. At least 48 hours had to pass between a person's arrest and trial.[67] Before

61 Thomas J. Coyne, born 1901, educated in Clongowes Wood College, he served in British airforce during World War I, and later obtained a legal and political science degree from UCD. Called to the Bar in 1922, he became private secretary to Kevin O'Higgins in 1923. He was appointed to the permanent civil service in 1925, and later seconded to the department of External Affairs, he returned to the department of Justice in 1934, becoming principal officer in 1939. He was assistant controller of censorship from Sept. 1939, and controller from Sept. 1941. He became assistant secretary of the department of Justice in 1946, and secretary in 1949. He retired in 1961. 62 Resident of Youghal, Co. Cork, he worked in a solicitor's office. Fought in the war 1914–1918, and during the Civil War organized local volunteers to defend Youghal for the provisional government. 63 The growth in the size of the army necessitated the appointment of clerical staff to assist the legal section. One of those employed in this capacity was Louis Carrig (brother of John Carrig of Bourke and Carrig, Ballina, Co. Mayo, who later worked in the chief state solicitor's office). 64 SRO, 1922, xix, 515. For jurisdiction and powers of these proposed tribunals see Iris Oifigiúil 3 Oct. 1922, press of 12 Oct. 1922. 65 Campbell, *Emergency law*, pp 199–201. 66 Gen Reg. 3(1). 67 Gen. Reg. 7.

being tried, the accused was given a copy of the list of charges against him, an abstract of the evidence, and a list of the names, ranks, and corps of the officers constituting the court.[68] In cases of unauthorized possession of firearms, ammunition or documents or armed robbery, the burden of proof was shifted to accused. Otherwise, the ordinary rules of evidence applied.[69] In addition, the accused was entitled to be represented by counsel and by a solicitor, was to be afforded every reasonable facility 'consistent with military exigencies',[70] and had the right to challenge for cause any court member, save the legal officer.[71] (In practice, though, the anti-Treaty IRA, as a matter of policy, did not recognize any military tribunal, though this policy was eased somewhat after February 1923.)[72] Each court was to determine its own procedure, except as prescribed in the general regulations.[73] Tribunals were held in secret and news of a death sentence was not communicated to relatives until after it had been executed.[74]

Each court was constituted by a president holding the rank of commandant or above, a legal officer nominated by the minister for Defence and certified by the law officer to be a person of 'legal knowledge and experience' and detailed by the convening officer for service of the court, and one other officer not below rank of captain.[75] The legal officer would direct on points of law, procedure and evidence.[76]

Except for 'not guilty' verdicts, sentences were subject to confirmation by a confirming authority – two members of the army council[77] – which could order a military court to revise the sentence; confirm or refuse to confirm a sentence or finding (in whole or in part); order a new trial; reduce the punishment; or suspend execution of the sentence.[78] The confirming authority could not increase a sentence, nor could a sentence sent for revision be increased.[79] When considering a court's sentence, the judge advocate general was available to assist the confirming authority on points of law and to indicate if inconsistencies or legal error existed.[80] In one case, a UCD student named Mallin had been convicted of unauthorized possession of a revolver, but Davitt urged that the death sentence be reduced because of the prisoner's age. On 30 November 1922, his co-accused, Joseph Spooner, Patrick Farrelly and John Murphy, were shot, though Mallin's life was spared because, as Diarmuid O'Hegarty (the army's director of organization) later explained, the prisoner's father,

68 Gen. Reg. 10. 69 Campbell, *Emergency law*, p. 207. 70 Gen. Reg. 9. 71 Gen. Reg. 14. 72 Minutes of the Provisional Government, 22 Nov. 1922, Campbell, *Emergency law*, pp 203–4. 73 Gen. Reg. 15(1). 74 *Irish Times*, 28 and 29 Nov. 1922, Campbell, *Emergency law*, p. 205. 75 Gen. Reg. 4. 76 Gen. Reg. 15(3). 77 Gen. Reg. 21. 78 Gen. Reg. 23. 79 Gen. Reg. 24. 80 The General Regulations were carried in *Iris Oifigiúil*, 21 Nov. 1922.

Michael Mallin, who had commanded the IRA on Stephen's Green during the Easter Rising, had been executed by the British in May 1916.[81]

Military courts did not begin functioning until 3 November 1922.[82] By 15 November 1922, only 12 cases had been investigated and one sentence confirmed.[83] Those 12 included Peter Cassidy, John Gaffney, James Fisher and Richard Twohig, who were tried on 8 November 1922. They were the first to be executed, dying on 17 November 1922. Charlie Casey was on hand to ensure that the sentences were properly executed, and, afterwards, in the place of an inquest, Eugene Sheehy presided at a court of inquiry. Davitt objected to this, believing it inappropriate to involve the prosecution in the execution of a tribunal's sentence and in post-execution matters.[84]

Later that day, Richard Mulcahy said that the men in question 'were found on the streets of Dublin at night, carrying loaded revolvers, and waiting to take the lives of other men',[85] adding that he had 'the utmost detestation of street ambushes' and 'not the slightest sympathy for those involved'.[86] Speaking of the first executions, O'Higgins explained:

> it was better at first to take an average case, to take the cases which had nothing particular, no particular facts about them to distinguish them from the cases of thousands all over the country who are leading the Nation to death. If you took as your first case some man who was outstandingly active or outstandingly wicked in his activities the unfortunate dupes through the country might say, 'Oh, he was killed because he was a leader,' or 'He was killed because he was an Englishman.'[87]

Undoubtedly, the provisional government had far more important republicans in mind.

Erskine Childers, the IRA's English-born director of propaganda, had been arrested in November in possession of a revolver,[88] and convicted by a military court.[89] Relying on *Egan v. Macready*,[90] his counsel applied to Lord Justice O'Connor (who had delivered the ruling in Egan's case) for a writ of habeas corpus on the grounds that the provisional government was precluded from establishing military tribunals unless it did so by statute

81 Davitt memoir. 82 Dáil Debates vol. 1 col. 2057, Campbell, *Emergency law*, p. 196. 83 Valiulis, *Mulcahy*, p. 178. 84 Davitt memoir. 85 Dáil Debates vol. 1 col. 2264, 17 Nov. 1922. 86 Quoted T. de Vere White, *Kevin O'Higgins* (1986), p. 124. 87 Dáil Debates vol. 1 col. 2267. 88 At Childers' trial, Coyne served the charge sheet, and Sheehy prosecuted. Childers was defended by P. Lynch KC, M. Comyn KC, and Conor Maguire. See Davitt memoir. 89 See Campbell, *Emergency law*, pp 247–50. 90 [1921] 1 IR 265.

(counsel argued that the Army (Special Powers) Resolution was not law) because the Restoration of Order (Ireland) Act, 1920 was still in force.[91] (In Egan's case, O'Connor had ruled that the 1920 act prevented the British army employing prerogative martial law powers.)

Dismissing these arguments, O'Connor declared that the provisional government was 'de jure as well as de facto the ruling authority', and was bound to administer the law and to suppress attempts to overthrow the state: 'Those duties carry with them the right to organize an army for the protection of the people in any case of emergency.' He accepted the provisional government's contention that war was raging and that a duty to restore order existed. That duty, he concluded, undoubtedly fell on the government, either the provisional government or the finally constituted Free State government. 'No Government can exist unless there is some physical force behind it ... independently of any statute the Executive Government is bound to protect the subjects of the State from aggression', he said, adding that the right to organize an army for the protection of the people was 'a right inherent in any Government'. That, he added, 'gets rid of a technical point ... against the validity of [the Army (Special Powers) Resolution] passed by the Dáil, the House of the Irish Parliament.' He also ruled that the Restoration of Order (Ireland) Act, 1920 applied only to the British army and, therefore, that no statute limited the Irish army's powers; its actions while suppressing the rebellion were not justiciable by the courts.[92] He explained: 'However doubtful the law may have been in the past, it is now clearly established that once a state of war arises the Courts have no jurisdiction over the acts of the military authority during the continuance of hostilities. The matter has been so recently and frequently discussed, I do not consider it necessary to do more than refer to Marais' Case, Tilonko's Case, and Allen's Case.'[93] Childers was executed on 24 November 1922.

Almost simultaneously, in *R (Johnstone) v. O'Sullivan*,[94] a mother and daughter sought to prevent their trial by a military court on the grounds that the military courts established by the provisional government were wholly illegal because they were not created by an act of parliament, which required royal assent. Counsel also contended that the provisional government had no express power to create an army. While article 8 of the Treaty would empower the Irish Free State to establish an army, article 9 of the Provisional Government (Transfer of Functions) Order, 1 April

91 *R(Childers) v. The Officer commanding the Troops and the Adjutant-General of the Forces of the Irish Provisional Government*, [1923] 1 IR 5, before Lord Justice O'Connor, Master of the Rolls, 20–3 Nov. 1922. 92 J. Kelly, *Constitution of Ireland* (1984), p. 415. 93 [1923] 1IR 13–15. 94 [1923] 2 IR 13–14, 19.

1922 declared, 'Nothing in this order shall effect the control or administration of any of the existing naval, military or air forces of the Crown, or transfer to any department of the Provisional Government any of the powers of any existing department in relation to any of those forces.' Indeed, counsel argued, 'the only lawfully constituted army in Ireland is the British Army, which could have been used in quelling the rebellion.'

But the habeas corpus application was dismissed. Although Chief Justice Molony accepted that the National Army 'was not formed in accordance with Clause 8 of the Treaty, or in pursuance of an Act of Parliament of Ireland similar to the Army Act', he continued, 'but when the Government of a country is attacked, it has, apart from any statutory or other provisions, an inherent right to organize a force and to take such steps as it may deem necessary to quell the insurrection.'[95] Further, the provisional government had obtained Dáil approval for the establishment of military tribunals and other powers. The chief justice added that a state of war existed in Co. Donegal (where the two women had been arrested) and this justified the application of martial law: 'We have no jurisdiction *durante bello* to inquire into or pass judgement upon the conduct of the military authorities in repressing the rebellion.'[96]

In the court of appeal, Lord Justice O'Connor admitted the provisional government had 'no paper title to raise an army.' He concluded, however,

> But that by no means disposes of the matter, many a title is good which is not a paper title ... Not only had the Government the right to protect itself but it was its bounden duty to do this, and in doing so to use any force which was necessary, and to call on all well-disposed persons to assist it. It required no transfer of powers to enable the Government to do this.[97]

The appeal was dismissed.

One consequence of Childers' court actions was that the four sentences of the first military court held in Co. Kerry, handed down against Matthew Moroney, Thomas Devane, Cornelius Casey, and Dermot O'Connor, while confirmed, had not been executed, pending the outcome of his case.[98] Disagreement had developed in the army council regarding the men's fate; some members argued that one month awaiting execution was sufficient punishment, while others contended that one month was the normal period between conviction and execution and that the execu-

95 [1923] 2 IR 15. 96 [1923] 2 IR 17. 97 [1923] 2 IR 25. 98 Campbell, *Emergency law*, p. 212.

tions should proceed. The judge advocate general's opinion was sought, but he saw no legal grounds for reprieve, the prisoners' fate was a question of policy. When pressed, Davitt suggested that these men could be held as hostages for the good behaviour of the anti-Treaty IRA in the county, and suggested that General Murphy of the Kerry command issue a proclamation declaring that the four men had been tried, convicted, and their sentences confirmed, but that execution had been suspended on condition that there were no further attacks on the army in the county. Some members of the army council also objected to this, but Richard Mulcahy reiterated that the alternative was that the men be shot.[99] A proclamation was duly issued.[1]

The IRA finally responded to the executions on 28 November 1922 when Liam Lynch, IRA chief of staff, warned the Ceann Comhairle (the speaker of the Dáil) that 'very drastic measures to protect our forces' would be taken. He had ordered his men to shoot on sight any TD who had voted in favour of the Army (Emergency Powers) Resolution.[2] Subsequently, on 7 December 1922, two TDs were shot; one, Seán Hales, was killed, the other, Pádraic Ó Máille, was badly wounded. (The provisional government passed into history on 6 December 1922, when the Irish Free State came into existence, the first anniversary of the signing of the Treaty.)

The executive council and the army council immediately resolved to introduce military committees, as provided in the Army Resolution.[3] Committees composed of lower ranking officers would dispose of charges of unauthorized possession of arms, ammunition, and explosives,[4] thus permitting a more summary administration of military rule on a more decentralized basis. One committee member, though, could be no lower in rank than captain. Military courts continued to operate, but only in cases of doubt – that is where the prisoner was not caught 'red-handed', or if there were doubts regarding facts, witnesses etc.[5] Persons arrested in possession of arms would be brought before a committee as soon as possible,[6] which would investigate the arrest and report in writing if there had been unauthorized possession. There appears to have been no provision for an accused to consult with a solicitor or a barrister, though he

99 See Davitt memoir and minutes of the executive council, 12 Dec. 1922: 'The minister of Defence reported that in view of the improved situation in the Kerry area, he proposed to adopt a certain procedure in regard to the cases of four men who had been captured in arms, and tried before a Military Court. His proposal was approved.' 1 The Kerry hostages' sentences were commuted to ten years' penal servitude on 18 Jan. 1923. See generally Campbell, *Emergency law*, pp 211–14. 2 Hopkinson, *Green*, p. 190. 3 Proclamation dated 7 Dec. 1922 and issued to the press, 8 Dec. 1922. 4 Paragraph 2. 5 Davitt memoir. 6 Paragraph 1.

would have an opportunity to make a defence and could have an officer assigned to defend him.[7] On receipt of a committee's report, the army council would decide on a punishment – 'death or such other punishment as they shall think fit'.[8] Punishments were to be carried out summarily.[9]

Richard Mulcahy ordered that the necessary regulations and proclamation be issued to the press on the night of 7 December or the following morning in order to bring them into effect immediately.[10] When consulted, however, Cahir Davitt explained to the army council that as the proposed committees were more in the way of drumhead courts martial, having no judicial function, simply investigating and reporting, and since investigations were not a trial, there was no actual need for rules of procedure or regulations. Nevertheless, to keep the committees within the terms of the September resolution, each would include an officer nominated by the minister for Defence and certified by the law officer to be a person of legal knowledge – a command legal officer – who would ensure that committees were conducted properly and that reports were correctly presented. Revealing Davitt's disapproval of the committee system, he argued that as the proposed committees were not judicial in nature, neither he nor his office should have any part in their operation, and that the legal officers overseeing committees should do so as soldiers obeying orders.[11]

In addition to the establishment of the military committees, four anti-Treaty IRA leaders who were captured after the fall of the Four Courts (Rory O'Connor, Liam Mellows, Richard Barrett, and Joe McKelvey), each representing one of the four provinces,[12] were taken from their cells in Mountjoy jail on the morning of 8 December 1922 and shot. There was no pretence of legality; these were killings ordered by the executive in retaliation for the shooting of the two TDs the previous day. The minister for Home Affairs, Kevin O'Higgins, argued that all states rely on the threat and the use of violence, adding 'while the existence of the nation is at stake there can be but one code … *Salus Populi Suprema Lex*.'[13] W.T. Cosgrave said of the executions that it was 'really a psychological question', to show those involved in the conspiracy against the Dáil and the government 'that terror will be struck into them'.[14] Perhaps indicating the efficacy of the government's actions, no further pro-treaty TDs were shot during the Civil War.

The IRA was initially spurred into new activities by the Free State's hardened approach, concentrating more on arson, sabotage, pulling up railways, and blowing up bridges. While the National Army had been in

7 Campbell, *Emergency law*, p. 216. 8 Paragraph 4. 9 Paragraph 5. 10 P4/569, 7 Dec. 1922. 11 Davitt memoir. 12 Coogan, *De Valera*, p. 342. 13 Dáil Debates vol. 2 col. 68, 8 Dec. 1922. 14 Dáil Debates vol. 2 col. 94–5. See Campbell, *Emergency law*, p. 167.

a superior and dominant position since the outbreak of war, after six months of fighting, disorder persisted. Impatience grew within the executive council until it finally confronted the army council on 10 and 11 January 1923 to discuss 'the lawlessness prevailing throughout the country, with a view to bringing it to a speedy end', and to consider the army's position *vis à vis* the civil government.[15]

Kevin O'Higgins[16] believed that continuing lawlessness had been 'fostered by the idea that there is a breakdown of law and the sanctions of law, that the existing Government is unable to function effectively' and that only a small amount of it was 'due to genuine dissatisfaction with the Treaty'. The problems to be confronted were simple:

> Not only must the Irregulars be crushed, but illegal holding of land, refusal to pay debts,[17] not to mention poteen making, must be stamped out immediately. The problem is *psychological* rather than *physical*, we have to vindicate the idea of law and ordered government, as against anarchy.[18]

Looting and the illegal holding of land and property were, he argued, the 'practical fruits of the revolt of the last year ... the whole revolt against all idea of morality, law and social order. If these things cannot be vindicated there is no future for the Nation.'[19] O'Higgins later told the Dáil that:

> Officers were appointed by the Four Courts Executive whose special function and duty it was to stir up agrarian trouble of this kind, and stir up this spirit of confiscation and wanton illegality. It has to be visualised in that way and has to be tackled in that way. To fail to utilise the military to cure this evil would mean that the evil was not going to be cured at all.[20]

O'Higgins proposed the establishment of 'a mobile column of 40 or 50 men' in each county to deal with agrarian offences – this led to the cre-

15 D/T S.3306, and generally Hopkinson, *Green*, pp 221–7. 16 See De Vere-White, *Kevin O'Higgins*, pp 1–3; Lee, *Ireland*, pp 97–8. 17 Obstructions to legal remedies for debt were tackled by the Enforcement of Law (Occasional Powers) Act, 1923. Those powers continued in operation until March 1926. Figures given in Dáil Debates vol. 14 col. 890 are as follows: on 11 Mar. 1924 there were 7,000 decrees outstanding, valued at £170,000, by 31 Jan. 1926 there were 3,434 decrees outstanding valued at £69,910. See D/J H.171/5 and H.171/12. 18 D/T S.3306, memorandum by O'Higgins, 11 Jan. 1923, O'Higgins' emphasis. 19 D/T S.582, O'Higgins to Cosgrave, 5 Apr. 1923 and O'Duffy to O'Higgins, 29 Mar. 1923. 20 Dáil Debates vol. 3 col. 990, 17 May 1923. See also Hopkinson, *Green*, pp 90–1; Dáil Debates vol. 4 col. 1862, 24 July 1923, regarding stock seizures up to 6 Dec. 1922.

ation of the Special Infantry Corps.[21] He also sought more widespread executions: 'the psychological effect of an execution in Dublin is very slight in Wexford, Galway or Waterford,' he complained.

The president of the executive council, W.T. Cosgrave, was also unhappy with the scale of executions: 'We have had executions confined to Dublin, Kildare[22] [and] Kilkenny.[23] According to that the whole country with the exception of these counties must be in excellent order or free from arrests. [Commanding officers] who are neglecting their duty in this respect might as well be losing battles.' He demanded more executions on a wider geographical basis.[24]

The government shortly increased the jurisdiction of the military courts and committees, empowering them to deal not only with active IRA members but also with those who commanded them, those who gave then material support, intelligence or held communications with persons with the intention of committing offences under paragraph 1 (a), (b) and (c) of the September resolution.[25] The 17 January 1923 order extended the offences triable by the military courts and committees to include murder, aiding and abetting murder, attempting and conspiracy to commit murder and commanding, procuring, inciting, counselling, soliciting, encouraging, persuading or endeavouring to persuade any person to commit murder.[26] It also covered the unauthorized possession of army uniforms and assisting persons to escape from civil or military custody, among other offences. Richard Mulcahy called it a 'Stand Clear Order'.[27]

November had seen 11 executions, and December 8. In January, 34 were put to death, with 5 shot on 15 January[28] and 12 on 20 January.[29] While continued anti-Treaty opposition prevented the complete exercise of sovereignty and jurisdiction by the state, it was clear by January 1923 that the IRA was collapsing. On 19 January 1923 Liam Deasy, IRA deputy chief of staff was captured and his death sentence reprieved only after he called on the IRA to surrender immediately. An amnesty period followed from 9 to 18 February 1923, and the already flagging IRA was thrown into greater turmoil. Although February witnessed only one execution, that appears to have been linked to the Deasy's surrender call. There was no softening on the part of the executive council or the army, the latter deciding on 12 February 1923 that 'bad cases' should be prepared for execution, and after

21 D/T S.3306. 22 On 8 Jan. 1923, five ex-National Army soldiers were shot for earlier engaging in treachery at Leixlip, Co. Kildare. 23 Two were shot on 29 Dec. 1922. 24 D/T S.3306. 25 General Order of 17 Jan. 1923. 26 Paragraph 1 (a)(b)(c). 27 Dáil Debates vol. 2 col. 887, 17 Jan. 1923. See Campbell, *Emergency law*, p. 167. 28 Four in Roscrea, one in Galway. 29 Five in Athlone, four in Tralee, two in Limerick, one in Galway.

18 February 'it must be anticipated that no clemency will be shown in any case.'[30] On 13 March, 8 were executed;[31] 4 were shot the following day in Donegal; on 11 April, 6 were executed in Tuam, Co. Galway; on 25 April, 3 were shot in Tralee, Co. Kerry; the following day, one was executed in Ennis, Co. Clare; on 2 May, 2 more were put to death in Ennis. The last executions occurred on 30 May 1923, when Michael Murphy and Joseph O'Rourke were shot for robbing a bank in Co. Galway.[32]

Speaking with neutral republicans in February 1923, W.T. Cosgrave said, 'The executions have had a remarkable effect ... once the people saw we were in earnest they came along. We never got so much information as we are getting now.' There would be no concessions or change in policy. He warned, 'I am not going to hesitate and if the country is to live and if we have to exterminate ten thousand Republicans, the three millions of our people are bigger than this ten thousand.'[33]

Approximately 140 persons came before the military courts and 9 were executed, with 85% of suspects being convicted. Of the 1,039 who came before the committees, 64 were put to death, with about 46% of suspects being found guilty.[34] In total, 77 were officially executed.

Writing 35 years after the end of the Civil War, Cahir Davitt concluded that

> It was clear that it was not punishment which was the main purpose of the executions; and their justification as a policy had to be sought in their efficacy in helping to crush the insurrection. This I think must have been considerable; but I have no doubt that even without them the anti-Treaty forces would have been completely defeated in any event.

The IRA executive met on 23 March 1923 to discuss Tom Barry's motion that further resistance would not further the cause of independence. Though his motion was lost by five votes to six, the executive would reconsider it April.[35] Incredibly, even at that stage, Liam Lynch, the IRA's chief of staff, believed that victory was still possible. But after Lynch was shot by the National Army on 10 April, it was only a matter of days before a ceasefire was called.

30 Quoted in Campbell, *Emergency law*, pp 222–3. 31 One in Dublin, one in Cork, three in Wexford, three in Mullingar. 32 'Departmental Notes', pp 205–7. 33 Quoted in Garvin, *1922*, p. 163. 34 Interned: 0, Acquitted: 563, Convicted: 476. By 8 Apr. 1924, of these: 64 executed, 274 in custody, 31 escaped, 107 released, see C. Campbell, Emergency law, pp 206–20. 35 J.B. Bell, *The secret army: the IRA, 1916–1979* (1990), p. 37; Hopkinson, *Green*, pp 228–38.

On 31 March 1923, army intelligence reported that although the country could not yet be considered satisfactory, from a military point of view the situation was very positive: 'Even in the worst areas which we are dealing with at present the position is such that it cannot cause the least anxiety.' It assured the government that those remaining areas would be 'cleaned up' in a matter of weeks if the IRA formations within them could be found. There were some weak columns operating in mountainous districts, and although large army sweeps failed to locate them, they had broken IRA formations into smaller bands. Outside of the remaining difficult areas, the army believed that the maintenance of order was now the responsibility of an armed police force.[36]

It was clear to the IRA's leadership that the war was lost. It ordered a suspension of hostilities for 27 April 1923. The government would not entertain surrender terms, and Lynch's successor, Frank Aiken, ordered the IRA to dump its arms. Although he had reportedly spoken of a renewed 'short and sweet ... war with the Staters',[37] most anti-Treatyites wanted no further fighting. As Éamon de Valera explained to the Associated Press: 'The war, so far as we are concerned, is finished.'[38] At best, anti-Treatyites could only content themselves with agitating for the release of prisoners and concentrating on the forthcoming general election.

By 19 May 1923, the army reported that most anti-Treatyites in the south of the country were 'convinced of the hopelessness of their military and destruction campaign'. In fact, military intelligence reported no IRA activities from Cork. The Kerry IRA had yet to be dispensed with, however, because of difficult terrain and effective IRA intelligence. Nonetheless, the resumption of train services in the county had a very positive effect. It reported, 'the sense of normality thus restored has gone some way towards breaking down the reticence of the people which has helped considerably to prolong the War in Kerry'. Elsewhere in Munster, the army concerned itself with searching for arms. In Donegal, the Midlands and the East, it claimed, 'the situation is so normal and sufficiently well in hand from the Military view point as to call for no comment.' In addition, the Gardaí and the courts were operating in Mayo.[39] Indeed, as the weeks passed, circumstances rapidly recovered. The department for Defence noted on 16 June 1923 'a little improvement shows itself every week and if the present "peace atmosphere" lasts the country will not long be getting back to normal.'[40] Nevertheless, a high incidence of crime continued after the end of hostilities.[41]

36 D/T S.3361, report on the military situation, 31 Mar. 1923. 37 *Irish Times*, 23 July 1923. 38 Quoted in D. O'Sullivan, *The Irish Free State and its senate* (1940), p. 129. 39 D/T S.3361, general weekly report, week ending 19 May 1923. 40 Quoted in Bell, *The secret army*, p. 40. 41 D/T S.3527.

On 16 April 1923, the government began to formally consider legislation to deal with the post war situation.[42] The department of Home Affairs explained that the army's special powers of search, arrest and detention would, following the termination of the state of war, have to be transferred for 'a limited period' to the civil authorities with the necessary support of the Oireachtas. It maintained that once peace and normality were achieved 'no exceptional powers will be needed.'[43] Nevertheless, between war and peace there would be a '"middle period", the waves will continue to run high for some time after the storm has blown itself out'. During this time, 'exceptional powers' would be required.

Éinrí Ó Frighil,[44] secretary of the department of Home Affairs, immediately anticipated several problems: 'The Constitution as it stands does not give the freedom and the elasticity which the Legislature and the Executive … should have in such a period.' For instance, article 72 precluded the use of jury-less special courts, similar to that envisaged by the Criminal Procedure (Northern Ireland) Act, 1922,[45] which had been planned to deal with circumstances similar to the post-Civil War situation in the south of Ireland. That he regarded as 'the one outstanding example' of the constitution blocking legislation necessary to restore order in times of national emergency. Ó Frighil was convinced that special jury-less courts would have to be introduced: 'when the question is between the State and the individual the ordinary jury is inclined to be swayed by anti-Governmental bias, by the feeling that the State can afford to lose prestige and even security better that the prisoner can afford to lose life and liberty.' Acknowledging the long history of domination in Ireland, he warned that it would take many years for citizens to respect the state:

> The State is still, in this country, for too many of its citizens, the butt of all vague complaint and abuse, the machine that insists on collecting taxes instead of giving away money to everybody for nothing, the tyrant that wants to hang and imprison people whose only fault was using a gun in a manly and careless way, or burning down

42 Minutes of the executive council, C.1/84, 16 Apr. 1923, D/T S.3063. 43 D/J H.171/17 annex, undated memorandum by Ó Frighil, given to the acting secretary, the executive council, for distribution on 22 May 1923. See also C.1/109, and D/T S.3063. 44 Éinrí Seosamh Ó Frighil (1892–1977), born Co. Cork and educated in UCD. He worked in the Estates Duty Office of the British civil service, but was dismissed in 1918 because he refused to take an oath to the British king. Dáil court judge during the War of Independence, he became secretary of the department of Home Affairs (replacing P. Ó Síocháin) in Apr. 1922, a post he held until 1933, when Daniel Browne succeeded him. He was chairman of the Dairy Board, 1933–1958. 45 These courts, to consist of two judges, were never established. See Campbell, *Emergency law*, pp 276, 313–15.

the house of a family whose politics are notoriously unpopular. From these people, juries are picked.

Unless the constitution were amended, once the courts deemed the Civil War to have ended, serious offences against the state would have to be tried by jury, which would, he believed, doom the most elaborate legal measures designed to defend the state. Indeed, he feared that majority jury verdicts would also be unconstitutional. But rather than simply recommend a formula that might permit jury-less tribunals, Ó Frighil proposed a constitution amendment authorizing the suspension of the constitution for a definite period 'so to give full effect to any laws which the Oireachtas may think fit to pass within and for the space of such period'. Neither of these options, though, would be seriously explored at this time.

The department of Home Affairs was particularly concerned that internment might be unconstitutional, especially as the Free State constitution neither expressly permitted nor forbade it. Indeed, Ó Frighil wondered if internment was 'foreign to the Constitution … [or was it] at least *extremely doubtful* whether the Superior Courts would recognize the legality of [an internment].' He feared that these questions would only be answered '*ex cathedra* and *post eventum*, when it is too late'.[46] Hugh Kennedy swiftly allayed this concern, however, explaining that, in his opinion, deterrent detention as opposed to punitive imprisonment without trial was not prohibited by the constitution.[47] Work on the provisionally entitled the Peace Establishment Bill began immediately.[48]

A 'draft skeleton' of a bill permitting internment in certain cases, the punishment of offences, the seizure of stolen property and trespassing livestock, and dealing with poitín making and selling was quickly prepared. It proposed that persons interned during the previous year would be 'deemed to have been interned by an order validly made in pursuance of this Act'. Regarding the possession of firearms, the department of Home Affairs felt it would be necessary to define what constituted legal possession as the government intended severe punishments for the unlawful possession of either arms or explosives: 'It is suggested that no civilian should have possession of anything of this nature, except a sporting gun and ammunition … held on licence signed by a District Justice on the recommendation of a Peace Commissioner.'

46 Ó Frighil's emphasis. 47 Executive council minutes, 28 May 1923, C.1/113. His opinion appeared to be based on the judgment delivered in *R (Zadig) v. Halliday*, [1917] AC 260. 48 D/J H.171/17, the department of Home Affairs was unhappy with the title suggested by the attorney general and proposed something akin to the Maintenance of Public Order (Emergency Powers) Act. Ó Frighil to the attorney general, 1 June 1923.

The substance of this draft was approved by the executive council on 2 June 1923,[49] and a more substantial draft was drawn up by the attorney general. Following discussions on 11 June 1923, it was accepted by the executive council, subject to amendments. Two days later, the executive approved a new short title: Public Safety (Emergency Powers) Bill, 1923.[50]

O'Higgins defended the bill and, more particularly, internment, declaring that, 'We would not be executing fairly or decently or honourably our stewardship to the people of this country and to the interests that look to us for protection if we were to contemplate the wholesale, indiscriminate release of these men on a day or date that the courts would decide that there was no longer a state of war or a state of armed rebellion.'[51] He added, 'no slaughter is proposed by this bill. Six months' detention, six months' internment … I guarantee the Bill asks for no more than that.' Because IRA arms had not been 'definitely put aside', he asked, 'what is the alternative?'[52]

Section 1 permitted an executive minister[53] to order an arrest and internment when 'satisfied' that there was reasonable grounds for suspecting a person of 'being or having been engaged or concerned in the commission' of part 1 scheduled offences,[54] or 'that the public safety is endangered by such person being allowed to remain at liberty'[55] or on receipt of a report from the military authorities[56] that the detention of persons was a 'matter of military necessity arising out of the existence of a state of war or armed rebellion, whether local or general'.[57] A 'responsible officer' (an army officer not below the rank of commandant or a Garda officer not below the rank of superintendent) was empowered to arrest and detain persons 'found committing or attempting to commit or whom such officer suspects of having committed' part 2 scheduled offences. Such detainees would have to be released within one week, charged or interned.[58] Initially, it had been proposed to restrict this to 48 hours, but

49 Minutes of the executive council, C.1/114. Regarding the position of the parliamentary draftsman and relations between the attorney general and Kevin O'Higgins, see P4/760, 31 May 1923 and 1 June 1923. 50 P4/602/4, D/T S.3063, Minutes of the executive council, C.1/121, 13 June 1923. 51 Dáil Debates vol. 3 col. 2003–4, 15 June 1923. 52 Dáil Debates vol. 3 col. 2501–3, 26 June 1923. 53 In practice, only the minister for Defence issued warrants, see Campbell, *Emergency law*, p. 233. 54 Section 1(a). 55 Section 1(c). 56 'the army council for the time being of the National Army, or a General Officer commanding a district or any other officer, not being below the rank of commandant, having executive command of troops.' 57 Section 1(b). Office of director of intelligence of the chief of staff, 17 Dec. 1923 on the subject of 'Warrants for wanted Irregulars still at large':– warrants issued on grounds (a) and (c) but none on grounds (b). See Campbell, *Emergency law*, p. 237. See also D/D A.9010, D/J 93/2/6, minute of 6 June 1928, numbers interned under the 1923 Public Safety Act given as 274, numbers arrested 95, of whom 88 were sentenced. It has not been possible to verify these figures. 58 Section 2(2), (3).

the department of Home Affairs argued that such a limit presupposed 'an almost impossible degree of coordination and efficiency in the administration of the Act ... A half-staffed Ministry, composed almost altogether of inexperienced officers, cannot be expected to perform wonders.'[59] Regarding interments, the minister for Home Affairs said,

> We are not prepared even to lend colour to the implication that [an] arrest is based on anything [other] than ... the statement of the military authorities of that area that they deem the arrest a matter of military necessity. You cannot place the military in a particular area in a situation when they may feel that the arrests they make or the things they do are to be reviewed by a Court while [conflict continues].[60]

Any person detained since the Civil War would remain in custody if, in the opinion of the 'military authorities', their detention was a 'military necessity' or if an executive minister was 'of opinion that the public safety would be endangered by such person being set at liberty'.[61]

Part 1 of the schedule covered 'offences committed expressly as part of a revolt against the State ... [and] may be summarized as "Active treason or insurrection"', and included:

1. An armed revolt against the Government of Saorstát Éireann.
2. Threatening, coercing, assaulting or attempting to threaten, coerce or assault any person in furtherance of any such revolt.
3. Destroying, damaging or removing or attempting to destroy, damage or remove any property in furtherance of any such revolt.

Part 2 dealt with 'offences which are not necessarily part of such revolt but may be committed in pursuance of such revolt or merely by ordinary criminals.' It covered the unlawful possession of arms, ammunition or explosives; unlawful possession of army or police uniforms or equipment; unlawfully assuming the name designation, description or uniform of a policeman or soldier; unlawful occupation or use of land or property; armed robbery; arson; damage or destruction of property; illicit distillation; selling illicit spirits; assisting, abetting or encouraging these offences or assisting any person guilty of them.

One or more appeal councils consisting of at least three members, one of whom was a practicing barrister or solicitor of at least five years' standing were to be established to investigate the detention of internees who requested an inquiry. In such cases, an appeal council was to be 'furnished

59 D/J H.171/17. 60 Dáil Debates vol. 4 col. 448–9. 61 Section 3(1).

with the reports or certificates' authorizing the internment and if it reported there were no reasonable grounds for suspecting an internee of having 'committed or being engaged or concerned in the commission' of any scheduled offences, he was to be released within one month, unless the minister presented the council with new evidence, or the internee was charged with an offence.[62]

While providing for a maximum penalty of death on conviction for part 1 scheduled offences, five years' penal servitude on conviction on indictment for part 2 scheduled offences and twelve months' imprisonment of summary conviction, the act also permitted flogging on conviction for arson and armed robbery, 'where medically permissible'.[63] The department of Home Affairs wrote 'that these criminals escape lightly if they escape with a flogging and that a flogging every week … would help to deter them from repeating their offences, or to deter other people from imitating them.'[64] O'Higgins claimed that the executive council had considered capital punishment for persons convicted of armed robbery.[65]

The department of Home Affairs had raised a significant concern if district justices could summarily try charges as serious as arson, given article 72 of the constitution. But this concern was also allayed – O'Higgins' notes explained, 'Incidentally this assumes that all the offences in Part II of the Schedule are "minor" offences within the meaning of article 72 of the constitution. This is a highly important point but the Ministry is assured by the attorney general that the Constitution is not violated by the proposed provisions of the Bill.'[66]

Section 6 empowered executive ministers to order the seizure of trespassing livestock, which could be held until a fine was paid or the animals were sold to cover costs and to compensate losses suffered by landowners.[67] Firearms regulations covered firearms licences, the registration of manufacturers and dealers, and restrictions on importing, exporting and transporting firearms.[68] The act also permitted district justices to freeze assets (land, property, money, etc.)[69] and bank accounts[70] which an executive minister alleged were the proceeds of robbery or should rightfully be in the possession of the minister or of a government department.

62 Section 4(1), (2), (3), (4). **63** Section 5, D/T S.3063, C.1/119, Minutes of the executive council, 11 June 1923. **64** D/J H.171/17, notes for second reading. **65** Dáil Debates vol. 3 col. 2505. For Dáil criticism see Dáil Debates vol. 3 col. 2547–606, 2 July 1923. **66** O'Higgins' notes for the second reading of the bill. **67** Section 6(1), (3) and (4). **68** Section 8. **69** Section 10. **70** Section 11. Only one case seems to have been dealt with under this section. On 12 Oct. 1923, an application was made to the district court in Naas, Co. Kildare for an order that the sum of £1145 deposited in the name of a T.J. Williams be transferred to the minister for Finance after the bank manager had frozen the account. See D/J H.171/44, 1 Feb. 1924, Ó Frighil to the secretary of the department of Finance.

On application by the attorney general to the high court 'upon his certificate that he believes a more fair and impartial trial can be had at a court and in a county to be named in such certificate, shall make an order … that the trial shall be had at the court and in the county named in the Certificate'.[71] This provision was based on section 4 of the Criminal Law and Procedure (Ireland) Act, 1887,[72] though the British system worked in 'proclaimed districts', while the Free State system was available throughout the state.[73]

Section 15 preserved the special powers of the army in case of military necessity in order to 'suppress rebellion' or for 'securing the public safety and restoring order throughout the country.' O'Higgins defended the granting of such wide powers to the army:

> We are endeavouring to pass out of a military situation and it is not duplicating of powers but the explicit preservation of the powers of the military in the event of a military situation arising that is sought … I am advised that such explicit preservation is necessary, lest the Courts should think that in legislating along the lines of this Bill that we are thereby depriving or seeking to deprive the military of the fullest powers in order to deal with situations that may arise.[74]

The bill was heavily criticized in the Dáil (the debate saw its first all-night sitting on 12 and 13 June 1923):[75] Thomas Johnson likened it to legislation in Northern Ireland,[76] and George Gavan Duffy described the proposed appeals councils as only offering 'fraudulent appeal',[77] but it became law on 1 August 1922.

Although there were several applications for habeas corpus after the ceasefire, each was refused.[78] Lord Justice O'Connor discharged an application on behalf of detainee Nora O'Brien[79] on 15 June 1923,[80] concluding that there was still a state of war: 'the Irish Republican Army did not state that a state of war had ceased to exist'.[81]

Finally, on 31 July 1923, the court of appeal held that the state of war had ended in Dublin. On 1 August the Public Safety (Emergency Powers)

71 Section 12(1). 72 50 and 51 Vic, ch. 20. 73 An example of this procedure is given in D/J H.8/876. Section 54 of the Courts of Justice Act, 1924 made this a permanent aspect of the law. 74 Dáil Debates vol. 4 col. 437, 10 July 1923. 75 A. Gaughan, *Thomas Johnson, 1872–1963: the first leader of the Labour Party in Dáil Éireann* (1980), p. 219. 76 Dáil Debates vol. 3 col. 2513, 26 June 1923. 77 Dáil Debates vol. 3 col. 2529. 78 Campbell, *Emergency law*, p. 256. 79 P4/658, 9 June 1923, the chief state solicitor, M.A. Corrigan to Hugh Kennedy. 80 O'Sullivan, *The Irish Free State and its senate*, p. 126. 81 [1924] IR 36–7. He added that the affidavit filed on behalf O'Brien was insufficient; the only evidence produced that the war had ended was an *Irish Times* article, 29 May 1923.

Act, 1923 was enacted, and detention orders were made continuing O'Brien's internment. O'Brien persisted in her attempts to gain release,[82] though now on the grounds that her detention was illegal because the terms of article 47 of the constitution had not been invoked when the Public Safety Act was enacted. Article 47 permitted 40% of TDs or a majority of senators to request the president of the executive council to suspend for 90 days any bill within a week of its being passed or being deemed to have been passed and subsequently to submit it to a referendum if 60% of senators or 5% of registered voters so demanded within that 90-day period. This provision would not apply to money bills or to bills declared by both Houses of the Oireachtas to be necessary 'for the immediate preservation of the public peace, health or safety'. Internments would, therefore, counsel argued, be unlawful until this seven-day period had elapsed as the act made no explicit reference to the declaration. The attorney general countered that once the act received the governor general's assent, the court was compelled to assume that article 47 was not applicable. He further maintained that even if the required number of members of the Oireachtas demanded a referendum, the president could, at his discretion, ignore the demand, and could, if he chose, send the bill to the governor general immediately. He added that the third recital in the act constituted a declaration as required by article 47.

The attorney general's arguments were dismissed. The chief justice, Mr Justice Molony, ruled that article 47 imposed a duty on the president of the executive council if a referendum were sought, noting

> A written demand requires time. What time is to be given for that written demand? The Article says seven days. Consequently the scheme of the Article so far is this: A Bill passes both Houses, but notwithstanding that it passes both Houses two-fifths of the members of the Dáil or the majority of the Seanad may think that there should be a referendum and may express their thoughts in a constitutional manner under Article 47 by presenting a petition to the President of the executive council.

The bill could, therefore, not operate until seven days after it had been passed. Molony rejected the argument that the recital in the bill fulfilled the requirements of article 47.[83] The prisoner was to be released immediately.

Although the court had insisted that the legislature adhere to a particular provision of the constitution, it had certainly not ruled that the

82 [1924] 1 IR 32. *R (O'Brien) v. Military Governor NDU*. 83 [1924] 1 IR 48–9.

state had no right to intern civilians in peacetime. This minor inconvenience was overcome by incorporating the Public Safety Act into the schedule of a new act – the Public Safety (Emergency Powers) (No. 2) Act, 1923 – which invoked the declaration making article 47 inapplicable.

Other prominent republicans continued to seek their freedom through the courts. For instance, Mr Justice Pim dismissed an application for habeas corpus on behalf of Seán T. O'Kelly (the future minister for Finance), ruling that the objections he raised did not affect the validity of the minister for Defence's internment order.[84] Éamonn Donnelly, who had been released by order of the court of criminal appeal on 2 August 1923, was later rearrested and made repeated applications for habeas corpus, but each was discharged.[85] Having appealed to several judges, Lord Justice O'Connor finally declared that his 'appeal was perfectly hopeless'.[86]

A further challenge to the Public Safety Act was brought in *R (Murphy) v. Military Governor, Mountjoy Prison*.[87] Murphy's counsel contended that the third Dáil had been improperly convened given the terms of article 24 of the constitution and was, therefore, incapable of enacting legislation. Secondly, counsel argued that any act would have to be passed at least seven days before the end of a parliamentary session; otherwise the provisions of article 47 could not be invoked. Counsel claimed that as both Public Safety Acts had been passed sooner than seven days before the Dáil was dissolved for the general election, they were invalid. Lord Justice O'Connor rejected the first argument on the simple grounds that the third Dáil was only bound to the transitory provisions of the constitution while acting as the constituent assembly. He also dismissed the second argument: 'it would certainly be a curious Constitution under which a Parliament should continue to sit for seven days doing absolutely nothing', adding that a demand to suspend legislation would be made directly to the President of the executive council.[88]

With security issues satisfactorily resolved, in the short term at least, the government could turn its attention to further re-establishing peace and normality in the country. An important step in that direction would be the holding of a general election. The 27 August 1923 poll represented a massive endorsement of the new state: Cumann na nGaedheal (as pro-Treaty Sinn Féin was christened in 1923) received about 415,000 votes and returned 63 candidates. Despite many factors militating against them,

84 *Irish Times* 29 Aug. 1923. 85 *Irish Times* 22 Aug. 1923, *Evening Herald* 5 Sept. 1923, *Irish Independent* 6 Sept. 1923. 86 *Evening Herald*, 26 Oct. 1923. 87 [1924] 58 ILTR 1, Murphy was a TD, see Campbell, *Emergency law*, pp 261–2. 88 [1924] 58 ILTR 3.

anti-Treatyites also polled strongly, receiving approximately 286,000 first preference votes and securing 44 seats.[89]

Military intelligence reported very little IRA activity during August 1923, limited to looting, and holding up of Gardaí and postmen.[90] A number of IRA bands still roamed parts of the country, some in column formation in the Wexford-Tipperary-Waterford areas, and others in the west of the country simply avoiding arrest. Generally, though it was believed that most anti-Treatyites 'desire for a trial of the Constitutional Method'. Nonetheless, some anti-Treatyites regarded the revival of the Sinn Féin clubs as an opportunity to reorganize the IRA. Some drilling was reported, and isolated attacks on the army were anticipated. Although military intelligence believed the IRA was well armed, it believed the organization possessed little ammunition. In the short-term, anti-Treatyites focused on securing the release of internees, future elections and the creation of 'an invisible machine that may be used more on terrorist lines amongst the civil population, than as a fighting force in the field'.[91]

Military victory and repeated pro-Treaty electoral success did not see an immediate or total hand-over of power and all non-military responsibilities from the army to the civil authorities. Very often, the police remained dependent on the army for the enforcement of the law. However, as the country became more peaceful, the process of disengaging the army would accelerate.

Éinrí Ó Frighil wrote, 'the maintenance of order and the enforcement of law are primarily the responsibility of the police and other authorities', and argued that the time had arrived for the army to act only when requested to by the civil authorities. In September 1923, the department of Home Affairs had sought to restrict this to dealing with cases of illegal possession of land, cattle driving, strikes, execution of decrees, protection of rate collectors in certain counties, arson, and the safe custody of prisoners. Ó Frighil also believed that responsibility for issuing firearms, ammunition, and explosives permits should be transferred to the civil authorities. The minister for Defence, Richard Mulcahy, felt agreement should be reached on how to delimit the areas of responsibility of the Gardaí and the army, and that the duties of the army and Gardaí should be considered in regard to armed robbery, illegal possession of land, the execution of decrees, and crime detection generally.[92] The Special Infantry Corps, which had arrested 123 persons suspected of agrarian offences, was disbanded in September 1923.[93]

89 Hopkinson, *Green*, p. 262. A revision of the constituencies increased the number of seats from 128 to 153. 90 D/T S.3361, chief of general staff to the minister for Defence, 20 Sept. 1923. 91 Ibid., 15 Oct. 1923. 92 D/T S.3306, Ó Frighil to Joseph McGrath, 24 Sept. 1923. 93 D/T S.3306.

A partial solution to this problem lay with the Dublin based Criminal Investigations Department (CID). The CID had acted as a division of Michael Collins' military intelligence during the War of Independence.[94] Following the transfer of administrative functions on 1 April 1922, it took over various duties of the Dublin Metropolitan Police's detective branch ('G Division'). After February 1923, it became responsible for all intelligence gathering for the Dublin Area. By October 1923, the CID claimed to have '2,200 files dealing with the activities of as many active and suspect Irregulars'.[95] In post Civil War circumstances, however, the executive council had begun to consider its disbandment.[96]

The CID was widely regarded as brutal,[97] and its relationship with both the army and the police was poor.[98] Further, the force had no statutory basis and the department of Home Affairs felt that the required legislation was undesirable at that time. As an alternative, it suggested that the best CID men could be formally transferred to the Dublin Metropolitan Police and merged with its 'G' Division to form a new detective special branch for Dublin. Out of a total of 86 CID men, the department of Home Affairs regarded 31 as 'useless', 30 as merely 'mediocre', and only 25 as being of a 'good type'. On 23 October 1923, 24 members of the CID and 4 members of the Protective Corps were formally inducted into the DMP. The new special detective force was headed by David Neligan and numbered 62. While it was conceivable that that number would not fall for quite some time, if 'normal' conditions returned reductions might be undertaken.[99]

Law enforcement problems persisted in many parts of the country. The department of Home Affairs described the problem thus:

> It is the opinion of this Ministry that while the operations of those armed bands undoubtedly create police problems – as did, indeed the whole 'Irregular' campaign – their immediate dispersal is a task for the Defence forces. The military campaign for the suppression of the 'Irregular' revolt cannot be said to be complete whilst so

94 See minutes of meeting of Provisional Government, 24 Aug. 1922. 95 D/T S.3331. Captain Ó Muireadhaighe to the minister for Industry and Commerce, McGrath, 12 Oct. 1923. 96 See D/J H.169/46/2, 6 Oct. 1923 and minutes of the executive council, C.2/11, 13 Oct. 1923. 97 See for example Coogan, *The IRA*, p. 62; Brady, *Guardians*, p. 125; Campbell, *Emergency law*, pp 161–2, 183–5. 98 See for example D/J H.169/33 and C. Brady, 'The police and government in the Irish Free State, 1922–33', MA thesis, UCD, 1977, ch. 6, pp 27–37. 99 D/J H.169/46/2, department of Home Affairs memorandum to each member of the executive council, 5 Oct. 1923; on the take over of the DMP see D/T S.3460, 9 July 1923, and minutes of the executive council, C.2/30, 10 Dec. 1923; Brady, 'The police and government', ch. 6, p. 22.

> many armed Irregulars roam about the country some of whom are even banded together in 'columns' quite definitely under the standard of Irregularism, and under the leadership of [elected TDs].

A Garda report had identified West Cork as 'by far the worst area in the state':

> Small gangs move at will … and so completely intimidate the public that even people whose property they loot or destroy dare not assist the Garda Síochána in the prevention or detection of crime … The position is so bad in north West Cork that unless conditions improve it may become necessary to remove the Gardaí

Further, south Leitrim was reported to be 'becoming worse every day'. Problems were also identified with, for example, Co. Galway and East Cork, while bands of robbers were said to be roaming in Tipperary.[1] But in most counties, including Kerry and Longford, the situation continued to improve. Clearly, there had been a vast improvement in circumstances in the country six months after the end of hostilities. In early March, there were 120 'incidents' per week; by 26 October 1923, this had fallen to about 10 per week.[2]

On 30 November 1923, the executive council decided that the army and Gardaí 'should cooperate in rounding-up and arresting armed criminals'. In addition, it divided the country into three areas: thirteen counties where conditions were 'normal'; six counties where Gardaí could undertake the maintenance of order 'provided they had the moral support of military garrisons stationed at larger centres'; seven counties or parts thereof where 'owing to the presence of bands of armed men, the Civic Guard could not take responsibility for the prevention of crime.'[3]

Despite these arrangements, some disorder persisted, and the minister for Home Affairs pressed for new tactics. On 7 February 1924, he wrote of continuing 'chronic lawlessness' in counties Leitrim, Sligo, Mayo, Kerry, Cork (east and west riding), Tipperary and Clare, requesting that 1,000 additional Gardaí (armed with rifles) be sent to deal with the unrest and disorder. But Richard Mulcahy urged caution, fearing that O'Higgins' pro-

1 D/J H.186/7, 28 Nov. 1923. 2 See Campbell, *Emergency law*, p. 170, 'incidents' included attacks on troops (including ambushes), attacks on army posts, destruction of property, stations burnt, cabins burnt, bridges destroyed, lines taken up, wire destruction, burnings, houses attacked, post offices attacked, Garda barracks destroyed, house robberies, road robberies. 3 Executive council minutes, 30 Nov. 1923 and Dáil Debates vol. 5 col. 1942, 14 Dec. 1923.

posal would 'destroy the [Garda] ... injure its position in the minds of the people, and destroy its present prestige.'[4] He argued that arming the Gardaí with rifles would 'spoil' the force's ability 'to put its finger on the pulse of the people in the thorough way in which I feel they certainly will after a further short space of time if the general position of the force remains at present.' Instead, the minister for Defence recommended closer communications between Gardaí and the army in areas of continuing difficulty.

Regardless of O'Higgins' claims, Eoin O'Duffy reported that of the problem areas pointed to, only in West Cork did Gardaí need military back-up. Accordingly, a decision on O'Higgins' plan was postponed,[5] and not re-examined until May 1924 when Éinrí Ó Frighil proposed sending the DMP's special detective branch outside of Dublin, suggesting that an enlarged force could be broken up into groups of about twelve men, armed and supplied with transport and sent to each Garda division. Each group would be responsible to the local superintendent vis à vis pay, discipline and administration, but would remain under centralized direction. This was agreed to and the Garda special branch began operating outside of Dublin in March 1925 when units were sent to Leitrim.[6]

Although O'Higgins had given assurances that internment powers would not be needed after 1923, Éinrí Ó Frighil notified the department for Defence on 2 November 1923 that most of the provisions of the Public Safety Act, 1923 would have to be continued after the act expired on 1 February 1924.[7] The department for Home Affairs proposed dividing the original act into three separate statutes: permitting and continuing internment in certain cases; providing for the punishment of offences committed due to or because of opportunities afforded by the Civil War; and a firearms act.[8]

Meeting on 8 December 1923, Kevin O'Higgins and Hugh Kennedy decided that the bill dealing with internment would re-enact sections 1, 2, 3, 4, 13, 15 and 16 of the original act, though the preamble, the division in the schedule and any reference to armed revolt would be dropped. It would last for 12 months.[9] Although, the army believed that circumstances no longer required it to make arrests under sections 1 or 2 of the 1923 act, the executive council decided to continue these powers.[10]

4 22 Feb. 1924. 5 Minutes of the executive council, 26 Feb. 1924. 6 Brady, 'The police and the government', ch. 6 pp 31–5, Dáil Debates vol. 9 col. 2677, 12 Dec. 1924. Postal services remained precarious in parts of Leitrim even as late as 1929, however. Gardaí warned that the resumption of service would 'merely be an act of provocation'. See D/J H.197/32. 7 See D/J H.171/38. 8 Ó Frighil to the attorney general, 10 Dec. 1923. 9 C.2/31, D/T S.3463, Ó Frighil to Hugh Kennedy, 10 and 11 Dec. 1923. In addition, the offence of threatening (with view to intimidation) to commit offences 5, 6, 7, 8, 9 of part 2 of the schedule of the 1923 Act was to be added. Draft ready by 11 Dec. 1923. 10 The secretary of the department of Defence to Ó Frighil, 22 Nov. 1923.

Defending the Public Safety (Powers of Arrest and Detention) Temporary Bill, the minister for Home Affairs explained that the hunger strike of late 1923 had slowed releases by about a month, but by December, they were again proceeding at a satisfactory rate. O'Higgins promised that releases would 'proceed gradually, and judicially. We do not desire to hold any of these men for one half hour longer than we think the public safety requires.' But he warned the camps could not be emptied 'before we are quite sure that we have our foundations laid, and that those foundations are staid, and that our Executive forces and the machinery of our administration of the country will be able to deal with any situation that may arise.'[11]

The attorney general, Hugh Kennedy, explained that he had hoped TDs would regard the bill as 'a non-political, non-party measure', necessary because of the difficult transitory period from war to peace. 'It is not a matter of politics or of holding certain opinions, but of dealing with offences against the law,' he declared. Because juries in certain areas refused to convict, and because panellists were often guilty of offences covered by the bill 'it is impossible to convict', he asserted. Kennedy insisted that he would not 'pack juries', adding that 'it is absolutely impossible to impose on the jurors of Dublin the trial of all the crimes in the Country'.[12]

Internments could now be ordered only if an executive minister certified 'in writing that he is satisfied that there is reasonable ground for suspecting such person of being or having been engaged or concerned in the commission of any' scheduled offences.[13] A 'responsible officer' was empowered to arrest and detain in custody for a period not exceeding one week 'any person found committing or attempting to commit or whom such officer suspects of having committed' any scheduled offences. When making an arrest, the responsible officer could 'enter on and search any premises in which any such person is known or reasonably believed to be'.[14] Detained persons were to be charged, interned or released within one week of arrest.[15] Section 6(1) provided that the minister for Home Affairs could attach conditions to the release of internees, requiring them to be of good

11 Dáil Debates vol. 5 col. 1946, 14 Dec. 1923. 12 Dáil Debates vol. 5 col. 1974–6. 13 Section 1. The schedule was copied from part 2 of the schedule to the 1923 Act, with the addition of the offences of attempting to overthrow the government by violence; inciting or inducing officers of the state to neglect or refuse to do their duty; obstructing or attempting to obstruct the administration of justice. 14 Section 2(1). 15 Section 2(3), D/J H.210, Ó Frighil to the commissioner, 17 Apr. 1924. See D/J 93/2/6, number detained under the Public Safety (Powers of Arrest and Detention) Temporary Act, 1924 given as 104. Instructions of 17 Apr. 1924 added that section 2 was to be relied upon in cases of emergency when circumstances did not permit consultation with the department of Home Affairs.

behaviour and keep the peace for up to three years. This condition would have to be guaranteed by two sureties.[16] Further, the army's powers were preserved, but only 'by virtue of military necessity arising in the course of the performance of their duty to suppress the rebellion.'[17]

Proposals to continue the army's special powers of arrest drew serious criticism in the Dáil. One TD argued that 'that the state of organisation in the army today is such that this power should not be given to officers in the Army. It is not good for the army itself; it is not good for the State; it is bad for the citizens and it is bad for the peace of the State.'[18] It was decided, therefore, that the army would, in general, no longer be involved in searches and raids unless armed resistance was expected, and if a responsible army officer expected that he would have to enter a premises when making an arrest, he was, 'wherever reasonably practicable', to arrange that a Garda or DMP officer was on hand.[19]

On 30 January 1924 an emergency resolution was passed making article 47 of the constitution inapplicable and the bill became law on 1 February 1924. Nevertheless, new internment orders had to be issued if persons detained under the 1923 act were to be held further – section 4 permitted the continued detention of any unsentenced internee by 'an order of an Executive Minister if such Minister is of opinion that the public safety would be endangered by such person being set at liberty.'[20]

The only challenge of note brought against these internment powers occurred in *R (O'Connell) v The Military Governor of Hare Park Camp.*[21] Counsel for O'Connell sought release on the grounds that section 4 deprived O'Connell of the right to habeas corpus under article 6 of the constitution; counsel further argued that in ordering the continued internment, the minister was not acting in due course of law and therefore breached articles 70 and 72; the minister was acting as an extraordinary court which was prohibited by article 70; and that the making of the detention order was exercising 'judicial power' as contemplated by article 64.[22]

16 D/J H.171/38, Ó Frighil to Duff, 1 Jan. 1924, Ó Frighil to Kennedy, 3 Jan. 1924. John Edwin Duff (1895–1949), UCD educated, he entered the British civil service 1914, London, later joining the British-run Irish Local Government Board. After the burning of the Customs House in 1921 he was seconded to the Finance division of the chief secretary's office, and in January 1922 entered the Provisional Government department of Home Affairs. Appointed principal officer and called to the Bar in 1923. Appointed assistant secretary in 1938 and secretary in succession to S.A. Roche in January 1949. 17 Section 8. 18 Patrick Baxter, Dáil Debates vol. 6 col. 24, 10 Jan. 1924. 19 Section 3. 20 D/J H.171/38, Ó Frighil to secretary of the department of Defence, 29 Jan. 1924. Section 5 provided that the appeals councils created under the 1923 act would continue in operation, and for the establishment of additional councils. 21 [1924] 2 IR 104. 22 Campbell, *Emergency law*, p. 262–3.

Citing *R (Zadig) v. Halliday*,[23] Chief Justice Molony ruled that the Public Safety Act came within the meaning of 'law' as enunciated by article 6 and therefore did not contravene the constitution.[24] Quoting Lord Atkinson, he said that habeas corpus was not infringed by legislation 'if the legislature chooses to enact that he can be deprived of his liberty and incarcerated or interned for certain things for which he could not have been heretofore incarcerated or interned, that enactment and the orders under it, if intra vires, do not infringe the Habeas Corpus Acts in any way whatsoever.'[25] Molony dismissed the view that a minister was exercising judicial power under section 4 – 'He is to form an opinion in whatever materials he deems sufficient; but there is no cause, no trial, no hearing, nothing except the inner consciousness of the Minister expressed in the written order.' It was simply 'a power … conferred by the legislature to meet a threatened danger to the state'.[26] He also ruled that the minister was not acting as an extraordinary court when ordering an internment, and that the order was made 'in due course of law'.[27] He added, 'there is nothing in the Treaty or the Constitution, or the statutes confirming the same, which limits the power of the Oireachtas to make such a provision [for internment].'[28] Mr Justice Pim conceded, however, that a law to deprive persons permanently of their freedom without having been first tried and convicted might be 'contrary to the spirit' of article 6, but that would not be true for temporary laws introduced in times of emergency.[29]

The Public Safety (Punishment of Offences) Temporary Act, 1924 re-enacted sections 7, 9, 10, 11 and 12 of the 1923 Act,[30] with slight modifications.[31] Originally, section 5 restricted judges to inflicting punishments available under the act, precluding the imposition of ordinary law penalties; this anomaly was removed.[32] The department of Home Affairs also requested a separate section dealing with 'shebeening', explaining it was practically impossible to charge persons with selling illicit liquor.[33] Further, it proposed an undivided schedule, as in the internment act, though the parliamentary draftsman[34] successfully argued that the offences covered

23 [1917] AC 260. 24 Kohn, *Constitution*, p. 133. 25 [1924] 2 IR 109, quoting [1917] AC 272. 26 [1924] 2 IR 112. 27 [1924] 2 IR 113. 28 [1924] 2 IR 111. 29 [1924] 2 IR 118. 30 Covering, respectively, punishments, agrarian offences, the return of stolen property, possession of stolen property, land or other property acquired using stolen funds, funds in bank accounts acquired illegally. 31 D/J H.171/11, Ó Frighil to O'Higgins, 6 Dec. 1923, D/J H.171/44, Ó Frighil to the attorney general, 20 Dec. 1923. 32 Section 1(5). 33 It proposed provision for a maximum fine of £20. The schedule would be the same as that of the Public Safety (Powers of Arrest and Detention) Bill. 34 Arthur Victor Matheson (died 1945), appointed parliamentary draftsman in September 1922, he was joined in 1923 by John Hearne and Gerald McCarthy who had been assistant judge advocates general and in 1925 by Denis Stephens who had been secretary to the Boundary

were of varying gravity: he believed that incitement to overthrow the government deserved more than five years penal servitude and a £100 fine;[35] it would be punishable by penal servitude for life (section 1(1)).[36]

Addressing the Dáil on 20 February 1924, O'Higgins said 545 indictable offences under the 1923 Public Safety Act had been reported to Gardaí during January 1924, though he believed the true figure could not be determined.[37] While O'Higgins conceded that 'there is no definite challenge to the fabric of the State at the moment', he argued the bill was necessary because 'there is a challenge to the rights of the ordinary quiet, peace-loving citizens, a menace to their property rights, a menace occasionally to the security of their person. That is not a normal situation nor a proper situation.'[38] The minister for Home Affairs remained convinced of the benefits of flogging:[39] 'it is a deliberate policy of the Ministry to stigmatize this crime as a cowardly and disgraceful crime, and it is the deliberate policy of the Ministry to remove every vestige of a halo from the head of the man who goes out with a gun to rob his neighbour.'[40]

Section 2 permitted an executive minister to order the seizure, removal and detention of trespassing animals,[41] though the practice of selling seized cattle had essentially ceased,[42] Gardaí simply held trespassing livestock on occupied land until an appropriate ransom was paid.[43] Only unredeemed animals were to be sold, with the proceeds used to cover costs and to compensate affected landowners. Any remainder was to be paid into the exchequer.[44]

The minister for Home Affairs was eager to have sections 6 and 7 (which re-enacted sections 10 and 11 of the original act) fully exploited as the reciprocal powers under the 1923 Act had not been used. Ó Frighil wrote:

> It is common knowledge that in many parts of the country persons are now in possession of farms which they purchased in recent years notwithstanding that up to the commencement of the disturbed

Commission. The Ministers and Secretaries Act, 1924 assigned the office of the parliamentary draftsman's office to the attorney general's office. Matheson retired in 1943. **35** D/J H.171/44, parliamentary draftsman to the attorney general, 31 Jan. 1924. **36** D/J H.171/44, Duff to the attorney general, 12 Jan. 1924. **37** Dáil Debates vol. 6 col. 1216, 20 Feb. 1924. **38** Dáil Debates vol. 6 col. 1256, 21 Feb. 1924. D/D A.9010 gives a figure of 157 persons arrested and sentenced under the act. **39** It was repeated in section 1(4) for conviction on indictment of arson or armed robbery. **40** Dáil Debates vol. 6 col. 1217. Section 1(4). **41** Section 2(1). **42** D/J H/171/44, note by O'Duffy, 6 Feb. 1924. **43** Schedules attached to D/J H.171/17 and D/J H.171/44 detail the fixed fines, e.g. £10 for a horse, £5 for a cow and 10*s* for a goat. See D/J H5, which gives various examples of agrarian unrest. Memorandum by Duff, 12 Jan. 1924, D/J H.171/44. **44** Section 2(4), (5).

> times they had no means whatsoever of making such purchases. The inference in many such cases is that the land was purchased out of the proceeds of bank or other robberies.[45]

Sections 3, 4 and 5 dealt with the possession and return of stolen property; section 8 permitted changes of trial venue.

Also enacted was a temporary Firearms Act that prohibited the possession of firearms without a licence, punishable on summary conviction by a maximum six months' imprisonment or, on indictment, to a term not exceeding two years.

The ending of hostilities would, however slowly, be followed, by the release of prisoners and internees. Releases had begun in July 1922 provided prisoners sign a suitable undertaking. Exceptions were made if the CID or the army believed prisoners were important anti-Treatyites or had a previous criminal record.[46] Following Liam Deasy's surrender call in February 1923, the government offered an amnesty to internees who accepted his call.[47]

The end of the war was not followed by immediate or mass releases. After June 1923, a continuing review of internees by committees of army officers and by the Protective Corps in Dublin saw 35 of the 'harmless type' released per day. The Protective Corps, though, reported difficulties 'owing to the extreme difficulty in obtaining information relative to the men who are imprisoned. In many cases it was found next to impossible to verify the address given by the prisoners.'[48] By this time, the Protective Corps had investigated over 1,100 cases and recommended continued detention in 20% of cases.[49]

In July 1923, the government decided to class internees into four groups: those no longer regarded as a threat to the state; those who might be released on signing an undertaking, or who might be kept in detention until normality had returned to some particular area; those who might be released when the country had returned to absolute normality; those to be held indefinitely, against whom a serious charge was or would be preferred.[50] While provision for other systems to oversee releases would be planned, most releases appear to have taken place as a result of the continuing reviews carried out by the army and the Protective Corps.

45 D/J H.171/44, Ó Frighil to the commissioner, 6 May 1924. 46 Minutes Provisional Government, 17 July 1922, Dáil Debates vol. 2 col. 1218, 1 Feb. 1923. 47 See minutes of the executive council, 16 Feb. 1923. The executive council decided prisoners would not be given another opportunity to sign out. 48 D/T S.3331, Ó Muireadhaighe to Joseph McGrath, 12 October 1923. 49 See generally Campbell, *Emergency law*, pp 227–32, and 239–42. See also C. Foley, *Legion of the rearguard: the IRA and the modern Irish state* (1992), pp 36–7. See table 1 for a list of the numbers held and released between 1 June 1923 and 21 May 1924. 50 Campbell, *Emergency law*, p. 232.

The minister for Defence presented proposals for the mass-release of internees to the executive council on 14 November 1923. There was, however, some unease in the executive council at the prospect of the prison camps being cleared. Kevin O'Higgins said that he had been informed 'Cork County has not been in a worse condition this three years and that there are other areas which are very little better.'[51] Echoing O'Higgins' views, the postmaster general, J.J. Walsh, wrote, 'I believe that a very large percentage of these prisoners are of the robber type and to release them would only land the country in another crime wave.'[52] He suggested that 'those of this class' be segregated and treated as criminals awaiting trial. The executive council agreed to this and directed that all military prisoners who could be charged before the civil courts should be transferred to civil custody. Investigations were to be carried out by army post intelligence officers in cooperation with local Garda superintendents, and subsequently, the military would hand over all relevant information to the Gardaí. By 5 February 1924, 79 internees had been transferred.[53] During November, 2,304 were released, with 3,574 freed the following month. Numbers fell from 11,480 on 1 July 1923 to 1,852 on 1 January 1924.[54]

Although the Public Safety Act, 1923 provided for internment appeals councils, the department of Home Affairs had neglected to investigate how these might work, forcing it to write urgently to the Irish high commissioner in London on 28 August 1923 enquiring about what it knew of the British experience.[55] It appears that the British had no definite regulations governing the 'Advisory Councils' established under regulation 14B of the Defence of the Realm Act, 1914. After the war, the 'Aliens Repatriation Committee'[56] considered applications submitted by interned enemy aliens who sought exemption from compulsory repatriation. The committee devised a series of 'categories' – a list of conditions to be fulfilled – which it used as a simple guide when deciding whether or not enemy aliens should be allowed to stay in Britain. Based on these investigations, plans were made to present finalized appeal council provisions to the executive council sometime in October 1923,[57] though no council was established.[58]

51 Ernest Blythe Papers, UCDAD, P24/193, O'Higgins to Cosgrave, 15 Nov. 1923. 52 To Richard Mulcahy, 5 Oct. 1923, D/D A.10231. 53 For IRA views on this policy, see *Irish Independent*, 18 Jan. 1924 and Dún Mhuire, Killiney, De Valera Papers 320, 2 Aug. 1924. 54 D/T S.1369/4. 55 See D/J H.210, M.H. Eliasnoff to Duff, 31 July 1923. 56 Command Paper 383, 'Report of Committee appointed to consider applications for exemption from compulsory repatriation submitted by interned enemy aliens'. 57 D/D A.10138, though by 8 Nov. 1923, the department of Defence was still uninformed of progress. 58 A copy of these regulations is in D/J H210, see also Campbell, *Emergency law*, pp 239–40. O'Connor, department of Defence reported to the chief of staff on 18 Sept. 1923 that it took two weeks to investigate queries regarding cases of military detention, and that this would clearly lead to

A rather different system dealt with persons convicted by military courts and committees. A board of commissioners, comprising judges Doyle and Dromgoole, was established under the Indemnity Act, 1923 to investigate these cases, as well as those of National Army defaulters.[59] The minister for Defence devised the board's procedural rules in January 1924, and hearings were held between 27 February and 19 May 1924.[60] IRA prisoners showed little interest in the process – of 323, only 17 made applications to the board.[61] Jeremiah Stapleton of Kinsale, Co. Cork, for instance, had been tried by a military tribunal on 2 February 1923 on charges of unauthorized possession of arms and ammunition and sentenced to death, though the sentence was reduced to ten years' penal servitude on 20 February 1923. The particulars of the sentence were not conveyed to Stapleton until 29 January 1924 when he was supplied with the necessary form to apply to have his sentence reviewed by the board of commissioners, though he refused to avail of the opportunity.[62]

Failure to attract IRA interest forced the government to formulate an alternative approach not requiring prisoner cooperation. W.T. Cosgrave (acting minister for Defence) explained that in making recommendations to the minister for Home Affairs two rules were, as far as practicable, to be adhered to by the judges: the unexpired portions of sentences for acts of war or rebellion pure and simple should be remitted, and sentences in excess of three years for murder, robbery, arson, receiving money under threat or other serious criminal offence should be reduced at least to three years from the date of conviction, without taking into account remissions for good conduct which would accrue in the normal way.[63]

In total, the commissioners wholly remitted 295 sentences, 8 sentences were partially remitted and one was confirmed. Nevertheless the department of Justice did not act immediately on the boards' recommendations, because 70 prisoners were still detained on 30 June 1924 – 14 because of military objections to their release, and 63 because of pending civil charges.[64] All 44 army prisoners held applied to the board for release.[65]

Most of the camps and prisons were cleared by the beginning of 1924. By 1 July 1924 there were 209[66] internees in custody and by 21 July, only

great difficulties were the appeals councils to operate. **59** The act gave retrospective validity to the sentences of military tribunals and committees created after 27 June 1922. The board could contain no fewer than two members, each holding a specified judicial office. Under section 3(3), the board was empowered to review sentences of the military tribunals established during the Civil War, and could confirm, reduce or remit, though not increase the sentences imposed. **60** D/T S.1369/5. **61** Copy of form available in P4/1522; 9 sentences totally remitted, 8 partially remitted. **62** P4/1522, D/D A.6842/1894. **63** P4/569, Cosgrave to Kennedy, 24 May 1924. **64** See Campbell, *Emergency law*, p. 224. **65** Seventeen sentences totally remitted, 18 partially remitted, 9 confirmed. **66** Dáil Debates

two remained.[67] On 4 November 1924, the executive council decided to cease instituting prosecutions against persons believed to have committed offences arising directly or indirectly from the Civil War.[68]

Having comprehensively defeated the IRA, cleared the prison camps and essentially brought the emergency to an end, while establishing ordered conditions which allowed the Gardaí and the courts, for the most part, to operate, the one outstanding matter facing the Government was the reduction of the size of the army to peace time requirements. By May 1923, it numbered 52,000 soldiers and 3,000 officers. Under Richard Mulcahy's direction, numbers would be drastically reduced during the coming year: the army numbered 32,821 by 17 November 1923,[69] and 13,306 by 31 March 1924.[70]

The speed and the manner of the reduction in difficult economic times quickly led to friction. In November 1923, several officers refused their demobilization orders. The minister for Industry and Commerce, Joseph McGrath, resigned from the executive council on 7 March 1924, protesting at the 'mishandling and incompetence' of the department of Defence. More seriously, on 9 March 1924, several officers presented an ultimatum to the executive council demanding an end to demobilization and the removal of the army council. They also accused the government of pursuing policies 'not reconcilable to the Irish people's acceptance of the Treaty'. The ultimatum was immediately denounced by the executive council, which ordered the arrest of the officers' leaders, Major General Liam Tobin and Colonel Charles Dalton. But the whole incident ended abruptly on 19 March 1924 when troops acting under Richard Mulcahy's orders arrested soldiers believed to have been planning attacks on the executive council.[71] By 7 April 1924, the Garda commissioner Eoin O'Duffy, reported that 96 officers had resigned and 6 had deserted.[72] The minister for Defence, however, had failed to inform O'Duffy or the executive council of his plans or developments. Despite Mulcahy's swift and effective

vol. 8 col. 88, 1 July 1924. **67** See D/T S.1369/4. **68** P24/134. See also minutes of the executive council 6 Nov. 1924 and reply to a question from Patrick Ruttledge given by Fitzgerald-Kennedy, 10 Nov. 1927, Dáil Debates vol. 21 col. 1185. On the return of the remains of those executed to relatives after the army withdrew from several posts and the ensuing disturbances see C.2/110, 24 June 1924, minutes of executive council, Eoin O'Duffy to William Cosgrave, D/T S.1884, 27 June 1924, and the *Dundalk Democrat*, 1 Jan. 1924, *Irish Times*, 13 Nov. 1924, Eoin O'Duffy to Ó Frighil, 7 Nov. 1924, D/J H.197/45. **69** On 2 Nov. 1923 massive cuts in army expenditure were announced, falling from £10.5 million in 1923–4, to £4 million in 1924–5. See Fanning, *Independent Ireland*, pp 48–9 and Valiulis, *Mulcahy*, p. 209. **70** P24/222, 7 Apr. 1924, E. O'Duffy to executive council. See also J.J. Lee, *Ireland*, p. 99. **71** 'Departmental Notes', pp 210–1, Ó Broin, *Revolutionary underground*, p. 210–12, Valiulis, *Mulcahy*, pp 199–220. **72** P24/221.

action, the executive council claimed the minister for Defence had overstepped his authority and had endangered the safety of the state.

Within a very short time, Mulcahy was forced to resign and Kevin O'Higgins' ascendancy to a position of dominance in the government followed. Of greater importance to the Irish state, though, was that these events finally ensured the subordination of the military to the civil government. Cosgrave initially took over at Defence, and was eventually replaced by Peter Hughes. Patrick McGilligan replaced McGrath as minister for Industry and Commerce on 3 April 1924.

A further, highly significant, effect of the 'Army Mutiny' was the greater pressure it placed on anti-Treatyites. Because the mutiny led to the resignation of nine Cumann na nGaedheal TDs who sought re-election as the 'National Party' (on the basis of their support for the mutineers and their desire to get a popular mandate for a more proactive policy towards Northern Ireland), the post-Civil War anti-Treatyite stance would shortly be adjudged by the electorate.

2

Civil War aftermath, 1924–1927

By the summer of 1924, the government of the Irish Free State had successfully established the Gardaí and the ordinary courts as the primary law-enforcement agencies. It had also significantly reduced the size of the army, while simultaneously purging its ranks of militant secret societies. Gradually, peace and stability were taking hold. But there remained two major unresolved issues. First, the Boundary Commission, created under article 12 of the Treaty, had yet to conclude its work.[1] Second, although the anti-Treatyites had been decisively defeated, they had not been eradicated, and the threat they posed in post Civil War Ireland remained unclear.

Twelve months after the ending of the Civil War, army intelligence reported that the anti-Treaty movement was imbued with renewed optimism: 'in Sinn Féin and Irregular circles the belief is not only entertained, but is most industriously and continuously propagated, that the Government will be forced to appeal to the country in a few months' time'.[2] Some months earlier, Sinn Féin had re-established a network of clubs throughout the country and was actively collecting funds, spreading propaganda and training members for the forthcoming elections.[3] Nonetheless, the Garda commissioner, Eoin O'Duffy, was unimpressed by anti-Treatyite activities: 'the real weakness of their position, however, lies in the fact that their increase in strength, etc is due to no inherent virtue of themselves or their policy', but because of the widespread unemployment and other social and political issues.[4] He believed that the anti-Treaty political organization had reached its zenith, and without a national crisis would decline. Of concern to O'Duffy, though, was widespread IRA drilling with arms and that on several occasions members held firing practice in public.[5]

The security situation remained unsatisfactory in various parts of the country, especially in southern and western counties. In the West Cork

1 See *Irish Independent*, 4 Feb. 1922; Lee, *Ireland*, pp 141–50, D. McArdle, *The Irish Republic* (1968), pp 793–809. 2 Ernest Blythe papers, UCDAD, P24/222, 'Confidential Report for period ending 26 May 1924', O'Duffy to the executive council, 29 May 1924. 3 See for example captured documents in the National Archives, Dublin, D/T S.1759. 4 P24/222, 29 May 1924. 5 Drilling was reported in Kerry, Limerick, Wexford, Meath, and Louth. O'Duffy also reported that Frank Aiken's assistant had been to Liverpool purchasing arms.

town of Drimoleague, for example, the IRA threatened local Gardaí, warning them not to supply information to the army.[6] Other parts of west Cork remained poor because of robbery and agrarian agitation, though the Gardaí and the army were actively seeking to curb these problems.[7] IRA columns were said to be roaming in the districts around Rathmore, Kilcummin, Beaufort, and Derreen in Co. Kerry, though they were not interfering with the public. In Leitrim, 'the people are stated to be hostile and unwilling to assist the Garda'; while a group of ten or twelve IRA men that was blamed for two bank robberies in the county continued to evade arrest. Also worrying was the increase of the IRA in south County Dublin: 'it is reliably reported that we are losing ground rapidly.'

Nonetheless, improvements were reported in Co. Sligo following the establishment of a military post at Grange, though, when charges were brought against IRA members, witnesses would not attend court unless they were first arrested. Generally, the country was becoming more peaceful. Indeed, Gardaí reported that in East Cork, one of the most troubled areas during and after the Civil War,

> There is less of the feeling of terror and more confidence among the people, who appear to be reverting to the ordinary activities of life, the tendency to have recourse to deeds of violence is receding, and a better moral tone seems to be emerging from the chaos and suspicion and uncertainty of the past two years.[8]

As the security situation improved, far-reaching political developments began to unfold. By November 1924, there were 14 vacancies in Dáil Éireann. Nine had arisen when Joseph McGrath and eight other members of the National Party resigned their seats following the 'Army Mutiny', protesting at 'government by a clique and officialdom of the old regime'.[9] Five by-elections were held on 18 November 1924[10] and there was a marked increase in Sinn Féin's vote, resulting in the election of two members. The frantic organizational work that had begun in early 1924 continued well into 1925 as the party prepared for the remaining by-elections and the general election which it expected at any time. These activities, though, could not conceal the very grave discord growing within anti-Treatyite political ranks.

Military intelligence reported an 'acute difference of opinion in the inner circles – almost amounting to a split.' Within Sinn Féin and the

6 P24/222, 29 May 1924. 7 Ibid., monthly police report for May 1924, Mac Donnchadh to the secretary to the executive council, 16 June 1924. 8 Ibid., police reports 29 May 1924. 9 Quoted in McArdle, *The Irish Republic*, p. 801. 10 In Dublin, Cork and Donegal.

IRA there was, however, agreement on one point: the party would win next general election. While certain elements 'look forward to this event as the date upon which the Republic may be legitimately re-established as the Government of the country', others sought a clearer definition of policy regarding England, Northern Ireland, and existing government services, maintaining 'their party could take over the existing machinery of Government without having any internal troubles.' Doctrinaire republicans denounced this as 'trimming' and 'weakness'.[11]

Regardless of disagreements among senior anti-Treatyites politicians, the IRA's policy and outlook had become much clearer. Working on the assumption that Sinn Féin would be the majority party in less than a year, the IRA was reported to be organizing

> at a feverish rate with the general objective of being in a position to take over the country from a military point of view when their party is in a majority. If a suitable opportunity of effecting a coup by which the various Military Barracks etc., can be captured, presents itself it will be taken advantage of, provided the political situation justifies such action. Members of GHQ Staff have stated that they could take over every Barracks in Ireland outside Dublin, the Curragh and Athlone within a few days if their organisation proceeds according to plan during the summer.

IRA divisions in the south and west had, apparently, been ordered to prepare to advance on the army barracks in the Curragh and in Athlone respectively.[12]

It was against the background of IRA reorganization and potential Sinn Féin schism that the executive council sought to legislate for the public safety in post Civil War Ireland. The unusual powers of arrest and detention, search and seizure exercised by the army and the Gardaí during the Civil War and afterwards had gone through a number of changes, but all had been of an extraordinary and temporary nature, justified by the exigencies of the situation. As the country moved further from war, the Gardaí became primarily responsible for the maintenance of order,[13] and the continued use of extraordinary legal powers became increasingly difficult to defend. Given Ireland's particular circumstances though, it appeared that permanent public safety measures would be unavoidable.

As early as 1923, the government sought permanent and rigid firearms control. Further, while a violent IRA resurgence was expected, the minister for Defence, Richard Mulcahy, anticipated anti-Treatyites pursuing

11 P24/222, report for period ending 15 Feb. 1925. 12 Ibid. 13 D/J D.53/36, T.A. Finlay to the secretary of the department of Defence, 29 Jan. 1925.

other avenues. In October 1923, he asked the attorney general, Hugh Kennedy, to consider how charges for treason and other offences against the state might be brought, believing 'the possible attitude of the Irregulars is to set up an authority in the country as distinct from the Government, to call themselves Minister for this and that, and to keep armed forces. We must have native laws that will enable us deal with persons guilty of such offences.'[14] Permanent legislation dealing with treason, treasonable offences, and sedition was required. Finally, the executive council sought powers to regulate public meetings.

The Free State inherited the English law regulating public meetings. It dealt with questions such as the right of passage on a street, the reasonableness of those holding a meeting, etc. Although the law did not recognize a specific right to hold public meetings, it was one 'which has long since passed out of the region of discussion or doubt', Mr Justice Wills explained in *ex parte Lewis*.[15]

Circumstances in Ireland were complicated by several factors, however. For instance, the department of Justice contended that persons attending meetings in Ireland were often reasonably suspected of carrying arms, though the English law had never evolved to deal with this.[16] Further, article 9 of the constitution guaranteed very wide rights 'to assemble peaceably and without arms' so long as 'not opposed to public morality', and provided that laws regulating this right could contain 'no political, religious or class distinction'.[17] The department of Justice also claimed that public meetings in Dublin were causing 'considerable loss and inconvenience' to business people.[18]

A draft Public Meetings Bill drawn up in November 1923 proposed to outlaw any public meeting in any public place 'unless such permission as is authorized by this Act shall have been previously given for the holding of such meeting.' The Garda commissioner, with the approval of the minister for Home Affairs, might, by proclamation, give general permission and apply various conditions for the holding of such meetings 'in any specified public place or places', and could revoke permission at any time. Proclamations were to be advertised in newspapers 'and in such other ways as the [Garda] commissioner shall think expedient.' If a person sought to hold a public meeting 'not authorized by any general permission', he would be required to apply at least three days in advance 'to the chief officer of

14 Hugh Kennedy Papers, UCDAD, P4/662, Mulcahy to Kennedy, 29 Oct. 1923. 15 [1888] 21 QBD 196. 16 D/J D.53/36, memorandum prepared by Duff, 18 Nov. 1936. 17 D/T S.3400, memorandum prepared by John A. Costello, sent by Hugh Kennedy to Ó Frighil, secretary of the department of Home Affairs, 18 Dec. 1923. 18 Ibid., 14 Nov. 1923, Éinrí Ó Frighil to the executive council.

the police of the area' where the meeting was to be held, detailing its purpose, proposed time, where it would be held, and giving his name and address, or the name of the organization on whose behalf the meeting was planned. Permission could be refused if the meeting was expected to interfere with traffic, to be prejudicial to the preservation of public peace and order, or if it passed near an industrial dispute.

Hugh Kennedy concluded, however, that the draft bill was 'unconstitutional and bad'.[19] An amended draft that sought to prohibit meetings that obstructed traffic was prepared by October 1924 and regarded by the attorney general to be constitutional.[20] Nevertheless, the legislation was abandoned. Years later, when drafting the Offences against the State Act, 1939, the secretary of the department of Justice, Stephen Roche,[21] explained that it was impossible to satisfactorily draft public meetings legislation because the terms of article 9 were so broad.

Less challenging, however, was firearms legislation. The provisions of the 1923 Public Safety Act dealing with firearms were continued as temporary measures in 1924[22] and 1925. Statutory firearms' control existed under the British Firearms Act, 1920,[23] but the Irish government never enforced it and was very reluctant to bring charges under it.[24] Instead, a permanent and native measure was devised.[25]

A draft bill was prepared by 8 January 1925, though a number of technical matters delayed its introduction to the Dáil.[26] Kevin O'Higgins explained, 'there is no particular necessity for me to argue from the point of view of the preservation of peace and order in the country that it is necessary to have the possession of firearms restricted and controlled'.[27]

19 Ibid., 18 Dec. 1923, Kennedy to Ó Frighil. **20** Ibid., O'Higgins to the executive council, 23 Oct. 1924. **21** Stephen Anselm Roche (1890–1949) Born in Co. Kerry, he spent much of his childhood on Barra off Scotland where his father worked for the Excise. Educated in Blackrock College and TCD where he gained a BA and LLB. He entered the British civil service, working first in Edinburgh and then in the estate duty office, in Dublin. He entered the Free State department of Home Affairs in 1922. He was involved in drafting every Courts of Justice act after 1924 and played a significant role in devising public safety legislation after 1930, he became secretary of the department of Justice in 1934. **22** Became law on 5 Apr. 1924, and remained in force for 12 months. **23** 10 and 11 Geo. 5 c.43. **24** D/J H.171/38, department of Home Affairs to District Justice Flattery (Sligo), 9 Feb. 1924. Such prosecutions would have been possible, though, under the Adaptation of Enactments Act, 1923. **25** On discussions regarding the consolidation of the Gun Licence Act, 1870 and the Game Licence Act, 1860 see D/T S.4111, Ó Frighil to the secretary of the department of Finance, 16 July 1924. **26** The department of Finance wanted fees dealt with in the Finance Bill; therefore, the Firearms Bill had to be redrafted. The resulting delay meant that the permanent firearms measure was not ready for enactment once the temporary legislation lapsed, which had to be continued until 1 Aug. 1925. See also Dáil Debates vol. 11 col. 427, 28 Apr. 1925. **27** Dáil Debates vol.

The Firearms Act, 1925 prohibited the possession of firearms and ammunition without a certificate,[28] and prescribed that a firearms certificate would only be granted if a Garda superintendent or the minister for Justice was satisfied that an individual 'has a good reason for requiring the firearm ... can be permitted to have in his possession, use, and carry a firearm or ammunition without danger to the public safety or to the peace; and is not a person declared by this Act to be disentitled to hold a firearm certificate'.[29] The legislation created a register of firearms dealers,[30] restricted the manufacture and sale of firearms,[31] required firearms dealers to keep a register 'of all purchases, hiring, sales, repairs, and other transactions of or in relation to firearms or ammunition made by him',[32] and regulated the import and export of firearms and ammunition.[33] Conviction for possession of firearms 'with intent to endanger life or cause serious injury to property', or 'with intent to enable any other person by means of such firearm or ammunition to endanger life or cause serious injury to property' could be punished by a maximum of 20 years' penal servitude.[34]

A Garda was entitled to demand the production of a firearm certificate 'from any person whom he observes or believes to be in possession of, using, or carrying a firearm or any ammunition'; if no certificate was produced, the Garda could demand the person's name and address. Persons refusing to give their name and address could be arrested without warrant. Further, a Garda could stop, search and arrest without warrant any person whom he believed was in possession of or using or carrying a firearm or ammunition in contravention of the Act and seize any firearm or ammunition in the person's possession.[35] A Garda superintendent could issue a search warrant 'to any one or more' Gardaí under his command if 'there is reasonable ground for supposing that an offence under this Act has been, is being, or is about to be committed.'[36]

The final element of the Irish Free State's public safety legislation programme was the development of a permanent measure dealing anti-state organizations and offences against the state. Work finally began in late 1924 when Thomas Finlay,[37] assistant secretary of the department of Justice[38] asked the attorney general, John O'Byrne, to appraise existing treason and sedition legislation in the Irish Free State.[39] Finlay was con-

11 col. 426, 28 Apr. 1925. **28** Section 2. **29** Section 4. The grounds for revocation were similar, section 5. **30** Section 9. **31** Section 10. **32** Section 12. **33** Sections 16 and 17. **34** Section 15, **35** Section 22. **36** Section 24. **37** (1893–1932) Born in Co. Cavan, educated in Clongowes Wood College and UCD. Called to the Bar in 1915, he was appointed a district justice in 1922, but resigned in 1924 when he entered the department of Justice. He returned to the Bar in 1928, taking silk in 1930. He was elected to the Dáil as a Cumann na nGaedheal TD in 1932. **38** The department of Home Affairs was renamed the department of Justice in 1924. **39** D/J H.266/15, no date, approximately

cerned that a prosecution for treason, for example, would only be possible with reference to the English king – a person would have to be charged under the Treason Act, 1351 with either compassing the king's death or levying war against him.[40]

The 1351 Act defined treason as:

1. compassing the death of the king, queen, or prince, and declaring the same by an overt act;
2. violation or carnal knowledge of the king's consort, the king's eldest daughter unmarried, or the prince's wife;
3. levying war against the king;
4. adhering to the king's enemies within the land or without, and declaring the same by some overt act;
5. counterfeiting the great seal or privy seal;
6. counterfeiting the king's coin, or bringing counterfeit coin into the realm;
7. killing the chancellor, treasurer, justices of one bench or the other, justices in eyre, justices in assize, justices of *oyer* and *terminer* in their places doing their offices.[41]

Treason consisted of four basic elements: treachery; the breach of the feudal bond; that the duty to the king was greater than the feudal duty to the lord; the adoption of the Roman law *laesa majestas*. The first, third and fourth elements sought to protect the king, though the fourth was not extended by judicial construction in the way that first and third were.[42]

Clearly, the provisions of the 1351 Act could not be directly applied in the independent Irish state. Regardless of that obvious difficulty, the offence of 'treason' presents substantial legal and political problems, elegantly described by the American legal historian James Willard Hurst:

> Accurate definition of the intent and act elements and the policies underlying their definition provides the central and most difficult problems in the law of treason. Treason is the betrayal of allegiance owed a sovereign either because of citizenship or because of accept-

17 Oct. 1924. **40** A comprehensive account of the development of treason law from the time of the early English writers Bracton and Glanville, through to Coke and Foster, and, later, James F. Stephen, can be found in J.W. Hurst, *The law of treason in the United States: collected essays* (1971). It also deals with the history of treason prior to American independence, treason under the American constitution, and cases since the 1940s, including the Cramer case. An earlier, comprehensive discussion is in Hale, *The history of the pleas of the crown* (1972), vol. 1, pp 58–382. **41** Hale, *Pleas*, vol. 1, p. 91. **42** W. Holdsworth, *A history of English law* (1966), vol. 8, p. 307.

> ance of the protection of laws. Obviously the intention is at the heart of such a crime. Is an act a distinct element of the offense, in addition to the showing of the intent to betray? Must the act be of some peculiar character, or must it be such as to furnish some evidence, or evidence beyond a reasonable doubt, of the existence of the treasonable intention? The crime is the most serious against the safety of the state; but, by the same token, the stigma it carries, and the vagueness of its reach have made it a notorious instrument of arbitrary power and political faction. This contrast poses the further question, whether in a doubtful case policy calls upon the court to extend the scope of the offense for the protection of the state, or to restrict it for the protection of the individual.[43]

The only relatively recent cases brought under the 1351 Act and related to Ireland are *R. v Lynch*,[44] and *R. v Casement*.[45] For the most part, offences falling within the 1351 Act's definition of treason were, since 1848, disposed of under the Treason Felony Act, 1848. Although not repealing the 1351 Act, it dealt with conspiracy to depose the king, levying war for the purpose of altering the law or intimidating parliament, or urging foreigners to invade the United Kingdom. Conspiracy was to be expressed in printing, writing or by overt act or deed.[46]

There were several other offences to be considered. At the end of 1924, the only power dealing with revolt was contained in part 1 of the schedule of the Public Safety (Punishment of Offences) Act, 1924, which was due to lapse on 21 April 1925. The department of Justice was eager to have this provision made permanent and expanded to cover actions designed to prevent or impede the functioning of Dáil Éireann.[47] In addition, Finlay recommended that section 3 of the Treason Felony Act, 1848 be adapted to declare that conspiracy to commit a treasonable offence would constitute an offence of equal gravity. He further suggested that 'sedition' be redefined to include the offences of declaring in speech or writing that the Oireachtas was not the lawful legislature of Saorstát Éireann or that it did not have the power to make valid laws. He also proposed outlawing the use, without lawful authority, of the titles of government ministers or other titles that might lead to misapprehension. Additionally, offences including unlawful drilling, establishing unlawful courts and incitement to mutiny were examined.[48] The department of

43 Hurst, *Treason*, pp 14–15. 44 [1903] 20 CCC 468. 45 [1916] 25 CCC 480. 46 Notable cases include *R. v. Gallagher and others* [1883] 15 CCC 291, *Mulcahy v. R.* [1867–8] L.R. 3 H.L. 306, *R. v. Davitt* [1870] 11 CCC 676, *R. v. Deasy and others* [1883] 15 CCC 334. 47 D/J H.266/15, no date, approximately 17 Oct. 1924. 48 D/J

Justice prepared heads of legislation by 30 October 1924, and following a conference on 26 January 1925,[49] drafting of the Treasonable and Seditious Offences Bill, 1925 was completed on 30 January 1925.

Addressing the Dáil on 11 February 1925, Kevin O'Higgins explained that the bill would 'equip the Executive with sufficient powers to deal with offences directly against the State and provide suitable punishment for such offences.' Reliance on temporary public safety legislation was 'an eminently undesirable state of affairs', he said, adding 'every modern civilised State, as far as I know, equips itself with powers to meet a challenge at an earlier stage than when the matter would come to one of actual physical combat.'[50]

Section 1 defined treason as:

(a) levying war against Saorstát Éireann;
(b) assisting any state or person engaged in levying war against Saorstát Éireann;
(c) conspiring with any person (other than his or her wife or husband) or inciting any person to levy war against Saorstát Éireann;
(d) attempting or taking part or being concerned in an attempt to overthrow by force of arms or other violent means the Government of Saorstát Éireann as established by or under the Constitution;
(e) conspiring with any person (other than his or her wife or husband) or inciting any person to make or to take part or be concerned in any such attempt.[51]

Citizens or persons ordinarily resident in Saorstát Éireann who committed treason outside the state would also be guilty of treason.[52] Punishment would be death. Persons convicted of encouraging, harbouring, or comforting persons levying war against the state or attempting to overthrow the government by violence could be punished by a maximum of 20 years' penal servitude.[53]

Persons charged with treason were to be indicted, arraigned, and tried in the same manner as if charged with murder.[54] Initially, though, the bill provided that the evidence of one witness would suffice to convict. The

H.266/15, attorney general to Finlay, 21 Oct. 1924. **49** In attendance were Kevin O'Higgins, the attorney general (John O'Byrne), the parliamentary draftsman, Mr Hearne, Ó Frighil and Finlay. **50** Dáil Debates vol. 10 col. 118. 11 Feb. 1925 and vol. 10 col. 271, 18 Feb. 1925. **51** Section 1(1). **52** Section 1(2). **53** Section 1(3). **54** Section 1(4).

department of Justice believed this was a justifiable departure from the English law, arguing that a rebellion or armed uprising would lead to many deaths and, thus, to difficulty obtaining witnesses. But several TDs argued that the two witnesses rule protected against the perjured evidence of one informer and Ó Frighil concluded that incorporating such a provision[55] would not compromise the general fabric of the section.[56]

Section 2 provided for misprision of treason – failing to immediately inform a district justice or a Garda or 'other person lawfully engaged on duties relating to the preservation of peace and order' that an act of treason 'is intended or proposed to be, or is being, or has been committed.'

Section 3 outlawed attempting, taking part or being concerned in an attempt 'by force of arms or other violent means to overawe or intimidate in any way' the governor general, executive ministers, members of the Oireachtas, or any judges 'with a view to influencing their or his actions'; assisting, encouraging, harbouring or protecting any person engaged or taking part or concerned in any such attempt; conspiring with or inciting any person to make or to take part or be concerned in any such attempt.[57] These subheadings were adapted from the Treason Felony Act, 1848,[58] and had 'simply been altered to suit the conditions of the Saorstát', the department of Justice explained.[59] Section 3 also prohibited the establishment of pretended courts and courts-martial,[60] and the incitement of Gardaí or soldiers to desert or to mutiny or of any civil servant to commit any act or omission in dereliction of his duty.[61]

Also proscribed was the usurpation of the functions of any government minister or person in the service of Saorstát Éireann (police, army or civil service);[62] membership of an assembly purporting or attempting to exercise the powers of either House of the Oireachtas.[63] Unlawful drilling and military exercises were also outlawed;[64] the burden of proof that drilling was authorized would be shifted to the accused.[65] Forming, organizing, promoting or maintaining secret societies in the army or Gardaí was also proscribed,[66] as was the administration of oaths that bound persons to commit, plan, promote, conceal or assist in any crime or any breach of the peace or to abstain from giving or disclosing information on such offences or to

55 This was inserted as section 1(5). **56** D/J 93/2/5, Dáil Debates vol. 10 col. 1061, 12 Mar. 1925. **57** Section 3(1)(a), (b) and (c). **58** 11 Vic., c. 12. **59** D/J 93/2/5. **60** D/J 93/2/5 and Dáil Debates vol. 10 col. 416, examples were given of pretended courts operating in South Leitrim where suspects were tried for offences after having been kidnapped. Following conviction, these courts order convicted persons imprisoned; prisoners were detained in remote farmhouses and outhouses. In Galway, an unauthorized court dealt with an eviction problem. **61** This subsection was an adaptation and extension of the terms of the Incitement to Mutiny Act, 1797, 36 Geo. 3, ch. 70. **62** Section 4. **63** Section 5. **64** Section 7(1). **65** Section 7(5). **66** Section 8(1).

abstain from giving evidence against persons who committed such offences; or to become members of organizations whose object was committing crimes or breaches of the peace; to abstain from disclosing or giving information regarding the existence, formation or proposed formation or giving evidence against persons involved in the formation of such organizations.[67]

A district justice could issue a search warrant if 'satisfied on the information on oath' given by a Garda not below the rank of chief superintendent that there was a reasonable ground for suspecting that there are treasonable documents in any specified building, land, premises, or other place.[68] A warrant would last 48 hours and would name a specific Garda officer not below the rank of superintendent, who would be accompanied by other Gardaí as the officer thought proper, permitting them to search the specified building, land or premises and to seize all documents that appeared to the officer to be treasonable.[69] A Garda officer conducting a search was entitled to demand the name and address of any person found during a search and to arrest without warrant persons who refused to give their name or address or who gave a name or address which the officer knew or suspected to be false or misleading, using force if necessary.[70]

When first introduced, the bill defined seditious libel as declaring or publishing by speech or writing that:

(a) the Constitution was not the lawful Constitution of Saorstát Éireann, or
(b) the Executive Council, or the president, or the vice-president, or a Minister duly appointed under and in accordance with the Constitution was not the lawful executive council, president, vice-president, or minister of Saorstát Éireann, or
(c) the Oireachtas is not the lawful legislature of Saorstát Éireann, or that the Oireachtas had not power to make valid laws for Saorstát Éireann, or
(d) any lawfully established Court duly functioning under and in accordance with the Constitution was not a valid and lawful Court, or
(e) uttered or published any speech or writing with a seditious intention as defined by this section.

It defined seditious conspiracy as agreeing 'with any person (not being his or her wife or husband) to do any act for the furtherance of a seditious

67 Section 9(1). This section was derived from the Unlawful Oaths Act, 1797. 68 Section 10(1). 69 Section 10(2). 70 Section 10(3), 'In this section the expression 'treasonable document' includes any document which relates, directly or indirectly, to the commission of any act which is by this Act declared to be treason or to be a felony or a misdemeanour.'

intention common to both such persons.' Seditious intention was defined as the intention to

> (a) to bring into hatred or contempt or to excite disaffection against the Constitution, or the Executive Council or any member thereof or any other minister duly appointed under and in accordance with the Constitution, or the Oireachtas or either House thereof, or any lawful court or any judge of any such court, or
> (b) to incite any person to attempt to bring about or effect (otherwise than in accordance with law) the alternation of the Constitution or of the law established by or under the Constitution, or the repeal or alteration of any British Statute or Act of the Oireachtas, or
> (c) to raise, promote, or foment discontent or dissatisfaction among the citizens of Saorstát Éireann or feelings of ill-will or hostility between different classes of such citizens, or
> (d) to incite any person to commit any crime in breach of the peace.[71]

In the department of Justice's view, it was simply adapting the English jurist James Stephen's unchallenged definitions of seditious libel, of speaking seditions words, and of seditious intention to Irish circumstances. While it expected Labour Party opposition to these provisions, it did not believe they represented any danger.

Many TDs, however, expressed outright hostility towards the bill. One described treason as 'feudal'.[72] Darrell Figgis (a member of the drafting committee of the 1922 constitution) conceded that there was a need for offences against the state legislation, but asked that the words 'treason' and 'sedition' be dispensed with: 'they are words with no happy history in this country'.[73] Richard Mulcahy, free to criticize the government since March 1924, wondered where 'usurpation of the functions of Government' was occurring. He conceded, though, there was some drilling. He further contended that, for instance, that in place of a mandatory death penalty for treason, judges ought to have some discretion and power to impose lighter sentences in certain cases.[74] The department of Justice dismissed this: 'treason should be dealt with by the death sentence only … provid-

71 Punishment was set at a fine not exceeding £500 or, at the discretion of the court, to imprisonment with or without hard labour for any term not exceeding two years or to both such fine and such imprisonment. 72 Major Cooper, Dáil Debates vol. 10 col. 347, 18 Feb. 1925. 73 Dáil Debates vol. 10 col. 356. 74 Dáil Debates vol. 10 col. 365–371.

ing an alternative punishment would be that the death sentence would never be imposed ... it must be remembered that the prerogative of mercy always exists.'[75] More specifically, Mulcahy maintained that there could be one very serious and undesirable consequence if section 1(c) were retained: 'the arrest of one, or two, or more persons attending what might be called a battalion or brigade council meeting of the Irregulars, and discussing among themselves the purchase say of arms for arming themselves, would mean, according to my reading of the clause, that any of these persons might be sentenced to death.'[76] Kevin O'Higgins agreed – a new provision (section 6) was added making it an offence to be a member of or to take part or assist 'in the formation, organization, or maintenance of any association or other body which purports to be a military or police force, and is not established and maintained as such by law'. Maximum punishment would be five years' penal servitude.

The department of Justice, however, dismissed criticism that section 3 came almost verbatim from the Treason Felony Act, 1848[77] as 'purely sentimental'.[78]

Clearly much more than expected, the section covering sedition was the most highly criticized of the bill. Thomas Johnson and Richard Mulcahy, among others, contended at length that the provision not only amounted to an attack on free speech, but would be exploited by those opposed to the state intent on generating propaganda for their policies and activities.[79] Because of the scale of opposition, the department of Justice proposed more clearly defining sedition – fomenting violence was a fundamental aspect of the offence. The parliamentary draftsman prepared an alternative:

> Every person who shall by speech or writing incite any person to offer active resistance to any person in the service (whether military, police, or civil) of Saorstát Éireann or the service of any local authority in the exercise of his powers or performance of his duties in such service or to attain by violence or breach of the peace any object or to commit any crime shall be guilty of the misdemeanour of seditious libel and shall be liable on conviction thereof to a fine not exceeding five hundred pounds or, at the discretion of the court, to imprisonment with or without hard labour for any term not exceeding two years or to both such fine and such imprisonment.

75 D/J 93/2/5, no date, department of Justice notes for second reading. 76 Dáil Debates vol. 10 col. 1024, 12 Mar. 1925. 77 Dáil Debates vol. 10 col. 294, 18 Feb. 1925. 78 D/J 93/2/5, department of Justice notes for second reading. 79 See for example Dáil Debates vol. 10 col. 298.

W.T. Cosgrave felt that this offered no improvement on the common law position: 'the [original] section in the Bill is foolproof, but this amendment is much worse. It would be better to leave it out all together.' He concluded, 'Personally, I don't mind an occasional outburst of sedition or seditious libel. It is tolerated to an almost alarming extent in England, and has been generally regarded as a safety valve. An otherwise negligible minority might achieve notoriety by seditious libel in Bill form.'[80] The words 'and seditious' were removed from the title on 3 April 1925 and the section was deleted.[81]

There was strident opposition to the measure in the Dáil; each vote was notable for the large number of abstentions. As *An Phoblacht* pointed out on 24 July 1925, an average of 28 TDs supported the bill at each vote, 14 voted against, with 63 TDs abstaining; there were a further 48 Sinn Féin TDs outside the Dáil. The bill finally passed on 3 April 1925, 30 votes to 13. Indeed, opposition was such that O'Higgins asked:

> If Deputies think there ought to be no prosecutions for such offences, they should say so. If they think there ought to be prosecutions, they should equip the Executive with power for such prosecutions. Prosecutions must be brought under some Act, under some section, under some subsection ... Because you have a State you will have treasonable offences, and if they are treasonable, let us not be afraid to call them so. Similarly, you will have sedition ... Sedition leads up to treason. It is the preparation for treason.[82]

Reminding deputies of the difficulties experienced when the Dáil considered the first Public Safety Act in 1923, and of the relative ease of passage of similar legislation in late 1923 and early 1924, he remarked, 'in regard to Bills of this kind you have to experiment. You have to see to what extent the Dáil has developed in a political sense towards maturity.'[83]

The lapsing of the Public Safety Acts in early 1925 left the Gardaí with significant difficulties. *An Phoblacht* reported that Gardaí in Co. Kerry had resorted to bringing charges under the eighteenth-century Whiteboy Act when two men were charged before Judge O'Donoghue in Tralee with 'uttering a threatening letter' to a former army officer.[84] There were other

80 D/T S.4263, memorandum by W.T. Cosgrave to the executive council, 27 Feb. 1925. For O'Higgins' comments on the alternative draft, see Dáil Debates vol. 10 col. 1259–60, 19 Mar. 1925. 81 D/J H.266/15, the attorney general to O'Higgins, 2 Mar. 1925; Dáil Debates vol. 10 col 1259–1264, 19 Mar. 1925. 82 Dáil Debates vol. 10 col. 411–12, 19 Feb. 1925. 83 Dáil Debates vol. 10 col. 1261–2, 19 Mar. 1925. 84 *An Phoblacht*, 17 July 1925.

problems. For instance, James O'Brien, state solicitor for Tipperary, reported the failure of juries in the county to convict.[85] Following one particular case, he complained, 'In my opinion the verdict of the jury was perverse. The case was conclusively moved against the accused and on the return of the verdict the Judge told the Jury he did not agree with it', but added, 'it is useless to repine because country jurors disregard their oaths. There is little or no sense of civic duty in the country.' The attorney general reminded the minister for Justice that Gardaí could apply for changes of venue 'in all cases in which it is feared the juries in that County will not perform their duty with impartiality' under section 54 of the Courts of Justice Act, 1924.[86]

Alternative proposals had been put forward to deal with the IRA in early 1925. The general officer commanding, Southern Command, suggested that the houses of prominent and active IRA members be periodically searched for arms. The Garda commissioner, Eoin O'Duffy, wrote he would 'be slow to adopt' such a proposal in the absence of reasonable grounds for believing arms would be found, adding he was 'rather disposed to question the utility of the wisdom of searching houses of certain people in the absence of any definite suspicions, and in order merely to harass them.'[87] Thomas Finlay added that the general searches contemplated 'would probably cause some irritation and would not be likely to afford any corresponding advantages.'[88] In any event, as the Firearms Bill and the Treasonable Offences Bill would shortly become law, such tactics appeared unnecessary.

July 1925 saw nationwide raids for arms and documents and the first arrests under the Treasonable Offences Act, 1925. Initial results were both promising and noteworthy.[89] The most significant raid occurred on 30 July 1925 when the Garda special branch arrested Michael Carolan, IRA director of intelligence, Seán McBride, IRA director of finance, and Dr Con Lucy, IRA director of medical services, in Dublin.[90] Gardaí also recovered an enormous number of IRA intelligence and medical reports, and documents detailing every IRA volunteer, covering the whole period from 1922 to 1925. The arrested men were charged under section 6 with unlawfully taking part and assisting in the 'organisation and maintenance' of an unlawful military force.[91] The department of Justice was keen that more serious

85 D/J H.8/876, 23 May 1925. 86 Ibid., on 28 May 1925. 87 D/J H.197/51, 14 Feb. 1925, Eoin O'Duffy to the secretary of the department of Justice. 88 D/J H.197/51, Finlay to the secretary of the department of Defence, 16 Feb. 1925. 89 P24/122, 15 Sept. 1925. 90 D/J H.264/16, 31 July 1925. Preliminary report by the chief superintendent, detective branch, to minister for Justice. 91 D/J H.264/16, 31 July 1925, initialled by Finlay, approved by the attorney general.

charges were not brought against IRA members under section 1 which the minister for Justice did not consider 'desirable in present conditions'.[92]

When Michael Carolan was tried before Green Street courthouse in Dublin, he refused to recognize the court, though addressing it in Irish, he admitted membership of the IRA. The trial judge, Thomas O'Shaughnessy, who was unable to understand the language, was forced to ask for help from an uncooperative *An Phoblacht* reporter. Eventually, the jury retired and after 25 minutes returned a guilty verdict but added, '[we] do not consider [Carolan] a criminal'. An exasperated O'Shaughnessy interjected, 'That is not the question, the accused is a criminal in the eyes of the law.'[93]

It quickly became clear that securing convictions against republicans would be difficult.[94] Peter McMahon and Gerald O'Reilly had been tried on charges of forming an illegal military force, but both refused to plead, and the jury found each man 'not guilty'. The presiding judge afterwards claimed that it was impossible to have found McMahon, in particular, 'not guilty': 'Any men who are capable of bringing in such perverse verdicts ... are unfit to discharge the duties of jurors ... The necessary result must be that persons in this country can be deprived of the right, possessed by persons in other countries of being tried by juries of their fellow countrymen. They have to be tried in some other venue.'[95]

Although prosecutions were instigated against members of other anti-Treaty organizations, there were similar results. When charges were brought against 12 members of the Fianna Éireann boy scouts for illegal drilling all were discharged.[96]

Worse still was the realization that section 6 was largely ineffectual. In a case before District Justice Louis Walsh, documents relating to an illegal military force were used as the sole evidence against an accused, but because the documents were dated prior to the enactment of the Treasonable Offences Act, 1925 the charges were dismissed. Walsh ruled, 'Article 43 of the Constitution expressly laid down that no Act to be passed by the Oireachtas could make any offence punishable which was not punishable at the passing of this Act, or, in other words, that Acts were not retrospective.'[97] If documents were left undated or carried notional pre-June 1925 dates, charges under section 6 would fail.

92 D/J H.264/16, 6 Aug. 1925, Ó Frighil to the Commissioner. See also A/G 229/25, 3 Nov. 1925, chief state solicitor, Michael Corrigan, to the attorney general. 93 U. Mac Eoin (ed.), *The IRA in the twilight years, 1923–1948* (1997), p. 120. Carolan was sentenced to 12 months' imprisonment. 94 See for example, *An Phoblacht*, 20 Nov. 1925, and table 2 for a summary of prosecutions under the Treasonable Offences Act, 1925, 1925 to 1937. See Mac Eoin (ed.), *The IRA*, p. 120. 95 *An Phoblacht*, 23 Apr. 1926. 96 Ibid., 15 Jan. 1926, 5 Mar. 1926. 97 A/G 233/25, Finlay to the attorney general, 16 Oct. 1925. See also *An Phoblacht*, 14 Aug. 1925.

Writing in 1930, Eoin O'Duffy identified other problems with the act:

> the procedure to be followed renders [section 11] impractical. If, for example, a [detective officer] has reasonable grounds for suspecting that there are treasonable documents in any place, he must report the matter to his sergeant who, in turn, reports to his Superintendent who, in turn, reports to his Chief Superintendent who must swear an information before a District Justice in a matter in which he has no personal knowledge, and the latter may issue a search warrant. The warrant must be executed by a Superintendent within 48 hours, and it has been held after all this that the possession of such documents is not itself an offence.[98]

Throughout this period, Sinn Féin continued its frantic preparations for the remaining nine by-elections, while some in the IRA still spoke of renewed hostilities. Military intelligence reported that the IRA's leadership sought 'a trained and organised force to resist a feared military dictatorship in the event of a defeat of the Government in a general election. The dictatorship is being freely discussed in Irregular circles.' It added: 'Much attention is being paid to the new detective force which is regarded as having been purposely organised to help in the setting up of a dictatorship should the need arise.'[99] But most republicans conceded that there was no hope of attaining republican objectives in 'the present generation'. Some spoke of entering the Dáil, arguing it would hasten the government's downfall. This naturally increased friction within anti-Treaty circles.

Internal anti-Treatyite difficulties were dismissed by members of the government, particularly the minister for Justice:

> We have got to face facts. Mr de Valera hates facts like a cat hates water, and we have got to rub these facts into him during the next few weeks. It is time we grew up and recognised that we cannot just live in a world of make believe. If we denounce the Treaty and tear up the Constitution it does not mean that by the mere act of doing that you will get international recognition of the sovereign and independent Republic. It is more likely to mean a Crown Colony, and it is certain to mean the loss of the Northeast, as well as the economic ruin of the State.[1]

98 Desmond Fitzgerald Papers, UCDAD, P80/856/11, report by the commissioner on organizations inimical to the state, period ended 30 Mar. 1930. 99 P24/222, 14 Mar. 1925. 1 *Irish Independent*, 9 Feb. 1925.

O'Higgins had indicated some weeks previously that his attitude to any possible IRA threat remained unchanged in three years. Addressing an election rally in Sligo, he said, 'I stand over those seventy-seven executions and over seven hundred and seventy-seven more if they become necessary.'[2]

As the government clearly knew, renewed war was most unlikely: 'The rank and file in most places show no anxiety for further fighting,' army intelligence reported.[3] Ireland in the mid-1920s was, economically, an unpleasant place. For many internees released from the prison camps in 1923 and 1924, the only future lay in emigration.[4]

The long-awaited by-elections proved a major disappointment for Sinn Féin, returning only two TDs.[5] Although the anti-Treaty vote had increased since the 1923 poll,[6] the anticipated landslide failed to materialize.[7] The situation was compounded by the local government elections in June 1925, when Sinn Féin recorded only 11% of the vote and marked 'the almost complete elimination of Sinn Féin from the field of local administration.'[8] Sinn Féin's political plans were in tatters. Military intelligence reported that many TDs were anxious to enter the Dáil, but only 'on the understanding that they do not recognise the Free State nor the Treaty as the final settlement of Ireland's claims; that they are not prepared to take the Oath'.[9] Many attributed the disastrous local elections results to public apathy engendered by abstentionism. Significantly, army intelligence reported, 'that certain members of the political group regard the "Army" as a grave menace to political progress. The extreme political section and the militarists naturally regard the "Army" as the backbone of the whole organisation.'[10]

As 1925 slipped by, an ever greater sense of despondency pervaded anti-Treatyite ranks:

> The only outstanding feature of the political position is the fact [d]e Valera has during the past month, made a tour of the greater part of the country in an effort to revive enthusiasm in Sinn Féin circles. It was noted that there was a marked absence of interest in his meetings almost everywhere. It is significant that at a meeting in Tralee on August 16th, Tom McEllistrum, one of the local Irregular T.D.'s was not on [d]e Valera's platform although he was observed in the audience.[11]

2 *Irish Times*, 19 Jan. 1925. 3 P24/222, 14 Mar. 1925. 4 Bell, *The secret army*, p. 50. 5 Held on 11 Mar. 1925. Oscar Traynor returned in North Dublin, and Samuel Holt in Sligo-Leitrim. 6 See McArdle, *The Irish Republic*, p. 803. 7 See comments by de Valera, *Irish Times*, 18 Mar. 1925, R. Dunphy, *The making of Fianna Fáil power in Ireland* (1994), p. 65. 8 P24/222, 15 July 1925. 9 Ibid., memorandum to the executive council, 8 July 1925. 10 Ibid., 15 July 1925. See also Mac Eoin, *Survivors*, pp 100–1. 11 Ibid., 15 Sept.

Army intelligence reported that McEllistrum was anxious to enter the Dáil and had 'repeatedly expressed his disgust at the aimless tactics pursued by de Valera and other political leaders'.

The deep fissures within anti-Treatyite ranks were finally exposed at the IRA general army convention of 14 and 15 November 1925.[12] Frank Aiken, IRA chief-of-staff, caused consternation when he admitted that he would enter the Dáil if the oath were removed. He was quickly demoted and replaced by Andy Cooney.

This occurred just days after the proposed Boundary Commission settlement was leaked to the press.[13] Promoted by Treaty supporters as a formula that would dismember Northern Ireland and make it unviable, the Boundary Commission had, instead, decided to redraw the border in a manner that did not leave the Northern government in 'a less advantageous position that it occupied under the [Government of Ireland Act, 1920].' Cosgrave and O'Higgins had to rush to London, Cosgrave reportedly saying that the commission's report should be 'burned and buried'.[14] In return for scrapping the agreement, the Irish government assumed additional financial liabilities on behalf of Britain; Cosgrave consoled the country saying, 'the Free State will lose nothing. It will gain good will'.[15]

By 10 March 1926, as Sinn Féin held its árd fheis (annual congress), the strains within anti-Treaty political ranks could no longer be contained. After de Valera was unable to propose a resolution recommending that the party should enter the Dáil if the oath were removed,[16] he resigned the presidency. A short time later, de Valera and his supporters founded Fianna Fáil. The rump of Sinn Féin remained wedded to abstentionism and rapidly decayed.[17]

Although the IRA claimed to number between 20,000 and 25,000 in October 1926, in reality, its support, like that of Sinn Féin, was dwindling.[18] Eoin O'Duffy described the 1926 Easter commemorations as 'an abject failure', writing there was

> a general wail of disappointment at the apathy displayed by the public towards the Commemoration Services. Few prominent or influential people would appear to have identified themselves with the proceedings with the exception, of course, of the usual prominent

1925. See also Mac Eoin, *Survivors*, p. 348. 12 Frank Aiken wrote a new constitution for the IRA which changed the structure of the organization, and forbade members of the IRA recognising the institutions of either jurisdiction on the island of Ireland. 13 McArdle, *The Irish Republic*, pp 793–818. 14 *Irish Times*, 23 Jan. 1968. 15 Quoted G. Boyce, *Nationalism in Ireland* (1982), p. 362. 16 Bell, *The secret army*, p. 55. 17 Dunphy, *Fianna Fáil*, pp 74–5. 18 Bell, *The secret army*, p. 57.

> 'Republicans', and in some instances these were conspicuous by their absence.[19]

Efforts to hold military parades were dismissed as 'feeble'. The Easter demonstration fixed for Mohill, Co. Leitrim had to be abandoned because only six persons attended. This reflected a pattern identified a few months earlier that although drilling continued countrywide, attendances were down.[20]

By late 1926, the IRA was at a low ebb. Its leadership, however, was determined to prevent the organization's demise and pushed for some form of action, especially as the training of 1924 and 1925 had not been followed by IRA operations.[21] Seeking arms and information, IRA units raided twelve Garda stations on 14 November 1926, leaving two Gardaí dead – Garda Ward in Hollyford, Co. Tipperary, and Sergeant Fitzsimmons in Cork City.[22] Within hours of the attacks, Gardaí had arrested most of the active IRA members in Cork, Tipperary, Kerry, and Waterford; *An Phoblacht* reported that 110 had been detained.[23]

Kevin O'Higgins directed 'in view of the recent epidemic of attacks on Garda Síochána barracks throughout the country … that provision be made at once for the revival of certain powers conferred by the Public Safety (Powers of Arrest and Detention) Temporary Act, 1924.' Although some thought was given to adding provisions permitting the suppression of publications regarded as being 'designed to produce disorder or to incite persons to attempt to overthrow the Government or … concerned with the establishment of an illegal organisation,' because under the existing law, 'it would be difficult to secure a conviction',[24] the new bill dealt solely with the declaration of an emergency and internment provisions.[25] The executive council approved the immediate introduction of the Public Safety (Emergency Powers) Bill, 1926 on 15 November.[26]

Addressing the Dáil on 17 November, W.T. Cosgrave explained that the bill would 'provide for the preservation of public safety and the protection of persons and property during national emergencies and for matters connected therewith.'[27] It would be a permanent measure, operating whenever the executive council made a proclamation declaring that it was

19 D/J H.197/58, Eoin O'Duffy to the minister for Justice, 16 Apr. 1926. 20 P24/222, 15 Sept. 1925. At this time, military intelligence's responsibilities in regard to surveillance of the IRA, and other militant political groupings were transferred to the Gardaí. See E. O'Halpin, 'Intelligence and Security in Ireland, 1922–45', in *Intelligence and National Security* (5.1, 1990), pp 55–7. 21 Bell, *The secret army*, pp 57–8. 22 'Departmental Notes', p. 212. 23 Brady, *Guardians*, p. 144; *An Phoblacht*, 19 Nov. 1926. 24 D/J H 266/44, 15 Nov. 1926. 25 Hand written note on margin, 18 Nov. 1926. 26 Meeting of the executive council, C.2/295; the scheme of bill was approved the following day, C.2/296. 27 Dáil Debates vol. 17 col. 39–40.

of opinion that 'a state of national emergency exists'.[28] A proclamation would last for three months unless continued,[29] and either House of the Oireachtas could pass a resolution revoking a proclamation within 21 days of its being laid before them.[30]

During a proclamation, an executive minister could order the internment of any person whom he certified in writing that 'he is satisfied that there is reasonable ground for suspecting such person of being or having been engaged or concerned in the commission' of any scheduled offences.[31] A responsible officer[32] was empowered 'to arrest and to detain in custody for any period not exceeding one week any person found committing or attempting to commit or whom such officer suspects of having committed' a scheduled offence, and for the purpose of effecting 'any such arrest to enter on and search any premises in which any such person is known or reasonably believed to be'.[33] The act also provided for an appeal council[34] and permitted internees to 'enter into a recognizance with two solvent sureties before a justice of the District Court in such amount as may be approved by the Minister', on condition that the internee be of good behaviour and keep the peace for a period of up to three years.[35]

Cosgrave told the Dáil that although a resurgence of IRA activity had been expected, he did not believe that the organization was capable of repeating the station raids. While the government hoped for prosecutions, he cautioned, 'it is clearly difficult to deal with a conspiracy of this kind by the ordinary criminal processes ... the real criminals – though they are well known to the police, are very careful to avoid, as far as possible, leaving evidence which would secure their conviction in a court of law.'[36]

Although Dáil opposition was no way as strident as that seen during the passage of the Treasonable Offences Bill, 1925, Thomas Johnson said the measure revealed the government's inability to stabilize the country and was 'a confession of inefficiency of the Defence Forces and the Garda Síochána.'[37] W.T. Cosgrave dismissed opposition to the bill as hysterical.[38] The state, he conceded, had faced greater dangers in the past, but insisted the government was bound to show its support for the unarmed Gardaí. The legislation's simple aim was to interfere with the liberty of the few who sought to upset the law and the order of the state; it became

28 Section 1(1). 29 Section 1(2). 30 Section 1(4). See also Kohn, *Constitution*, pp 150–1. 31 Section 3. The schedule was taken from the Public Safety (Powers of Arrest and Detention) Act, 1924 with the addition of '14. Any act the commission of which is under or by virtue of the Treasonable Offences Act, 1925 (No. 18 of 1925) treason or misprision of treason, or a felony or a misdemeanour.' 32 The definition was taken almost verbatim from section 9 of the 1924 Act. 33 Section 4(1). 34 Section 6. 35 Section 7. 36 Dáil Debates vol. 17 col. 134, 17 Nov. 1926. See also D/T S.2257 37 Dáil Debates vol. 17 col. 141–2. 38 Dáil Debates vol. 17 col. 155–8.

law on 19 November 1926,[39] and the executive council made a proclamation[40] under section 1 the following day.[41]

The government's swift response to the IRA attacks was matched by how quickly it had to suspend the legislation (on 15 December 1926), following reports of Garda violence towards detainees in Co. Waterford. All 58 internees had been released on 13 December 1926 because, 'in the opinion of the executive council, a situation does not now exist in the country which would warrant the continued detention of persons against whom it has not been found possible to formulate any charge'. Referring to the incidents in Waterford with 'deep regret and a feeling of humiliation',[42] O'Higgins conceded that the IRA had successfully evaded the provisions of the Treasonable Offences Act, though regarding the Public Safety Act, he said, 'I do not want to comment now by way of criticism on what the shortcomings of a Bill which was hurriedly passed to meet a special situation.' Notwithstanding this climb down, O'Higgins warned, 'if there is a recurrence of incidents of that kind I will have advice to give to the Dáil and proposals which are not covered by the [Public Safety] Act'.[43]

The end of 1926 brought no improvement for the IRA. Some members proposed greater involvement in politics. Prominent among these was Peadar O'Donnell who began using *An Phoblacht* in 1927 to expound his socialist ideas and to publicize his land annuities campaign in Donegal.[44] The IRA army council, however, showed little interest in his activities. Of more immediate concern was reuniting the disparate threads of republicanism – the IRA, Sinn Féin, and Fianna Fáil. Agreement was impossible because Sinn Féin maintained its abstentionist stance, while Fianna Fáil would wait for an appropriate opportunity to enter Dáil Éireann, even as a minority.[45]

The long awaited general election was finally held on 9 June 1927. Although Fianna Fáil strength was undiminished, the party made no progress on the questions of removing the oath or of entering the Dáil. But these on-going issues were suddenly overshadowed on 10 July 1927, when three IRA members, Archie Doyle, Bill Gannon, and Tim Coughlan,[46] unintentionally came upon a lone Kevin O'Higgins as he walked to Mass.[47] He was shot several times and died a few hours later.

39 D/J S.62/39. 40 *Iris Oifigiúil*, 22 Nov. 1926. 41 D/T S.2262, 20 Nov. 1926, note to the controller, the Stationery Office, 'Departmental Notes', p. 213. For comments by O'Higgins, who was attending the imperial conference in London, see *Irish Times*, 23 Nov. 1926. 42 Dáil Debates vol. 17 col. 692–7, 15 Dec. 1926. On the dispute that arose between O'Higgins and O'Duffy on disciplining the Gardaí involved, see Brady, *Guardians*, pp 145–7. For details of the disciplinary inquiry, compensation, etc, see 'Departmental Notes', p. 212, P80/853 and Dáil Debates vol. 30 col. 93, 22 May 1929. 43 Dáil Debates vol. 17 col. 695–7, 15 Dec. 1926 44 See for example *An Phoblacht*, 14 Jan. 1927. 45 Bell, *The secret army*, pp 59–60. 46 Foley, *Legion of the rearguard*, p. 66. 47 R. English,

Fianna Fáil condemned the attack[48] and the IRA denied responsibility.[49] Although intensive Garda investigations followed, no conviction was ever gained. Ten persons were arrested on 12 July, two more on 28 July, and Seán McBride on 25 August.[50]

The government, on the other hand, was sent into panic by the shooting. Thomas Johnson recorded, 'Fitzgerald, O'Sullivan ill; Cosgrave, McGilligan, Hogan worn out.' After overcoming its initial shock, the executive council sought an immediate and definite response to the assassination. On the night of the killing, Ernest Blythe explained to Johnson that, although the government had not discussed reprisals, he feared unauthorized attacks would be carried out by Gardaí and the army.[51]

The executive council met on 15 July 1927 to consider which steps it should take to counter what it believed was an assassination conspiracy directed against it.[52] It decided to vacate the seats of abstentionist TDs, to oblige every elected TD to take the oath or lose their seat, and to remove articles 47 and 48 (which permitted the initiation of legislation following a petition) from the constitution. In addition, the Treasonable Offences Act was to be amended, giving greater powers to deal with offences against the state.[53] The secretary of the department of Justice, Éinrí Ó Frighil, was asked to present public safety legislation proposals to the cabinet on 17 July 1927.[54]

A rough draft public safety bill was quickly prepared. It proposed the establishment of a special court, staffed by three high court judges sitting without a jury, to try offences under the proposed act, the Treasonable Offences Act, 1925, the Firearms Act, 1925 and the Explosives Acts, or on application by the attorney general. The second significant element of these proposals was the definition of an 'unlawful association', initially described simply as a treasonable and seditious organization. Proof of membership would be established by the possession of documents emanating from an unlawful association, with the burden of proof shifted to the accused. This was not a new concept for Ireland, however. Under section 6 of the Criminal Law and Procedure (Ireland) Act, 1887, the lord lieutenant could declare any association to be a 'dangerous association' if satisfied it was

(a) formed for the commission of crimes; or

Radicals and the Republic: socialist republicanism in the Irish Free State, 1925–1937 (1994), p. 268. **48** *Irish Times*, 12 July 1927. **49** Bell, *The secret army*, pp 61–2. **50** 'Departmental Notes', p. 213. **51** The National Library of Ireland ms 17,162. **52** D/T S.5486, CAB 3/4. **53** It also decided that these matters could, if necessary, be declared by resolution of the Dáil to be necessary for the immediate preservation of the public safety. **54** D/J 93/2/6.

(b) carrying on operations for or by the commission of crimes; or
(c) encouraging or aiding persons to commit crimes; or
(d) promoting or inciting acts of violence or intimidation; or
(e) interfering with the administration of the law or disturbing the maintenance of law and order.

The draft also proposed that all periodicals should be registered with the government; Garda powers of search and detention would be extended; executive ministers would be empowered to deport persons. It also suggested punishing the guardians of minors who permitted their charges to remain in unlawful organizations.[55]

An unsigned note to Ó Frighil suggested that all those sentenced by the special court should be subject to military law and should be held in military custody. Further, it proposed that death sentences should be executed within 24 hours of being passed, adding 'no use having Pierrepoint over to hang these people with a month's delay and the usual petitions and threats.'[56]

Regarding how it should deal with the seats of abstentionist TDs, the executive council sought the views of the Labour party leader.[57] On July 19, Thomas Johnson and T.J. O'Connell met with W.T. Cosgrave, Patrick McGilligan and Ernest Blythe.[58] Cosgrave argued that executive council ministers were physically unable for the mini-general election that would necessarily follow the vacation of these seats; he sought an accommodation between Dáil parties to minimize the number of contests, and that the election be held almost immediately. Johnson estimated that up to 35 anti-Treaty TDs would lose their seats under this plan.

Armed with army and Garda reports that warned of further attacks, Cosgrave explained that he believed O'Higgins's killing was part of an assassination plot designed to topple the government. Perhaps indicating executive council alarm, Johnson recalled, 'The number of people on the list of those likely to be expelled from the country rose during the discussion from ten or twelve to a hundred.'[59]

Despite the government's warnings, Johnson regarded proposals to remove the initiative and the referendum from the constitution and to oblige all TDs to take the oath as unacceptable. Further, no agreement was possible on the formation of a national government and the executive council decided 'not to vacate the Irregular seats'.[60] Nonetheless, the gov-

55 Ibid., unsigned and undated. 56 See also D/T S.5486, Cab 3/5. 57 Minutes of the executive council, CAB 3/6, 18 July 1927. 58 See NLI ms 15740 (i): '1927 political crisis and the Enniskerry Affair'. 59 See Gaughan, *Thomas Johnson*, pp 296–7. 60 Minutes of the executive council, CAB 3/7, 19 July 1927. See NLI ms 17162.

ernment would implement the other proposals: it would remove the initiative and the referendum from the constitution,[61] oblige TDs to take the oath within a specific period or else lose their seats,[62] and, in addition, would introduce the Public Safety Bill.

On 20 July 1927, the executive council decided that if the special court were established, the unlawful possession of arms would carry a maximum penalty of death. On 26 July,[63] it was forced to alter the special court's composition to include only army officers not below the rank of commandant and one person certified by the attorney general to have legal knowledge and experience, because two members of the high court, Mr Justice Fitzgibbon and Mr Justice Murnaghan, threatened to resign when asked to sit on the special court.[64] In any case, the special court was never established.

Addressing the Dáil on 26 July 1927, Cosgrave explained that

> Ever since the days of the civil war the Government has not been ignorant of the existence of disappointed and vindictive revolutionaries, who have sought, by every means in their power, to subvert the State, its representative institutions and the public peace and security. Measures such as the Treasonable Offences Act, 1925, were passed to enable their activities to be dealt with by ordinary processes of law within the Constitution.[65]

Because the Firearms Act, 1925 and the Treasonable Offences Act, 1925 were regarded as insufficient, a new public safety measure containing the 'minimum powers' the executive council deemed necessary 'to cope with the present situation' was devised.[66]

Thomas Johnson dismissed the government's reaction to the assassination:[67] 'it seems to indicate that the conspiracy against the State is very much more widespread and has very much more support in the country than I or any other members outside the executive council believes or believed.'[68] He had met with the National League's leader William Redmond the previous day to plan a campaign to delay the bill, hoping that the government might reappraise the situation with clearer minds. Certainly, mem-

61 Constitution (Amendment No. 10) Act, 1928, enacted in July 1928. **62** Electoral (Amendment)(No. 2) Act, 1927, became law in November 1927. **63** Minutes of the executive council, CAB 3/11. **64** See D/J 93/2/6, D/J S.55/34, Dáil Debates vol. 20 col. 1406, Dáil Debates vol. 40 col. 45, 14 Oct. 1931. **65** Dáil Debates vol. 20 col. 825. Cosgrave gave a short account of IRA developments since 1923, Dáil Debates vol. 20 col. 826–39; see also Gaughan, *Thomas Johnson*, pp 299–302. **66** Dáil Debates vol. 20 col. 839. **67** Johnson's call for the second reading to be postponed for two weeks was ruled out of order, Dáil Debates vol. 20 col. 843. **68** Dáil Debates vol. 20 col. 846.

bers of both parties spoke at exhaustive length during the debate, leading Patrick Baxter of the Farmers Party to accuse them of obstruction.[69]

By the end of July, O'Higgins' death had not been followed by other attacks and it was becoming clear that the situation was no way as serious as the government initially feared. In fact, Ernest Blythe believed that the IRA was practically finished as a force in the country – the splits in the organization had made renewed warfare very unlikely.[70]

Nonetheless, the government proceeded with the bill. Part 1 provided that the bill would last for five years and overcame any potential constitutional conflicts by providing that, 'Every provision of this Act which is in contravention of any provision of the Constitution shall to the extent of such contravention operate and have effect as an amendment for so long only as this Act continues in force of such provision of the Constitution.'[71]

Part 2 covered unlawful associations, other offences and special Garda powers. Section 4 permitted the executive council to declare any association to be an unlawful association if it:

(a) has among its professed objects, or advocates or encourages, or professes to encourage the overthrow by force of the Government of Saorstát Éireann or the alteration by force of the Constitution or the law,
(b) without lawful authority organizes or maintains or endeavours or purports to organize or maintain an armed force,
(c) promotes or encourages the unlawful possession of firearms by its members,
(d) engages in, promotes, encourages, or advocates any act, enterprise, or course of action of a treasonable or seditious character, or promotes, encourages or advocates the attainment of any object of a treasonable or seditious character,
(e) promotes, encourages or advocates the commission of crimes or interference or the obstruction or interference with the administration of justice or the enforcement of the law,
(f) promotes encourages, or advocates the non-payment of moneys payable to the Central Fund or any other public fund whether by way of taxation or otherwise or the non-payment of local taxation.

In order to overcome the problems that had emerged with section 6 of the Treasonable Offences Act, this act provided that proof to the satis-

69 Gaughan, *Thomas Johnson*, pp 294–325. 70 Dáil Debates vol. 20 col. 856–9. 71 Section 3.

faction of a court that a document '(of whatsoever date or bearing no date) issued by or emanating from or appearing to be issued by or to emanate from an unlawful association or purporting to aid or abet an unlawful association or otherwise relating to or connected with an unlawful association' was found on a person or in his possession or in premises belonging to or occupied by him or under his control would suffice to convict of membership of an unlawful association.[72] The maximum penalty for membership of an unlawful association was five years' penal servitude.[73] Persons under 16 years convicted of membership of an unlawful association could be detained 'during the pleasure of the Minister for Justice' for up to one year.[74] Parents or guardians of persons under 16 years convicted of membership of an unlawful association would also be guilty of an offence, punishable by six months' imprisonment unless they could satisfy the court they had not 'conduced to the commission of the offence' by neglecting to exercise a due care of the offender.[75]

Part 2 also prohibited the printing, publication, distribution or sale of material that contained statements made by, on behalf or in support of unlawful associations.[76] It also empowered the minister for Justice, on application to a high court judge, to suppress publications containing seditious libel, statements that incited or encouraged seditious or treasonable offences or the commission of part 1 scheduled offences,[77] or contained statements on behalf of, emanated from or aided and abetted an unlawful association.[78]

Additionally, the minister for Justice was empowered to issue 'expulsion orders' against persons who, in his opinion, were 'associated with any

---

72 Section 7. 73 Section 5, unless he could prove that he was not a member of an unlawful association, as set out in section 7. 74 Section 8. 75 Section 18. 76 Section 9(1). Punishment would be up to six months' imprisonment and/or fine up to £100, and the forfeiture of printing machinery.

77 PART I

1. Any offence which is declared by the Treasonable Offences Act, 1925 (No. 18 of 1925) to be treason or a felony or a misdemeanour.
2. Any offence which is declared by this Act to be a misdemeanour.
3. Murder or attempted murder of or conspiracy to murder the Governor-General or any member of the Oireachtas or any Judge of the Supreme Court, the High Court, or the Circuit Court or any Justice of the District Court.

PART II

1. The offence under the Firearms Act, 1925 (No. 17 of 1925) of having possession of or using or carrying a firearm without holding a firearm certificate therefor.
2. Any murder or attempted murder or conspiracy to murder in respect of which the Attorney-General, while Part IV of this Act is in force, directs that the person charged therewith shall be sent forward for trial by a special court under the said Part IV.

78 Section 10(1). Section 11 permitted the executive council to prohibit the importation of such publications.

of the activities of an unlawful association' or 'associated with or concerned' in any part I scheduled offences or any offence of a treasonable or seditious nature or any murder or 'other crime of violence and whose continued presence in Saorstát Éireann' was in the opinion of the minister 'prejudicial to the public safety or the maintenance of law and order'.[79] Expelled persons could not return to the country until an order had expired or was revoked; persons who defied an order could be punished by six months imprisonment. The British authorities, however, expressed concern at how the government intended to use this power: 'if the power of expulsion were to be exercised in such a manner as to result in the deportation to this country of persons who could not properly be regarded as belonging to it, awkward questions might arise'.[80]

While the act empowered Garda superintendents to issue search warrants for treasonable or seditious documents,[81] and any Garda to stop, search and arrest without warrant any person he believed 'to be carrying any treasonable or seditious documents' (and in both cases to seize those documents),[82] the most significant Garda power was contained in section 16. A Garda superintendent could arrest or order the arrest of persons whom he suspected of 'being or having been engaged or concerned in the commission of any' part I scheduled offences, and whose detention was, in his opinion, 'necessary or desirable for the proper investigation of such offence or any other like offence'. The statement of this opinion before a district justice would be sufficient for a district justice to order the suspect detained for seven days. An executive minister could extend detention for a further two months, with a detainee having to be either released or charged within three months of having being first arrested, though he might be released at any time by order of an executive minister. W.T. Cosgrave argued, 'This is an unusual power to give to the Garda Síochána and it is the unusual circumstances of the case which warrant it.'[83]

Persons who refused to recognize a Free State court, or did any act equivalent to a refusal to recognize a Free State court, 'other than standing mute or lawfully objecting in due form of law to the jurisdiction of the court to try him on such charge', would be guilty of contempt. While a 'not guilty' plea would be entered on their behalf, an accused would not be entitled to legal representation. Further, his refusal to recognize a court would be taken into account at sentencing: if an accused was found not guilty of the initial charge or charges, he still faced a maximum two years' imprisonment for contempt, or up to a maximum of five years' penal servi-

79 Section 13. 80 D/T S.5486, 2 Nov. 1927, signed by Lovat for the secretary of State. 81 Section 14(1). 82 Section 15. 83 Dáil Debates vol. 20 col. 1264, 2 Aug. 1927.

tude if found guilty of the charge or charges, even if the normal punishment was only a fine.[84]

Persons convicted under this act or under the Treasonable Offences Act, 1925 and paid by the state would lose their jobs and forfeit their pensions; convicted persons would be disqualified from employment paid by the state.[85]

Under part 3, special courts could be established by proclamation 'whenever the Executive Council is of opinion that it is necessary in order to secure the due administration of justice and the sure punishment' of scheduled offences. A proclamation would remain in force for three months, unless continued, and could be annulled within 21 days by a resolution of either house of the Oireachtas 'without prejudice to the validity of anything previously done under such proclamation.'[86]

After a proclamation was made, one or more special courts were to be established under part 4. Each was to consist of three or more members, one of whom was certified by the attorney general 'to have legal knowledge and experience', though not necessarily an army officer, the others being army officers not below the rank of commandant.[87] Although the act made no mention of how these courts should arrive at decisions, if, for example, unanimity was required, or if the normal rules of evidence would apply, section 27 empowered an executive minister to make regulations prescribing their procedure and practice and provided that an accused was entitled to be represented by a solicitor and counsel. Once part 4 came into force, persons charged with scheduled offences and sent forward for trial to any court before part 4 came into force would be deemed to have been sent forward for trial by a special court. Persons charged with scheduled offences while part 4 was in operation would be been sent forward for trial to a special court.[88]

Special court convictions and sentences would be subject to confirmation by a confirming authority – an army officer not below the rank of colonel nominated by the executive council.[89] He could confirm with or without modification or refuse to confirm the conviction or sentence imposed by a special court or order a new trial.[90] There was to be no appeal from any conviction, sentence, order, or judgment of a special court and 'no special court shall be liable to be restrained in the execution of its powers under [part 4 …] by any other court nor shall any proceedings before a special court be removed by certiorari to any other court.'[91]

84 Section 17. 85 Section 19. 86 Section 20(1, 2, 4). 87 Section 22(1). 88 Section 23. 89 Section 24(1)(2). 90 Section 24(3). 91 Section 25(5). Certiorari is an order of a superior court directing that the records of a lower court be sent up for review.

While part 4 was in operation, the maximum sentence for the possession of firearms without a certificate was death.[92] Otherwise, the normal punishments available to the central criminal court would be imposed. Sentences, orders and judgments of a special court were to be carried out 'by the civil authorities and officers ... in the like manner' as those of the central criminal court 'is required by law to be carried out.' Similarly, its convictions, sentences, orders, and judgments would, unless otherwise specified, have the same consequences in law as those of the central criminal court and would confer the same protections and immunities on those carrying them out.[93]

Records indicate that four persons were arrested under the act. Seán McBride was detained between 25 August 1927 and 24 October 1927. P.J. Tuohy, John Murphy and Éamon Horan were arrested on charges of treason and conspiracy on 13 and 14 September following a Fianna Fáil election meeting in Knocknagoshel, Co. Kerry. Tuohy, Murphy and Horan were remanded to Tralee district court on 20 September 1927 when they were further remanded under section 16. The three were shortly released and they sought damages for conspiracy, trespass, false imprisonment, malicious prosecution, and slander, but the jury was unable to reach a verdict when their case was heard in February 1929.[94]

The courts reviewed the act on only one occasion in *The Attorney General v. McBride*.[95] Following Seán McBride's arrest on suspicion of complicity in the killing of the Kevin O'Higgins, superintendent Peter Ennis of the Garda special branch made an application under section 16 to district justice Little for an order to detain McBride for seven days on the grounds that his detention was necessary and desirable for the proper investigation of the offence.[96] On 31 August 1927, Little rejected the application, not because of any deficiency in proof (the prosecutor had fulfilled his duties as required by section 16) but on two more fundamental grounds. Firstly, Little concluded that section 16 was an alteration or an amendment of an individual's rights as set out in article 6 of the constitution, and because the necessary constitutional amendment formalities required to amend article 6 had not been adhered to, the Public Safety Act, 1927 was null and void. Secondly, he ruled that the act could not operate retrospectively: O'Higgins was shot on 10 July; the act became law on 11 August 1927.

These grounds were successfully contested by the attorney general before Mr Justice Hanna in the high court, where Little's actions were judged to be unsustainable in law. Although Hanna said the amendment

92 Section 28. 93 Section 25(1, 2, 3, 4). 94 See D/J H.308/37. 95 [1928] IR 451. 96 McBride was remanded in custody on a charge of conspiracy to murder.

in section 3 left the citizen 'in the dark as to what is really altered in the Constitution … An "omnibus" amendment of this kind is contrary to the spirit of Article 50, if not to the letter',[97] he concluded, 'with great hesitation', that the amendment fulfilled the requirements of article 50 (which allowed constitutional amendments by ordinary legislation until 1930). He added, though, 'it is a precedent that should not be followed.'

Regarding the retrospective nature of section 16, he referred to Mr Justice Denman's ruling in *R v Griffiths*: 'unless the intention of the Legislature is clearly expressed to that effect, criminal offences are not created by giving retroactive operation to Acts of Parliament'.[98] In section 16, he concluded that the words 'suspects of … having been engaged' in the commission of an offence were 'clearly open to a reference to past acts', though, in the case of murder, the section could only apply to the murder of particular persons – 'the Governor-General or any member of the Oireachtas or any Judge of the Supreme Court, the High Court, or the Circuit Court or any Justice of the District Court'.[99]

Although nobody was ever convicted of the assassination of Kevin O'Higgins, the legislation that followed his death was significant in so far as it forced Fianna Fáil to enter the Dáil, taking the oath and its seats on 12 August 1927.[1] The importance of Fianna Fáil's entry into the Dáil was that a large majority of those who had opposed the Treaty and had lived in opposition to the constitution and the institutions of the Irish Free State since 1922 now accepted their lot as a defeated minority. Fianna Fáil, though somewhat reluctantly, accepted the legitimacy and sovereignty of the Free State and while opposing certain government policies, would work within the constitutional framework of the state.

In late 1927, Fianna Fáil tabled a motion calling for the repeal of the Public Safety Act, 1927. Their call was not wholly ignored and, on 10 November 1927, the Dáil resolved 'in view of the altered circumstances which have arisen since that Act was passed that its duration might reasonably be limited to the 31st December, 1928.' The date was chosen by Cosgrave,[2] and necessitated the amendment of the original 1927 Act.[3] The act was repealed in December 1928, though without reference to the Garda commissioner, Eoin O'Duffy. More than likely, the government was simply hoping to appease the main opposition party.[4] More dramatically,

97 The temporary nature of the amendment was not discussed. 98 [1891] 2 KB 145. 99 [1928] IR 457. 1 Gaughan, *Thomas Johnson*, p. 314. 2 D/J H.266/66, 5 Nov. 1928, Ó Frighil to the attorney general. 3 See D/T S.5793, 1 Jan. 1929, note from Mac Donnchadha to the private secretary of the minister for Justice. The Public Safety Act, 1928 received assent on 26 December 1928. 4 D. O'Sullivan, *The Irish Free State and its senate*, p. 255.

though, the assassination of O'Higgins began a period of increased friction between the Garda special branch and the IRA, the Gardaí doing their utmost to make the lives of IRA members intolerable, the IRA discovering new methods to oppose the Free State.

3

IRA resurgence, 1927–1932

Fianna Fáil's entry into Dáil Éireann in August 1927 appeared to mark the emergence of a viable alternative to the Cumann na nGaedheal-dominated administration. Five years would pass, however, before de Valera's party assumed power. Following two Cumann na nGaedheal by-election victories in the wake of the minister for Justice's assassination, the government called a second general election in September 1927. Both Cumann na nGaedheal and Fianna Fáil polled well, but as the historian Richard Dunphy noted, 'Fianna Fáil was on the offensive, conquering new ground, Cumann na nGaedheal was on the defensive, absorbing its allies.'[1]

While the election proved an unexpected boost, Fianna Fáil continued its definite move away from militant republicanism. Party election posters for the September 1927 campaign declared: 'What Fianna Fáil does not stand for: Attacking the North East: Fianna Fáil does not stand for attacking "Ulster". It will accept existing realities, but will work resolutely to bring partition to an end.'[2] Although Fianna Fáil would challenge the government on many issues during its first five years in Dáil Éireann, by the very act of taking its seats, the party formally submitted itself to the Irish Free State, its constitution and laws and, ultimately, would not fundamentally oppose the government's right to govern. In the famous words of Seán Lemass, Fianna Fáil was a 'slightly constitutional party', adopting 'the method of political agitation' because it believed that to be 'in the interests of the nation and of the Republican movement'.[3]

Fianna Fáil's growth was in marked contrast with the IRA's situation. In 1927, the organization reported a trying and difficult period to its American supporters, Clan na Gael, especially because of the loss of experienced men through emigration. Furthermore, the organization believed that 'the bad economic conditions have produced a depression of feeling and hopelessness amongst the people, which reacts on all the National morale. The people appear to submit rather than actively protest against the horrible conditions.' Nevertheless, while some weapons were prone to deterioration, and occasionally difficult to find, the IRA claimed 'a very

1 Dunphy, *Fianna Fáil*, p. 133. 2 Quoted in Bowman, *De Valera*, p. 102. 3 Dáil Debates vol. 22 col. 1615–16, 21 Mar. 1928.

small quantity had been captured by the enemy since 1923, notwithstanding constant raiding, and the offers of huge bribes'.[4]

Without doubt, Fianna Fáil's taking its Dáil seats further deepened the IRA's political isolation; the organization was unable to offer an alternative to Fianna Fáil's political programme. Peadar O'Donnell had attempted to move the organization leftwards,[5] but most of the IRA leadership was uninterested in political experiments and persisted in preparations for renewed war against the Free State. It procured arms and drilling continued, but the prospect of large-scale conflict was remote. Indeed, late 1927 and early 1928 saw no proposals that might advance any IRA aims. Preventing the organization's disintegration sapped most of the leadership's energy.[6]

Continuing IRA weakness, however, did not result in an end to the activities of militant republicans. On 23 January 1928, IRA members shot at the principal warder of Mountjoy Prison. Five days later, Seán Harling shot and killed Tim Coughlan, one of the trio who had assassinated Kevin O'Higgins. Harling, a Garda agent, was later sent out of the country with the aid of secret service funds. On 11 November 1928, the IRA attempted to blow up the statues of George II in Stephen's Green and of William of Orange on College Green, Dublin. Moreover, Garda pressure on prominent and active IRA members had continued unabated since the killing of Kevin O'Higgins. The Garda special branch began a policy of regularly searching the premises of known republicans for treasonable documents and arms, as well as repeatedly arresting, detaining and questioning them, and later releasing them without charge.[7]

While members of the government spoke of its eventual demise, not all republicans were content to allow stagnation overwhelm the IRA and some sought to develop new tactics and to revisit older ones that would enable republicans challenge the Free State. For instance, Cumann na mBan (the women's auxiliary to the IRA) printed pamphlets, signed by 'Ghosts', seeking to subvert Gardaí and soldiers.[8] More importantly, the Juries Act, 1927 entitled members of the public to purchase copies of any jury panel in any county. As early as November 1927, Cumann na mBan began canvassing jury panellists not to convict republicans if selected for jury duty.[9] In addition, members of Cumann na mBan regularly attended hearings and jury selections in order to more precisely identify those actually serving on juries.

4 M.V. Tarpey, *The role of Joseph McGarrity in the struggle for Irish independence* (1976), pp 241–2. 5 See English, *Radicals and the republic*. 6 Bell, *The secret army*, pp 73–4. 7 'Departmental Notes', p. 214, Brady, *Guardians*, p. 150. 8 Bell, *The secret army*, p. 75, Mac Eoin, *Survivors*, p. 348 and D/T S.5631. 9 Dáil Debates vol. 29 col. 1648–52, 8 May 1929.

A Garda raid on Sinn Féin's Dublin offices, 10 April 1928, and a follow-up raid on a member's house unearthed a copy of the central criminal court jury panel for February 1928 and circulars addressed to each member of the jury panel signed by 'Ghosts'. The following day, Gardaí discovered a copy of the jury panel for the March 1928 sitting of the central criminal court in Dublin in the home of the Cumann na mBan leader Sighle Humphries.[10]

It is quite difficult to gauge the overall effectiveness of the Cumann na mBan campaign. Certainly, several prominent IRA and Cumann na mBan members were found guilty despite the campaign, while other juries clearly refused to convict because jurors were sympathetic to those tried. Although juries regularly failed to agree verdicts, disagreements by no means resulted in the automatic release of those tried. More often than not, the attorney general insisted on retrying known republicans. Indeed, it was not unusual that, by the time a second jury either convicted or acquitted a prisoner, the period spent on remand equalled the sentence that would have been imposed had the prisoner been initially convicted. When asked if persons charged with treasonable offences would be discharged after three separate juries failed to reach a verdict, the minister for Justice, James Fitzgerald-Kenney,[11] explained:

> I cannot undertake to make any arrangements whereby, as a matter of course, any particular class of person returned for trial will, in the event of the jury disagreeing at the first trial, be put on trial again before another jury, at the same sitting of the Court; neither can I guarantee the formulation of the practice suggested … All these matters must be considered in the light of the public interest, and in light of attempts made by persons awaiting trial or their friends to tamper with juries.

Sighle Humphries, for example, was tried on 22 June 1928 but the jury could not agree a verdict. By 14 November 1928 she remained incarcerated, awaiting retrial. The minister for Justice explained, 'if persons are in fact kept in custody for a considerable time awaiting trial, the fact is

10 Florence McCarthy was sentenced to six months by the circuit court, 3 May 1928, 'Departmental Notes', pp 214–15; Dáil Debates vol. 29 col. 742–3, 24 Apr. 1929. 11 (1878–1956) Born Galway, educated Clongowes Wood College, and Royal University of Ireland, called to Irish Bar 1899, and Inner Bar 1925. Active in Conradh na Gaeilge in Galway, founding a branch in his own area. Joined the Irish Volunteers 1914 and remained a follower of John Redmond until the signing of the Treaty. Elected TD for South Mayo in June 1927, he was appointed minister for Justice in September 1927; he remained in the Dáil until the 1940s.

entirely accidental as far as the prosecution is concerned and very often it is due to the person himself or herself.'[12] A second jury found Humphries guilty of embracery (attempting to illegally influence a jury) and she was sentenced to six months, but because she had been on remand for so long, she was released immediately.[13]

Despite these developments, the situation in late 1928 was regarded as tolerably peaceful and sufficiently under control. W.T. Cosgrave told the American press that '[Ireland] is a crimeless country today. The fact is that the Irish people in general are one of the most law-abiding peoples in the world.'[14] On 26 December 1928, the government repealed the Public Safety Act, 1927.

Within a few weeks, however, the anti-Treaty jury campaign took a violent turn. On 23 January 1929, John White, the foreman of the jury that had convicted IRA member Con Healy,[15] was shot in the stomach, though he later recovered.[16] More seriously, Albert Armstrong, who had given evidence against four men charged with removing a 'union jack' from his workplace in August 1928, was shot dead on 20 February 1929. Although a large number of arrests followed, nobody was charged with his killing. *An Phoblacht* expressed no sympathy for those shot: 'the slave-minded jurors ... are responsible, and are paying for their treachery, one lying in a Dublin hospital'.[17] Fianna Fáil's weekly *The Nation*, while certainly not condoning the violence, declared the party 'did not wish to associate [itself] with the equally brutal, inefficient, useless methods of repression adopted by the Free State Government.'[18]

Unquestionably, convictions against republicans would become even more unlikely. The Garda commissioner complained that since the attack on White

> no jury has convicted for political or quasi-political offence, and for a considerable time past State Solicitors request a change of venue

12 Dáil Debates vol. 27 col. 7–8, 14 Nov. 1928. 13 Mac Eoin (ed.), *Survivors*, p. 348. 14 *New York Times*, 12 Apr. 1929. 15 D/T S.5838, Con Healy (pre-truce and anti-treaty IRA, the 'one-eyed gunner', born *c.*1900, so named because he had a glass eye and had control of a Lewis gun which he carried strapped to his back), shot at two Gardaí while resisting arrest following a disturbance at a dance in Blarney, Co. Cork. Unanimously convicted of using a firearm with intent to cause grievous bodily harm, he was sentenced to five years. 16 'Departmental Notes', p. 215. 17 *An Phoblacht*, 23 Feb. 1929. A number of copies of this issue were seized by Gardaí because, as Fitzgerald-Kenney explained, it was treasonable and encouraged the killing of jurors 'who carry out their duty'. When pressed for what authority the Gardaí had to do this he said, 'I take the attitude that it is correct and proper ... for the Guards to carry out the law and to seize documents of this nature.' Dáil Debates vol. 28 col. 591–3, 28 Feb. 1929. 18 *The Nation*, 23 Mar. 1929, quoted in Bell, *The secret army*, p. 76.

> to Dublin for all such cases. This is really an admission of failure there is little doubt that the ordinary juryman will not convict in such cases henceforth, and members of my staff inform me that strong supporters of the State – citizens who were formerly conscientious jurymen – now assert that they will pay any fine rather than act as jurymen henceforth.

Following Armstrong's killing, O'Duffy feared that witnesses would no longer assist the Gardaí:

> from the point of view of their outlook on so-called political crime, the Irish public is rotten. Their sense of citizenship is negligible. It was improving, though slowly it is true, in recent years, but one or two attacks on the person of citizens has thrown them back into the abyss of moral cowardice ... A policeman bereft of the cooperation and helpfulness of the general public is impotent.

He also complained of the 'nonchalance' and 'weakness' of the judiciary when dealing with the IRA, adding, the 'Treasonable Offences Act, 1925, as administered ... brings the law into contempt. Imagine two months' sentences (in the rare event of a conviction) for treason.'

O'Duffy gave no definite proposals on how to effectively counter the IRA, other than writing, 'All one can do is to hamper and hinder the movements of the criminals as much as humanly possible; make them suffer, make their lives a burden, apply unremitting surveillance to their every movement and generally make their connection with conspiracy and murder a non-paying proposition.' He also proposed that IRA members be sacked from their jobs. He was certainly concerned about what view the judiciary might take if Garda tactics were challenged in the courts, though he argued they were legally justified:

> My view is that, [according] to the common law, a policeman can arrest a man whom he suspects committed an outrage and detain him until he is satisfied that no outrage has been committed. A policeman can also ask a man to account for his movements if an outrage has been committed.

IRA members had been ordered 'under threat of dismissal' not to answer any questions, to make or to sign any statements, or to account for movements, activities or associates when arrested by Gardaí. IRA general order No. 24 explained:

> There is no obligation, even from the standpoint of the enemy's laws on a person to make a statement or answer questions, and refusal to do so does not constitute a 'charge'. Volunteers should, therefore, remain silent and let the enemy make his charge. Remember, interrogation or extracting of statements is always an attempt on the part of the enemy to get evidence against the person immediately concerned, or against his comrades or associates.

Writing in March 1929, Eoin O'Duffy explained how Gardaí exploited this tactic:

> In the first case we used their refusal to make a statement as a means to keeping them in prison for twenty-four hours, during which time 'their movements were being enquired into' ... In the second place we allow a suspect to see the inside of the Bridewell [Garda station] a sufficient number of times until he is civil enough to be asked to sign a form of undertaking.[19]

The department of Justice summarized Garda policy thus, writing that when an offence occurred indicating

> at once the work of the Irregulars the Police know dozens of persons who are likely to have been implicated and as a matter of Police art apart from questions of legal practice the obvious thing to do is to arrest everyone of the suspects ... The Police might by accident find amongst the number one man with a revolver which had been recently used. The guilty person might by his conduct and behaviour show he was guilty and although this might have no legal value it might be an important matter for the Police at that stage of their investigation'

Holding persons for a day or two prevented IRA members conferring after an offence was committed, adding, 'The arrest and detention without subsequent charge might have to be repeated several times for tactical reasons.' Furthermore, the department contended that at times, 'the only sure way to prevent a violent crime may be to arrest a certain group of persons and detain them throughout what is considered to be the crucial period.' For instance, Gardaí might arrest dozens of IRA members on 10 November and hold them throughout 11 November to prevent attacks on persons commemorating Armistice Day.[20]

19 P80/856/5–6, which also contains a copy of IRA general order no. 24. **20** D/J S.66/29, no date, 1929.

Inevitably, Garda tactics were criticized in the Dáil. In response to Seán Lemass, Fitzgerald-Kenney said, 'the Guards have to do their duty and will continue to do their duty.'[21] Cosgrave explained to Patrick Ruttledge that 'persons who by their behaviour give grounds for suspicion that they are engaged in a conspiracy to murder must realise that they cannot be allowed to pursue their activities without interference', adding, 'there is ample legal authority for any action taken in connection with the detention of suspected criminals'. The president conceded, however, that there were cases of persons being arrested 8 or 9 times, and that 28 persons were being held without charge that day.[22]

Naturally, the failures of juries to convict and the attacks on witnesses and jurors were issues the government could not ignore. The problem exhibited other undesirable features. Employing Gardaí to protect jurors and witnesses involved in the trials of republicans cost £16 per person per week.[23] The minister for Finance, Ernest Blythe, suggested that the government arm and pay the relatives of jurors and witnesses to protect them. Relatives would sleep in a juror's or witness's home and be inconspicuously accommodated at his place of work. £3 per week was offered to cover the loss of earnings. Everybody concerned was approached and this suggestion 'tactfully outlined', though in only two cases were relatives amenable and revolvers were issued in both instances. Garda protection of other jurors and witnesses continued, but the number was reduced from six to two per person. That freed 48 Gardaí daily, though 28 remained engaged in the special duty.[24] Clearly, though, something would have to be done in respect of jury and witness intimidation, but also in respect of juror sympathy for republicans. But it was clear that the canvassing of jurors and difficulties in achieving jury unanimity were widespread problems, regardless of the political views of those involved. The under-sheriff for Tipperary, John Buggy, wrote, 'So far as my experience goes in this county there has not been much intimidation but there has always been a great amount of canvassing and I suspect bribery.'[25] Stephen Roche later echoed this view:

> The real object in getting a list of the panel is, frequently, if not usually, to carry out the systematic canvas of the persons on it, on behalf of the accused, in the course of which canvass the accused

21 Dáil Debates vol. 24 col. 2057–8, 5 July 1928. **22** Dáil Debates vol. 28 col. 1882–4, 22 Mar. 1929. By 10 Apr. 1929 Fitzgerald-Kenney was unwilling to give any further information on the numbers being held without charge, Dáil Debates vol. 29 col. 4–5. **23** Dáil Debates vol. 29 col. 1818, 9 May 1929. **24** P80/918, 8 Apr. 1929, note by Ernest Blythe. **25** D/J H284/24, 17 Aug. 1929, John W. Buggy to Ó Frighil.

> gets a fair idea as to which of the persons on the panel are likely to do their duty honestly, to which persons the accused, if he is guilty, then proceeds to object.[26]

The department of Justice began by examining the jury system. The under-sheriff was responsible for jury selection in each county. He possessed a 'jurors book', which contained an alphabetical list of the names and addresses of all persons liable and qualified for jury service in the county. Before a jury could be chosen to hear a civil or criminal case, the under-sheriff was required to fill a 'panel' of about 400 names. Beginning at the point in the jurors book where he stopped when filling the last panel, he took a name under each letter of the alphabet, repeating the process until he was satisfied he had a sufficient number of names. A copy of the panel was then posted in the courthouse and given to the defence, if demanded.[27] Panellists were next summoned to attend the courthouse on a specified date (defaulters were fined), when a sufficient number of panellists' names were selected at random by a court-officer, having regard to probable 'challenges and standings-to'.[28] Defence counsel and counsel for the state next had an opportunity to challenge the inclusion of any number of jurors 'with cause shown' (on grounds of bias, etc),[29] and up to five jurors 'without cause shown'.[30] When 12 jurors were secured (not ordered to stand by or challenged), they were sworn in to try the issue.

Take, for example, the trial of Thomas Connors who was accused of murdering Annie Connors on 25 September 1928. In the circuit court, Green Street, Dublin, the March 1929 panel, numbering 400, was called on 19 February, with a supplementary panel of 200 called on 11 March. The panellists were summoned to the courthouse, their names were placed in a box and a number were drawn at random. Counsel for the defence and for the state proceeded to identify and challenge prospective jurors until a jury of 12 was eventually selected after 29 names had been drawn.[31]

Initial discussions in the department of Justice centred on three basic points: ensuring panel secrecy, providing for majority jury verdicts and creating new offences. Some thought was given to expanding juries to 15 in certain circumstances, with a majority of 12 sufficient to gain conviction. This proposal was dropped, however, because it would 'increase the burden of jury service' and because jury boxes could not hold the increased

26 D/T S.6520, memorandum, 8 Feb. 1933. 27 Juries Act, 1927, section 50. 28 Sections 46 and 47. 29 Section 58. 30 Section 57. 31 D/J S.49/29, department of Justice memorandum; Séamus Ó Conchubhair (county registrar, Green Street) to secretary of the department of Justice, 27 Mar. 1929. See R.L. Sandes, *Criminal practice, procedure and evidence in the Irish Free State* (1930), pp 92–6.

numbers. Instead, Ó Frighil wrote, 'the same result can be fairly achieved by a majority of nine out of twelve.' A proposal to try all political offences *in camera* was also rejected: 'We have always resisted any attempt at a definition and have always taken the view that crime is crime and that motive is immaterial to us', Ó Frighil noted.[32]

The Juries (Protection) Bill, 1929 was introduced into the Dáil on 1 May 1929, and given a second reading a week later. The minister for Justice reminded TDs of Albert Armstrong's killing on 20 February 1929 and of the wounding of John White on 23 January 1929: 'We are striving always to safeguard the lives and the liberties of jurymen and witnesses.'[33] Essentially, the law would revert to the situation that existed prior to 1854,[34] when no person indicted for any offence was entitled to a copy of the jury panel. The 1854 act introduced to Ireland the law in force in England since the time of Queen Anne,[35] and permitted persons charged with treason or the misprision of treason to view a copy of the jury panel. In Ireland, the system was altered by the Juries Act, 1871,[36] apparently because of widespread 'jury packing' by the authorities, and entitled anybody, whether connected to a case or not, to a copy of a jury panel list.[37] (Jury legislation in Ireland was consolidated by the Juries Act, 1927.)

The bill was to be permanent, and would apply to all trials in the central criminal court and the circuit court, not just those involving republicans.[38] Although never used, it provided for the transfer of the responsibility of selecting and then summoning jury panels from the under-sheriff the county registrar. The department of Justice believed that as the county registrar was directly responsible to the minister for Justice (the under-sheriff employed private staff) leaks could be more effectively traced.[39] Jury panel lists became 'confidential official documents' and would not be available to the accused before jury selection.[40] During jury selection, only

32 D/J S.49/29, memorandum commenting on this list of proposals by the department of Justice, no date (sometime in March 1929), no signature, corrected by Ó Frighil. 33 Dáil Debates vol. 29 col. 1553–4. 34 The minister for Justice did not name the act, simply describing it as an 'An Act to assimilate the Law and Practice existing in Ireland to the law and practice existing in cases of High Treason in England', 17 and 18 Vic. ch. 20. 35 7 Anne, ch. 21. 36 The 1871 Act was introduced following jury fixing in a case in Co. Monaghan, though packing continued afterwards. The English Lord Chancellor explained in 1908 that 'packing juries is one of the methods by which alone a government determined to depart from the ordinary law and determined to govern against the sympathies of the people could govern Ireland.' See E. Mulloy, *Dynasties of coercion* (1986), pp 19–20 and J.F. McEldowney, 'The Case of *the Queen v. McKenna* (1869) and jury packing in Ireland', [1977] *Irish Jurist*, pp 339–54. 37 On the payment of a small fee 38 Dáil Debates col. 29 col. 1554–61, 8 May 1929. The bill was amended and duration set at two years, continuing in force until 30 Sept. 1931 when it was renewed for a further two years. 39 Section 2. 40 Section 3(2). Section 50 of the Juries Act, 1927 would not apply.

the judge, court officers, Gardaí and panellists would be permitted in the courthouse.[41] Although panellists' names would be used when initially confirming attendance, they would be subsequently assigned a number, and afterwards reference would be to this number only, unless a panellist was suspected of leaving the courthouse.[42] Jury selection would then proceed as before, with the accused and his counsel having an opportunity to challenge the jury, or particular jurors, as normal.

Section 5 provided that 'a majority vote of nine members of the jury … or upwards' would be sufficient to determine a verdict 'without disclosure of the number or identity of dissentients'. In capital cases, however, the foreman was obliged to inform the presiding judge 'privately in writing, whether the verdict was or was not unanimous and the number of the dissentients (if any).' This was to be communicated to the minister for Justice.[43]

Judges were given a number of new powers. They would determine if a prisoner was 'mute by the visitation of God', when the normal consequences would follow, or if he was refusing to recognize the court, in which case the judge would enter a plea of 'not guilty'.[44] Persons who displayed 'gross disrespect' or acted 'disrespectfully or contumaciously towards the Court' or refused to recognize the court other than 'standing mute or lawfully objecting in due form of law to the jurisdiction of the Court to try him' could be punished by six months' imprisonment.[45] At the judge's discretion, the trial could be postponed until this sentence was completed, or the sentence could be imposed after the trial, regardless of the verdict.[46] In theory, at least, a prisoner who defied a judge could be held indefinitely.

These powers were used only twice, however. In the *State v. Coughlan*, in Cork circuit court on 14 January 1930, the accused refused to plead when charged with unlawful possession of firearms under section 2 of the Firearms Act, 1925. A plea of 'not guilty' was entered on behalf of the accused and he was found guilty; he was sentenced to 12 months' hard labour and fined £50. On the other occasion, William Daly was charged with malicious damage to Russell Hotel on Stephen's Green, Dublin. On arraignment before the central criminal court on 16 December 1930, he refused to recognize the court and was imprisoned for six months for contempt. When he came before the court again on 16 March 1931, he pleaded guilty to the original charge and was sentenced to three months imprisonment from 16 December 1930.[47]

Judges were also empowered to clear the court if a Garda not below the rank of superintendent stated on oath that it was necessary for the pro-

41 Section 4(c). 42 Section 4(a), (b) and (d). 43 Section 5(2). 44 Section 6(1) and (2). 45 Section 6(3). 46 Section 6. 47 See D/J H.284/25.

tection of witnesses and jurors at a trial. Only the presiding judge, court officers, jurors, witnesses and barristers and solicitors specifically involved in the trial could remain on the premises. The court was to remain cleared until the jury delivered a verdict. Reporters could also be barred from a cleared courthouse until the completion of a trial if a Garda superintendent produced copies of their newspaper which, in the judge's opinion, were calculated to intimidate or influence jurors or witnesses in a particular trial or generally.[48] The judge could also adjourn a trial twice until the next sitting of the court if he believed there was intimidation of jurors or witnesses, during which time the accused would remain in custody.[49]

Additionally, under section 9, it became an offence to distribute any information regarding persons 'called, sworn, or engaged' as jurors, whether correct or not. Section 10 provided for jury summonses to be sent by ordinary post (and not delivered by the Garda Síochána).[50] Section 11 prohibited 'urging, encouraging or exhorting' jurors not to act as jurors or to disregard their oath, making statements or publishing threats of violence against jurors or potential jurors. Section 12 provided for the prosecution of persons found loitering 'without lawful reason' on the roads or the streets leading to the central criminal court or to a sitting of the circuit court.

Regardless of these provisions, James Fitzgerald-Kenney warned that 'trial by jury is only a means to an end ... if after the passage of the Bill, it fails, reluctantly – regretfully that such a situation should arise – but unhesitatingly, we shall adopt some other method, while the need lasts, for a certain class of criminal.'[51]

The bill was strongly opposed by Fianna Fáil, objecting to the first public safety measure introduced since it entered the Dáil. De Valera described it as part of 'an evil continuity' since the time of English rule,[52] adding, 'I am not to be taken as sympathising with attacks on or intimidation of jurors ... [but] if you want to have the law respected you will have to have the law people can respect.'[53] Rather less dismissive. Labour's T.J. O'Connell contended that while the bill aimed to alter the jury system as a whole to suit a special set of circumstances, it seemed to him that if the problem were as serious as the government claimed provision should be made abolishing jury trials for certain classes of offences.[54] He claimed he would support such an initiative. Because of the large number of oppo-

48 Section 7. Green Street courthouse was cleared on either two or three occasions in late 1929 or early 1930, D/J H.284/25. 49 Section 8(1) and (2). D/J H.284/25: this section was never used. 50 This amended section 44 of the Juries Act, 1927. 51 Dáil Debates vol. 29 col. 1561, 8 May 1929. 52 Dáil Debates vol. 29 col. 1576. 53 Dáil Debates vol. 29 col. 1599. 54 Dáil Debates vol. 29 col. 1606.

sition amendments tabled (Ruttledge proposed 94), the executive council introduced a 'guillotine resolution', and the bill passed both Houses of the Oireachtas on 31 July 1929.[55]

Despite the department of Justice's efforts, most juries remained unwilling to convict republicans. In one case, the accused had been arrested on 11 November 1929, allegedly in possession of a loaded revolver and a mine. The first jury failed to agree a verdict and the attorney general ordered a retrial. Eoin O'Duffy reported:

> Enquiries were made regarding the reason for the Jury's failure to arrive at a decision in the case and it was ascertained that immediately they retired to consider their verdict they agreed to disagree, several members stating that if they convicted [the accused] it would mean that they would have a policeman standing outside their door guarding them for the rest of their lives. It was also ascertained that the fact of the court being cleared under the Jurors' Protection Act had the effect of making the Jurors more nervous than if such action had not taken place.[56]

But as a change to the ordinary law, the act clearly had benefits. The Cork county registrar, D.M.J. O'Connell wrote:

> The full benefit of the Juries Protection Act was gladly availed of by both County and County Borough Jurors in my Circuit. No hitch ever appeared in its practical working. The calling of jurors by numbers and not by name and address, worked smoothly from the commencement and gave satisfaction to the summoned jurors and to the Court. The procedure greatly shortened the calling and empanelling of Jurors, which used take considerable time under the old method – In my opinion the secrecy of the ballot of Jurors was a great inducement and encouragement to Jurors to discharge their duties fairly and independently – Every opportunity was given to the accused and his legal advisers to identify the Juror with the name and address on the panel handed to them and I never received any complaint in respect of the change. Apart altogether from political consideration the Act was the means of effectually stopping the general canvass of Jurors on behalf of accused persons when the Sittings opened, and this open scandal, familiar to me for a great many years back as Clerk of the Crown and Peace of the County, is now ended.[57]

55 Minutes of the executive council, CAB.4/87, 22 May 1929, D/T S.5838. 56 P80/856/14, O'Duffy's report for the period ending 31 Dec. 1930. 57 D/J H 284/24,

With the continuing failure of juries to convict republicans, apparently the only remaining means to counter IRA activities was the Gardaí's regularly criticized harassment policy.

Undoubtedly, Garda tactics caused very serious problems for the IRA.[58] They forced the prominent left-wing IRA leader George Gilmore to bring a civil action against the Gardaí, eventhough it necessitated recognizing the Free State's courts. O'Duffy reported, 'the pace has got too hot for Gilmore ... It is an extraordinary position but there can be no doubt that this method is the most efficacious yet hit upon.' Nevertheless, the commissioner was concerned that the courts would not support Garda policy. He had little confidence in District Justice Little who was hearing Gilmore's case. His detachment when deciding such matters was, he wrote, 'amusing were it not contemptible'.[59] Gilmore won his case and it was conceivable that a flood of similar litigation might follow. Patrick Rooney, another IRA member, brought a case against the Gardaí in March 1929 for alleged assault and battery after he was held without charge for 11 hours.[60] While superintendent Peter Ennis of the Garda special branch gave assurances that no violence was used, he worried that 'complications may arise owing to the number of times Rooney has been arrested in recent weeks (eight in all).'[61] Although that case was dismissed,[62] it appeared that the only effectual system employed against the IRA was in danger of being prohibited by the courts.

Clearly, though, Garda tactics constituted very fundamental departures from the ordinary law, forcing the department to ask the attorney general two specific questions. First, after an offence was committed, were Gardaí justified in arresting known IRA members where 'they can conscientiously say that any member arrested is likely to have been engaged in felony directly or as an accessory before or after the deed.' Second, if Gardaí possessed information of 'a reliable character' that a felony was to be committed but which they 'could not possibly disclose' were they justified in making arrests in order to prevent the crime and or must they afterwards satisfy the court that they had reasonable grounds and how far would the courts investigate that those grounds were reasonable.[63]

To properly understand the situation, it is necessary to consider the Gardaí's legal powers of arrest, detention, and interrogation in 1930.[64]

4 June 1931. **58** Coogan, *The IRA*, pp 87–8. **59** Brady, 'The police', ch. 7, pp 16–17, report for period ending 31 Mar. 1929. **60** D/J S.66/29. **61** Ibid., 25 Mar. 1929. **62** Ibid., Garda HQ memorandum to the secretary of the department of Justice, 4 Apr. 1929. **63** Ibid., no date. **64** Based on a memorandum in P24/167, prepared by Finlay and Lavery, Ó Frighil to Mac Donnchadha, 31 Mar. 1930, and D/J S.66/29 Ó Frighil to O'Duffy, 12 May 1930. See also Sandes, *Criminal practice*, pp 70–8.

A Garda may make an arrest without a warrant, in certain circumstances, under the common law or under various statutes. Under the common law, a Garda may arrest without warrant:

- if a felony is committed or is about to be committed in his presence[65]
- on a reasonable suspicion that a felony has been committed, where he has reasonable and probable cause to suspect the person whom he has arrested of committing the felony
- to prevent the occurrence or the continuance of a breach of the peace
- where an offence, though not a breach of the peace, is publicly scandalous and prejudicial to public morals
- occasionally, where an arrest is the only method to prevent damage to property

Reasonable grounds for suspicion include:

- 'The common fame of the country', though this fame would require some probable ground
- 'Being found in such circumstances which infer a strong presumption of guilt'
- 'Behaving oneself in such manner as betrays a consciousness of guilt'
- 'Being found in company with one known to be an offender at the time of the offence, or generally at other times keeping the company of persons of scandalous reputation'
- 'Living an idle, vagrant and disordered life without having any visible means to support it'
- 'Facts stated to [the Garda] by a third party'
- 'Being pursued by a hue and cry'.

When an action is brought against a Garda for assault or false imprisonment, where the Garda justified the arrest without a warrant on the grounds that at the time of the arrest he suspected the plaintiff had committed a felony, the Garda is obliged to state, for the court's information, the particulars of the alleged felony and the grounds of the reasonable and probable cause of his suspicion.[66] When those grounds and particulars are given at a trial before a judge and jury, the judge must decide if there was reasonable suspicion or not. A Garda cannot refuse to disclose the grounds for his reasonable suspicion because of privilege or otherwise, such as the public interest.

It is difficult for a Garda to justify making an arrest on the orders of a superior officer and not on the suspicion being entertained by himself

65 *R. v. Hunt* 1 Mood 93. 66 *Green v. Garbutt* 28 TLR 575.

unless immediate action were necessary. The superior officer would normally be expected to obtain a warrant, though an arrest might be justified in cases where the superior officer was able to establish reasonable grounds for such suspicion.[67] Where a Garda arrested on grounds advanced by a third party, it must be reasonably supposed that the third party had first-hand knowledge of a felony.

Arrest without warrant is also possible under a number of statutes:

- a person found committing any indictable offence at night, section 11 of the Prevention of Offences Act, 1851
- a holder of a licence granted under the Penal Servitude Act, 1864, whom a Garda reasonably suspected of having committed any offence or breaking any condition of his licence
- any person found committing any offence against the Malicious Damage Act, 1861
- any person on any highway or public place who was guilty while drunk of riotous or disorderly conduct, section 12 of the Licensing Act, 1872
- any person on a highway who was so drunk as to be incapable of taking care of himself, section 25 of the Licensing (Ireland) Act, 1874
- any person found in premises where an illicit still was working, section 19 of the Illicit Distillation Act, 1831
- the Dublin Police Act, 1842 gave wide powers of arrest to officers of the Gardaí in the Dublin Metropolitan area in respect of summary offences.[68]

Following an arrest without warrant, a Garda is obliged to bring the prisoner at the first available opportunity before a peace commissioner or a district justice to be charged immediately with the offence in respect of which, or on the suspicion of which, the arrest was made. A Garda may not detain a person arrested by him if he allows an opportunity to have the prisoner formally charged pass. If the person is simply detained without charge, it is open for the judge and jury to hold that the imprisonment was wrongful because the prisoner had been detained without reasonable charge or legal commitment.

A Garda may not detain suspected persons for the purpose of questioning them or making inquiries concerning them. No person may be detained against his will unless he is formally arrested and then charged as soon as possible. Mr Justice Hugh Kennedy demolished the contention

67 Though knowledge that an arrest warrant for the person suspected had been issued is sufficient ground for reasonable suspicion, see *Creagh v. Gamble* [1888] 24 LR Ir 458. 68

that there was in any way a difference between the detention of a person by Gardaí during preliminary investigations and the formal arrest and cautioning of a person in *Dunne v. Clinton*:

> In law there can be no half-way house between the liberty of the subject, unfettered by restraint, and an arrest. If a person under suspicion voluntarily agrees to go to a police station to be questioned, his liberty is not interfered with, as he can change his mind at any time. If, having been examined, he is asked, and voluntarily agrees, to remain in the barracks until some investigation is made, he is still a free subject, and can leave at any time. But a practice has grown up of 'detention', as distinct from arrest. It is, in effect, keeping a suspect in custody … without making any definite charge against him, and with the intimation in some form of words or gesture that he is under restraint, and will not be allowed to leave … this so-called detention amounts to arrest … the expression 'detention' has no justification in law in this connection.[69]

While it may be convenient for Gardaí to take a statement from someone suspected of having committed an offence in a Garda station, if that person is unwilling to go, Gardaí must decide whether or not to make an arrest.

Statements made to Gardaí must be taken without any hint of coercion, and it must be clear that the person giving the statement did so as a free act. The admissibility or otherwise of statements by accused persons amounting to confessions is a question that can only be answered by the trial judge. Mr Justice Kennedy described the breadth of this discretion in *Attorney General v. McCabe*:

> it is not the law that a statement must be excluded from evidence on the sole ground that either the statement was made in answer to questions put by a police officer or that it was made without a caution having been first administered. But in such cases it is a matter for the judge at the trial to decide whether, in his judicial discretion, he will admit the statement or not, having regard to all the circumstances, and observing the legal requirement that the statement shall be voluntary, though not necessarily volunteered. He will differentiate between statements led to by questions put to a person not in custody for the purpose of investigation of crime and the

See generally E. Ryan and P.P. Magee, *The Irish criminal process* (1983), pp 525–8. 69 [1930] IR 370; J. Kelly, *The Irish Constitution*, ed. G. Hogan and G. White (1994), pp 831–2.

> tracing and arrest of the guilty party and confessions resulting from questions put to a person in custody, not so much to clear up doubtful matters in a narrative by him as to trap or put pressure upon him.[70]

In the court of criminal appeal, counsel for the accused may challenge the admission of a statement successfully, but counsel for the state is not entitled to object to the exclusion of an alleged confession at the trial. Essentially, the admissibility of a statement depends on whether or not it was voluntary. Mr Justice Fitzgibbon ruled in *State v. Treanor*:

> A confession made to any person under the influence of a promise or threat held out by a person in authority, calculated to induce the confession, is inadmissible, unless it be clearly proved to the satisfaction of the Judge, whose duty it is to decide the question, that the promise or threat did not operate upon the mind of the accused, and that the confession was voluntary notwithstanding, and that the accused was not influenced to make it by the previous promise or threat.[71]

If a statement, amounting to a confession, 'flows from hope [of some promise or prospect of a temporal benefit] or fear exacted by a person in authority, it is inadmissible. On this point the authorities are unanimous', Mr Justice Cave explained in *R. v. Thompson*.[72] Statements obtained in answer to searching questions will more than likely also be excluded if challenged. Inducements that amount to no more than moral or religious exhortations would not render a confession inadmissible, however.[73]

In addition to the Treasonable Offences Act, 1925, the primary measure employed by the Gardaí in the investigation of IRA activities was the Firearms Act, 1925, sections 21, 22 and 24. But as the assistant secretary of the department of Justice, Stephen Roche, later explained to the first Fianna Fáil minister for Justice

> These provisions have not been found effective in the face of anything like a determined conspiracy to carry arms. Before an officer can search a suspect he must be prepared to establish the fact that he 'observes or believes' the suspect to be carrying arms and very

70 [1927] IR 134. 71 [1924] 2 IR 208. 72 [1893] 2 QB 15, see also Baron Parke in *R. v Moore* (3C. and K. 157). 73 *R. v. Picham*, [1828] 1 Mood 186.

> often the grounds on which such 'belief' is based, while perfectly genuine, will not stand a cross-examination in Court. As regard the searching of premises under section 24 it will be observed that first of all there must be 'reasonable ground' for suspicion: secondly, nobody lower than a superintendent can issue the necessary warrant and thirdly the members ... must be named under the warrant. These conditions seriously limit the utility of the powers in practice.[74]

In short, the ordinary law was ineffectual when used in the investigation of IRA offences. The courts shortly prohibited the unusual measures adopted by Gardaí to deal with IRA activities when several IRA members challenged Garda tactics, claiming false arrest and unlawful detention.[75]

On the night of 26 August 1929, Superintendent Ennis of the Garda special branch instructed detectives Sherlock, Corry, Hussey and Byrne to arrest Patrick McKee on suspicion of involvement in the murder of Albert Armstrong. McKee was arrested the following morning and removed to the Bridewell Garda station in Dublin where he was held for a 'considerable period' without charge and was subsequently released.[76] He brought an action against the four detectives. The court held that it was no defence in law for the defendants to claim that they were acting under the orders of their superior officer. Because Corry and Hussey could not say that they had any reasonable suspicions, and Sherlock refused to disclose his grounds for suspicion, Judge Shannon ruled, as a matter of law, that the defendants had not proved any facts justifying the arrest and imprisonment of McKee.[77] When Ennis was examined, he said he had a reasonable suspicion but refused to disclose it. The only question considered by the jury was that of damages, which it fixed at £75.[78]

Special branch detectives arrested Charles O'Neill at 8.30 a.m. on 30 June 1929 as he walked to the annual Wolfe Tone commemoration in Bodenstown, Co. Meath after he refused to tell them of his destination. Other detectives subsequently detained him and removed him to the Bridewell Garda station at about 11 a.m., where he was detained without charge until 12.30 p.m. the following day. The detectives who initially arrested O'Neill explained that because they believed O'Neill was an IRA member, they acted in order to prevent a breach of the peace which they

74 D/J D.7/35, Roche to James Geoghegan, 11 Mar. 1932. 75 Account in P24/167. 76 *Irish Independent*, 19 Mar. 1930. 77 The plaintiff could not cite any evidence against detective Byrne and at the close of McKee's case the judge directed in favour of Byrne. 78 The department of Justice's law officers concluded, 'In our opinion the learned Judge was right in the conclusion at which he arrived and the judgement and verdict could not be successfully challenged on appeal.' P24/167, no date March 1930.

expected at Bodenstown during the day. While O'Neill denied that he was going to an IRA assembly, he refused to answer whether or not he was an IRA member because he might incriminate himself. But it was against the other detectives who subsequently detained him that O'Neill brought the action.[79] Judge Shannon ruled that two of them were answerable for the imprisonment of O'Neill, because they had not justified the imprisonment in evidence as neither could state that he feared a breach of the peace. They were liable to pay damages, which the jury fixed at £80, and to pay costs. The jury concluded that a third detective was not on the road to Bodenstown or at the Bridewell on the day in question and the case against him was dismissed with costs.[80]

Detectives arrested John Sugrue early on 26 March 1929 on suspicion of involvement in the murder of Albert Armstrong. He was held without charge in the Bridewell for 46 hours until his release late on 27 March 1929. Between noon and 1 p.m. on 27 March, Detective Byrne interrogated Sugrue regarding his movements on the night of 20 February 1929, but he refused to answer any questions and Byrne ordered Sugrue returned to his cell (Byrne admitted as much in evidence). Although the jury felt that the Gardaí involved had reasonable grounds to suspect that Sugrue was involved in Armstrong's murder,[81] it held that Sugrue had been assaulted and detained for an unreasonable length of time. Compensation, in addition to costs, was set at £40.

Finally, detectives arrested Dónal O'Donoghue on the morning of 27 August 1929 on suspicion of involvement in the murder of Albert Armstrong. He was brought to the Bridewell where he was held without charge. Around 6 p.m., O'Donoghue told his jailer that if he was not released or charged before 6.30 p.m. that he would break his cell's windows; 6.30 p.m. came and went and O'Donoghue duly broke the windows. Gardaí charged him under the Malicious Damage Act, 1861, and brought him before the district court the following morning. But when District Justice Cussen questioned the legality of O'Donoghue's initial detention, the charge was dropped and he was released at about 4 p.m. on 28 August 1929. The jury concluded that the defendant, detective Rogers, had assaulted O'Donoghue and detained him for an unreasonable length of time; it assessed damages at £50.[82] Rogers gave as his reasonable suspicion that O'Donoghue matched a description given by a resident on the South Circular Road of a man seen in the vicinity of Armstrong's house before the killing, and when questioned, O'Donoghue refused to account

79 See also *Irish Independent*, 20 Mar. 1930. 80 The department of Justice concluded that no satisfaction could be gained by appealing as the Judge's ruling was correct in law. 81 See also *Irish Independent*, 21 Mar. 1930. 82 See also *Irish Times*, 22 Mar. 1930.

for his movements on that night. But when Rogers asked the informant to identify O'Donoghue, he refused. Rogers refused to reveal the name of his informant because it would prejudice further investigation of the case.

The size of the awards was explained because the plaintiffs could show that they had been arrested and detained without charge on more than one occasion. A dismayed O'Duffy complained that 'it is remarkable that on every occasion [juries] give verdicts for huge sums against the police in civil actions brought by the Irregulars, whether through fear, or ignorance, or influence of certain Judges, is not clear. It is impossible to even surmise what Judges are aiming at; it is certainly an object lesson on the weakness of democratic rule.'[83] Eight further cases were brought against the Gardaí in early 1931, and although damages awarded were smaller,[84] they confirmed the illegality of Garda activities.

Following Mr Justice Shannon's rulings, O'Duffy wrote that the Garda policy of surveillance and harassment was undoubtedly 'efficacious, and the people it was aimed at have suffered considerably as a result, and their organisation was crippled. They had to go into the courts, or else witness an impotent organisation vanishing.' In fact, he believed that 'there was a great chance of finishing up the problem [of the IRA] were it not for the Court decisions.' He now asked, 'What weapons are left to the police to deal with the menace? The Treasonable Offences Act as a weapon is not worth the paper it is written on.' He added:

> Bad as the [Treasonable Offences] Act is it was never administered seriously by the Judiciary. Judge Hanna and District Judge Louis Walsh sneered openly at cases brought under it. The sentences awarded under it brought contempt to the proceedings. The original Bill was all that it should be, but before it became law it had been disembowelled.[85]

Six years after its enactment, O'Duffy wrote, 'without fear of contradiction that [the Treasonable Offences Act, 1925] did not help us in dealing with the actual problems confronting us.' The prospect of charging members of the IRA with 'levying war against the State' or 'usurpation of executive authority' would make a 'laughing stock' of the Gardaí. Further con-

83 P80/856/14, period ended 31 Dec. 1930. 84 D/J 66/29. Cases heard before judge Cahir Davitt and a jury, in the circuit court, Dublin Castle, on 3 and 4 Mar. 1931. The juries awarded £10 damages with costs to Laurence Farrell, Edward Thackaberry, Robert O'Brien, and Joseph Vaughan; and £5 damages with costs to Gerard Dempsey, Robert Hamilton, Christopher Holden, and James Holden. 85 P80/856/10–11, 'Report on organisation inimical to the state', period ended 31 Mar. 1930.

tributing to Garda difficulties, he described the terms of section 22 of the Firearms Act, 1925 as 'very obscure ... it is very difficult for a policeman to *prove* that he was satisfied a man was armed, unless he actually saw the gun in his pocket.'[86] The department of Justice described the situation thus: 'The Government seemed, therefore, to be placed in an almost ludicrous position of helplessness, and the only comfort in the situation was that the IRA did not take anything like full advantage of their position of practical immunity'.[87] The government's legal difficulties were compounded by reports of increasing IRA radicalism, and of the organization's links with international socialist groups.[88]

Some senior members renewed attempts to move the organization leftwards, though their endeavours were unlikely to succeed. The historian Richard English wrote: 'the [IRA's] socialists were a definite minority within the organization.'[89] In reality, the efforts of republican-socialists bore little fruit, though, in February 1931, leftwing IRA members launched Saor Éire, with the official, albeit unenthusiastic, support of the IRA's leadership.[90]

Of much greater concern was the increasing violence that 1931 witnessed. Although the IRA had successfully frustrated Garda tactics and legislation employed against it was largely ineffectual, the two years following Albert Armstrong's death had seen little violence. That changed on 30 January 1931 when Patrick Carroll, a suspected Garda informer, was killed.[91]

The Gardaí continued to deal with the IRA as far as circumstances and the law permitted.[92] In February 1931, Seán Curtin, a Garda superintendent in South Tipperary, began proceedings under the Treasonable Offences Act, 1925 against local IRA members who had been arrested openly drilling.[93] Significantly, 14 members had sworn informations against their officers. Four were tried, but despite the evidence, and what Judge Sealy described as a 'strong case', all were acquitted.[94] Superintendent Curtin concluded that radical changes to the criminal law were necessary:

> On the whole it is useless to have anything in the nature of a political case ever again tried in this South Riding of Tipperary. The

86 O'Duffy's emphasis, following an earlier case in the high court, which he cited as *Jas. F. Morris, N.T. v Sergeant Doyle, Newport.* 87 'Departmental Notes', p. ix. 88 P24/169, 'Revolutionary Organisation', memorandum circulated to the executive council, 5 Apr. 1930. 89 English, *Radicals and the republic*, p. 113. 90 M. Milotte, *Communism in Ireland: the pursuit of the workers' republic since 1916* (1984), p. 110. 91 'Departmental Notes', p. 5. 92 Ibid., pp 5–8, small amounts of arms continued to be uncovered, and a few incidents of jury canvassing were reported. 93 The raid occurred on 6 Feb. 1931. 94 See A/G 11/31 and D/J D.20/35.

> result of this case should, I respectfully suggest, give rise for serious thought to abolish the jury system in cases of political nature. As far as the Garda were concerned in this case all possible was done at every stage of the case to make it successful and no pains were spared.[95]

While this only confirmed to the department of Justice and to the Garda commissioner the fundamental difficulties faced when using the ordinary law against the IRA, the 'Tipperary Drilling Case' was noteworthy for the IRA's response to Curtin's persistent, though futile, investigations – he was shot on 20 March 1931 and died the following day.[96] *An Phoblacht* predicted a familiar response:

> The shooting of Superintendent Curtin will, no doubt, be made an excuse for another attempt at the Last Conquest of Ireland, just as was the shooting of Kevin O'Higgins ... Like his English predecessors, O'Duffy has to admit that 'he can see no hope for the country's future' because 'murderers are being shielded by the people' who refuse 'to take a bold and courageous stand in the interest of order, peace and progress' (British Style).[97]

O'Duffy wrote:

> The laws of this state are laws meant for a civilised people, a normal people. They are the laws ruling England. That country is fortunate in having behind her hundreds of years of internal tranquillity. For hundreds of years no organisation has attempted to violently overthrow her government. The people too, have a highly developed civic sense and moral courage which is entirely lacking here. If there is anybody in this country who thinks that this state can be ruled by the present laws, he is making a cardinal error.[98]

Ernest Blythe suggested that civil actions against the Gardaí for alleged unlawful arrest or alleged assault should be heard by a judge sitting without a jury. If damages were awarded they should be measured by the actual loss suffered; damages should not be punitive or 'exaggerated'; a Garda found guilty of mistreating prisoners should be disciplined or charged. Additionally, he proposed small mandatory sentences for illegal drilling

95 Curtin to deputy commissioner C, 20 Mar. 1931, quoted in Bell, *The secret army*, p. 74. 96 'Departmental Notes', p. 5. 97 Issue of 28 Mar. 1931. 98 P80/856, O'Duffy's memorandum, 24 June 1931.

(fourteen days to three months) and for unlawful possession of arms, ammunition or treasonable documents (one to six months) which would be tried by a district justice. Persons suspected of membership of unlawful organizations or having knowledge of serious political crimes should be obliged to divulge any relevant information or otherwise face imprisonment. He also proposed empowering superintendents to detain suspected members of unlawful organizations without charge for questioning for up to seven days.[99]

The shooting of Superintendent Curtin certainly impressed upon the government and the Gardaí the need to reappraise the IRA situation. Less than a month after Curtin's death, Eoin O'Duffy wrote that limitations placed on Gardaí by the courts were 'responsible for the marked increase in activities by the Irregulars, [the IRA] feel that they have this field to themselves.'[1] At this stage, O'Duffy was confident that the Gardaí were in control of the situation, though he felt that circumstances might deteriorate: 'I do not consider that internment or deportation would be an effective remedy, nor is it a job for the army at least at this stage.' In the long run, though, he believed that 'more drastic measures, such as military courts may be eventually necessary to deal with all cases of a political value, which in the opinion of the attorney general cannot be properly tried before the ordinary tribunals.' The establishment of a military court would follow the outlawing of the IRA. O'Duffy also called for the suppression of *An Phoblacht*: 'Its continuance is an immediate danger to the lives of the members of the Garda. It is being distributed broadcast amongst the youth of the country.' Despite the apparent growth of the IRA and its increasingly violent activities, several months passed before O'Duffy's general proposals were seriously considered by the executive council.

In the meantime the Juries (Protection) Act, 1929 came up for renewal. The department of Justice identified the provisions it wanted made permanent (majorities verdicts), the provisions designed to counter the 'conspiracy against the functioning of the Courts of Justice',[2] and those dealing with the constant tendency 'apart from "political" conspiracies, where the accused person has any influence to defeat the course of justice by canvassing the panel of jurors.'[3] The act was renewed unaltered, however, and continued for a further two years. When guiding it through the Dáil, Fitzgerald-Kenny said that

> Unfortunately, the necessity for this Bill still continues. There is still a danger that jurymen would be intimidated and possibly assas-

99 D/J 93/2/7, Blythe's memorandum, 8 Apr. 1931. 1 D/J 93/2/7, hand-written note to the minister for Justice, 17 Apr. 1931. 2 Sections 3, 4, 6, 7, 11, 12. 3 D/J H.284/24, department of Justice memorandum to the executive council, 23 May 1931.

> sinated. The persons who are desirous of upsetting ordered government in this country by force of arms are not yet entirely quiescent. It is necessary that jurymen should do their duty as jurymen and carry out their obligations as citizens of this State and receive due protection from the law.[4]

The minister for Justice also noted that the opposition parties had not identified any problems with the legislation:

> No one opposite attempted to show that in its working it has not been a complete and admirable success. No one has attempted to show that it has not achieved its purpose. No one has attempted to show that in one single instance has it acted unjustly towards any single citizen of the State and, therefore, on the merits it demands the support of the House.[5]

Clearly, though, the government regarded the act as inadequate to deal with the IRA problem,[6] and had already begun examining alternative means to counter the organization's activities. Initially, the department of Justice did not consider abolishing jury trials. Instead, it drafted the Garda Síochána Bill, 1931 to give the Gardaí extra powers and to deal with the problem of civil actions by IRA members against Gardaí.[7] Indeed, the department of Justice claimed, 'the suggested provisions are considered to be the mildest possible having regard to the actual facts of the situation'.[8]

The draft bill proposed empowering a Garda not below the rank of inspector to order the arrest of persons whom he suspected of committing or about to commit a scheduled offence or had any knowledge regarding the commission or intended commission of a scheduled offence by another person. It would be lawful for that Garda or any Garda 'authorised in that behalf', to apprehend such person 'as if a warrant had been issued for such apprehension', search the suspect and his vehicle, and remove him to a Garda station, using 'such force as may be necessary'. An authorization might be 'verbal or in writing', could apply to 'a particular member, or a particular class of members, or all members of the Garda Síochána', and would 'identify or describe specifically the person

4 Dáil Debates vol. 38 col. 2550, 5 June 1931. 5 Dáil Debates vol. 38 col. 2570. 6 D/J H.284/24, notes for second reading, 4 June 1931. 7 D/J 93/2/7, Roche to the attorney general, 8 May 1931. 8 CAB 5/66, 11 June 1931. A number of other measures were approved by the executive council, including the issue of revolvers to district and divisional Garda Officers, increasing the special branch by 100, and establishing a special armed detective unit at Kilakee House, Co. Dublin.

or persons' in respect of whom these powers were to be exercised. A warrant would last two weeks and could be extended by a further two weeks. A statement on oath by a Garda not below the rank of inspector that a Garda who did anything in purported exercise of these powers was duly authorized would be 'conclusive and final evidence, incapable of being rebutted or questioned by cross-examination, rebutting evidence, or otherwise, that such member was so authorised when he did such act'.

Further, whenever a Garda observed a person whom he suspected of having committed or being about to commit a scheduled offence, the Garda would be empowered to stop and interrogate the suspect. If the suspect failed to give 'a satisfactory account of himself', the Garda could detain him, search him and his vehicle, and remove him to a Garda station, using 'such force as may be necessary'. The prisoner could be held for a maximum of 6 hours while a decision was made by a Garda not below rank of inspector to order him 'apprehended' for 72 hours from the time of his arrest or charged. Otherwise, the prisoner would be released.

Apprehended persons could be searched, photographed, and fingerprinted. More importantly, they would be obliged to give their name, address and a full account of movements and actions during the previous 14 days. Failure to do so or giving false or misleading information would, on conviction, be punished by up to three months' imprisonment. If the prisoner was to be prosecuted, he would have to be informed in writing within the allotted 72 hours. He would remain in custody and would have to be charged before a district justice within 10 days.

The draft also included a definition of unlawful associations taken directly from section 4 of the Public Safety Act, 1927 and a provision permitting district justices to summarily try felony charges under section 7 of the Treasonable Offences Act, 1925 (illegal drilling) on request of the attorney general. Civil actions against Gardaí for 'alleged illegal detention, or an alleged assault, or an alleged conspiracy' would be heard by a judge sitting without a jury.[9]

The IRA continued to expand during the summer of 1931. Maurice Twomey, the IRA chief of staff, reported an 'extraordinary growth of the Volunteer movement' to Joseph McGarrity.[10] The organization's public declarations became increasingly militant – *An Phoblacht*, for example, demanded that 'members of CID should be treated as "social pariahs" … that treatment must be extended to … Judges and District Judges, to uniformed police – to every individual who is a willing part of the machinery by which our Irish patriots are being tortured.'[11]

9 D/J 93/2/7. 10 Quoted in Dunphy, *Fianna Fáil*, p. 138. 11 20 June 1931.

These developments caused the O'Duffy to reassess the situation, contending that the IRA was pursuing a 'well considered' policy, warning, 'the State is going to suffer in consequence.' He believed the situation could now only be countered by radical new legislation, and proposed two alternative approaches.[12]

The chief superintendent of the Dublin Metropolitan Division (DMP) drew up the first. He sought the reenactment of parts 1 and 2 of the Public Safety Act, 1927, covering the constitution amendment, unlawful associations, and miscellaneous powers.[13] He also proposed establishing special courts constituted of one or more members of the high court, sitting without juries, to try scheduled offences,[14] on application by the attorney general.

Additionally, he proposed empowering superintendents to issue search warrants for firearms and treasonable documents or to search buildings where suspected unlawful assemblies were being held. (Gardaí would remain on premises for as long as necessary afterwards to prevent the commission of other offences.) The chief superintendent also proposed obliging persons suspected by superintendents of possessing information 'touching any offence committed under the Act' to furnish such information. He also sought to empower the Garda commissioner to prohibit meetings which sought to further the aims of unlawful associations, to provoke breaches of the peace, to intimidate peaceable citizens, or to obstruct the lawful use of roads or public places.[15]

The Garda special branch prepared the second proposal.[16] It had five basic elements:

- A schedule of offences including murder, attempted murder, any offence where firearms or explosives were used, carried or produced, and offences under the Treasonable Offences Act, 1925.
- Gardaí not below rank of sergeant would be empowered to arrest without warrant in order to detain and to interrogate persons suspected of committing scheduled offences or of possessing information relating to the commission of scheduled offences.

12 P80/856/44–5, memorandum, 24 June 1931, presented to the Executive Cabinet, 27 July 1931. 13 Sections 1 to 19 inclusive. 14 These would include offences scheduled under the Public Safety Act, 1927; assault, maiming, manslaughter or murder of Gardaí and soldiers; offences against persons to further the aims of an unlawful association; arson and assault or seizure of buildings with firearms; possession of firearms or ammunition with intent to endanger life or property; and malicious damage to property in furtherance of the aims of an unlawful association. 15 P80/856/38–41. 16 Memorandum by D. Neligan and É. Coogan.

- Persons could be detained in Garda custody for a period not exceeding 72 hours, when suspects would be obliged to answer questions posed by Gardaí relating to the commission of scheduled offences.
- Refusal to answer questions would lead to further remand by a district justice for up to eight days, and additional refusals would be punishable by a fine and/or imprisonment.
- Gardaí were to be indemnified against civil actions alleging wrongful arrest or ill-treatment. Complaints against Gardaí were to be dealt with under Garda discipline regulations.

O'Duffy believed if the special branch's proposals proved inadequate, a special tribunal, staffed by army officers, empowered to impose the death penalty, and from which there could be no appeal, would have to be established to deal with 'all cases of a political nature which in the opinion of the attorney general could not properly be dealt with in the existing courts'.[17]

The situation had not been formally re-evaluated by the government since the drafting of the Garda Síochána Bill when, on 20 July 1931, John Ryan, one of the witnesses in the Tipperary drilling case, was shot dead by the IRA.[18] Stephen Roche later recorded that Ryan's killing had 'naturally increased the tension'.[19]

O'Duffy identified Counties Tipperary, Kerry, Leitrim and Donegal as the most disturbed in the country,[20] and repeated that in light of the Gardaí's legal difficulties 'the Irregulars have the field to themselves.' He was clear about what had to be done:

> [Members of the IRA] should be deprived of the protection which enables them to endanger the security and peace of the State, by placing them outside the protection of a Constitution, which at the same time they are attacking and sheltering behind, and placing them in a position uninfluenced by the constitutional rights of citizenship where their activities can be met by suitable action. There is no good reason why an Organisation making war on the State should be afforded the protection which the State affords its loyal citizens.[21]

The executive council finally met to discuss the security situation on 30 July 1931 and to examine O'Duffy's various submissions. It ordered the

17 P80/856/42–4. 18 'Departmental Notes', p. 6. 19 D/T S.9249, 17 Aug. 1936. The Dáil, which adjourned on 17 July 1931, would have no way to question developments or the government's response. 20 D/T S.5864, O'Duffy to the secretary of the department of Justice, 10 Aug. 1931. 21 P80/857, O'Duffy to Roche, 27 July 1931.

minister for Justice to draft heads of a bill providing the 'necessary powers to deal with the situation.' In addition, a dossier on the IRA and related matters was to be prepared by the department of Justice for 'the information of the Bishops' and submitted for approval.[22]

The IRA was becoming increasingly brazen. Leading leftwing IRA member Frank Ryan declared that 'The Irish Republican Army is still at war with Britain. We regard the Free State Ministers merely as agents of Britain. We shall not lay down our arms until we have achieved the object Irishmen have been fighting for these many years – a completely independent republic for all Ireland.'[23] He claimed, 'I have only to give the word and every CID man would be wiped off the streets of Dublin tonight.' He described John Ryan as 'nothing else than a traitor' and said that Superintendent Curtin had 'exceeded his duty. He went out of his way to persecute the IRA.'

That day 'suggestions for a permanent measure to deal with treasonable offences' were ready for presentation to the executive council. The department of Justice sought the implementation of a definite and permanent set of procedures that would show that the days of 'leniency' and 'half measures' had passed. Heads of legislation were prepared based on 'the necessities of the situation' and not with regard to possible Oireachtas objections. The assistant secretary of the department of Justice, Stephen Roche, wrote, 'the existing situation is not to be met by minor remedies: the time has gone when it might have been cured by merely harassing the activists'. He believed that the only adequate deterrent 'to the leaders of disorder' was to 'drive into them the certainty that if they persist in their activities they will suffer death and that certainly cannot be achieved by the ordinary process of law'. He sought a special court, free from 'legal red-tape', which would be 'allowed to act much as a sensible man would act in his own case in a similar emergency'. While he recommended the taking of other powers, they were merely 'subsidiary … without the background of a summary tribunal which has the power of life and death and is prepared to exercise those powers freely all minor remedies are (in my opinion) merely playing the conspiracy of murder which faces us'.[24] These

22 CAB 5/75. In addition, the minister for External Affairs was asked to investigate measures taken by other states confronted with similar problems; Patrick McGilligan was to arrange a meeting between Cardinal McRory and executive ministers. See also D/T S.5864B for an August 1931 department of Justice report on the IRA which estimated its numbers at about 1,300 officers and 3,500 rank and file, and pointed to the organization's links with communistic groups. 23 *Daily Express*, 24 Aug. 1931. Quoted in Dáil Debates vol. 40 col. 34–6, 14 Oct. 1931. 24 D/J 93/2/7, Roche to the secretary of the executive council, 24 Aug. 1931.

extraordinary proposals would necessitate a constitutional amendment, though its exact form was to be left to the attorney general.[25]

The department's proposed tribunal would comprise two army officers and a president. It would have the same powers and privileges as the high court, and no other court could restrain it in any way and there would be no provision for appeal from its convictions or sentences. The department of Justice wanted the tribunal established as soon as possible after the enactment of this legislation and to remain in operation even if no immediate work existed, thus becoming a permanent feature of the state's legal machinery. Roche argued that the tribunal's mere existence and readiness to function at any time would act as a powerful deterrent. He added, 'The principle should be openly acknowledged that the task of dealing with anti-state activities of a violent character is no longer to be laid on the judges, juries, and state officials who are appointed to deal with the normal court business of a settled state.'

The proposed special court would prosecute offences under the Treasonable Offences Act, 1925, the Juries (Protection) Act, 1929, the Firearms Act, 1925; the Explosives Act, 1875; offences under the proposed act; any crime of violence that a Garda not below the rank of inspector certified 'to the best of his belief was committed from a "political motive".'

The department of Justice recommended that the tribunal should not be bound by the normal rules or laws of evidence or of examination or cross-examination of witnesses, suggesting that it could, at its own discretion, hear or consider any testimony, verbal or written, sworn or unsworn:

> It is considered essential that the tribunal should have the power to accept, for what it is worth, *anything* in the nature of evidence and to demand of the accused that he shall admit, deny, or explain the police allegations against him, and that refusal to explain or to give information, without some adequate reason, should be taken by the tribunal as sufficient evidence of guilt, even where there is no such positive proof of guilt as would satisfy an ordinary court.[26]

Further, it proposed permitting the tribunal to shift the onus of proof to the accused whenever it believed that to be fairer and for witnesses to give evidence privately if the tribunal feared for witnesses' lives or property.

There was a list of other proposals: the department wanted the tribunal to have power to inflict any greater penalty than normally available

25 Roche pointed out the that articles 64, 70, 72 and probably article 9 of the constitution would be amended by the draft. **26** Department of Justice emphasis.

under other legislation (including the death sentence) if it felt such was necessary in the public interest. When sentencing, the department proposed that the tribunal could take into account the convicted person's general character, his previous record, the circumstances in which the offence was committed and the general level of political offences occurring at the time of the offence. Further, it also suggested that a person might also be found guilty of an offence other than that with which he was charged.

The indispensable elements of the proposed tribunal were, Roche believed, that

- It had to have the power to convict 'notorious' IRA members 'on the strength of the Garda dossier alone', unless the accused made a genuine effort to exonerate himself
- The tribunal required not only special powers but to be staffed by persons who would use those powers 'fully and fearlessly'
- 'Every possible avenue of legal appeal must be closed'; its procedures were not to be open to investigation in any way by any other court.

There remained the issue of re-enacting provisions of the Public Safety Act, 1927 dealing with special police powers and unlawful associations,[27] and empowering the executive council to prohibit any meeting it expected would lead to a breach of the peace. Additionally, the department of Justice suggested that if a Garda inspector (or a Garda of higher rank) believed that persons were withholding information regarding the commission of a scheduled offence, persons should be brought before the tribunal where they would be obliged to answer questions. Failure to satisfy the tribunal would be punished as contempt.

These proposals were considered by the executive council on 2 September 1931.[28] While it broadly accepted them,[29] it raised several points. It wanted the offence of violence committed with a 'political motive' replaced by one along the lines of an armed attack on the institutions of the state. It also sought power to defer or suspend the execution of death sentences and a provision covering organizations that changed their name hoping to frustrate the unlawful associations provisions. It wanted the public to be clearly informed that membership of unlawful organizations was an offence. The executive council also had some difficulty with the pro-

27 Sections 4, 5, 6, 7, 9, 10, 12, 14, 15 and 19. 28 Cab. 5/79, 2 Sept. 1931; D/T S.4469/17, M. Ó Cuinneóin, assistant secretary of the department of Justice, to the attorney general, 7 Sept. 1931, when the attorney general was instructed to have the parliamentary draftsman draw up the necessary legislation. 29 D/T S.4469/17, Diarmaid Ó hÉigceartaigh to Roche, 2 Sept. 1931.

posed alterations to the laws of evidence, as well as with the proposal that the tribunal might convict persons of treasonable offences other than those charged, writing that 'as at present worded does not appear to be altogether reasonable.' This second proposal was dropped. Nevertheless, it was clear that the executive council was determined to overcome the difficulties experienced by the ordinary courts. Following cabinet discussions, the assistant parliamentary draftsman was informed that

> It is most important that the Tribunal shall have, and use to the full, ample powers to preserve its dignity. Members of the Tribunal may be murdered but the Tribunal must not be made ridiculous, as the ordinary courts have been. I think a section is desirable not only to give these powers but to advertise their existence. In particular, gross contempt in the face of the Tribunal should make the offender liable to corporal punishment. On the other hand if the *Irish Press* publishes a letter to the effect that the Tribunal takes its orders from the Government, the Tribunal should have power to inflict a heavy fine.[30]

A preliminary, though comprehensive, first draft of the provisionally entitled Treasonable Offences Bill was presented to the executive council on 18 September.[31] It had five basic parts: the constitution amendment, a special tribunal, special Garda powers, unlawful associations provisions and miscellaneous matters.

Originally based on section 3 of the Public Safety Act, 1927, the bill would override the constitution with a simple amendment:

> Article 3 and every subsequent Article of the Constitution shall be read and construed subject to the provisions of this Article, and in case of inconsistency between this Article and the said Article 3 or any subsequent Article, this Article shall prevail.

As soon as possible after being passed, a tribunal was to be established, consisting of three members, one of whom was to be certified by the attorney general 'to have legal knowledge and experience', the others would be army officers not below the rank of commandant. Its members were to be 'appointed and be removable at will by the Executive Council'.

The tribunal was to have jurisdiction to try, to convict or acquit persons charged with scheduled offences and to sentence persons convicted

30 Ibid., M. Ó Cuinneóin to the assistant parliamentary draftsman, 15 Sept. 1931. 31 D/J 93/2/7, draft prepared by 16 Sept. 1931, attorney general to the minister for Justice.

by it. Scheduled offences included any offence under the Treasonable Offences Act, 1925; any offence under the Juries (Protection) Act, 1929; possessing, using or carrying a firearm without holding a firearm certificate or any offence in relation to a prohibited weapon under the Firearms Act, 1925; unlawful possession of explosives under the Explosives Act, 1875; any offence under the bill. The tribunal would have the power to administer oaths to witnesses and would have, more importantly,

> full and absolute power to appoint the times and places of its sittings and to prescribe and regulate its own procedure in all respects and in particular in respect of the admission or exclusion of the public to or from its sittings, the examination of witnesses, the enforcing the attendance of witnesses and the production of documents, and the punishment of persons guilty of contempt of the Tribunal or any member thereof.

If the tribunal found a person guilty of a scheduled offence, in lieu of the normal punishment provided by law it could impose any greater punishment (including death), if it believed 'such greater punishment is necessary in the public interest.' Convictions, sentences, orders, and judgements were to be carried out in the same manner and would have the same consequences as those of the central criminal court. Persons carrying these out would enjoy the same protections and immunities as those carrying out 'a like conviction, sentence, order, or judgement of the Central Criminal Court.'

There was to be no appeal from 'any conviction, sentence, order or judgement of the Tribunal' and it was not to be restrained or interfered with 'in the execution of its jurisdiction or powers' by any other court nor could 'any proceedings before the Tribunal be removed by certiorari to any other court.' The executive council could, however, 'at their absolute discretion', freely pardon any person convicted by the tribunal and wholly or partially remit or modify (by way of mitigation only) any punishment imposed by the tribunal.

Initially, the department of Justice proposed that, on application of a Garda not below the rank of inspector, the tribunal would transfer trials to itself of persons charged with scheduled offences and awaiting trial by the central criminal court or the circuit court or those remanded by a district justice or peace commissioner.

Part 3 covered special Garda powers and was based largely on the Garda Síochána Bill. Any Garda was to be empowered to stop, interrogate and arrest persons whom he suspected 'of having committed or being about to commit or being or having been concerned in the commission' of a scheduled offence. Persons who failed to give 'a satisfactory account' of themselves could be apprehended without warrant, searched, and their vehicle searched, using 'such force as may be necessary'. Any person accompanying a suspected individual could be treated similarly. The Garda's statement on oath in any court that when he used these powers, he suspected the person of having committed or being about to commit a scheduled offence '(without specifying such offence) shall be conclusive evidence, incapable of being rebutted or questioned by cross-examination, rebutting evidence, or otherwise, that such member did at that time so suspect such person and was then entitled to stop and interrogate such person'. A Garda would also be empowered to stop, search and arrest without warrant 'any person whom he suspects to be carrying any treasonable or seditious documents', and to seize such documents.

Following arrest, suspects were to be removed to a convenient Garda station. Within 12 hours, a Garda not below the rank of inspector was to be informed of the arrest, who would direct if the prisoner should be 'apprehended' for 72 hours under the Act, arrested under warrant or released. Suspects were to be informed 'in writing' within the allotted 72 hours if a direction had been made ordering trial on a specified charge by the tribunal. Persons notified of trial by the tribunal would remain in custody and were to be brought before the tribunal within one month. Apprehended persons could be searched, photographed, fingerprinted, and any Garda could 'demand of such person his name and his address and a full account of his movements and actions during any specified period, beginning no more that fourteen days' before his detention.

Part 4 dealt with unlawful associations. The executive council could declare any association to be an unlawful association which, in its opinion, fell within one of the categories set out in the draft. (These definitions were taken directly from section 4 of the Public Safety Act, 1927.) Possession of a document 'of whatsoever date or bearing no date ... issued by or emanating from an unlawful association or appearing to be so issued or so to emanate purporting to aid or abet an unlawful association or otherwise relating to or connected with an unlawful association' was an offence, unless an accused satisfied the tribunal that he had no knowledge of the document or its contents. Possession of such documents would suffice to convict for membership of an unlawful association. The onus of proof would be shifted to the accused who would have to declare on oath that he was not a member since the association was outlawed and would have to produce two 'reputable witnesses' to support this.

The draft also proposed empowering the executive council to make suppression orders against periodicals that it believed contained seditious libel, statements appearing to emanate from or in support of unlawful associations, or statements inciting or calculated to incite scheduled, treasonable or seditious offences. Further, a Garda not below the rank of inspector could issue warrants to Gardaí under his command and named in the warrant to search any specified place or premises when of opinion that there was 'reasonable ground for suspecting that there are treasonable or seditious documents in any place or premises.' The draft also proposed empowering an executive minister to proclaim any public meeting he believed would 'lead to a breach of the peace or to promote or incite to the commission of acts of violence or intimidation or to interfere with the administration of the law or the maintenance of law and order.'

On 21 September 1931, the executive council examined alternative titles for the bill,[32] and decided that the bill should be introduced on the first day of the reassembly of the Dáil, Wednesday, 14 October 1931 with the hope of having the remaining stages 'pressed through as rapidly as feasible, if possible on the following day.' To that end, the Ceann Comhairle (speaker of the Dáil) was consulted on the question of a guillotine motion and the bill was given absolute priority.[33] A cabinet committee was also established to examine it more closely,[34] and the attorney general was asked to further examine the constitutional ramifications of the proposed amendment. In view of the suggested change to the bill's title, the tribunal's title also required attention. The legal qualification of one tribunal member was removed.[35]

The executive council worried that the tribunal would have to make formal procedural regulations, feeling that the words 'prescribe and regulate' were too rigid. M. Mac Donnchadha, secretary of the department of the President of the executive council, explained to the parliamentary draftsman, 'It is sufficient that the Tribunal should be empowered to adopt whatever procedure is desirable without the formulation of rules. It should also be empowered to determine what may be admitted as evidence'. The tribunal would have, in general, all the powers of the high court and was to have a seal. Regarding the tribunal's proposed jurisdiction, the executive council wondered if it was 'watertight enough' to prevent challenges on the grounds that there was an error in the manner in which an accused was brought before the tribunal, that the tribunal lacked sufficient jurisdiction to try an offence, or that the tribunal was not properly constituted.[36] Mac Donnchadha

32 A suggested alternative title was 'The Protection of the People Act'. Instructions sent to the parliamentary draftsman, 6 Oct. 1931. 33 D/T S.6193, M. Mac Donnchadha to the private secretary, minister for Local Government and Public Health, and to the attorney general, 29 Sept. 1931. 34 Consisting of Cosgrave, Blythe, Fitzgerald-Kenney, Desmond Fitzgerald (the minister for Defence), and Hogan (the minister for Agriculture). 35 Cab. 5/81, 21 Sept. 1931. 36 D/T S.4469/17, 22 Sept. 1931 Mac Donnchadha to

instructed the parliamentary draftsman that if the legality of any person's detention or punishment is questioned in the courts 'e.g. by way of *habeas corpus* – certificate under the seal of the Tribunal should be a final and conclusive answer.'[37] The executive council also requested redrafting of the provision permitting the tribunal to impose greater punishments than permitted by the ordinary law, and provision for death sentences to be executed in a manner other than hanging when 'desirable or necessary':

> The Tribunal in determining the punishment to be imposed on any person convicted before it shall not be bound by the penalties prescribed in this or any other Act but shall have regard to the circumstances of each particular case, and in particular to the prevalence, at the time, of treasonable and seditious offences. The Tribunal may inflict the sentence of death or imprisonment for any term, or a fine, or both such fine and imprisonment, or any other penalty recognised by law. The Tribunal may, if it thinks fit, specify the method in which any sentence shall be carried out and if it does not so specify then (subject to the provisions of the Act) every sentence shall be carried out in a like manner as near as may be as a similar sentence of the central criminal court would be carried out.[38]

The executive council was also concerned that the 12 hour limit during which a direction ordering a person's detention for 72 hours could be obtained from a Garda inspector was too short (it was extended to 36 hours). It also believed that the one-month limit during which a person had to be tried by the tribunal was too short (this provision remained unchanged). Further, in order to 'tighten up as far as possible so that the penalties cannot be evaded by rapid change in the name of the organisation', provisions were to be phrased along the lines that (a) any organization which does these things is an unlawful organization; (b) a declaration by the executive council would be conclusive proof. Regarding statements from unlawful associations, the executive council sought a provision allowing newspapers to print ministers' speeches that quoted IRA documents. Additionally, it wanted the power to suppress publications to be altered to prevent claims of interference with press freedom; *An Phoblacht* was to be specified by name, other publications by analogy. Regarding meetings, it requested power to prohibit meetings in any place for any period up to three months.[39] It was also concerned that the schedule was not wide enough.[40]

the private secretary, minister for Justice, instructions to parliamentary draftsman. 6 Oct. 1931. 37 Mac Donnchadha's emphasis. 38 Instructions to parliamentary draftsman, 6 Oct. 1931. 39 This was finalized as within one mile of the place. 40 D/T S.4469/17,

The Garda commissioner also made several observations and recommendations on the draft.[41] Initially, the bill proposed obliging suspects to account fully for their movements during the 14 days before apprehension, but O'Duffy argued, 'if a suspect were successful in keeping out of the way of the police for a fortnight he could not be interrogated in regard to an outrage committed prior to the commencement of the fortnight.'[42] He suggested expanding this power to compel suspects to give any information that was required for the detection and/or punishment of any scheduled offence. 'For example, the suspect might *have* seen or *heard* things which would be helpful to the police but he might claim that things which he had *seen* or *heard* did not form any part of his own "movements" or "actions".'[43] Essentially, O'Duffy had in mind something similar to the misprision of treason provisions of section 2 of the Treasonable Offences Act, 1925. These proposals were essentially implemented.

He also suggested empowering Gardaí to enter and search any lands or premises where, in the opinion of the Gardaí, a meeting or an assembly was being held, or about to be held and offences under the Act were being committed or contemplated. O'Duffy explained, 'it is a well known fact that meetings of known members of the Irregular organization are held where plans are laid, instructional classes held, etc., and the members attending these meetings are careful not to bring with them any documents or firearms.' Additionally, he wanted the Gardaí to be empowered to remain on the premises to prevent or detect the commission of offences. This was agreed to, but rendered as a tribunal power to close a building on application by a Garda inspector stating that the building was being used in relation to offences under the act.

O'Duffy also successfully argued for extended Garda search powers, finalized as whenever a Garda inspector was of opinion that there were reasonable grounds for suspecting there were treasonable or seditious documents or arms or ammunition in any place or premises he could issue a search warrant to any Garda named in the warrant.

The government did not implement every proposal O'Duffy made, though. He had proposed prohibiting 'the wearing of uniforms or badges indicating membership of an unlawful association' and prosecuting persons found in unlawful possession of firearms and ammunition as members of an unlawful association.

The executive council's observations and recommendations were sent to the department of Justice soon afterwards. Although it envisaged few

instructions to the parliamentary draftsman, 6 Oct. 1931. 41 Ibid., Eoin O'Duffy, in consultation with deputy commissioner Éamon Coogan and Colonel David Neligan, 28 Sept. 1931. 42 Instructions to parliamentary draftsman, 6 Oct. 1931. 43 O'Duffy's emphasis.

problems in the suggestions put forward on 21 September, a number of points had to be addressed.[44] A satisfactory title remained illusive – the 'Protection of the People Act' had been mooted, though the corresponding title of the tribunal was problematic.

The executive council had sought a provision which would allow the suppression of seditious periodicals that would not be regarded as curbing press freedom. But the department found 'it difficult to make any suggestion by which the power will remain equally effective in fact but will appear on the face of it less open to abuse.' The executive council opposed empowering the tribunal to suppress seditious periodicals, though this formula was eventually implemented.

The schedule that came before the executive council did not contain the complete list of offences suggested by the department. One serious omission, it believed, was a satisfactory definition of offences carried out for political ends. To avoid any ambiguity and because, as the draft stood,[45] it appeared that such offences would not automatically fall within the scope of the bill, it proposed adding the following to the schedule:

> Any crime of violence as regards which a member of the Garda Síochána not below the rank of inspector certifies that to the best of his belief such crime was committed with the object of impairing the machinery of Government or the administration of justice'.[46]

The executive council later substituted an 'Executive Minister' for 'a member of the Garda Síochána' not below the rank of inspector.

On the issues of sentencing and enforcement, the department emphasized that the minister for Justice should have 'an entirely free hand' in dealing with persons sentenced to imprisonment by the tribunal, who should be entirely segregated from ordinary prisoners. Any other approach would be 'foredoomed to failure', Roche believed. He wrote that such prisoners 'must be kept apart, not as a *privileged* class but as a class which is, in fact, distinct from the ordinary class of prisoner and which needs exceptionally firm treatment'.[47] Existing rules, he argued, did not anticipate detainees who challenged authority as IRA prisoners often did. It was to be made clear, he added, 'that these prisoners are not either convicts or ordinary short-term prisoners but a new class without any statutory rights

44 D/T S.4469/17, note by Roche, 28 Sept. 1931; suggestions by the commissioner had not been seen at this stage. 45 The initial inclusion of any crime of violence that a Garda not below the rank of inspector certified 'to the best of his belief was committed from a "political motive"' was omitted from this draft. 46 D/T S.4469/17, 28 Sept. 1931. 47 Roche's emphasis.

or privileges for whose proper detention and discipline special rules are necessary.' The department of Justice also sought the incorporation of the provisions of the Garda Síochána Bill permitting actions against Gardaí for alleged assault or false imprisonment to be heard by a judge sitting without a jury.

The executive council had expressed concern regarding possible jurisdictional challenges to the tribunal, but Roche believed that the bill had been drafted in such a way as to make investigation by any other court of the tribunal's orders, procedure or judgements very difficult, if not impossible. Clearly, there was no specific suspension of habeas corpus. He wrote, 'it would be … most undesirable, even if it were possible, to endeavour to restrict the existing constitutional right of making such applications'. If an order were sought, though, Roche urged that it be quickly disposed of in order to avoid a hostile inquiry into the tribunal's powers and procedure by way of an examination of signatures, seals, warrants, etc. If, for example, a detention ordered by the tribunal was challenged, it would be best disposed of by providing a clause that declared that a certificate, under the seal of the minister for Justice, that a person was lawfully held by order of the tribunal was conclusive proof as to the legality of the detention.

As drafting work reached its conclusion, the executive council began to advance against the IRA on a second front, described by Bowyer-Bell as 'a wide-scale attack on radicalism, revolution, and the contamination of Irish Catholic souls' by communism.[48] Ministers publicly demonized the IRA's links to left-wing organizations. The minister for Justice, James Fitzgerald-Kenney, warned that Saor Éire aimed 'to force by means of threats and crimes of violence, a republic of Soviet nature on this country'.[49] W.T. Cosgrave had privately warned Cardinal McRory of a secret IRA-communist conspiracy that operated under the banners of patriotism and physical force and appealed to the poor. He declared that the conspirators were intent on causing social revolution and sought 'the abolition of government as we understand it, the confiscation of property … and the creation of a state of anarchy'. He urged joint Episcopal action in the form of a concise statement of the Church's law on 'the present issue, and the penalties attached to its violation'.[50]

In the meantime, the executive council prepared to implement the legislation. Special precautions were to be taken to prevent information regarding plans leaking out. Cosgrave called for 'stern and stringent

48 Bell, *The secret army*, p. 88. 49 *Irish Press*, 14 Sept. 1931. 50 D/T S.5864B, Cosgrave to Cardinal McRory, 10 Sept. 1931. His letter was accompanied by a department of Justice memorandum concerned with the IRA and socialist groups in the state, and the legal difficulties being experienced by the state.

actions' in counties where Seán McBride and other prominent IRA members were active and similar treatment for members 'of the Irregulars apart from Fianna Fáil' in counties where land annuities were outstanding. Special protection was to be afforded to members of the Oireachtas for fear of 'spectacular displays of strength' once the legislation was introduced. The question of providing a special prison was to be addressed, and all formalities regarding the tribunal were to be finalized so that it was ready to operate once the legislation was passed.[51]

The executive council ordered section 19 of the Public Safety Act, 1927 re-enacted. In cases of civil actions against Gardaí for alleged conspiracy or assault and/or unlawful detention, if the Garda's defence was that he attempted to prevent the commission of an offence under the proposed Act, then the case was to be dealt with by a judge sitting without a jury. Further, *An Phoblacht* was to be immediately suppressed, all copies, posters, advertisements relating to it were to be summarily seized and destroyed whenever found. This power was to apply to any other periodical that appeared wholly or substantially to be a substitute or successor and if any question arose, then it would be determined by the tribunal. There was to be no coroner's inquest after the execution of a death sentence.[52]

The executive council approved additional instructions on 7 October 1931.[53] Because of difficulties with the name, it finally decided to call the tribunal simply the 'Constitution (Special Powers) Tribunal'.

The executive council also wanted every sentence pronounced by the tribunal to be subject to confirmation by a majority of the military members of the defence council. Roche, however, opposed this:

> the Tribunal, as originally conceived, is under no obligation to follow any definite procedure or to keep any notes of the evidence tendered or of the basis on which decisions are arrived at. But if a Confirming Authority is set up it follows of necessity that a complete record of the proceedings must be made and presented to the Confirming Authority: in fact, the Tribunal will be obliged to function under much the same conditions as the circuit court functions at present viz. attention cannot be concentrated on simply doing justice – a great deal of the time and energy of the Court must be

51 D/T S.4469/17, minute by Cosgrave, no date, between 22 and 29 Sept. 1931. A number of incidents occurred during September: the unoccupied Garda barracks in Kilreekle, Co. Galway was blown up, 12 Sept. 1931; William McInerney, a critic of the IRA and Saor Éire, was shot and seriously wounded, 13 Sept. 1931; and the home of Co. Clare state solicitor, James Lynch, was fired into, 15 Sept. 1931. See 'Departmental Notes', pp 6–7. 52 D/T S.4469/17. 53 Also in attendance were the attorney general and Éamon Duggan.

> devoted to getting into record form a complete justification, in writing, of the Court's decision. This has been held in many quarters to be a serious drawback to the circuit court: it will be a fatal drawback to the Tribunal and the original idea of a speedy and unfettered Tribunal will be completely nullified.[54]

The proposal was dropped.

The legislation was finally introduced into the Dáil on 14 October 1931, simply entitled the Constitution (Amendment No. 17) Bill, 1931. It set out to 'Amend the Constitution by inserting an article making better provision for safeguarding the rights of people and containing provisions for meeting the prevalence of disorder',[55] with the substantive provisions of the bill added as a schedule to the new article – 2A. W.T. Cosgrave described it as 'pre-eminently a Bill to safeguard the rights of the people and to ensure to them the full and peaceable enjoyment of those rights'. He explained:

> This is the best Bill that has been introduced in this house since it first sat. This is a Bill to secure life and property; it is to secure ordered conditions which are being menaced by a conspiracy and by a number of conspirators. This Bill will, we hope, put an end for all time to armed attacks upon citizens of this State to protect whom it is the duty of the Government of this State. It is the duty of this House to ensure every liberty and safeguard that it is possible in human experience to confer upon the citizens of this State. This Bill will do more than that. It will enable us for all time to get rid of a conspiracy against democracy, against religion, against authority, and it will give us an opportunity of ensuring that God's commandments will be obeyed in this country.

Turning directly to the question of the IRA, pointing to several violent incidents the organization carried out and to the Frank Ryan interview of August 1931, the president accused the organization of seeking to establish a dictatorship enforced by violence and intimidation, but declared, 'this time the menace must be removed once and for all.' He asked how a democratic government could remain idle while *An Phoblacht* proclaimed

54 D/T S.4469/17, note by Roche, 8 Oct. 1931. 55 *The Irish Times*, 15 Oct. 1931, commented the bill's most 'drastic proposals might have been unnecessary if sedition had been tackled at an earlier stage', and that the policy of Fianna Fáil in withholding support was 'at best, unintelligible … it knows, or it ought to know, that many of the forces which are arrayed against Mr Cosgrave's government, are equally hostile to itself.'

that the only true government of Ireland was the army council of the IRA, or described the Oireachtas as 'a mere cover or instrument of British usurpation'. The problem facing the state was simple: 'the Constitution and ... the law while adequate as regards ordinary crime have, in fact proved entirely ineffective to deal with [the IRA] ... In this Bill we are setting up a tribunal which will not be amenable to terroristic methods.'

Unlike several earlier public safety measures, Dáil opposition to article 2A did not appear to be resolute. Naturally, Fianna Fáil criticized it. Éamon de Valera claimed that the only policy the government employed was 'the way of force, the way of the big stick'. He predicted the government's measures would fail: 'If there are drastic measures taken, I have no doubt whatever they will drive [the IRA] more underground. This will prevent open drillings and things of that kind, but it will not drive out or kill or end the nature of the movement itself.' Nevertheless, de Valera declared that his own tolerance of the IRA was not unlimited. No authority outside the Dáil, he said, 'was entitled to take human life ... Our position in this matter is this – that there must be some authority in the country.'[56] Even more reserved was the Labour Party, whose opposition to the measure was neither unanimous[57] nor wholly dismissive. Nonetheless, Deputy T.J. O'Connell expressed some concern at the damage being done to the constitution[58] and wondered why the special court was not introduced in 1929 when the government acknowledged the existence of jury intimidation. The bill, unamended, became law.[59]

On 17 October 1931, the executive council, being of 'opinion that circumstances exist which rendered it expedient', declared that parts 2 to 5 of article 2A had come into force.[60] On 20 October 1931, it declared 12 organizations to be unlawful associations: Saor Éire; The Association styling and calling itself the Irish Republican Army, sometimes known as the IRA or Óglaigh na hÉireann; Fianna Éireann; Cumann na mBan; Friends of Soviet Russia; the Irish Labour Defence League; the Workers' Defence Corps; the Workers' Revolutionary Party (Ireland); the Irish Tribute League; the Irish Working Farmers' Committee; the Workers' Research Bureau. Also on 20 October, the governor general, acting on the advice of the executive council, appointed five army officers to the constitution (special powers) tribunal under section 4(2): Colonel Francis Bennett (acting assistant chief of staff), Colonel Daniel McKenna (deputy

56 Dáil Debates vol. 40 col. 375–6, 32–3, 45, 54–8, 16 Oct. 1931. 57 Two Labour deputies (Richard Anthony and Daniel Morrissey) were expelled from the Labour Party because they supported the bill. 58 Dáil Debates vol. 40 col. 62. 59 See O'Sullivan, *The Irish Free State and its senate*, p. 262. 60 Minutes of the executive council, C.5/94, 17 Oct. 1931.

quarter master general), Major John V. Joyce (deputy adjutant general), Commandant Connor Whelan (officer commanding, 3rd battalion), Commandant Patrick Tuite (training staff, Curragh district). The tribunal sat at Collins Barracks, Dublin.[61]

While article 2A was a permanent article of the constitution, it was not permanently nor did it automatically come into force.[62] Its provisions operated whenever the executive council made an order under section 1(2), which could be suspended at any time under section 1(3).

Special Garda powers under part 3 were not necessarily exercised, even when part 3 was in operation, and would not normally be used without a direction from the minister for Justice to the commissioner. A direction from the minister likewise controlled the operation of parts 4 and 5, dealing respectively with unlawful associations and miscellaneous matters.[63]

Under section 13(1), a Garda (or soldier) could stop, search, interrogate and apprehend any person whom he suspected of 'having committed or being about to commit or being or having been concerned in the commission of an offence mentioned in the Appendix to this Article or of having knowledge of the commission or intended commission of any such offence'. The statement on oath that when a Gárda or soldier

> stopped and interrogated a particular person under this section he suspected such person of having committed or being about to commit or of being or having been concerned in the commission of an offence mentioned in the Appendix to this Article or of having knowledge of the commission or intended commission of any such offence (without specifying such offence) shall be conclusive evidence, incapable of being rebutted or questioned by cross-examination, rebutting evidence or otherwise, that such member did at that time so suspect such person and was then entitled to stop and interrogate such person under this section.[64]

If a suspect was removed to a Garda station (or other convenient place) under this section, a Garda inspector would have to be informed within 36 hours. Before the expiry of this 36-hour period, the inspector could order the suspect detained, charged or released.[65] Where a detention was ordered, the prisoner could be held for a maximum of 72 hours (from the

61 Iris Oifigiúil, 23 Oct. 1931, 'Departmental Notes', p. 7, D/J 93/2/7, 16 Oct. 1931; D/T S.2433, memorandum distributed to the executive council, 19 Oct. 1931; D/T S.9249 and D/T S.2437; D/T S.2433, 15 Oct. 1931. 62 See also D/J H.308/39, for the years 1931–4. 63 See D/J D.7/35, Roche to Geoghegan, 11 Mar. 1932. 64 Section 13(5). 65 Section 13(3).

time of his initial arrest) during which time he would either be given notice in writing that he was to be brought before the tribunal or released.[66] After an inspector ordered a suspect detained, any Garda could demand of the detainee (until the 72-hour period after initial arrest elapsed) his name, address and a full account of his movements and actions during any specified period and 'all or any information in his possession in relation to the commission or intended commission by another person' of any offence under article 2A. Detainees who failed or refused to give this information, or gave information that was incomplete, false, or misleading, or obstructed Gardaí searching, photographing or fingerprinting them, assaulted Gardaí, injured property, behaved in a disorderly manner, or attempted to escape would be guilty of an offence and 'liable on conviction … to suffer such punishment as the Tribunal shall think proper to inflict.'[67] Persons to be tried by the tribunal would remain in custody until their trial, and were to be brought before the tribunal within one month.[68]

Additionally, any Garda could stop, search and arrest any person whom he suspected of carrying treasonable or seditious documents, and seize all such documents, regardless of whether he made an arrest.[69] Under section 30, a Garda not below the rank of inspector was empowered to issue search orders to Gardaí named in the order to search any place or premises when 'of opinion that there is reasonable ground for suspecting that there are treasonable or seditious documents, firearms, or ammunition in any place or premises.'

Section 19(1) defined unlawful associations, while section 22 provided that possession of documents 'of whatsoever date or bearing no date … issued by or emanating from or appearing to be issued by or to emanate from an unlawful association or purporting to aid or abet an unlawful association or otherwise relating to or connected with an unlawful association' would be sufficient to convict of membership, unless 'in addition to such other evidence as satisfies the Tribunal of such non-membership', a suspect declared on oath that he was not a member of an unlawful association and had not been a member since article 2A was inserted into the constitution.

Preparations for implementing these new powers began immediately.[70] Eoin O'Duffy planned to bring the nine IRA members on remand when the article 2A became law before the tribunal. He also requested each Garda division to furnish him with a list of all 'undetected political outrages', and of the persons suspected of involvement. Gardaí planned to apprehend about 100 members of the IRA and Saor Éire from whom it

66 Section 14(1). 67 Section 15(1) and (2). 68 Section 17(2). 69 Section 29(1). 70 P80/477, Eoin O'Duffy to the minister for Justice, 20 Oct. 1931. Considered by the executive council on 22 Oct. 1931.

hoped to learn the names of officers and men in IRA units, the amount and location of arms, meeting places, etc. Failure to answer all questions truthfully would be dealt with under section 15. O'Duffy instructed Gardaí that under no circumstances were the special powers to be used in the investigation of ordinary offences. He further warned that 'anything in the nature of so-called third degree methods, flourishing of guns, or bullying tactics, will be severely punished ... The new Act gives the force all the powers required as to interrogation, etc. and there can be no justification for exceeding these powers.'

The commissioner, however, sought more than simply the conviction of active and prominent IRA members. He hoped that several IRA leaders would declare on oath under section 22 that they had ceased to be members, believing such individuals would 'no longer pose before the youth as fearless men'.[71] He also expected that the act could also be employed to check the activities of IRA organizers operating outside Dublin who often travelled about posing as insurance agents. It was intended to photograph and to fingerprint the principal IRA leaders while in custody. Further, the 'Communist agitators here from England – Stuart, Ward, Ferguson, Bell, McLay, Pullock, Fox, etc' were to be warned to leave the country.[72]

The commissioner made no recommendation for internment, believing 'the Act gives sufficient scope to frame some charge against any person worth arresting. There will always be a popular demand for the release of any person against whom no charge is preferred'. Furthermore, O'Duffy advocated that IRA members be imprisoned in the Curragh because 'if detained in Dublin or other cities they will be a source of annoyance. It is unlikely that women will arrange processions or prayer meetings at the Curragh'.

The tribunal quickly dealt with several newspapers under section 26. It declared issues of *An Phoblacht* dated 31 October and 7, 14, and 21 November 1931 to be seditious. The *Irish World* of 24 and 31 October, and 7 November 1931; the *Workers Voice* of 7 and 14 November, and 12 December 1931; the *Irish Worker* of 24 and 28 November, 19 December 1931, and 23 January 1932; the *Republican File* dated 19 December 1931 were also declared to be seditious. The executive council proclaimed several meetings in Dublin City and County under section 24: on 7 November 1931 (the anniversary of Russian Revolution), and on 10 November 1931 (Anti-Imperialist League, a similar meeting in Cork was also proclaimed that day). The executive council also proclaimed meetings at Findlander's Place, Dublin on 8, 22 and 29 November, and 5 to 6 and 12 to 13

71 O'Duffy had put forward a similar proposal in a report for the period ended 31 Mar. 1929. 72 P80/477.

December 1931.[73] Additionally, under section 27(1), the tribunal could make closing orders against buildings (lasting up to six months) on application by a Garda not below rank of inspector stating that a building was being or had been used for 'the purpose of or in relation to the commission of an offence mentioned in the Appendix to this Article'.

The most important element of this legislation was the constitution (special powers) tribunal. Persons would only be brought before the tribunal if a Garda not below the rank of inspector took some active steps to that end. Gardaí normally notified the attorney general's office and the minister for Justice simultaneously when seeking to send a person for trial by the tribunal, though approval or otherwise usually came from the attorney general only, who did not consult with the minister for Justice.[74] Otherwise, the ordinary courts would deal with an accused in the normal way. The tribunal could try a person charged with a scheduled offence if a Garda not below the rank of inspector issued a direction under section 14(1) followed by the necessary steps under section 17. Alternatively, the tribunal could, on application by a Garda not below the rank inspector, make an order under section 11(1) transferring to itself the trial of a person charged with a scheduled offence sent forward for trial by the central criminal court or by the circuit court. In the case of persons on remand, either in custody or on bail, on application by a Garda not below the rank of inspector, the tribunal could make an order under section 11(2) sending them forward for trial. Where a district justice or a peace commissioner remanded persons for scheduled offences and the tribunal ordered their trial transferred to it under Section 11(2) and depositions had already been taken, there was no need to serve a summary of the facts on the accused. In practice, though, a copy of the charges was supplied to the accused which he furnished to his solicitor. In other cases, that is those under section 17, when a member of the Gardaí not below the rank of inspector informed the prisoner that he would be tried by the tribunal, a short statement of the facts on which the prosecution was based, together with a copy of the charges, was given to the accused before trial to facilitate the preparation of a defence. The statement was to be sufficiently informative, containing dates and places, though not necessarily the names of witnesses. When the tribunal transferred cases to itself under section 11(1), the registrar of the tribunal sent a copy of the certified order to the county registrar or other appropriate court officer, to the secretaries of the

73 'Departmental Notes', pp 7–8, and D/T S.2445, D/T S.9249. 74 D/J. D.29/36. the commissioner's office to each chief superintendent, 29 June 1936, though there were occasions when the attorney general ordered prosecution which the minister for Justice regarded as 'contrary to the public interest', D/T S.8974, 15 June 1936.

departments of Defence and Justice, and to the governor of the prison if the accused was imprisoned. If a person was in custody, the minister for Defence was required to make an order, under seal, authorizing his transfer to Arbour Hill detention barracks.[75]

Despite the preparations made and the instructions issued, by 4 November 1931 it was clear to the department of Justice that some Gardaí were experiencing difficulties.[76] For example, under section 17(1) it was necessary to advise a prisoner in writing within 72 hours of initial apprehension that he was to be brought before the tribunal. In several instances, however, Gardaí found it impossible to get written sanction from the attorney general within the prescribed period, and had prisoners remanded before peace commissioners, while instructions were awaited. The assistant secretary, Stephen Roche, objected to this on three grounds: it exposed the peace commissioner 'to the very odium and danger from which we have just rescued jurors and judges'; the ordinary courts were being involved in matters which this legislation specifically sought to remove from them; the procedure was not contemplated under article 2A. Therefore, Roche directed that the commissioner inform all superintendents that:

> if a local superintendent is of the opinion that a person who has been detained under the Act should be tried by the Tribunal, the superintendent should on his own responsibility (or after consultation with the chief superintendent if there is time) serve the detained person with notice required by the Act, viz.: a notice in writing that he will be brought before the Tribunal. Immediately after serving such notice he should lodge the prisoner in the nearest convenient prison, lodging with the Governor at the same time, by way of warrant, a certified copy of the notice which has been served upon the prisoner. Immediately the prisoner has been lodged the Garda Officer should report the whole facts, through the usual channels, to this Department.[77]

Roche emphasized that Gardaí had to employ the utmost care when using these powers and only against persons where evidence of 'recent and serious offences' under the act was available. Trivial cases, cases where the offences were not covered by the act, or cases where there was insuffi-

75 D/J H.308, finalized at a conference on 27 Oct. 1931 involving the secretary of the department of Defence, General Mac Mathghamhna, Commandant Feeley, registrar of the tribunal and M. Ó Cuinneóin, memorandum by Desmond Fitzgerald, 31 Oct. 1931. 76 Ibid., Roche to the minister for Justice, 4 Nov. 1931. 77 Ibid., Roche to the Commissioner, 4 Nov. 1931.

cient evidence were not to be sent to the tribunal. The department was aware that a number of persons had been arrested under the act, but Gardaí had failed to prove that they had been recently active.[78] He added, 'It should be remembered in this connection that once the notice has been served the prisoner *must* be brought before the Tribunal.'[79] He also reminded the commissioner that the powers of section 15 were only available against a person 'detained on suspicion' after an inspector or Garda of higher rank made a direction under section 14 and before a notice under section 17 was given, not when the prisoner was first brought to the Garda station.

The department of Justice explained some years after the abolition of the constitution (special powers) tribunal that it 'had been planned (so far at least as the Department of Justice knew or was concerned) as a court of the highest and most unquestionable authority, not subject to any other court, and completely the master of its own procedure and verdicts.'[80] Under section 5(2), it had 'full and absolute power to appoint the time and places of its sittings and full and absolute control of its own procedure in all respects and, in particular, in respect of the admission or exclusion of the public to or from its sittings, the enforcing the attendance of witnesses and the production of documents.' It could punish persons it found guilty of contempt as it thought fit.[81] It also had an 'official seal which shall be officially and judicially noticed and every document sealed with such seal and purporting to be an order or other act of the Tribunal shall be received in evidence in all Courts without further proof and be deemed to be an order or other act (as the case may require) of the Tribunal made or done with competent jurisdiction.'[82] It had jurisdiction to try, convict and sentence or acquit persons charged with offences contained in the act and scheduled to article 2A.[83] It had jurisdiction 'in lieu of or in addition to inflicting any punishment' to require a person to enter into recognisance to keep the peace for a specific period.[84] Further, no appeal 'shall lie from any order, conviction, sentence, or other act of the Tribunal, and the Tribunal shall not be restrained or interfered with in the execution of its jurisdiction or powers under this Article by any court nor shall any proceedings before the Tribunal be removed by certiorari to any court.'[85] Revealing the breadth of its powers, section 7(1) provided:

78 It was claimed in the Dáil that the provisions of section 14 (power to detain for up to 72 hours without charge) were used on repeated occasions to increase the maximum period of detention. See Dáil Debates vol. 57 col. 908–10, 26 June 1935. 79 Roche's emphasis. 80 'Departmental Notes', p. xv. 81 Section 5(3). 82 Section 5(4). 83 Section 6(1). 84 Section 6(4). 85 Section 6(5).

> Whenever the Tribunal finds any person guilty of an offence mentioned in the Appendix to this Article the Tribunal may, in lieu of the punishment provided by law (other than this Article) for such offence, sentence such person to suffer any greater punishment (including the penalty of death) if in the opinion of the Tribunal such greater punishment is necessary or expedient.[86]

Procedure included all necessary steps taken by the tribunal in order to exercise effectively the powers and jurisdiction conferred upon it. It was not obliged to create a permanent set of rules or procedures and it could modify and alter procedure (rules as to the admissibility of evidence, etc.) as it saw fit. The department of Justice hoped that:

> In a general, elastic and simple way the Tribunal will find it convenient to establish certain general lines on which to conduct its business. It will be helpful to bear in mind however that any rules may at any time be altered and also that it may be necessary to decree in certain instances that non-compliance with such rules will not invalidate proceedings or prejudice the prosecution or defence as the case may be.[87]

Indicative of other substantial departures from the ordinary law, the tribunal was not obliged to give the public automatic access to trials. Additionally, members of the press required special permission to attend hearings, which was dependent on 'a fair report of proceedings being given and no descriptive commentary or sensation mongering articles' being made. Strict rules also applied to the attendance of defence solicitors and barristers. Contempt of court or disrespect shown to the tribunal by the press or by lawyers could attract penalties and denial of future entry.

Normal trial practice dictated that members of the tribunal took their seats in order of seniority. The registrar then enquired whether the accused was present and whether counsel was appearing on his behalf. Once the presence of the accused was confirmed the registrar read aloud all charges preferred and then called upon those accused to plead to each charge separately. The tribunal normally entered a plea of not guilty on behalf of the accused where he ventured no plea himself or refused to recognize the tribunal, though it could punish as contempt a failure to plead or behaviour it considered disrespectful. The prosecution then presented a statement of the case against the accused and then the evidence of witnesses in support of its case.[88] At the conclusion of their examination by coun-

86 Section 7(1). 87 P80/479, no date, corrected by Commandant Feeley. 88 It was ini-

sel for the prosecution, witnesses were liable to cross-examination by or on behalf of the accused. Re-examination by the prosecution was possible. Counsel for the defence would then present its case. Consideration of the verdict was always to be done in private and was not promulgated in open court.[89]

The accused was to be assigned legal assistance, if he requested. In the Seanad, Thomas Johnson, the former Labour Party leader, had suggested that at least one member of the tribunal be certified by the attorney general to be a person of legal knowledge and experience, but Ernest Blythe rejected this:

> It might not be possible to get a suitable citizen to undertake the task. Remember he is a man who would get appointed for perhaps six months or a year. He might incur very considerable enmity. He would not always be living in barracks and perhaps carrying arms as a military officer would be. He would be a man who, having undertaken this difficult and dangerous work, would have to go out perhaps finding his practice at the Bar gone and finding himself in considerable difficulties about recovering it. We have come to the conclusion that in the circumstances we are up against, it would not be fair to put a man into that position and it might not be easily possible to get a really suitable man, because for this work you would certainly have to get a very good man. I am satisfied that with a section drawn as [section 4] is, you do not really require a legal man. You require simply three intelligent, resolute and conscientious men who will bring commonsense to the problem. Legal technicalities will not come into the procedure of this court.

He further explained, 'this court has no civil jurisdiction ... It is not going to be trying difficult, intricate matters at all. It will simply have to sift the evidence that may be put before it with regard to whether a man, say, was found in possession of a gun or not, the evidence as to whether a man was in possession of a seditious document or not, the evidence as to whether a man was a member of an illegal organisation or not. As I say, no very intricate or difficult problems will come before it'.[90]

The tribunal began hearing cases in November 1931, trying mostly charges of membership of unlawful organizations, unauthorized possession of firearms, and failure to account for movements. Although it pos-

tially suggested that witnesses should give their testimony on oath separately and should not be permitted to hear the testimony of others. **89** P80/479, no date, corrected by Commandant Feeley. **90** Seanad Debates vol. 14 col. 2006, 2015–6, 16 Oct. 1931.

sessed apparently limitless powers, sentences were generally quite light.[91] Excluding a *nolle prosequi* entered in each year, the tribunal tried 34 republicans in 1931,[92] finding 30 guilty (88%) and 20 in 1932, finding 18 guilty (90%). In 1931, the tribunal tried 5 on firearms charges, 12 for membership of an unlawful association, 8 for failure to account for movements, and 7 for perjury (arising out of the Tipperary drilling case). It sentenced one person to 2 years, 11 to sentences of a 6 months or less, and it deferred 17 sentences or the accused entered into recognisance. In 1932, 10 were tried for membership of an unlawful association and 8 on firearms' charges. It sentenced one person to 2 years, 3 persons to 6 months or less, the remainder entered into recognisance or their sentences were deferred.

The post November 1931 period also witnessed a return to the old-style Garda harassment of IRA members. Certainly, article 2A enabled the government and Gardaí to reduce IRA activities to a minimum, though the beginning of 1932 was marked in many areas by the lowest point in relations between Gardaí and the rural population since 1922.[93]

Despite the tribunal declaring several issues of the *Irish World*, the *Irish Worker* and the *Worker's Voice* to be seditious, and the executive council outlawing several socialist organizations it was clear that the IRA and Saor Éire were the primary focus of government attentions. The other groups outlawed in October 1931 seem to have escaped active suppression. Admittedly, there were a number of groups with revolutionary aims, however, they were generally very small, Dublin based, and prominent persons were often members of several organizations.[94]

Regardless of the true scale of leftwing politics in Ireland, the Catholic Church responded positively to government calls for a denunciation. On 18 October 1931, a joint pastoral attacked Saor Éire as a 'frankly communist organisation' that wanted to impose on Ireland 'the same materialistic regime, with its fanatical hatred of God, as now dominates and threatens to dominate Spain'.[95] The IRA pointed to what it regarded to be a historical pattern: 'again, as in 1922, the hierarchy are lending their sanction to brutal and repressive measures against republicans.'[96]

91 See tables 3a and 3b. 92 This figure does not include the three non-IRA persons charged with firearms offences in Galway, November 1931. 93 See Brady, *Guardians*, pp 158–60. Allegations of Garda violence surfaced when James Vaugh of Leitrim (who had been arrested on 5 Dec. 1931 and released on 24 Dec. 1931) died on Christmas day 1931. See Bell, *The secret army*, p. 91, 'Departmental Notes', p. 8. 94 See D. Keogh, 'De Valera, the Catholic Church and the red scare', in J. O'Carroll and J.A. Murphy (eds), *De Valera and his times* (1983), p. 139, English, *Radicals and the republic*, pp 154–5 and D/T S.5074, S.5864, P24/169. 95 See Keogh, 'The red scare', p. 140. 96 P7/C/88, 'The Coercion Act: our attitude and tasks'. For an account of communism (or the absence of it) in November 1932, see Garda reports read to the Dáil by de Valera, 1 Mar. 1934, Dáil

There were probably strong reasons for Cumann na nGaedheal government creating or at least exaggerating the 'red scare'. The republican-socialist Peadar O'Donnell certainly believed so: 'the red scare of 1931 was nonsense, in relation to Irish life, but it was necessary to make a climate for new, terrorist legislation ... The government raised a great din, press and pulpit forming a jazz band that bare throats could not cut through to reach the people.'[97] On the other hand, the historian Richard Dunphy speculated that the government chose to focus on the insignificant numbers of socialists because it was becoming desperate in the face of growing Fianna Fáil support.[98]

As 1932 approached, the Cumann na nGaedheal government was confronted with the daunting task of seeking re-election. It had to contend with the effects of a world economic crisis and growing unemployment. Its prospects were further damaged when it introduced a number of unpopular economic measures. Doubtless, certain members of the party felt that an election campaign could not focus on the economy. In September 1931, ignoring the potential benefits that might accrue from the Eucharistic Congress which was to be held in June 1932, or from the forthcoming Imperial Conference, the minister for External Affairs, Patrick McGilligan, urged that an election be contested

> on consideration of the Irregular and Bolshie situation alone. When I do go to consider other things – failing revenue, increasing demands for services, falling prices, increasing unemployment, absence of emigrants' remittances and almost the entire failure of dividends from foreign investments – I feel it would be sheer madness to think of trying to operate repressively throughout a miserable and poverty-stricken twelve months.[99]

The government waited until the following January to announce the election. In the meantime, it compounded its unpopularity by prosecuting the *Irish Press* and its editor, Frank Gallagher, on charges of sedition when the paper alleged ill-treatment of prisoners in Garda custody. Finding against the *Irish Press*, the constitution tribunal imposed two £100 fines. It was clear, however, from the tribunal's judgement that it was not satisfied that the paper's allegations were entirely groundless.[1]

When the government announced the election in January 1932,[2] the IRA was without any strategy or plan of campaign. Years later Seán

Debates vol. 50 col. 2496–500. 97 Quoted in English, *Radicals and the republic*, p. 139. 98 Dunphy, *Fianna Fáil*, pp 141–2. 99 Quoted Fanning, *Independent Ireland*, p. 105. 1 'Departmental Notes', p. xi. 2 The Dáil was dissolved on 19 Jan. 1932, and the election held on 16 Feb. 1932.

McBride remarked, 'I would agree that in the run up to de Valera's election success of 1932, the IRA itself had lost direction; had lost *political* direction.'[3] The IRA's leadership rescinded a November 1927 order prohibiting members voting in Free State elections, while IRA members assisted Fianna Fáil, with levels of enthusiasm varying from place to place, liaised with candidates, protected meetings, canvassed, obtained election registers and voted on behalf of the sick, the dead and the emigrated. *An Phoblacht* called on IRA members and supporters to 'put Cosgrave out'.[4]

3 Mac Eoin (ed.), *Survivors*, p. 122 4 Bell, *The secret army*, pp 92–3. 5 i.e the achievement of co-equality within the commonwealth through the Statute of Westminster. 6 Keogh, 'The Red Scare', pp 144–6. 7 *Irish Independent*, 27 Feb. 1932. 8 Ibid., 11 Feb. 1932.

4

Fianna Fáil in power, 1932–1937

After nine years of the Cumann na nGaedheal government, the Free State electorate voted for change. There was a smooth handover of power[1] and de Valera became president of the executive council on 9 March 1932, immediately appointing James Geoghegan minister for Justice and Frank Aiken minister for Defence.

Directly fulfilling one of its election promises, the new government granted free pardons under section 12(1) of article 2A to the 17 IRA members still imprisoned following conviction by the constitution tribunal.[2] It also released three other republicans imprisoned since the 1920s.[3] Several of those freed resumed their IRA activities immediately. Although imprisoned for nearly seven years, on release, Seán McGuinness was reported to have declared that 'the members of the defunct Executive Council were ... a menace to society and the independence of Ireland, and it behoved all Republicans to unite and wipe out that menace at all costs'.[4] On 18 March 1932, the Constitution (Suspension of Article 2A) Order, 1932 suspended parts 2 to 5 of article 2A. The article was not repealed – it would remain a permanent aspect of the constitution until deleted or until the constitution was replaced.

If some in the IRA hoped that Fianna Fáil's accession would bring their dream of a 32 county republic closer to reality, they would be disappointed. Shortly after coming to power, de Valera met several IRA leaders to discuss his intentions, essentially calling on them to disband the organization. 'We cannot have a Republic', he explained to Maurice Twomey and George Gilmore, 'until we get the Six Counties, and neither you nor we have a solution for that.'[5] He would emasculate the governor general's office[6] and promised to remove the oath.[7]

1 T.D. Williams, 'De Valera in power', in F. MacManus (ed.), *The years of the great test* (1967), p. 30. Fianna Fáil was dependent on the Labour Party for support. 2 Minutes of the executive council C.6/1,2,3, 10–14 Feb. 1932 and D/T S.2419. 3 Con Healy, imprisoned in Portlaoise, sentenced by the central criminal court, 2 Dec. 1928; Seán Hogan, imprisoned Portlaoise, sentenced by the Dublin City Commissioners, 30 Oct. 1923, for the murder of James Cullinan on 3 Oct. 1922; Seán McGuinness, imprisoned Mountjoy, sentenced by the central criminal court, 29 Oct. 1925. The remaining three non-IRA members convicted of robbery in Co. Galway were transferred from Arbour Hill to an ordinary prison to complete their sentences. 4 *Irish Times*, 14 Mar. 1932. 5 Mac Eoin (ed.), *Survivors*, pp 395–6. 6 James Mac Néill resigned on 31 Oct. 1932 and was replaced by Domhnall Ua Buachalla. 7 Bowman, *De Valera*, p. 125.

Seán McBride, the future IRA chief of staff, barrister and Nobel Prize recipient, who met de Valera around July 1932, later reported to US based IRA supporter Joseph McGarrity that de Valera had continually emphasized that 'the recognition of majority rule was essential [and that] once the oath was removed there could be no objection to such a recognition of majority rule and to recognising the Free State parliament as a legitimate body upon which rested the function of leading people.'[8] McGarrity shortly called on the government to come to an agreement with the IRA 'as a national necessity', but was rebuked. It had taken Ireland ten years to recover from the Civil War and de Valera asked, 'are we to abandon all this in order to satisfy a group who have not given the slightest evidence of any ability to lead our people anywhere except back into the morass?' De Valera held five meetings with Seán McBride in the eighteen months after he came to power, McBride reporting that at their final meeting de Valera 'got excited and said that he would maintain law and order even if it cost him his life'.[9]

In spite of de Valera's stated position, Fianna Fáil's first term in office was marked by what some regarded as leniency towards the IRA. The organization's numbers grew as many believed that membership would improve employment prospects, among other matters, under the new government.[10]

Fianna Fáil's accession to power coincided with the founding of the Army Comrades Association (ACA), an organization that claimed to promote the welfare of ex-army officers. It was quickly politicized, however, when members of Cumann na nGaedheal came to prominence within it, horrified by what they believed was government tolerance of the IRA. By mid-1932, the ACA claimed that Cumann na nGaedheal meetings were being heckled and disrupted by IRA members or Fianna Fáil supporters. Dr Thomas O'Higgins TD, who was elected ACA president on 11 August 1932, declared that the organization deemed it its 'bounden duty to resist any counter-attempts to interfere with free speech or the free expression of opposition'.[11]

The government watched developments uneasily. On 21 August 1932, de Valera described the ACA as 'unwanted and unnecessary'.[12] Eoin O'Duffy reported the organization's links with prominent members of Cumann na nGaedheal, and that a large number of members had held onto their arms since the War of Independence and the Civil War. The

8 McBride to McGarrity, 19 Oct. 1933, quoted in English, *Radicals and the republic*, p. 172. 9 McBride to McGarrity, 19 Oct. 1933, quoted in Bowman, *De Valera*, p. 124. 10 Bell, *The secret army*, pp 101–2. 11 Quoted in Manning, *The Blueshirts* (1987), p. 29. 12 Ibid., p. 30.

commissioner added, 'certain members of the organisation hold extreme views and would be prepared to urge the use of force in the pursuit of their policy.' He warned that the organization had access to a sufficient number of arms and ammunition to render 'it a very formidable insurrectionary force and a source of extreme danger to the peace and stability of the country'.[13]

Adding to the tension, in October 1932 *An Phoblacht* demanded 'No free speech to traitors' – to members of Cumann na nGaedheal.[14] Inevitably, there were scuffles between the ACA and its opponents. It was clear, though, that the government would not tolerate lawlessness from either the ACA or the IRA. Speaking at the November 1932 Fianna Fáil árd-fheis, de Valera warned both organizations:

> We have tried to avoid coercive measures because this has failed with our people in the past … but I want to give warning: it is our duty as a Government to proceed vigorously against anybody found in possession of arms. In future, anyone found in possession of arms will be given the full vigour of the law.[15]

Almost immediately after taking office, Fianna Fáil began implementing its political programme. On 20 April 1932, de Valera introduced the Constitution (Removal of Oath) Bill, dismissing the oath as a relic of medievalism. He had told the *Irish Times* on 6 March 1932 that he believed this would end all republican objections to Dáil authority. The Dáil passed the bill but the Seanad insisted on amendments in May and again in July. Subsequent Seanad opposition to a similar bill the following year meant that the oath was not removed until May 1933. More dramatically, on 1 July 1932 the government defaulted on semi-annual land annuity payments of approximately £1.5 million (of £76 million outstanding) to Britain (though the government continued to collect the money from farmers). On 12 July, the British responded by imposing extra duties on Irish livestock and farm produce. By the end of the month, the Irish government retaliated by taxing a range of British goods, including coal, cement, steel and electrical equipment. The 'Economic War' between Ireland and Britain had begun, and many, especially the larger agricultural exporters to Britain, regarded it as a threat to their livelihoods.[16]

Then, on 2 January 1933, after less than a year in government and apparently without warning, de Valera called a general election.[17] While

13 Quoted in Dáil Debates vol. 49 col. 1577–8, 9 Aug. 1933. See also D/J H.306/23. 14 Bell, *The secret army*, p. 102. 15 *Irish Press*, 9 Nov. 1932. 16 Manning, *The Blueshirts*, pp 20–2; 'Departmental Notes', p. 9. 17 Lee, *Ireland*, pp 178–9.

some regarded Fianna Fáil policies towards the IRA as alarmingly lenient, on the eve of the 1933 general election *An Phoblacht* criticized Fianna Fáil for jailing IRA members and for not disbanding the Garda special branch. It also expressed disappointment that 'no practical steps' had been taken to break the connection with the British empire.[18] Again, though, many IRA members supported the Fianna Fáil campaign, and worked and voted against W.T. Cosgrave and his party.[19]

Five ACA members stood as Cumann na nGaedheal candidates in the election, revealing the growing links between both organizations.[20] The British government considered the emergence of the ACA and the Economic War to be significant threats to Fianna Fáil's electoral prospects. As the historian Deirdre McMahon noted, the British believed 'Cosgrave would be returned with "a surprising majority", in addition the White Army (the Army Comrades Association) was numerically stronger than the IRA and "recruited from a far better class of person".'[21]

The general election on 24 January 1933 returned Fianna Fáil with a one-seat majority.[22] It also resulted in a hardening of the ACA – in February 1933 the organization began wearing blue shirts, lending it a particular nuance given the world political climate. The election also saw a stiffening of the position of many farmers whose refusal or inability to pay rates or annuities became a common tactic of opposition to the Economic War. Inevitably, there was confrontation and conflict when sheriffs sought to seize livestock where monies fell due. By the winter of 1933–4, 36% of rates remained uncollected nationwide, with 55% owing in Tipperary, and 40 per cent in counties Kilkenny, Waterford, Clare, Limerick, Wexford, and Westmeath.[23]

A refusal to pay land annuities would normally result in the land commission initiating legal proceedings, though this was a slow and laborious process. With the widespread non-payment of annuities, this system became quickly overloaded. The government responded with section 28 of the Land Act, 1933 which provided that a warrant issued by the land commission would take the place of legal proceedings. Between the 12 semi-annual gale-days, beginning November/December 1933 and ending May/June 1939, 403,088 land commission warrants were issued on foot of which £2,591,474 was levied or collected. In particularly difficult areas, special Garda stations were established, each with facilities for impounding and selling seized livestock. A number of court messengers were based

18 *An Phoblacht*, 7 Jan. 1933. **19** Bell, *The secret army*, pp 104–5. **20** M. Cronin, 'The Blueshirts in Ireland: The movement and its members, 1932–5' (1993), p. 22. **21** D. McMahon, *Republicans and imperialists: Anglo-Irish relations in the 1930s* (1984), p. 107. **22** 'Departmental Notes', p. 11. **23** Manning, *The Blueshirts*, p. 109.

at each station, controlling cars and lorries to transport confiscated animals. Five court messengers (later ten) were based in Westmeath from October 1934. Special stations were later established in counties Kilkenny, Kildare, Cork, Longford, Kerry, and, finally, in Wicklow in September 1937.[24]

There were regular attacks on court messengers, efforts by Blueshirts to intimidate purchasers of seized cattle, and riots and disturbances at cattle sales, leading eventually to a campaign of sabotage (blocking roads, cutting telegraph wires, interference with railways) seeking to prevent the arrival of messengers or the removal of livestock.

But there was another aspect to the emerging security problem. The government had doubts about the reliability and loyalty of some senior Gardaí, as well as various members of Garda special branch and military intelligence. On 17 February 1933, Colonel Michael Hogan of military intelligence and E.M. O'Connell, David Neligan's second in command in the Garda special branch, were arrested under the Official Secrets Act.[25] On 22 February 1933, O'Duffy was dismissed from his post as Garda commissioner: 'We want a police chief of whom no section of the community can say that that man is deliberately and politically opposed to us, and is likely to be biased in his attitude because of past political affiliations', de Valera later explained.[26]

Almost simultaneously, the Juries (Protection) Act again came up for renewal. The act had been devised because of difficulties involved in trying IRA members, but two points had proved its inadequacy: persons whose guilt was beyond doubt were acquitted while the act was in force; more revealingly, Cumann na nGaedheal introduced the constitution tribunal. Nevertheless, Stephen Roche saw merit in continuing sections 3 (panel secrecy), 5 (majority decisions), 6 (refusal to recognize the court), 9 (prohibition on publishing jurors' names),[27] 10 (delivering summons),[28] and 11 (intimidation of jurors) which the government could stand over without exposing itself 'unduly to the charge of having completely abandoned the views expressed whilst in opposition.'[29]

Sections 4 (calling the panel) and 7 (clearing the court) had proved ineffectual, he conceded, while section 2 had never been used. Further, the power under section 8 to adjourn a case because of suspected juror or witness intimidation was ineffective and clearly unfair to an accused.

24 See 'Departmental Notes', pp 99–100 and D/J S.55/34. 25 Bell, *The secret army*, p. 105; 'Departmental Notes', pp 11–13; Brady, *Guardians*, pp 176–7, D/J S.136/33. 26 Dáil Debates vol. 46 col 758–814, 14 Mar. 1933. 27 Saw no reason why the publication of jurors' names should not be prohibited permanently. 28 No juror, wrote Roche, ever complained of non-delivery. 29 D/T S.6520, memorandum by S.A. Roche, 8 Feb. 1933.

However, Roche envisaged using section 7 in non-political offences, particularly the trial of 'indecent and unnatural offences … regarded by many people as a cheap and effective substitute for the kind of books and picture plays which the censorship has made impossible in this state'.

There were, however, other, basic political issues to consider. Fianna Fáil would face awkward questions should it re-enact a measure it so strenuously opposed in 1929. Writing to the minister for Justice on 24 July 1933, and regardless of comments made in 1929, the secretary of the department of Justice, Daniel Browne,[30] argued that much of the act was simply repressive, and other portions ineffectual and absurd.[31] He proposed dispensing with sections 2, 3 ('rather a despotic Section'), 4 ('scarcely capable of justification'), 7 (of no use), 8 (most unfair to the prisoner in custody), 12 ('absurd'), though he conceded that sections 5, 6, 9, 10 and 11 had certain value.[32] Other than the difference of opinion on section 3, Browne's comments were similar to Roche's. While he was keen to retain the majority verdict, he felt that allowing the whole act to lapse was the only prudent path to follow.

The office of the attorney general, on the other hand, recommended more strongly that the act, or a large portion of it, should be continued. The attorney general's legal adviser, P.P. O'Donoghue,[33] admitted that sections 3, 4, and 9 failed to ensure the secrecy of the panel, and that the penal provisions of section 6(3) and (4) failed to justify themselves.[34] He felt, however, that section 6(1) and (2) constituted an intelligent replacement for the archaic procedure of establishing whether a person was mute of malice or by visitation of God. Clearly, a judge could establish the facts for himself.[35] The subject rested there, though. While the minister for Justice suggested that provisions covering majority verdicts and contempt of court might be included in future courts legislation, he felt that 'the

30 Daniel J. Browne (1895–1959) Born Co. Kerry, qualified as a solicitor in 1917. Joined the Irish Volunteers in 1914, he worked in the courts section of the Dáil department of Home Affairs, acting as secretary of the department in P. Sheehan's (Ó Síocháin) absence. Returned to Kerry to practice law after the signing of the Treaty. Involved in the Kilrush inquiry of 1932, and secretary of the department of Justice from 1933 to 1934, when he was appointed to the Land Commission. 31 D/J H.284/28. Browne to the minister for Justice. 32 Sections 1 and 13 were for interpretation and citation. 33 Philip O'Donoghue (1896–1987) educated in UCC and King's Inns. Appointed a district justice in 1922, in 1929 was invited by John A. Costello (attorney general at the time) to become his legal assistant. Involved in the Constitution Committee of 1934 and the drafting of Bunreacht na hÉireann in 1936. Called to the Inner Bar in 1939. Served 12 attorneys general, retiring in 1959. Appointed to the European Commission on Human Rights in 1965, became a Judge of the Court of Human Rights in 1971, retiring in 1980. 34 The attorney general did not oppose the deletion of these sections. 35 D/J H.284/28, 20 Sept. 1933, P.P. O'Donoghue to D. Browne.

passage of any special legislation on this subject through the Oireachtas at this particular time, as a matter of urgency, would be attended with so much friction that it is on the whole preferable not to move in the matter'.[36] Further, more pressing, political developments were of greater concern to the government, as the country entered a period of disturbance that witnessed major legal and constitutional change.

The former Garda commissioner, Eoin O'Duffy, returned to a position of national prominence very shortly after his dismissal from the force. He was appointed leader of the ACA in July 1933. On 20 July 1933, he laid down the movement's constitution and renamed it the 'National Guard'. O'Duffy declared that the aims of the organization were to safeguard the national honour, the national interests, and the national culture in the widest sense, and promised that 'the organisation will keep within the law, and illegalities will not be tolerated.[37] Physical drill will be practised only as a means to promoting good health, character and discipline.'[38] O'Duffy opened membership to all. Numbers rose from 8,337 in October 1932 to a height of 47,923 in August 1934.[39]

The government was understandably alarmed by O'Duffy's pronouncements and by the general Blueshirt situation. De Valera said, 'we believe the organisation has come to a dangerous stage … and it is the duty of the government to step in.'[40]

The government's first action was to withdraw all firearms certificates for revolvers and pistols.[41] The minister for Justice, Patrick Ruttledge,[42] explained that (under section 5 of the Firearms Act, 1925) certificates could be withdrawn at any time for certain reasons, a good ground being that a person had no reason to possess a firearm. He rejected Cumann na nGaedheal claims that portions of the population and banks would be left undefended or that the government was victimizing O'Duffy and the former governor general. Addressing the security situation, de Valera explained:

> We have two forces, one going to arm against the other: two forces each of which would be used for the growth and increase of the other. The Government would not be worthy of the confidence placed in it by the people if it permitted any such thing as that to go ahead. We are going to see, as far as we can, that people who have arms that we can get will not retain them in these circumstances.

36 D/J H.284/28, 21 Sept. 1933, Roche to the attorney general. 37 Manning, *The Blueshirts*, pp 73–4. 38 *Irish Times*, 21 July 1933. 39 Cronin, 'Blueshirts', p. 59. 40 Dáil Debates vol. 48 col. 2770, 14 July 1933. 41 Dáil Debates vol. 49 col. 903, 1 Aug. 1933. 42 James Geoghegan's successor.

Turning first to the IRA, he explained, 'my present attitude is that the moment that the Oath was removed, and it was possible for all sections of the people to be freely represented in this House, there was no excuse for anybody trying to use force or arming for the purpose of securing national freedom.' Regarding the National Guard, he promised that 'we are not going, so far as we can do it, to allow public parades in which uniform is worn, and we are not going to allow any guns in public'.[43]

The situation appeared to deteriorate when O'Duffy announced plans to march to Leinster House on 13 August 1933 to commemorate Michael Collins, Arthur Griffith, and Kevin O'Higgins. With claims that 20,000 members of the National Guard would march, the government could only have anticipated serious disorder.[44] Indeed, it seemed plausible that O'Duffy was planning to seize power in a coup d'état. Other factors added to the government's anxiety, not least of which was the dependability of the Garda special branch. Because the force's attitude to the former commissioner remained unclear, the senior Fianna Fáil politician Oscar Traynor TD and Éamon Broy (O'Duffy's successor) organized a loyal body of mostly IRA men, with very strong anti-Cumann na nGaedheal sentiments, to protect Leinster House (the Oireachtas) and to take over the duties of the Garda special branch.[45] The situation was viewed with such seriousness that the executive council reactivated parts 2 to 5 of article 2A on 11 August and proclaimed O'Duffy's planned march. W.T. Cosgrave dismissed rumours of a coup,[46] and the threat of confrontation receded when O'Duffy cancelled the procession, announcing instead a series of church parades to be held in provincial centres.[47] But the government also objected to these. On 18 August, Ruttledge warned that if any parades took place the Blueshirts organization would be outlawed.[48] While the church parades were cancelled, a number of uniformed marches proceeded and the National Guard was proclaimed on 22 August 1933.[49]

O'Duffy's immediate response was to rename the organization the 'Young Ireland Association' (YIA). One effect of the proclaiming of the National Guard was that it pushed a number of Fianna Fáil's opponents

43 Dáil Debates vol. 49 col. 904, 1030–5, 1059, 1065–7, 1 Aug. 1933. 44 'Departmental Notes', p. 14; Manning, *The Blueshirts*, p. 79, pp 84–8. 45 A new detective force was recruited, trained, armed and in place within three days, and all constituted completely within the terms of the Garda Síochána Act, 1924. Several special branch men were demoted or transferred to other duties during the coming months. See also Dáil Debates vol. 49 col. 1424–7, 9 Aug. 1933, Dáil Debates vol. 49 col. 1628–30, 27 Sept. 1933, Bell, *The secret army*, pp 107–8, Brady, *Guardians*, pp 196–200, 'Departmental Notes', p. 14. 46 *Irish Times*, 19 Aug. 1933. 47 Bell, *The secret army*, p. 107–8 and Manning, *The Blueshirts*, pp 79–80. 48 See 'Departmental Notes', pp 14–15. 49 *Iris Oifigiúil*, 25 Aug. 1933, the members of the tribunal were also reappointed on this day.

into closer unity. On 8 September 1933 the Blueshirts and Cumann na nGaedheal merged with the National Centre Party to form Fine Gael.[50] The National Guard's headquarters were closed by order of the tribunal on 15 September 1933.[51]

Opposition to the Economic War continued to increase.[52] Efforts to sell cattle seized for the non-payment of monies due in Tipperary had failed on two occasions, and the animals were brought to Dublin on 20 September 1933. Following the disorder that accompanied their sale, four prominent Blueshirts, E.J. Cronin, P. Belton TD, P.L. Ryan (chairman, South Tipperary County Council), F.B. Barton of the Farmers and Ratepayers League, Co. Kildare, were arrested, becoming the first to be tried by the resurrected constitution tribunal.[53] At their trial, counsel for the state argued that the disturbances were the public inauguration of a 'no rates campaign'. The tribunal found all four guilty.[54]

There was rioting between Blueshirts and opponents in Cork and Limerick during September, and there were several shooting incidents involving Blueshirts and the IRA.[55] But as confrontation and disorder continued, the government began to move decisively against both organizations, while depicting its actions as even handed. In Professor Lee's words, 'The Blueshirt episode permitted Fianna Fáil to pose as, and even to become, constitutionalists, defenders of law, order and majority rule against a militaristic threat.'[56]

The IRA contributed to the economic war by campaigning against English imports,[57] particularly Bass beer.[58] These disturbances resulted in damage to ten public houses, and large amounts of stock were destroyed throughout the country. The YIA took it upon itself to protect these imports, which led to further disturbances. By the end of September 1933, 13 were in custody for involvement in this disorder.

One of the most serious incidents of 1933 occurred in Tralee on 6 October when Eoin O'Duffy's appearance at a Fine Gael convention led to rioting involving several hundred people.[59] Seventy-five extra Gardaí had been drafted in to cope with the anticipated disturbances, supported by soldiers armed with rifles and fixed bayonets. In the course of the evening, several volleys of shots were fired at the local Garda station and

50 Manning, *The Blueshirts*, p. 109. 51 'Departmental Notes', p. 16. 52 See generally 'Departmental Notes', pp 101–8. 53 See Dáil Debates vol. 49 col. 1629–30, 27 Sept. 1933 and col. 1850, 28 Sept. 1933. 54 'Departmental Notes', pp 101. 55 Bell, *The secret army*, p. 109, 'Departmental Notes', pp 16–17. 56 Lee, *Ireland 1912–1985*, p. 180. 57 Beginning in May 1933, 'Departmental Notes', p. 16. 58 'Departmental Notes', p. xvii, pp 16–17. De Valera dismissed the campaign as 'damn foolacting business', quoted in Cronin, *The McGarrity papers*, p. 156. 59 See A/G 70/33, 7 Oct. 1933 and Bell, *The secret army*, p. 109.

baton charges and teargas were used to disperse the crowd. O'Duffy had to be spirited out of the town in a Garda special branch car.

Gardaí identified 12 persons as having taken part in the riot, though they believed that a total of 26 persons, members of Fianna Fáil or the IRA, could be successfully prosecuted.[60] The Co. Kerry state solicitor recommended charging the suspects with riot and unlawful assembly. Anticipating that the suspects would not recognize the circuit court and because of the effect that that tactic might have on witnesses and jurors, he recommended that they be tried in the district court.[61] The assistant commissioner, Éamon Coogan, called for a sterner response, however. He proposed that the constitution tribunal try the 12, arguing that a trial in Tralee district court could lead to local disorder, and that riot was so serious it should not be disposed of summarily.[62] He was also concerned that the safety of Eoin O'Duffy and other prominent Blueshirts, as well as the safety of Gardaí who witnessed the riot, could not be guaranteed if they were called to give evidence. The government agreed to this on 3 November 1933, and the minister for Justice granted the necessary certificate on 7 November 1933 permitting the tribunal to try the charges. The tribunal convicted all twelve and sentenced each to between three and six months' imprisonment.[63] But the government had already decided to use the tribunal against IRA members. The robbery of the film 'Gallipoli' from a travelling cinema proprietor by armed IRA members on 18 September 1933 was the first offence involving republicans to be tried by the resurrected tribunal on 6 November.[64]

Although the government was beginning to bring the full force of law to bear on the IRA, the main opposition party, Fine Gael, claimed that the organization was exerting extraordinary influence on the government. Fine Gael's Dr O'Higgins remarked 'that when a thing is demanded this week in the journal, *An Phoblacht*, within one or two months that demand becomes a government act … the removal of the Governor General … the removal of the [Garda] Commissioner.'[65] Speaking in Wexford on 15 October 1933, de Valera conceded that the IRA had been enjoying a degree of tolerance, but added:

> We have a very solemn duty … to use all the resources at our disposal to prevent disorder and to avert the violent overthrow of rep-

60 A/G 70/33, assistant commissioner to Roche, 20 Oct. 1933, note by P.P. O'Donoghue, and Dáil Debates vol. 49 col. 2207, 11 Oct. 1933. **61** Ibid., referred to by chief superintendent E. Duffy to the Garda commissioner, 19 Oct. 1933. **62** Ibid., É. Coogan to the secretary of the department of Justice, 31 Oct. 1933. **63** 'Departmental Notes', p. 17 and figures, table 3c. **64** See 'Departmental Notes', p. 16. **65** Dáil Debates vol. 49 col. 2466, 12 Oct. 1933.

> resentative institutions. If we failed in that duty we would be guilty of an act of treachery towards the people who entrusted us with power ... I have repeatedly promised, and I renew that promise today, that we will do our duty.[66]

Serious disorder followed in Kilkenny on 22 October when Gardaí were forced to call in the army to restore order after two baton charges failed to disperse a mob.[67] Within two weeks the government sanctioned Garda action under article 2A in all 'cases of outrage in which arms are used.'[68] The attorney general's express consent would have to be obtained before any person could be sent for trial by the tribunal. Conor Maguire explained that using powers under article 2A did not oblige Gardaí to send persons for trial by the tribunal:

> Article 2(a) does not oust the jurisdiction of the ordinary Courts. I consider it necessary that the question as to whether any particular case is to come before the ordinary Courts or before the Military Tribunal should be decided by me, and even if the powers conferred on the Guards by Article 2(a) have been made use of, I take the view that it is open to me to allow the ordinary Courts to deal with the case.

Only exceptional cases were to be tried by the tribunal. He added, 'The extent to which the powers of interrogation, arrest etc are to be used by the Guards, is a matter for the Commissioner.'[69]

Clearly, de Valera was completely serious when he warned IRA leaders he would enforce the law. Addressing the Fianna Fáil árd fheis on 9 November 1933, he said, 'I have been disappointed that the removal of the oath did not, to the extent I had hoped, bring about the possibility of cooperation with all Republican groups.'[70] Writing to Joseph McGarrity on 26 October 1933, IRA chief of staff, Maurice Twomey, explained that Fianna Fáil was pressing the IRA to disband and for its leadership to join the Irish Free State's army reserve. Indeed, he believed that the Fianna Fáil leadership was 'more bitter to [the IRA] than they were to the Blueshirts'.[71]

An Phoblacht complained that Blueshirts were being treated more leniently than IRA members. The 23 December 1933 issue protested that a prominent Blueshirt only received a £3 fine when convicted of unlaw-

66 Brady, *Guardians*, pp 211–12. 67 'Departmental Notes', p. 17. 68 D/J D.55/34, Roche to commissioner, 6 Nov. 1933, referred to in a note from the attorney general to D. Browne, 23 Nov. 1933. 69 Ibid., attorney general to Browne, 23 Nov. 1933. 70 'Departmental Notes', pp 9–10. 71 Quoted in Townshend, *Political violence*, p. 378.

ful firearms possession by the district court. The constitution tribunal declared that issue to be seditious on 20 December 1933. Without doubt, the deterioration of the IRA's position was reflected in government policy towards *An Phoblacht*.[72] The tribunal declared two issues in January and three issues in March and April 1934 to be seditious.[73] Further, on several occasions the Gardaí had cautioned the paper's publishers[74] and printers,[75] both orally and in writing, that by publishing seditious material they were exposing themselves to prosecution. Nevertheless, Stephen Roche believed that 'this form of sedition will continue until some more drastic action is taken'.[76]

The circumstances of late 1933 and early 1934 began to seriously concern the IRA's leadership. Speaking in Tralee, Co. Kerry, on 14 January 1934, Maurice Twomey complained of a 'lack of discipline' in the Kerry IRA.[77] Privately, though, he maintained that 'these attacks are very largely made by members of the Fianna Fáil organisation and active supporters of Fianna Fáil … Fianna Fáil leaders are using the commotion their own followers are largely responsible for creating, to attack us.' He believed that, ultimately, the government was attempting to 'isolate the IRA from the mass of Republican opinion, by representing the [IRA] as dangerous to political and economic progress'.[78]

Regardless of criticisms of the government's handling of the Blueshirts and the IRA, the government had taken the politically difficult step of re-establishing the constitution tribunal, and had begun employing article 2A for the purpose for which it had been designed – to deal with unlawful associations. While a mass of legal questions would shortly emerge, the courts would quickly explore them.

One of the most important matters to be probed was the meaning of an 'unlawful association'. Unquestionably, the emergence of the Blueshirts and their proscription in late 1933 brought the question of the IRA into sharper focus. Section 19(1) of article 2A defined unlawful associations, section 20 made membership of an unlawful association an offence triable by the tribunal, section 21 made possession of documents relating to unlawful associations an offence, and section 22 provided that possession of such documents alone could be used as evidence to prove membership.

72 The 23 Dec. 1933 issue was suppressed simultaneously with the *United Irishman*. See D/J A6/37/34, 22 Dec. 1933. 73 'Departmental Notes', 20, D/J A6/37/34. 74 'The Republican Press', Dublin, Liam McGowan was sub-editor at this time. 75 Longford Printing and Publishing Co. Ltd, Messrs. Aloysius and Matthew Farrell were the principle proprietors. 76 A/G 31/34, 23 Apr. 1934, S.A. Roche to the attorney general. Chief Superintendent G. Brennan to the department of Justice, 1 Jan. 1934, D/J A6/37/34. 77 See 'Departmental Notes', p. 20. 78 Quoted in Cronin, *The McGarrity papers*, p. 157.

Clearly, if any of the IRA's aims or activities were covered by section 19(1) it was an unlawful association within the meaning of the Act. If the IRA was unlawful, printing, publishing, and distributing *An Phoblacht* would most likely be an offence under section 23, while possession of the paper could be used to establish membership. Similarly, the YIA would be unlawful if its aims came under one or more headings in section 19(1). Significantly, the wearing of a uniform or a blue shirt was not specifically prohibited under article 2A. Section 19(2), which enabled the executive council to proclaim any specified association, was in the opinion of one civil servant 'intended merely to facilitate proof that the Body is unlawful.' Unless an association professed or pursued one or more of the six objects set out in section 19(1), a proclamation would have little or no effect. This anonymous civil servant cautioned that article 2A was 'a very unwieldy instrument save for the one purpose it was designed viz. to deal with the IRA or similar organisations'.[79]

Notwithstanding this unresolved issue, increased pressure was brought to bear on the Blueshirts. Gardaí raided the offices of the YIA and the homes of prominent members, including Eoin O'Duffy, Ernest Blythe, and Commandant E.J. Cronin, on 30 November 1933.[80] Ruttledge read some of the seized documents to the Dáil, claiming they proved the revolutionary and conspiratorial nature of the Blueshirts.[81] The YIA was proclaimed on 8 December 1933. The following day, its offices in Dublin and Cork were closed by order of the tribunal, and E.J. Cronin was arrested in Donegal on charges of membership of an unlawful association.[82]

Simultaneously, all chief superintendents were instructed to take adequate steps to prevent meetings, assemblies, parades, etc where a substantial number of those in attendance wore blue shirts (openly or covered by coats), armlets, blue sashes, ribbons, or berets. Once Gardaí were satisfied that a meeting was a YIA assembly, no person in attendance wearing a blue shirt or other Blueshirt insignia was to be permitted to address the gathering. Additionally, searches were to be carried out under sections 18, 29, and 30 of article 2A as deemed necessary, though Gardaí were instructed to avoid indiscriminate searches and to restrict house searches to daytime only. Chief superintendents were ordered to enforce article 2A in a manner that left 'no room for justifiable complaint against the Gardaí.'[83]

There remained the question of what legal consequences the wearing of a blue shirt would entail. Blue shirts and berets were undoubtedly the

79 D/J D.55/35, no date, no signature. 80 'Departmental Notes', p. 18. 81 Dáil Debates vol. 50 col. 862–872, 30 Nov. 1933. 82 'Departmental Notes', pp 18–19. The tribunal convicted him on 29 Dec. 1933 and sentenced him to three months. 83 D/J D.55/35, Chief Superintendent G. Brennan, detective branch, to all chief superintendents, 8 Dec. 1933.

attire of the National Guard and the YIA, and their adoption was noted in Fine Gael's newspaper, the *United Irishman*, in September 1933. Instructions to Gardaí on this point were unclear, however, leading the commissioner to ask if persons wearing blue shirts could or should be arrested for membership of an unlawful association.[84] P.P. O'Donoghue of the attorney general's office explained that blue shirts, berets, etc. could be used as 'some evidence' in support of a charge of membership of the YIA before the tribunal and, therefore, seizure could be justified, though the onus of proof would not be shifted to the accused. Otherwise, article 2A gave no authority to seize blue shirts etc. It followed that it was not an offence simply to wear a blue shirt.[85] The high court would shortly confirm this view.

Meanwhile, O'Duffy attempted to keep ahead of the government by renaming the YIA the League of Youth (LOY) on 14 December 1933, and the organization's supporters served an order on the high court seeking to establish the legality of the new organization.[86]

O'Duffy[87] was finally arrested in Westport, Co. Mayo on 17 December 1933 on charges of membership of an unlawful association.[88] He challenged his arrest and detention before Mr Justice O'Byrne on 21 December 1933, claiming that his arrest was for an offence unknown to law, namely wearing a blue shirt. O'Byrne considered the various powers of article 2A, and explained that

> Under Art. 6 [of the Constitution] a person may be detained in accordance with law, and once the court is satisfied that a person is so detained it has no power to interfere by way of *habeas corpus* or otherwise. Art. 2A of the Constitution undoubtedly enlarges the methods whereby a person may be lawfully detained. Apart from that there is no inconsistency between the two Articles.[89]

He concluded, nevertheless, in light of Garda statements and affidavits, that O'Duffy was not arrested on suspicion of being a member of an unlawful association as set out by section 19(1) of article 2A, but because 'he was proceeding or attempting to proceed into Westport, or because he was attempting to speak while wearing a blue shirt'.[90] O'Duffy was not

84 Ibid., Brennan on behalf of Broy to the secretary of the department of Justice, 11 Dec. 1933. 85 Ibid., memorandum by P.P. O'Donoghue, 15 Dec. 1933. He proposed that persons arrested for wearing blue shirts, etc. be bound to the peace. 86 *Blythe and Others v. the Attorney General* [1934] IR 266. 87 Two other prominent Blueshirts, O'Sullivan and Kilcoyne were also arrested, 'Departmental Notes', p. 19. 88 *In re O'Duffy* [1933] IR 550. 89 [1933] IR 561. 90 [1933] IR 570.

arrested on suspicion of being concerned in the commission of any offence under article 2A, and therefore the detention was unlawful. The former Garda commissioner was released.[91]

Almost immediately, O'Duffy was rearrested on five new charges: being a member of an unlawful association (the YIA) from 8 to 17 December 1933 and the National Guard from 22 August to 9 December 1933, both in contravention of section 20 of article 2A; sedition; incitement to murder; and attempting to incite murder.[92] On 2 January 1934, O'Duffy was granted a conditional order of prohibition[93] directed to tribunal member Colonel Francis Bennett, preventing the tribunal from proceeding and determining the charges set out in a summons dated 22 December 1933.[94] He told the press that the importance of the proceedings was 'to secure for him a trial of the charges according to law, whether that be before a jury of his fellow-citizens or the Military Tribunal'. He intended to be cleared of all charges 'beyond question'.[95]

The case turned on whether the constitution tribunal was an inferior court. The term 'inferior court' was determined in *James v. South Western Railway Company*[96] to include a court of limited jurisdiction. Blackstone further explained that courts that had extended and general jurisdiction were 'superior courts' compared to courts that have 'partial jurisdiction, and confined to particular districts'.[97] Matthew Hale defined the functions of the superior courts or the common law courts as:

> the superintendency over those [lower] courts to keep them within the limits and bounds of their several jurisdictions, and to judge and determine whether they do exceed those bounds or not; and, in case they do exceed their bounds, the Courts at Common Law issue their prohibitions to restrain them, directed either to the Judge or party, or both … Secondly, the common law and the Judges of the Courts of Common Law have the exposition of such statutes or Acts of Parliament as concern either the extent of their jurisdiction

91 All three brought successful actions against the Gardaí for assault. O'Duffy was awarded £200, Sullivan £75, and Kilcoyne £75, 'Departmental Notes', p. 20. 92 O'Duffy was ordered to appear before the tribunal on 2 Jan. 1934. 93 W. Blackstone defined an order of prohibition as one 'directed to the Judge and parties of a suit in any inferior Court commanding them to cease from the prosecution thereof, upon a suggestion either that the cause originally or some collateral matter arising therein does not belong to that jurisdiction but to the cognisance of some other court.' W. Blackstone, *Commentaries on the laws of England* (1982), vol. 3, pp 111–12. 94 *The State (O'Duffy) v. Bennett,* [1935] IR 70, the hearing was held on 24, 25, 29, 30, 31 January, 1 February and 21 March 1934. 95 *Irish Press*, 4 Jan. 1934. 96 1 L.R 7 Ex. 287. 97 Blackstone, *Commentaries*, vol. 3, p. 37. See also Sandes, *Criminal practice*, pp 47–8.

> of those Courts (whether ecclesiastical, maritime, or military) or the matters depending before them, and, therefore, if those Courts either refuse to allow these Acts of Parliament or expound them in any other sense than is truly and properly the exposition of them, the King's great Courts of the Common Law (who next under the King and his Parliament have the exposition of those laws) may prohibit and control them.[98]

O'Duffy's counsel contended that the tribunal was, in fact, an inferior court. Therefore, before it could try any offence which was not specifically included in article 2A or within its appendix, a summons would have to show that the tribunal had clear and sufficient jurisdiction to hear the charge – an executive minister was required to certify in writing, as provided by paragraph 7 of the appendix, that 'to the best of his belief the act constituting such offence was done with the object of impairing or impeding the machinery of government or the administration of justice'. As the third, fourth and fifth charges were not offences included in article 2A or within its appendix, such a certificate was required. Because the summons directed to O'Duffy did not state that such a certificate had been prepared, counsel argued that the tribunal could not hear those charges and therefore prohibition lay.

On this point, the high court found for O'Duffy: the tribunal was an inferior court and its jurisdiction was confined to offences included in article 2A[99] and within its appendix.[1] This constituted 'undoubtedly a limited jurisdiction, and the extreme powers given within that jurisdiction cannot alter the status from that of a court over which the high court has control,' Mr Justice Hanna concluded.[2] Counsel for Bennett attempted to rely on the provisions of section 6(5) which provided that 'the Tribunal shall not be interfered with *in the execution of its jurisdiction or powers under this Article* by any Court.'[3] But the president of the high court, Mr Justice Sullivan, ruled section 6(5) could have 'no application … where a prohibition is sought on the ground that the Tribunal is entertaining proceedings which are not within its jurisdiction or powers under the Article.'[4] To have claimed that the tribunal had jurisdiction to deal with cases of

98 Hale, *Common law*, p. 24 99 Sections 16, 20, 21, 23, 24, 27. 1 1) Offences under the Treasonable Offences Act, 1925; 2) offences under the Juries (Protection) Act, 1929; 3) offences under the Firearms Act, 1925; 4) Seditious Libel; 5) any offence whatever in respect of which a certificate pursuant to the clause is given by the minister. 2 [1935] IR 99. Mr Justice Sullivan said, 'the Tribunal has extraordinary powers, but … is a court of limited jurisdiction', at 79. 3 Mr Justice Sullivan's emphasis. The italicized words governed this clause, [1935] IR 78 and 110. 4 [1935] IR 78.

every description (both civil and criminal) or that if it dealt with matters outside its own jurisdiction, its orders remained unimpeachable and therefore had to be accepted as valid, as counsel for Bennett had essentially argued, was 'a revolting absurdity', Sullivan believed.[5] He rejected any construction of section 5(4) leading to such a result. Furthermore, the argument that the extreme nature of the tribunal gave it exceptional jurisdiction was dismissed. Mr Justice O'Byrne explained:

> The extensive and drastic nature of the powers of the Tribunal within the limits of its jurisdiction, so far from being an argument in favour of the proposition that the Tribunal is not subject to prohibition, seems to me the clearest reason why this Court should restrict it to the clear limits of its jurisdiction and thereby prevent it from using such powers in cases not committed to it by the Oireachtas.[6]

Therefore, as charges 3, 4, and 5 were not offences mentioned in the article, an executive minister's certificate, as prescribed by clause 7 of the appendix to article 2A, was required to give the tribunal jurisdiction to hear the charges.[7] The summons directed to O'Duffy did not state that any certificate had been given and therefore did not show jurisdiction on its face. Although counsel for Bennett argued that the absence of such a certificate was not essential to the validity of the summons, Mr Justice Sullivan concluded:

> In the present case we are dealing with a Tribunal exercising a special limited jurisdiction. It has elected to formulate in writing the charges upon which it intends to adjudicate, even in the absence of the accused. To found jurisdiction there must be a proper charge, that is a charge within the jurisdiction of the Tribunal, and, in my opinion, where the charge is formulated in writing, the jurisdiction must appear on the face of the proceedings. The summons in the present case does not show on its face that the Tribunal has any jurisdiction to entertain the third, fourth, or fifth charges set forth in the summons.[8]

This left the first two charges. Counsel for O'Duffy objected to these, claiming they did not disclose offences under section 20 of article 2A because O'Duffy was charged after the organizations had been dissolved.

5 [1935] IR 77. 6 [1935] IR 118. 7 Mr Justice Hanna held that the certificate was given but was void for uncertainty and duplicity, at 113–14. 8 [1935] IR 85.

The high court, however, disagreed.[9] The resolution of this issue, explained Mr Justice Sullivan, depended on the construction of the words 'is a member' in section 20. The president of the high court determined that

> the effect of the section is that every person who is a member of an unlawful association at the time when Part IV of the Article containing that section came into operation or who becomes a member at any subsequent time while that Part of the Article remains in force is guilty of an offence triable by the Tribunal.[10]

That interpretation was only confirmed by section 22, he believed, despite of a small degree of ambiguity.[11] The high court made the conditional order for prohibition absolute in regard to charges 3, 4, and 5, though discharged it in regard to charges 1 and 2.[12]

The government did not await the outcome of this second case to tackle the first difficulty it had encountered, introducing the Wearing of Uniforms (Restriction) Bill on 23 February 1934. It proposed prohibiting the wearing of uniforms and insignia by or in support of any political organization, the use of military terms by political parties, the carrying of weapons at political meetings and would empower Gardaí to seize uniforms and badges. Its aim, explained the minister for Justice, Patrick Ruttledge, was 'frankly to deal with the Blueshirt position in this country'. He added, 'The wearing of uniforms in this country, as in other European countries, has resulted in the creation of disorders … and a strain that the authorities cannot adequately deal with.'[13] Fine Gael TDs, dressed in blue shirts, accused the government of failing to tackle the state's real enemy, the 'communist inspired' IRA. But quoting from O'Duffy's old reports, de Valera responded:

> I have never stood for communism in any form. I loathe and detest it as leading to the same sort of thing that I loathe in the type of state that General O'Duffy would set up … This country is not a natural breathing ground for communism and everybody knows it. It is

9 Held by Sullivan and O'Byrne, Hanna dissenting. 10 [1935] IR 81, O'Byrne agreeing, Hanna dissenting. 11 Sullivan felt that the words 'at any time after this Article was inserted in this Constitution' were 'inserted in error' in place of 'at any time after Part IV of the Article came into force' as existed in section 20. [1935] IR 81–2. 12 O'Duffy appealed to the supreme court to have the order of the high court discharging the conditional order for prohibition in respect of charges 1 and 2 on the summons of the tribunal dated 22 Dec. 1933 itself discharged and in its place the conditional order of 1 Jan. 1934 made absolute in respect of the said charges. On 19 Dec. 1934, though, O'Duffy informed the supreme court he had abandoned the action. 13 Dáil Debates vol. 50 col. 2210–3, 28

> opposed to our religion; it is opposed to our individualistic tenancies; it is opposed to our whole scheme of life. If there is one country in the world which is unsuitable soil for communism, it is this.[14]

Although the Dáil passed the Uniforms Bill, on 21 March 1934, the Seanad refused to give it a second reading, and as with the bill to remove the oath, it would be delayed for over a year.[15] Outraged, de Valera described the second chamber as an 'absolute menace to this country':

> This Second Chamber, regardless of its responsibilities, acted in the most partisan manner ... If this Government is to have the responsibility of the maintenance of order, we must be in a position to take the measures which are necessary. We feel that the action which the Seanad is taking is designed deliberately to hamper and prevent this Government from doing its duty ... whatever may be the ultimate decision as to whether there should or should not be a Second Chamber here, the present Chamber, anyhow, as a preliminary has got to go.[16]

On 22 March 1934, the government introduced Constitution (Amendment No. 24) Bill, 1934 to abolish the upper house of the Oireachtas.

The scrapping of Seanad Éireann forced the government to clearly define what it regarded to be fundamental constitutional rights that the Dáil should not easily interfere with. De Valera promised that the constitution was to be 'examined de novo':

> I am quite prepared that there should be a commission, if you like, set up to examine whether there are not certain Articles of the Constitution which should not be put in a privileged position at the present moment, those of a democratic character, without any further consideration except the consideration that is necessary to ensure, in cases of real urgency and real public emergency, that an Executive would not be prevented from taking the action that might be considered necessary to safeguard public interests. ... So far as this Government is concerned, there are fundamental things that we have committed ourselves not to do without consulting the people again. I do not want to go further into our attitude in respect to those.[17]

Feb. 1934, quoted in Manning, *The Blueshirts*, pp 121–2. **14** Dáil Debates vol. 50 col. 2495–500, 1 Mar. 1934. **15** Manning, *The Blueshirts*, p. 126. The bill never became law. **16** Dáil Debates vol. 51 col. 1461–2, 22 Mar. 1934. **17** Dáil Debates vol. 51 col. 2479–80, 26 Apr. 1934.

On 24 May 1934, Stephen Roche, M. Mac Donnchadha, secretary, department of the President; J.J. Hearne, legal adviser, department of External Affairs, and P.P. O'Donoghue, were appointed

> to examine the Constitution with a view to ascertaining what Articles should be regarded as fundamental, on the ground that they safeguard democratic rights, and to make recommendations as to steps which should be taken to secure that such Articles would not be capable of being altered by the ordinary process of legislation.[18]

Between its appointment and the presentation of its final report on 3 July 1934, the committee held ten meetings. By its second meeting[19] it decided that its report 'should take the form of an entirely new Constitution',[20] which necessitated the insertion of a broad range of other provisions.[21]

One of the fundamental issues examined by the committee was emergency law. It concluded that 'Article 2A in its present form is not a proper one for retention in the Constitution'.[22] Roche wrote that '[Article 2A] is grotesque ... It must go ... [but] so long as we have the idea of a "normal" written constitution, with all sorts of snags and pit-falls for the Executive, we must have something, somewhere, along the lines of Article 2A.'[23] The committee recommended including provisions dealing with 'disorder not amounting to armed rebellion or state of war', as well as power to temporarily suspend articles of the constitution.[24]

Under 'Scheme A', it proposed that:

> Power should be provided in the Constitution for the enactment of legislation to provide, as part of the permanent judicial machinery of the State, for the trial by special courts of persons accused of crime, in respect of whom the appropriate ordinary Judge or Justice certifies, at any stage of the proceedings, either on his own initiative, or on the application of the Attorney General, that it is desirable, in the interests of justice, that the trial should be removed to a special court.

This would function preventatively, dealing with problems before they became dangerous. The committee added that the exact constitution and

18 D/T S.2979. 19 On 29 May 1934. 20 D/T S.2979, meeting 9 June 1934, the committee identified the articles of the 1922 constitution which should be contained in any new constitution. 21 D/T S.2979. 22 D/T S.8211, covering memorandum, Constitution Committee to de Valera, 3 July 1934. 23 Roche, 'Note with special reference to Article 2A.' 24 D/T S.2979, 3 July 1934, covering memorandum. This would not include articles relating to the Dáil, the independence of the judiciary, or habeas corpus.

powers of special courts should be determined by legislation: 'we have in contemplation is something in the nature of the Constitution (Special Powers) Tribunal, with such changes as experience has shown to be desirable.'

Under 'Scheme B', it proposed that:

> A new Article should be inserted in the Constitution which would authorise the Oireachtas to provide by ordinary legislation such powers as the Oireachtas might consider necessary, (including power to suspend temporarily any Article of the Constitution), to meet the requirements of any period during which the ordinary laws are not adequate for the preservation of public order.[25]

That article would provide 'that nothing in the Constitution or in any Act should be capable of being invoked or cited as invalidating anything in the article or in any legislation enacted or any other action taken under it.' Legislation would, either by preamble or title, 'state expressly that its object is to carry out the provisions of the said Article.'

Roche wrote, 'I gathered from the President that he was anxious, for obvious and weighty reasons, to get some form of judicial, or at least non-political sanction for such a declaration.'[26] The committee proposed that 'whenever the Executive Council is of opinion that it is desirable so to do', it would summon all the country's senior judges (though not members of the supreme court or high court nor persons acting as temporary judges or justices) 'for the purpose of advising the Executive Council as to whether the state of the country is such that the ordinary laws are not adequate for the preservation of public order.' The judges would decide the matter by secret majority vote and a report would be sent to the executive council 'attested by the signatures of all present at the meeting' recording the result of the vote, without specifying the names or numbers of person voting for or against. Wilful abstentions would be punished severely, 'amounting if necessary to automatic removal from office.' The committee explained

> our proposal to exclude the High Court and Supreme Court Judges is deliberate, on the grounds: a) that their jurisdiction is in practice almost exclusively civil, that they function in Dublin only, and that they are accordingly not in the same position as District Justices and Circuit Court Judges to assess the general condition of the country from the point of view of maintenance of law and order; b) that these judges may have to decide Constitutional questions arising out of the operation of the Article.

25 D/T S.8211. 26 D/T S.2979, 14 June 1934.

Roche added: 'I have … taken pains to avoid giving any ground for the charge that the Executive will be in a position to mark down for victimisation any individual Judge or Justice who opposes the Government wishes.'

If the judges concluded that there was an emergency, the executive council would declare by order that emergency legislation would become effective on a specific date. That order would be published in the *Iris Oifigiúil* before the necessary legislation became effective and would summon the Dáil immediately, if not already in session. The Dáil would have 21 days within which to annul the order. The order would remain in force for six months, when it might be renewed. The executive council could revoke an order at any time.[27]

Thus, the idea that Ireland faced two forms of emergency was clearly expressed. The subject rested there, though, for a year, and article 2A continued in force for some time, as the government attempted to deal with the immediate problems it faced and to resolve the various difficulties, legal and otherwise, created by the Blueshirt situation.

Although the government had experienced two notable court reversals, it had not relied solely on the constitution tribunal and article 2A to counter Blueshirt militancy. One important element of government policy towards the League of Youth was the drafting of several hundred IRA members into the Garda special branch. Further reorganization of the special branch saw chief superintendent Brennan transferred to crime ordinary branch, replaced by Tomás Ó Coillte.[28] By 12 March 1934, 35 of the most active special branch officers under O'Duffy had been transferred from the detective special branch to the depot or into uniform.[29]

Simultaneously, the government took further steps to encourage members of the IRA to break their links with the organization. Speaking on 7 February 1934, de Valera announced plans to establish the Volunteer Reserve Force (VRF), an army reserve based on a Swiss model. He explained 'we are putting to the defence of the country men who defended it in accordance with the oath which they had taken. What we want to do is see that there are back again in the national forces both sections of men who defended it from 1919 to 1921.' By 13 April 1934, it was claimed that 10,000 had joined.[30] The IRA army council described the VRF as an undesirable alternative to the IRA and several armed attacks on VRF members were reported during 1934 and 1935.[31]

27 The committee held its tenth and final meeting on 3 July 1934; it presented its report to de Valera that day. 28 *Irish Press*, 27 Feb. 1934, Brady, *Guardians*, p. 180. Also transferred were detectives Byrne, Ennis, Coughlan, Mordaunt, Mahony and Sauris. 29 *Irish Press*, 12 Mar. 1934. 30 *Irish Press*, 8 Feb. 1934, 13 Apr. 1934. 31 'Departmental Notes', pp 28–34.

Blueshirts continued to challenge article 2A in the courts. On 8 June 1934, the high court granted Patrick Hughes a conditional order of habeas corpus directed to Captain Lennon (governor of Arbour Hill detention barracks) and a conditional order of certiorari directed to the members of the tribunal.[32] Hughes had been charged with four offences: corruptly offering or agreeing to give consideration to a Garda, contrary to section 1 of the Prevention of Corruption Act, 1906; inciting, soliciting, counselling, or attempting to procure a Garda to commit an offence under section 2 of the Official Secrets Act, 1911 and contrary to section 7 of the Official Secrets Act, 1920 (two counts); and inciting a Garda to commit an act in dereliction of his duties, contrary to section 3(e) of the Treasonable Offences Act, 1925.

Although Hughes' counsel advanced 14 grounds in support of the application,[33] the case again turned on the fact that the tribunal was an inferior court. Counsel argued that as the tribunal was an inferior court, the tribunal's order of 1 June 1934[34] detailing Hughes' conviction had to show on its face that the tribunal had sufficient jurisdiction to try three of the offences charged as they were not offences explicitly covered by article 2A – an executive minister's certificate 'that to the best of his belief the act constituting such offence was done with the object of impairing or impeding the machinery of government or the administration of justice.' Lacking this, the order was bad on its face, and therefore certiorari lay.

Counsel for the Lennon, while noting the effect of *O'Duffy v. Bennett* earlier that year, argued that that case was irrelevant because it was concerned with a summons. This case, they contended, was concerned with an order of the tribunal and asserted there was no need for a written order as the tribunal's decision could be expressed orally ('jurisdiction to make

32 *The State (Hughes) v. Lennon*, [1935] IR 128, 4–20 July 1934. 33 [1935] IR 137–9. 34 Order of 1 June 1934: 'Whereas … Patrick Hughes was charged on the 14th, 23rd, 24th, 25th, 28th, 29th, and 30th days of May, 1934 before the Constitution (Special Powers) Tribunal with the offences set forth in the Schedule Hereto. And Whereas the said Patrick Hughes was on the 1st day of June, 1934 adjudged guilty of the said offences charged, and was sentenced to be imprisoned for a period of two years to date from the 24th day of April, 1934, in respect of all the said offences of which he was adjudged guilty. Now, therefore, it is ordered by the Constitution (Special Powers) Tribunal in pursuance of the powers conferred upon it by section 6 of Article 2A of the Constitution and of the Constitution (Amendment No.17) Act, 1931, and each and every power in that behalf it enabling, that the above named Patrick Hughes be imprisoned in Arbour Hill Prison, or in such other place as may be from time to time determined by the minister for Defence, in pursuance of the provisions of subsection 3 of section 10 of Article 2A of the Constitution and of the Constitution (Amendment No.17) Act, 1931 for a period of two years to date from the 24th day of April, 1934. And for this the present order shall be sufficient authority to all whom it may concern.'

the order need not be stated'). If the tribunal erred, counsel argued, it did so within its jurisdiction and therefore habeas corpus and certiorari did not lie.[35] Further, sections 5(4), 6(1), 6(5), and 7(4) of article 2A protected the tribunal's proceedings from being removed to any other court.[36]

These arguments were dismissed. Mr Justice Sullivan, president of the high court, held that the conviction recorded in the order of 1 June 1934 was bad on its face in respect of charges 1, 2, and 3 because it did not state that an executive minister had given the necessary certificate granting the tribunal jurisdiction to try each individual charge. He concluded that the protection afforded documents sealed with the seal of the tribunal by section 5(4) was confined to orders and acts which were not open to objection on their face,[37] unlike the order of 1 June 1934. Likewise, section 6(5) could only apply where the tribunal's order was not open to objection. As Mr Justice Gibson explained in *R (Martin) v. Mahony*, 'In the case of [an inferior court], no-certiorari cannot apply to evidence or latent error of law, and such a clause does not protect against certiorari if the conviction is bad on its face.'[38]

Mr Justice O'Byrne ruled that section 7(4) only extended the protection and immunity enjoyed by persons executing the orders and sentences of the central criminal court to persons executing the orders and sentences of the tribunal.[39] It had been contended that this section put the sentences of the tribunal on the same footing as those of the central criminal court. If that were true, he concluded, there would have been no need for a no-certiorari clause and the earlier decision that the tribunal was an inferior court could be ignored, 'If it were the intention of the Legislature to give to convictions by the Tribunal the same force and effect and to place them for all purposes upon the same footing as convictions of the Central Criminal Court, this could and ought to have been done in plain and express terms.'[40]

There was a more fundamental question to be addressed, however – Mr Justice Meredith asked to what extent could the fact that the tribunal was an inferior court be permitted to limit article 2A's ultimate objective:

> The Tribunal was clearly established for the purpose of dealing more effectively than the ordinary Courts, and, in particular, the Central Criminal Court, are capable of doing with an extraordinary situation

35 [1935] IR 140. 36 As regards pronouncing sentence in the presence of the accused or his counsel, counsel for Lennon noted that this was only necessary in cases of felony or treason. See Hale, *Pleas*, vol. 2, p. 300. 37 [1935] IR 143. 38 [1910] 2 IR 742. 39 [1935] IR 159: section 7(4) 'is dealing with the position of third parties'. 40 [1935] IR 158.

> which makes the ordinary administration of justice particularly difficult. Consequently the Tribunal is a practical compromise between military efficiency and the ordinary and desirable methods of administering justice. Such a compromise is distasteful … [but the] alternative … would doubtless be something more unwelcome.[41]

Accordingly, there could be no justification for the higher courts controlling the constitution tribunal as they might other inferior courts. To allow such 'subtle ingenuity' would be 'perverse', he believed. Further, nothing could diminish the force of section 5(2) which gave the tribunal 'full and absolute control of its own procedure in all respects'. He rejected the view that the words which followed ('and in particular, in respect of the admission or exclusion of the public to or from its sittings, the enforcing the attendance of witnesses and the production of documents') in any way limited its procedure or powers, explaining that the tribunal did not have to lay down any fixed procedure and that it was not bound to follow any recognized common law procedure.

Meredith dismissed as 'merely technical and of little substance' the remaining 13 grounds advanced for impeaching the conviction. Indeed, he originally viewed the question of jurisdiction on the face of the order as rather trivial, where jurisdiction could be established as a matter of truth, but eventually concluded, 'the obligation to show jurisdiction on the face of the order has a salutary effect, and it is not by any means a burdensome requirement. Attention to the matter will only assist the Tribunal in keeping with their jurisdiction.'[42] In summary, Meredith explained, the high court 'has a useful, a salutary, control, at the door of the entrance to, and the door of exit from the proceedings of the Tribunal, but not such a control as would hamper the Tribunal in the discharge of its very difficult and responsible duties.'[43] The court made the conditional orders of certiorari and habeas corpus absolute,[44] and Hughes was released on 20 July 1934. The government shortly released 32 republicans and 6 Blueshirts because their convictions were also deemed unsafe.[45]

41 [1935] IR 148. 42 [1935] IR 152–3. 43 [1935] IR 153. 44 Although the fourth charge did not require a certificate, the conviction was deemed unsafe. Quoting Palles C.B., Mr Justice Sullivan, referring to convictions in inferior courts ruled, 'that every separate count in an indictment for misdemeanour is treated as charging a distinct and separate offence, and that any number of misdemeanours … may be included in one indictment. If you have a general judgement and sentence upon all, one bad count will vitiate the entire sentence' (ibid., 146–7). Mr Justice O'Byrne held at 157 that it was 'charged disjunctively with two possible offences.' 45 'Departmental Notes', p. 25. Twenty-four of these would have completed their sentences before the end of 1934, 11 before the end of July 1935, and one each in April and July 1936 and April 1937.

The primary effect of the rulings in the second O'Duffy case and the Hughes case was that greater care was required when preparing the warrants, summonses and orders of the constitution tribunal. These could not be viewed as anything more than technical setbacks, and the overall effectiveness of the tribunal had not been compromised. Commenting on the tribunal's conduct when hearing Hughes' case, Mr Justice Sullivan remarked, 'I think it is only right to say that I do not see anything to suggest [Hughes] did not get an absolutely fair and impartial trial at [the constitution tribunal's] hands.'[46]

Of far greater importance was the realization that the Blueshirt movement had failed to widen its support beyond those opposed to Fianna Fáil and the IRA, and farmers directly affected by the Economic War. The Cumann nGaedheal–Blueshirt alliance had witnessed no improvement in Cumann na nGaedheal's electoral fortunes. A hoped-for landslide in the June 1934 local elections never materialized for Fine Gael. In spite of a franchise that was more suited to the party, it won control of only 7 of 22 councils.[47] After that electoral disappointment, it seems that O'Duffy and other Blueshirts, lost faith in constitutionalism, and contemplated ever more radical and ultimately desperate policies.[48]

Certain prominent Blueshirts now openly called for the non-payment of annuities and rates (and more aggressive steps) in protest at the hardship being experienced by some farmers. While there was no specific anti-annuities or anti-rates campaign organized by Fine Gael, individual TDs had urged farmers to pursue such a policy. Inevitably, conflict between farmers and the authorities increased. Violence intensified after the local election, with Blueshirts being killed in June and August.[49]

At the LOY's annual congress in August,[50] the main resolution called on the government not to collect land annuities while the problems created by the Economic War continued. It also called on farmers not to pay land annuities or rates, and on labourers not to pay rent on cottages until the government established a tribunal to examine the general situation of farmers. The Fine Gael leadership was shocked. If the resolution became party policy, it would bring it definitely within the terms of section 19(1)(f) of article 2A. The end of Fine Gael's union with the Blueshirts followed almost immediately. Professor Hogan resigned from the Fine Gael executive at the end of the month, explaining that it was the strongest protest he could make against 'the general destructive and hysterical leadership

46 [1935] IR 147. **47** Manning, *Blueshirts*, pp 134–6. **48** D. Keogh, *Twentieth century Ireland: nation and state* (1994), pp 85–6. **49** Manning, *The Blueshirts*, pp 136–8. **50** On 18 and 19 Aug. 1934, in the Mansion House, Dublin, see 'Departmental Notes', pp 25–6 and Manning, *The Blueshirts*, pp 141–5.

of its President, General O'Duffy'. Finally, on 21 September 1934, O'Duffy stepped down. The department of Justice reported:

> General Mulcahy presided at a meeting of the Cabra branch of the LOY on October 10 [1934] and, speaking of the reasons which led up to General O'Duffy's resignation, said that O'Duffy wanted methods adopted by Fine Gael which would make government by the present administration impossible: as a political party Fine Gael must keep within the law, and in view of this could not entertain O'Duffy's policy.[51]

Historian Mike Cronin concluded:

> In the event Fine Gael were glad to see the back of O'Duffy. They promoted Cronin to the Directorship and under his guidance the membership and the activity of the LoY slowly diminished. It seems that this was an agreed policy. The belief amongst all involved was that extra-parliamentary politics had seen their day, and the future of Fine Gael as a party was far more important than the existence of the LoY.[52]

Public calls for farmers not to pay their rates or annuities did not go unheeded, however, igniting widespread resistance to the collection of monies due.[53] During 1934, there was widespread blocking of roads and railways, and cutting of telephone wires; attacks on, damage to and destruction of recreational halls, in addition to attacks on social functions, on public meetings and on individuals.

The campaign against road and rail communication required the transfer of 2 inspectors, 4 sergeants, and 97 Gardaí, with special units also being established to enforce the payment of land annuities in Mullingar, Claremorris House, and Naas, requiring the transfer of 2 inspectors, 5 sergeants, and 64 Gardaí. Normally though, Gardaí were transferred from within their division to deal with problems. During 1934, 1,826 Gardaí performed 144,000 extra hours of duty.[54] A total of 424 cases of obstruction to the collecting of rates were recorded during the year, leading to 133 prosecutions, the charging of 706 persons, and 492 convictions.[55] While a large number of cases were disposed of in the district court, the constitution tribunal dealt with most.[56] Twelve cases were pending at the end of 1934.

51 'Departmental Notes', p. 26. 52 Cronin, 'Blueshirts', p. 28. 53 See tables 4a, 4b and 4c. 54 See D/J D.28/24. 55 Mostly for rail and road obstruction and cutting telegraph wires. See D/J D.28/34. 56 See table 3j.

Indeed, the tribunal was so busy at the end of 1934 that the attorney general wanted to give its members 'a bit of a holiday', and asked the commissioner to keep the number of new cases to be tried to a minimum.[57]

Seventeen cases of unlawful interference with public meetings were recorded during the year. Prosecutions were instituted in 10 cases and 90 persons were convicted. Fifteen attacks were made on dances and other recreational parties and prosecutions were instituted in six cases. In addition, a large number of persons were detained under article 2A and released without charge during 1934.[58] Further, Kilkenny, Waterford, South Tipperary, and Laois County Councils were dissolved when they refused to cooperate with the collection of moneys due.[59]

Although the Blueshirts disintegrated rapidly after the summer of 1934, the use of article 2A against Fine Gael's former allies drew serious criticism from the party. For instance, James Fitzgerald-Kenney, minister for Justice when article 2A was introduced in 1931, claimed that in the case of Jeremiah Ryan, Hubert Johnson and John Harty, who had been charged with the attempted murder of a rate collector,[60] copies of the attorney general's brief, documents that 'were absolutely teeming with statements which no attempt was made to prove' were supplied to tribunal members:

> Does the minister not consider that it is very unfair to prisoners who are brought before the Tribunal that matters of conjecture, detrimental to the interests of the prisoners, should be supplied by the Attorney-General, or by anyone else, to the Tribunal, and is the minister not further aware that if depositions taken before District Justices, who know the law of evidence, were allowed before a jury and if the jury were allowed to see them, a conviction by that jury would not stand for five minutes in the Court of Criminal Appeal.

Ruttledge denied this: 'the practice settled by the Constitution (Special Powers) Tribunal requires the Attorney-General to serve upon each accused a copy of the statement of charges and a summary of evidence to

57 Roche to the commissioner, no date, D/J D.67/34.
58 Dáil Debates vol. 54 col. 2080, 20 Feb. 1935:

Wicklow	2	Limerick	82	Dublin City	4	Galway	4	Tipperary	88
Carlow	21	Louth	17	Waterford City	6	Kildare	–	Meath	38
Offaly	9	Waterford Co.	51	Kerry	56	Kilkenny	137	Laois	1
Wexford	14	Cavan	–	Longford	–	Monaghan	–	Westmeath	29
Clare	12	Mayo	–	Cork City	19	Roscommon	1	Cork Co.	369
Sligo	1	Donegal	–	Leitrim	3				

Total: 964.

59 Manning, *The Blueshirts*, pp 130–4. 60 Ibid., p. 130 and *Irish Times* 25 Mar. 1931.

be given against him and to lodge with the registrar of the Tribunal copies of the documents.' Not without irony, the attorney general added, 'the practice followed is the same as the practice followed since the Tribunal first started its operations, and I do not see how the Deputy can expect me to decline to obey the ruling of the Tribunal itself.'[61] He explained:

> Every effort possible is made to exclude from the summary of evidence anything which will not be admissible as evidence. It may have happened in some cases that something did creep into these summaries which perhaps it might have been wiser not to have allowed in, but, I assure the Deputy that every effort will be made to exclude such things. I cannot, however, refuse to file with the Registrar a copy of the charges and a summary of evidence.

Ryan, Johnson and Harty had been granted conditional orders of habeas corpus and prohibition and their trial before the tribunal was adjourned while they sought relief in the high court and then in the supreme court.[62]

Their counsel contended that article 2A was unconstitutional because of inconsistency with articles 6, 64, and 72 of the constitution. They further argued that Constitution (Amendment No.16), which extended the time during which the Oireachtas could amend the constitution by ordinary legislation from 8 years to 16 years, was invalid and, therefore, Constitution (Amendment No 17) was invalid. The high court unanimously rejected these arguments. Mr Justice Meredith explained, 'the Court must take the Constitution as it finds it.'[63]

Although this case is remembered for the minority judgement delivered by the chief justice, Hugh Kennedy,[64] the supreme court upheld the high court's ruling. Mr Justice Fitzgibbon conceded that several articles[65] were partially or wholly abrogated by article 2A, but he refused to consider arguments about fundamental or natural rights.[66] Ruling that the 16th constitution amendment was valid, he said, 'the same reasoning which applies to the power of the Oireachtas to amend article 50 applies with at least equal force to amendments of any other Article.'[67] He added:

61 Dáil Debates vol. 54 col. 1505–8, 18 Dec. 1934. 62 *The State (Ryan and Others) v. Lennon and Others* [1935] IR 170. 63 [1935] IR 181. 64 [1935] IR 189–219; J. Kelly, *Constitution of Ireland*, (2nd ed.), (1984), p. 407. 65 Articles 6, 43, 64, 65, 68, 69, 70, 72 66 [1935] IR 230–1 67 [1935] IR 228. 'Article 50 was to prescribe the method by which legislative sanction was to be given to those amendments of the Constitution which the Oireachtas was empowered to make, and the Oireachtas had full power during eight years, in the absence of any express prohibition, to alter modify or repeal the method prescribed', [1935] IR 227.

> In Article 6 it is declared that 'the liberty of the person is inviolable', but that is not a law of universal application, for the Article proceeds: 'and no person shall be deprived of his liberty *except in accordance with law*'. The law may, therefore, make provisions in accordance with which a person may be deprived of his liberty. It is for the legislature to prescribe those provisions, and for the Courts to enforce them.[68]

This was true, he said, 'even if, under Amendment no. 17, a person has been deprived of his liberty by the mere caprice of an executive minister,[69] on the unfounded suspicion "incapable of being rebutted or questioned by cross-examination, rebutting evidence, or otherwise ... of any member of the Garda Síochána[70] ... or of the Defence Forces of Saorstát Éireann",[71] such deprivation would be "in accordance with law" and the prisoner would have no redress'. Article 2A set out 'the conditions under which liberty is enjoyed and justice may be administered in [the ...] Saorstát'.[72] Mr Justice Murnaghan ruled that constitutional amendments could repeal articles of the constitution 'within the terms of the scheduled Treaty'.[73] In essence, he said, 'the only function of the Court is to see that the proposed amendment is within the scope of the power granted by the Constitution and that the requisite forms insisted upon by the Constitution shall have been duly observed.'[74]

Incidents involving Blueshirts continued into 1935. A Blueshirt march in Kilmallock, Co. Limerick on 17 March 1935 led to rioting,[75] and there was an attack on a dance-hall in Buttevant, Co. Cork on 6 May 1935. There were also armed attacks on Killdorrery Garda Station, Co. Cork on 5 and 29 June 1935. These incidents were accompanied by the cutting of telegraph wires in that general area.[76] One of the Blueshirts arrested following these incidents, William McCarthy, incriminated himself during interrogation and brought the last legal challenge to article 2A.[77]

McCarthy challenged his conviction on the single ground that the statement extracted from him by Gardaí under section 15(1)(d) of article 2A, which was used as the sole evidence to secure his conviction, was inadmissible because it was extracted under threat of violence under section 15(2):

68 [1935] IR 229. 69 Appendix, clause 7. 70 Section 13 and 29. 71 Section 13. 72 [1935] IR 237. 73 [1935] IR 241. 74 [1935] IR 242. 75 *Cork Examiner*, 18 Mar. 1935, 'Departmental Notes', pp 36–7. 76 'Departmental Notes', pp 40–3. 77 *The State (McCarthy) v. Lennon and others* [1936] IR 485. The constitution tribunal convicted William McCarthy on 25 July 1935 of membership of an unlawful organization and of downing telegraph poles. See *Irish Press*, 4 Apr. 1936, 'Departmental Notes', p. 43.

> Every person detained on suspicion under this Article who, while he is so detained ... when any information in his possession is demanded of him under this section by a member of the Garda Síochána, fails or refuses to give such information or gives information which is false, incomplete, inaccurate, or misleading ... shall be guilty of an offence triable by the Tribunal and shall be liable on conviction thereof to suffer such punishment as the Tribunal shall think proper to inflict.

His counsel argued that the statement would have been inadmissible under the common law and that the provisions of section 15 were contrary to the 'Natural Law'. The conditional orders for habeas corpus and certiorari were, however, discharged by the high court. Referring simply to *R. v. Scott*,[78] the president of the high court, Mr Justice Sullivan, said, 'Having regard to the scope and object of [Article 2A], the statement was admissible in evidence.'[79] McCarthy appealed to the supreme court where his arguments found favour with the chief justice, Hugh Kennedy, who, again dissenting, explained:

> My simple logic cannot trace any sequence from the sworn evidence given compulsorily in a court of law to a statement, not on oath, privately extracted by a policeman from a man, in his custody and unprotected, without eyewitness of the alleged examinations or record of what passed, without regulation of time or place or circumstance ... There is no trace in the Constitution amendment of a purpose of using a prisoner's extorted answers in evidence in any court for any purpose.[80]

He declared that the regulations introduced in article 2A were unsound. Although disagreeing with Kennedy, Mr Justice Fitzgibbon remarked sarcastically:

> To describe statements extracted under what was tantamount to a threat of capital punishment if they were to refuse, 'Voluntary Statements tendered to me by William McCarthy' must have required some hardihood, but it is not surprising to find that the subordinates who are employed to put into execution enactments such as Article 2A of the Constitution carry out their work in the same spirit as that which inspired the legislators who framed and passed the Act.[81]

78 7 Cox, C.C. 164, dealing with a bankruptcy case. 79 [1936] IR 490. 80 [1936] IR 495–6. 81 [1936] IR 498.

He explained he was bound to examine the law as it stood, however. Accordingly, he ruled that the Dáil had legislated 'that in case of any inconsistency between Article 2A and Article 73,[82] Article 2A shall prevail'[83] and that an accused could incriminate himself, despite the common law maxim *nemo tenetur se ipsum accusare*: 'statements ... obtained [under sections 15] are obtained lawfully, and I know no law which makes statements or confessions lawfully obtained or made, inadmissible as evidence in any legal proceeding'.[84] Rejecting 'Natural Law' as an unclear concept, he cited *Abel v. Lee* and quoted Mr Justice Willes: 'I utterly repudiate the notion that it is competent to a Judge to modify the language of an Act in order to bring it in accordance with his views of what is right or reasonable.'[85] The position of the court, Fitzgibbon explained, was that

> When the legislature has enacted a law, no court has power to disregard the plain provisions of that law because it thinks them unreasonable or unjust. If the language used be reasonably capable of two constructions, one of which would give rise to manifest injustice, the Court is free to, and will in most cases, adopt the other, but when the language or intent is plain, the Court must give effect to it, however unreasonable or unjust the result may appear to the Court to be. It is the right of the legislature to make laws, and the duty of the courts to enforce them.[86]

Mr Justice Murnaghan concurred and the order was discharged.

By now, though, the Blueshirts had more or less disintegrated. Maurice Manning wrote 'as far as Irish politics are concerned the Blueshirts were an aberration, the most fundamental explanation of whose origin lies in the fear and distrust harboured by the opponents of Fianna Fáil in 1932 and 1933.'[87] Neither the emergence of the Blueshirts nor Fianna Fáil's economic and political policies had seen the government's popularity fall. Prominent republican Sighle Humphries recalled, 'there were a lot of people that thought [de Valera] was going slowly, but that he was going somewhere – and they were happy with it.'[88] Although de Valera had not succeeded in achieving a 32 county Irish republic, he had delivered significant constitutional reform and removed many unpalatable aspects of the Treaty. Fianna Fáil also devised other inducements designed to encourage IRA members to break with the organization. Under one of those measures, the

82 Article 73 continued in force the laws operating in Ireland prior to December 1922. 83 Section 2. 84 [1936] IR 500. 85 LR 6CP 371; [1936] IR 503. 86 [1936] IR 502. 87 Manning, *The Blueshirts*, p. 245. 88 Quoted in English, *Radicals and the republic*, p. 162.

Military Service Pensions Act, anti-Treaty Civil War veterans were awarded pensions in August 1934. The IRA army council described the pension as outright bribery,[89] though by November 1937, the government reported that 4,155 veterans had broken with the IRA and accepted the pension.[90]

With the collapse of the Blueshirt movement and the continuing successes of Fianna Fáil, the IRA again found itself completely isolated in the Irish political landscape. Efforts to politicize by means of the Republican Congress had split the republican movement in two, and the Congress itself disintegrated as it held its first convention.[91] By late 1934, the IRA had little to focus on: its own anti-rates campaign was a failure and only the occasional attack on imperial or colonial symbols offered members the promise of action. Many simply drifted into Fianna Fáil.[92]

As the IRA's position deteriorated, department of Justice and Garda pressure on *An Phoblacht* increased, especially as 1934 drew to a close. In October 1934, Stephen Roche wrote that the newspaper was 'quite definitely a seditious publication ... any reference in it to the alleged Irish Republican Army is seditious, the intention being to encourage the idea that a separate army, not authorised by law, not only exists and functions, but is entitled to support and sympathy'.[93] The following week, he instructed the commissioner that

> every issue of this paper should be examined by the police before it is distributed and that the whole issue should be confiscated if it is seditious. It may be as well to add that the officer charged with this duty should not discuss with the printers or publishers the precise items to which he takes objection: he should wait until the paper is ready and he should then simply confiscate it as seditious, if he finds anything seditious in it.

Roche believed that 'the time has now come when the publishers of this Paper should be prosecuted and a sharp penalty sought'.[94] In a note to the attorney general, he argued, 'if the Police are to act in this matter at all, they must proceed by way of wholesale confiscation on the slightest provocation'.[95]

Roche explained the censoring system applied by the Gardaí thus:

89 Bell, *The secret army*, p. 188. 90 Dáil Debates vol. 69 col. 750, 10 Nov. 1937. 91 English, *Radicals and the republic*, pp 185–215; Bell, *The secret army*, pp 111–18; Keogh, *Twentieth century Ireland*, p. 80. 92 Bell, *The secret army*, p. 118; Foley, *Legion of the rearguard*, p. 149. 93 D/J A6/37/34, Roche to the commissioner, 11 Oct. 1934, referring to 13 Oct. 1934 issue. 94 A/G 31/34, Roche to commissioner, 19 Oct. 1934. 95 Ibid., Roche to the attorney general, 19 Oct. 1934.

> What happens is that if the police see anything seditious in an issue, they seize the whole issue without specifying the particular words or paragraphs to which they object. The offenders then print a new edition, omitting or modifying the matter which, so far as they can conjecture, was the cause of the offence. The police should examine the issue and either pass it or seize it as before, without explanation. In due course, if the publishers are patient enough, an edition is evolved which the police are prepared to pass, but at no time have the police objected to any particular phrase or asked that it be altered or omitted.[96]

The attorney general was unenthusiastic about Roche's proposals or Garda practice. He reminded the secretary that Dáil criticism of censorship of the *United Ireland* had upset de Valera. More importantly, he doubted if Gardaí had any legal power to censor newspapers. The attorney general had previously advised the publishers and printers on what constituted sedition, and they were warned that the tribunal might be called on to deal with them at any time in the future. He hoped this policy would 'put all the responsibility' on the publishers and printers.[97]

Desperation was beginning to pervade the IRA. In late 1934 and early 1935, it began intervening in trade and land disputes, inevitably bringing it into confrontation with the authorities. In one case, the Town Tenants Association in Edgeworthstown, Co. Longford, passed a resolution on 5 November 1934 calling for IRA assistance in their dispute with the village landlady, Maria Sanderson and the local estate agent, Gerald More O'Farrell. On 9 February 1935, members of the Leitrim–Sligo IRA descended on the estate agent's home, apparently intent on intimidating him. In the ensuing altercation, however, More O'Farrell's son was shot and later died. Four IRA members were charged with the killing. When tried in the central criminal court in Dublin, the first jury was unable to reach a verdict; a second jury found them not guilty.[98]

96 D/J A6/37/34, Roche to the attorney general, 28 Nov. 1934. 97 A/G 31/34, attorney general to Roche, 27 Nov. 1934. Superintendent Down to the commissioner, 22 Nov. 1934, reported that the printers were printing one side of the page with non-seditious matter (on Tuesdays) and a limited number of issues were completed the following day which could be seized by the Gardaí. D/J A6/37/34, on 25 Mar. 1935 Gardaí were instructed not to seize the newspaper until a large number of copies had been printed, and not to indicate which parts or articles were objected to. It was intended to put both the publisher and the printer to the 'maximum of expense and inconvenience.' Matter considered objectionable included portions of the issue of 7 Mar. 1935 which placed the word Dáil in inverted commas, and spoke of 'former comrades gone astray.' The 27 May 1935 issue was seized because the 'general tone … appeared defiant and offensive.' 98 Bell, *The*

The Longford incident raised very serious questions. Frank McDermott TD asked if the IRA would be proclaimed, but Ruttledge replied, 'Any action that may be necessary for the maintenance of public order will be taken in regard to the Irish Republican Army and other military and semi-military organisations, but it is not the opinion of the Executive Council that the necessity has arisen.' Frank McDermott resurrected the subject in June 1936, when he asked the then acting-minister for Justice, Gerald Boland, why the constitution tribunal had not tried the men. Boland explained that Ruttledge had not issued a certificate because he 'could not conscientiously state that the crime was committed for the purpose of interfering with the machinery of Government or the administration of justice'.[99]

The IRA also became involved in the Dublin tram and bus dispute of March 1935. The government moved to relieve the consequences of the strike on 20 March 1935 by sending in soldiers and army lorries to partially supplement public transport. A few days later, the IRA described the government's actions as a 'definite challenge to all workers' and announced its 'willingness to assist the workers in their struggle.' This proved unacceptable to the government and on 26 March 1935, Gardaí arrested 44 IRA and Republican Congress members. 'There was only one thing the Government could do', de Valera explained.[1]

Further confirming the stiffening of government policy, on 29 and 30 March 1935, newspapers were warned (under threat of prosecution by the constitution tribunal) not to carry any correspondence from unlawful associations. Closing orders were made against three buildings involved in the IRA sweepstake on 30 May 1935.[2]

Revealingly, the tribunal tried those arrested in March on charges of membership of an unlawful association. Before the constitution tribunal on 24 April 1935, the prosecutor, Mr William Black SC, argued

> This is a very important case in that the Government of the country have felt it their duty to challenge the right of any organisation to maintain itself as an armed body, intending by arms to achieve the overthrow of that Government … I propose to put the constitution of the IRA in evidence as one of the proofs that it is an unlawful association.[3]

This charge had never been brought against IRA members since Fianna Fáil came to power. By 1936, though, it was the offence most regularly charged.[4]

secret army, pp 119–20, 'Departmental Notes', pp 32–4; *Irish Times*, 3 May 1935. 99 Dáil Debates vol. 55 col. 1, 27 Feb. 1935, vol. 55 col. 342–5, 6 Mar. 1935; 'Departmental Notes', pp 33–4. 1 *Irish Independent*, 25 Mar. 1935, *Irish Times*, 28 Mar. 1935, *Irish Press*, 30 Mar. 1935. 2 See Dáil Debates vol. 55 col. 1896–9; 'Departmental Notes', p. 42. 3 'Departmental Notes', p. 39. 4 See figures, tables 3c–g.

Although Gerald Boland had proposed the government formally consider its policy towards the IRA in May 1935, the final break was a year away.[5] De Valera conceded that attempts to completely co-opt every member of the IRA into Fianna Fáil or to encourage all of the organization's members to join one of the various government schemes had failed. Those who remained in the IRA had failed to develop 'a sense of respect for law', in spite of its being 'Home Law' and not a British creation, he claimed. De Valera warned, 'there must be order. If the ordinary operations of law cannot be relied upon to maintain order and secure justice – if there is to be government at all – the Government have to seek and use the powers which make law operative.' He continued that if the government

> were introducing a [new] constitution tomorrow ... we would have to introduce in that Constitution certain emergency provisions which would give power to the Executive, in case the ordinary courts were set at defiance, to bring those acting in an unlawful and illegal manner before courts which could not possibly be intimidated.[6]

De Valera and his advisers were already working on a new constitution.[7] P.P. O'Donoghue speculated that it would 'contain ... machinery for bringing the emergency provisions into force and at the same time suspending what are regarded as the usual Constitutional guarantees.'[8] Provision for judicial sanction before declaring an emergency, which was a major factor in the 1934 discussions, was absent, however. Preliminary work on legislation to replace article 2A was also in progress.

Setting out the basic requirements of new legislation, P.P. O'Donoghue emphasized:

> Where conflict has occurred, as it frequently does, between a theoretical regard for Constitutional nicety and the provision of a practical scheme likely to stand the test of usage I have unhesitatingly adopted the latter course ... no question of legal formalism should be permitted to prevent the Executive, who must remain primarily responsible, from making adequate provision to tide over the period of emergency. We have seen to what extent these efforts can be thwarted where a clean cut has not been made.

5 D/T S.7494, Roche to assistant secretary of the executive council, 13 May 1935. 6 Dáil Debates vol. 56 col. 2090, 29 May 1935. 7 D. Keogh 'The Irish constitutional revolution: an analysis of the making of the constitution', in Frank Litton (ed.), *The constitution of Ireland, 1937–1987* (1988), pp 8–11. 8 D/J D.42/37, O'Donoghue to the attorney general, 8 Aug. 1935.

Heads of the provisionally entitled Protection of the Community (Special Powers) Act[9] would provide for the establishment of 'The National Emergency Tribunal', a censorship board, create special powers of arrest, search and detention, deal with unlawful organizations and assemblies, create a mechanism to investigate allegations of unlawful arrest, and provide for disqualifications and forfeitures of persons convicted by the proposed tribunal. Work on this, however, could not proceed far until civil servants had a clearer idea of the provisions of the new constitution.

In spite of the government's notable constitutional and political advances, it was now clear that it would not bring Ireland any closer to the IRA demand of a 32-county republic. Frustrated by the failure of its support for de Valera and Fianna Fáil, IRA members called for a new policy of action at the organization's August 1935 army convention.[10] Nevertheless, while a small number of incidents occurred in the second half of 1935, it seemed that the IRA no longer constituted a significant danger in the state.

The weakening of the IRA did not halt Garda pressure on *An Phoblacht*. On 28 May 1935, its acting editor criticized on-going censorship of the paper.[11] He claimed that the previous week's issue had been delayed for sixteen hours at the printers by the local Garda superintendent, who refused to allow it out until a number of items were deleted – 'as a matter of fact, the paper received a more severe censoring last week than ever before'. When the paper was finally circulated, however, Gardaí seized as many copies as possible from newsagents throughout the country, even relieving Dublin newsboys of their copies.[12]

The attorney general was unhappy that his earlier instructions had been ignored and demanded an explanation. 'There is … no legal justification for censorship', he complained, repeating that if a newspaper contained seditious matter it should be dealt with by the tribunal.[13] Roche responded:

> [Because *An Phoblacht*] is published with the primary object of advocating, promoting and encouraging treason and disloyalty … and because of the manifestly seditious character of the paper … the Government has authorised the police to seize seditious issues of 'An Phoblacht' before the paper can be put on the streets instead of awaiting actual publication and proceeding before the Courts in the ordinary way.

9 The act would operate upon a declaration of a state of emergency by the Dáil, otherwise by order of the executive council. 10 Bell, *The secret army*, pp 125–6. 11 T. Mac A'Bhaurd, letter to *Irish Press* 28 May 1935. 12 See D/J A6/37/34. On 25 Mar. 1935, Roche instructed the commissioner to begin seizing two and more print-runs of each week's issue of *An Phoblacht*. 13 A/G 31/34, attorney general to Roche, 28 May 1935.

He conceded Gardaí had no legal powers to censor and that the work posed an unfair burden on them. He again proposed that the printers of *An Phoblacht* be 'mulcted once or twice in sharp fines', but based on evidence provided by issues of the paper during the preceding twelve months. This seemed rather futile, though, because Gardaí had already sanitized most issues. Therefore, he proposed ending seizures, and warning the publishers and printers that they would be prosecuted by the tribunal if they offended again. If those warnings were unheeded, the paper would be seized as soon as possible and the publishers and printers charged.[14]

New instructions were issued to the Garda commissioner. Henceforth, Gardaí would supply John O'Connor, the solicitor in the attorney general's office, with copies of *An Phoblacht* who would take whatever steps were necessary to have them considered by the constitution tribunal. If the tribunal declared an issue was seditious, Gardaí would seize all copies. No prosecution would be brought, however, unless two or more successive issues were declared to be seditious, thus leaving the publishers and printers with no defence.[15]

As 1935 drew to a close, the country seemed more peaceful than for several years, prompting the Labour Party leader, William Norton, to call for the repeal of article 2A. De Valera responded, 'organised crimes of violence are still occurring'. He conceded, though, there was considerable opposition to article 2A, but said that the government would be irresponsible if it suspended it.[16]

The IRA continued to face sustained Garda pressure. Indeed, 1936 would be more difficult for the organization than 1935, with the call for action made in 1935 leading to disastrous results. On 24 March 1936, the Co. Cork IRA killed 72-year-old Vice-Admiral Henry Boyle Somerville because he had written references for locals wanting to join the British navy.[17] On 26 April 1936, John Egan was killed in Dungarvan, Co. Waterford, on suspicion of being an informer.[18] Four were arrested in connection with Egan's death and Michael Conway was sentenced to death by the constitution tribunal, though he was later reprieved.

These killings generated considerable public outcry and within three days of the second attack, Gardaí arrested a large number of IRA members in Dublin and Cork.[19] More significantly, the government decided in

14 Ibid., Roche to the attorney general, 3 June 1935, and 11 June 1935; attorney general to Roche, 14 June 1935. 15 D/J A.6/37/34, Roche to the commissioner, 15 June 1935, Thomas Coyne to P.P. O'Donoghue, 15 June 1935. 16 Dáil Debates vol. 59 col. 1535–6, 28 Nov. 1935. For department of Justice comments on Norton's proposal see D/J D.55/34, 25 Nov. 1935. 17 Bell, *The secret army*, p. 126. 18 Dáil Debates, 29 May 1946. William O'Donoghue, John Tobin, Edmond Carrigan, Michael Conway were arrested for the killing. 19 'Departmental

principle to formally outlaw the IRA during May 1936,[20] finally proclaiming the organization on 18 June 1936.[21] Gerald Boland expressed the government's position very simply when he told the Dáil:[22]

> the fact that these murders have occurred ... makes it clear that stern action must be taken against any organisation which claims to have power of life or death over its members, or ex-members, or other citizens, or claims that it is entitled to use force upon the community to compel obedience to its will. I now give definite notice to all concerned that the so-called Irish Republican Army, or any organisation which promotes or advocates the use of arms for the attainment of its object will not be tolerated.[23]

The following day he declared: 'we smashed [the Blueshirts] and we are going to smash [the IRA]'. When questioned about Fianna Fáil's earlier links with the IRA, de Valera asked rhetorically, 'Do I regret that policy? If that policy led in any way to murder of individuals in this State I regret it. I cannot say whether it is that policy that has done it but, if it has, I must regret it.'[24]

The final suppression of *An Phoblacht* occurred on 24 June 1936 when the premises of the Longford based printers were raided by Gardaí on foot of a warrant issued under section 30 of article 2A, and 5,500 copies of the newspaper seized.[25] The paper did not appear afterwards. By 31 July 1936, 77 republicans were serving sentences in military detention,[26] where they were subjected to a rigorous prison regime.[27]

The government could feel a degree of satisfaction with its handling of the security situation. Seán Cronin estimated IRA numbers fell from 8,036 in September 1934 to 7,358 in late 1935, and to 3,844 in November 1936, though 'parade strength was only 2,038'.[28] In fact, by the end of 1936 the government began to consider releasing those who had been convicted of the most serious offences and imprisoned during the previous year-and-a-half.[29] Two were released in November 1937, eight the following month, and the remaining nine, including Michael Conway and Maurice Twomey, in April 1938.[30]

Notes', pp 50–4. **20** Brady, *Guardians*, p. 229. **21** *Iris Oifigiúil*, 20 June 1936. The annual Bodenstown march was banned on 19 June 1936, enforced by 1,000 troops and 500 Gardaí. See also Brady, *Guardians*, pp 229–30 and 'Departmental Notes', p. 55. **22** On 30 June 1936, the attorney general offered a full amnesty to persons who severed their IRA links, Dáil Debates vol. 63 col. 661. **23** Quoted in 'Departmental Notes', p. 54, 16 June 1936. **24** Dáil Debates vol. 63 col. 112, 23 June 1936. **25** A/G 31/34, Roche to the attorney general, 25 June 1936. Issue of 27 June 1936. **26** See D/J D.69/34. There were also 8 Blueshirts. **27** 'Departmental Notes', pp 60–1, J.B. Bell, *The secret army*, p. 139, D/J H.308/39. **28** Cronin, *The McGarrity papers*, p. 166. **29** D/T S.9231, cabinet committee on political prisoners. **30** 'Departmental Notes', pp 118–20. On deferring and

Having removed the oath and references to the English king from the Irish constitution following the abdication of Edward VIII in December 1936,[31] de Valera could rename the Free State simply Ireland, and though not establishing the republic, was plainly intent on achieving a wholly independent and sovereign state.[32] That independence and sovereignty would find further expression in a new constitution, Bunreacht na hÉireann.

The Fianna Fáil leader explained that with Bunreacht na hÉireann he intended to prevent 'that sort of window dressing which was in the old Constitution. Wherever we have made statements here, side by side with them we have put the limitations which are absolutely necessary. There is a certain value in the statement of these principles, so long as we state them accurately.'[33] De Valera warned, though, that rights and their inclusion could be no more than 'headlines with regard to the things the Legislature should aim.'[34] He cautioned, 'all you can do is to give the fundamental principles; to state them clearly and correctly, and leave it to the sense of justice, the goodwill of the community to work in accordance with the spirit of the declaration.'[35] Regarding the courts, de Valera explained, 'as long as the Legislature acts properly, the Courts ought not to interfere … as long as it carries out the functions necessary for the life of the community, then the Courts ought not to interfere … interference in such a case would be harmful and would be to the public detriment.'[36]

Bunreacht na hÉireann did away with the executive council and, instead, created a cabinet, while the President of the executive council became the 'Taoiseach'. The new constitution also included several provisions dealing specifically with emergencies. Under article 28.3.2, it provided 'In the case of actual invasion … the Government may take whatever steps they may consider necessary for the protection of the State, and Dáil Éireann if not sitting shall be summoned to meet at the earliest practicable date.' Further, under article 28.3.3, it provided that 'Nothing in this Constitution shall be invoked to invalidate any law enacted by the Oireachtas which is expressed to be for the purpose of securing the public safety and the preservation of the State in time of war or armed rebel-

reviewing sentences under article 2A, disabilities, and pardons see D/T S.7824, D/T S.6860, S.9794, D/T S.2444, D/J S.51/36, D/J D.14/38 **31** See D/T S.2437, S.9430, Constitution (Amendment No 27) Act, 1936. In their haste to draft the amendment, the department of External Affairs neglected to delete reference to the governor general from section 25 of article 2A. **32** The constitution was introduced into the Dáil on 10 Mar. 1937. **33** Dáil Debates vol. 67 col. 1613–4, 3 June 1937. Quoted in J. Kelly, *Fundamental rights in the Irish law and constitution* (1967), p. 24. **34** Dáil Debates vol. 68 col. 217, 9 June 1937. **35** Dáil Debates vol. 67 col. 62, 11 May 1937. **36** Dáil Debates vol. 67 col. 1614, 3 June 1937.

lion, or to nullify any act done or purporting to be done in time of war or armed rebellion in pursuance of such law.'

The new constitution also provided for special criminal courts which 'may be established by law for the trial of offences in cases where it may be determined in accordance with such law that the ordinary courts are inadequate to assure the effective administration of justice, and the preservation of public peace and order'.[37] Their 'constitution, powers, jurisdiction and procedure' would be prescribed by law.[38] In addition, article 38.4.1 provided for 'military tribunals to be established ... to deal with a state of war or armed rebellion'. Article 38.5 exempted special criminal courts and military tribunals from requiring juries to determine guilt, and article 38.6 exempted them from provision for appeal to the court of criminal appeal and from requirements regarding the appointment and removal of judges under articles 35. Finally, article 39 defined treason:

> Treason shall consist only in levying war against the State, or assisting any state or person or inciting or conspiring with any person to levy war against the State, or attempting by force of arms or other violent means to overthrow the organs of government established by this Constitution, or taking part or being concerned in or inciting or conspiring with any person to make or to take part or be concerned in any such attempt.

Regarding article 28.3.3, de Valera told the Dáil that

> What we have here is a very mild form of an Article which is found in practically every written Constitution, an Article providing for a complete suspension of constitutional guarantees in order to be able to deal with cases where the ordinary machinery of Government is not capable of coping with the situation it has to deal with.[39]

He warned that if the constitution did not contain this power, provision would be made for far more extreme measures.[40]

37 Article 38.3.1. 38 Article 38.3.2. 39 Dáil Debates vol. 67 col. 1538–9. 40 The text of the constitution was published 1 May 1937, and passed by the Dáil 14 June 1937. The Dáil was dissolved and a general election and referendum was held on 29 June 1937. The constitution was passed 685,105 for, and 526,945 against. The number of seats in the Dáil was reduced from 153 to 138, with Fianna Fáil returning 69 TDs, Fine Gael 48, Labour 13, and Independents 8.

5

The new constitution, 1937–1939

Bunreacht na hÉireann marked, in many ways, a new beginning for the 26 Counties. It asserted a claim to the whole island, renaming the country simply Ireland. Although partition remained, the other distasteful terms of the Treaty had been, or very shortly would be, removed. Whatever reasons justified the IRA's continued existence in southern Ireland had, it seemed, finally and absolutely evaporated. In spite of its many political successes and constitutional advances, though, the government did not imagine that militant republicanism had been completely and permanently eradicated.

The question of emergency law had been central to the Constitution Committee's work in 1934, and de Valera promised the Dáil in 1935 that a new constitution would contain emergency provisions. True to his word, Bunreacht na hÉireann, provided for the establishment of a special criminal court whenever the government deemed that the ordinary courts were inadequate for the effective administration of justice and the preservations of public peace and order and for a declaration of a state of emergency in time of war or armed rebellion. Unlike 1931, when the constitution became subsidiary to a public safety act, emergency powers were inserted as ordinary articles of the constitution and the precedent of 1931 would not occur again unless there was an outbreak of war or armed rebellion. That the people had accepted the constitution in a referendum gave these emergency provisions added legitimacy. Further, as both main parties had relied on article 2A, the Oireachtas could not genuinely or honestly oppose these new powers. Ultimately, 15 years of the administration of the law in Ireland demonstrated that emergency laws would have to be permanent.

Bunreacht na hÉireann created a republic in the south of Ireland in all but name. Nevertheless, republican opposition to the independent Irish state and to Northern Ireland continued. Peadar O'Donnell criticized the privileged position the new constitution gave 'the Roman Catholic Bishops in the South';[1] Seán Russell, the future IRA chief of staff, attacked it because it did not 'drive the foe from our land'.[2] Generally, though, the circumstances of militant republicans were bleak. A demonstration against the coronation of George VI organized for 14 May 1937 in Dublin was

1 Quoted in Foley, *Legion of the rearguard*, p. 177. 2 *San Francisco News*, 1 July 1937, quoted in Tarpey, *Joseph McGarrity*, p. 316.

proclaimed,[3] while the Wolfe Tone gathering at Bodenstown a month later was permitted, but attracted only 1,500.[4] Despite many discouraging factors, Tom Barry, chief of staff of the IRA since 1936, unveiled plans to attack Northern Ireland in 1937. He envisaged not so much a guerrilla offensive, or a series of hit-and-run attacks, but a coup d'état. The operation was cancelled, however, when it emerged that republicans were openly discussing Barry's plans. Barry resigned soon after.[5] Whether or not the government was aware of these plans is unclear. While new public safety legislation was under consideration, no significant urgency was evident.

The question of new public safety legislation was becoming more pressing, however, as the repeal of the 1922 constitution necessarily included a repeal of article 2A.[6] Although the 1922 constitution would expire in December 1937, formal permission to draft replacement public safety legislation was not granted until August.[7] By 7 October 1937, the parliamentary draftsman had completed a preliminary draft Special Criminal Court Bill based on article 38.3, which dealt solely with the trial of offences, making no reference to the other powers provided in article 2A. Roche explained the draft was 'intended merely to provide a basis of discussion and my mind is quite open as regards all or any of its particular provisions.' It was clear, though, that definite departures from the constitution (special powers) tribunal were being contemplated.[8]

Under the first draft, a special criminal court would be established whenever the government was satisfied that 'the ordinary courts are inadequate to secure in all cases the effective administration of justice and the preservation of public peace and order,' as required by article 38.3 of the constitution. The court would consist of nine members, 'all of whom shall be officers of the Defence Forces of Ireland not below the rank of captain and shall be appointed and removable at will by the President acting on the advice of the Government.' Five members would normally constitute the court, though all nine would try capital cases; convictions would require unanimity. Significantly, the ordinary rules of evidence were explicitly stated to apply and there was provision for appeal to the court of criminal appeal. Further, the special criminal court would only impose penalties authorized by the ordinary law and convictions would not lead to disqualification from holding state employment or to the forfeiture of state pensions.

3 'Departmental Notes', p. 64. 4 Bell, *The secret army*, 138 and Foley, *Legion of the rearguard*, p. 178. 5 Bell, *The secret army*, pp 133–5. 6 D/J D.42/37, D/T S.9794, 14 Apr. 1937. 7 D/T S.9794, 7 Aug. 1937 and D/J D.42/37, Roche to Coyne, 19 July 1937. 8 D/J D.42/37, Roche to P.P. O'Donoghue, 7 Oct. 1937. 9 D/T S.10454A, memoran-

The department of Justice had initially proposed a larger court to dispel some of the criticism of the abolition of trial by jury,[9] though this view was not widely supported.[10] The parliamentary draftsman wrote:

> To my mind your court is much too large; I would have a court of five members for capital cases, and three members in other cases; I would, however, make the three members a minimum and not a fixed number. I do not think the Court should be obliged to be unanimous; I would have the decision pronounced by the presiding member and say no more, thus leaving it to the members to arrive at their decision in any way they like.[11]

Roche agreed, suggesting a five-member court that made decisions by simple majority.[12]

Additionally, P.P. O'Donoghue proposed that the special criminal court should be established as 'a permanent institution rather than to give the Government an option which would be very likely to prove an embarrassment.'[13] The attorney general had also suggested that the court would be strengthened by the addition, as a member or as an advisor, of a practising barrister of at least seven years' standing, particularly in view of proposals to include provision for appeal, though the department of Justice foresaw problems ensuring the safety of practising civilian lawyers and damage to their private business. As an alternative, it suggested the appointment of 'a person of legal knowledge and experience (not necessarily an existing practitioner) as certified by the Attorney General'.[14]

It seemed to the department of Justice that establishing a special criminal court would be a straightforward undertaking, and not necessarily overly controversial. But as Roche explained to Muiris Ó Muimhneacháin,[15] the secretary of the department of the Taoiseach, 'a [special] court … although likely to prove a strong deterrent so far as political crimes of violence are concerned, will not suffice of itself to enable the authorities to

dum of 25 Oct. 1937, circulated to the Executive Council, 21 Dec. 1937. **10** Ibid., P.P. O'Donoghue to the attorney general, 8 Oct. 1937. **11** Ibid., parliamentary draftsman to Roche, quoted in memorandum for the executive council, 25 Oct. 1937. **12** D/J 42/37, Roche to P.P. O'Donoghue, 7 Oct. 1937. The minister for Justice accepted this view by 25 Oct. 1937. **13** D/T S.10454A, O'Donoghue to the attorney general, P. Lynch, 8 Oct. 1937, memorandum for the Executive Council, 25 Oct. 1937. **14** Ibid., attorney general to Roche, 14 Oct. 1937, memorandum for the executive council, 25 Oct. 1937. **15** (1902–1999) Born Tralee, Co. Kerry, secretary of the department of the Taoiseach 1937–1960 and governor of the Central Bank 1961–1969. Later wrote *Currency and central banking in Ireland*, 1922–60 (1975), and edited *Speeches and statements by Eamon de Valera*, 1917–73 (1980).

deal with all emergencies in the event of an organised anti-state campaign'.[16] A range of other issues required examination.

While the Treasonable Offences Act, 1925 provided for treason and cognate offences, in view of article 39 of the new constitution, it was unclear if that act could be re-enacted with amendments or if new legislation was needed. Regarding unlawful associations, Roche proposed re-enacting section 19(1) of article 2A. He believed that permitting members of unlawful associations to appeal a proscription to the high court could be included 'without impairing the effectiveness of the provision' and would make the legislation 'more palatable to the Dáil'. Additional powers, providing for the confiscation of funds and the closing of buildings, for instance, were also proposed. Provisions were also sought covering newspapers, printing and publishing. Additionally, a completely new law would be required to regulate the right 'to assemble peaceably and without arms' as prescribed by article 40(6)(1) ii of the constitution. Roche envisaged legislation covering seditious or armed assemblies, traffic nuisances, placing certain areas (Bodenstown, for example) out of bounds to the public at certain times, and allowing the Gardaí to declare any meeting to be unlawful if persons did not disperse when ordered to. Further, there was apparently no English law dealing with collections made for seditious ends.[17]

Article 2A also provided special interrogation, search and arrest powers. Most criticized was that of 72-hour detention where a refusal to answer questions could be penalized: 'this was a most useful power and extremely effective in dealing with organised crime against the State.' Roche argued, 'very full powers [of search and arrest] will require to be conferred on the police in connection with treasonable and kindred offences.' While he believed Gardaí should retain the power to question suspects and to require them to answer questions under penalty, Roche opposed using self-incriminating statements in evidence against suspects. Additionally, he proposed that chief superintendents be empowered to issue warrants 'if the case is one of great emergency and the interests of the state require immediate action.'[18]

Special attention was given to treasonable offences. P.P. O'Donoghue set out the basic provisions of the Treasonable Offences Act, 1925: its relationship to the 1922 constitution, the institutions of Saorstát Éireann,

16 D/T S.10454A, Roche to M. Ó Muimhneacháin, 4 Jan. 1938. In the short term, the special criminal court was to be considered by a cabinet sub-committee on 21 Jan. 1938, see D/T S.10496. 17 Sections 21, 22, 23, 26, 27 of the 1931 act should, it was proposed, be re-enacted and, perhaps, strengthened. 18 D/J D.42/37, Roche to Ó Muimhneacháin, 4 Jan. 1938.

and the 1937 constitution.[19] Although article 39 of Bunreacht na hÉireann was quite close to the 1925 definition of treason, he cautioned the punitive provisions of the 1925 Act would be difficult to adapt to apply to article 39. Although possible to adapt some provisions of the 1925 Act dealing specifically with treason, such a path was not favoured by attorney general's office: 'The offence of treason in its nature is intimately connected with the Constitution to which it refers and while the old Statute law is capable of adaptation there is a deliberate omission to import any part of the old Constitution in to the present one.' Section 1 (1),(3) of the 1925 Act could not 'with any degree of safety be applied to Article 39 of the Constitution,' O'Donoghue wrote. He further believed that new legislation was necessary to prescribe trial procedure and to regulate the punishment of treason under the new constitution. Section 3(1)(a) was also problematic, as it referred to the governor general and to ministers 'duly appointed under and in accordance with the [1922] Constitution'. Nevertheless, he concluded that section 1(2), which mentioned treason occurring outside the state, was constitutional. In view of article 50 of the new constitution and the Interpretation Acts, 1923–1937, and because they made no express reference to the 1922 constitution, he believed sections 4 to 10 were not inconsistent with the new constitution.

Proposals covering six specific areas, in addition to the special criminal court, were resubmitted to the cabinet on 6 May 1938.[20] These included amendments to the Treasonable Offences Act, 1925 and proposals to deal with unlawful associations by re-enacting sections 19, 21, 22 and 23 of article 2A. The department of Justice proposed a less extreme form of interrogation than existed under article 2A, based on section 1 of the Criminal Law and Procedure (Ireland) Act 1887, though it anticipated criticism because of its source. It also submitted that public meetings should be banned on public highways unless tolerated by the Gardaí. Regarding sedition, Roche wrote:

> At the present time there is no way of dealing with loose talk of a seditious character (which is frequently the source of more serious evils, more particularly when reproduced by the press), except by way of a very cumbersome procedure and the chances of convicting any person of sedition are almost negligible. The word 'sedition' has a historical significance in this country which is fatal to the prosecution. By the creation of a new summary offence and a

19 Ibid., P.P. O'Donoghue to the attorney general, P. Lynch, 8 Feb. 1938, in response to a query made by Roche on 29 Jan. 1938. 20 Ibid., note by the department of Justice: 'Legislation to replace Article 2A of the former Constitution.'

> provision to make newspaper reports prima facie evidence it is believed that the nuisance occasioned by loose talk of a dangerous character can be effectively abated, and the press made more careful as to the publicity it gives such matters.

Additionally, the department of Justice sought provisions covering collections for seditions purposes and dealing with foreign flags and foreign military uniforms.

The department of Justice recommended 'if this kind of legislation is to be undertaken at all it should be sufficiently wide in its scope to cover all the matters which have been found by experience to be a source of embarrassment to the authorities in periods when political crime is common'. It suggested incorporating these provisions into a single measure, the Public Order (Miscellaneous Provisions) Bill, which would be in addition to a separate Special Criminal Court Bill. Although the minister for Justice believed it was neither necessary nor desirable to introduce the proposed legislation at that time,[21] the cabinet granted formal drafting permission on 17 May 1938.[22]

Drafting continued into the early winter of 1938, even though many believed that the IRA was defunct. Against a background of growing world tension and improving Anglo-Irish relations, however, certain militant republicans were intent on giving the movement new direction. Mick Fitzpatrick replaced Tom Barry as chief of staff in January 1938, though that was only a short-term measure.[23] Deep divisions had resurfaced in the organization in the late 1930s because many members believed its leadership had become reluctant to take action.[24] Nonetheless, growing discontent within the IRA did not prevent the government releasing eleven prominent republicans convicted by the constitution tribunal on 14 December 1937. Those freed included Maurice Twomey who simply wished to retire from the organization.

The December releases preceded a period of significant progress in relations between Ireland and Britain. Beginning on 17 January 1938, meetings between the Irish and British governments led to the ending of the Economic War and, on 25 April 1938, to the signing of a new Anglo-Irish agreement.[25] Inevitably, there was no progress on partition, but the British and Irish dropped all punitive tariffs, the land annuities were discontinued, and the British agreed to hand the Treaty ports over to Ireland in return for a payment of £10 million. De Valera assured the Dáil that he

21 Ibid., 6 May 1938. 22 Cabinet minutes, G.C. 1/27. 23 Mac Eoin (ed.), *Survivors*, p. 398. 24 Bell, *The secret army*, p. 145. 25 R. Fisk, *In time of war: Ireland, Ulster and the price of neutrality* (1985), pp 39–47.

had made no secret deal, but added, 'it is far better for Britain, far more advantageous for Britain, to have a free Ireland by its side than an Ireland that would be unfriendly because of liberties which Britain denied'.[26] He later said that if war did come, 'our desire would be for neutrality as far as possible', though he believed that in the event of an invasion Ireland could expect British assistance.[27]

One result of improved diplomatic relations was the British government giving the Irish government access to its 'War Book' during the summer of 1938.[28] By 6 September 1938, the department of the Taoiseach explained that because of the unfolding European crisis, it was of the 'greatest urgency to have legislation and regulations in readiness to enable the Government to deal with a war situation.' De Valera proposed establishing a non-executive committee to identify the most critical areas of responsibility and to assign them to departments. The 'Committee on Emergency Measures' was drawn from the secretaries of the departments of Agriculture, Defence, External Affairs, Finance, Industry and Commerce, and the Taoiseach. It was required to prepare an 'Emergency Book of Instructions' detailing the steps to be taken by departments in the event of an emergency and to monitor the relative priority of problems. Executive work, so far as possible, would be done within the existing departmental framework. Initial priorities included the maintenance of supplies of food and other essential commodities and the regulation of external trade; censorship, counter-espionage, and the control of communications and publicity; coast watching; financial and monetary policy; control of transport; military measures; air raid precautions; protection of vulnerable points, such as Government Buildings and the Shannon hydro-electric station; alternative accommodation for government and staffs; safeguarding important documents; safeguarding important works of art, etc; legislation. The first three issues were regarded as being the most important.[29]

A drafting sub-committee of T.J. Coyne (of the department of Justice) and P.P. O'Donoghue prepared the first heads of legislation. They contended:

> the range of the effect and influence of hostilities carried out on a present day scale by a powerful nation which would include a part of our own island can hardly be exaggerated. It is inevitable that a war in which Great Britain is engaged must constitute a menace to our safety and integrity to a greater or lesser degree and make it

26 Quoted in T.C. Salmon, *Unneutral Ireland*, pp 98–9, Dáil Debates vol. 71 col. 32–48, 27 Apr. 1938. 27 Salmon, *Unneutral Ireland*, p. 99, Dáil Debates vol. 72 col. 696–703, 13 July 1938. 28 Salmon, *Unneutral Ireland*, p. 100. 29D/T S.10823, department of the Taoiseach memorandum, (initialled by P. Ó Cinnéide), circulated on 6 Sept. 1938.

> necessary for us to take extraordinary legislative steps for the safety of our people.[30]

The legislation contemplated was essentially based on proposals put forward in Britain in the Schuster Report of July 1937.[31] In the event of war, the government would deal with the emergency by means of delegated legislation, permitting 'the widest possible powers to enable the Government to deal with an emergency. These powers would be such that in some respects at any rate, the ordinary constitutional rights of the citizen might have to be abrogated during the period of the emergency.'[32]

Writing of Britain's experience, the legal historian R.J. Sharpe argued:

> The significant aspect of twentieth-century experience with emergency powers has been the use of statutes conferring broad powers to enact subordinate legislation. In other words, Parliament has not itself conferred defined powers of arrest and detention, but has delegated its very legislative capacity so that the executive has defined the limits of its own powers by statutory instrument or regulation.[33]

The proposed heads of legislation contained significant differences from the British scheme, however. The most obvious was 'in regard to the trial and punishment of offences ... [the British] don't even contemplate that juries will be perverse.'[34] This necessitated provision for the trial of civilians by courts martial if the ordinary courts were deemed inadequate, Coyne and O'Donoghue argued. They proposed courts martial with jurisdiction to try more serious offences and to impose sentences of penal servitude for life downwards in cases of murder and treason (where the death penalty would normally be imposed). But the Committee on Emergency Powers and, subsequently, the government rejected this. Therefore, an alternative scheme, based on ideas developed for the Special Criminal Court Bill and contained in article 2A, would be devised. Coyne and O'Donoghue also argued, in view of the constitution, that the bill should clearly recite all the 'more drastic powers' the government intended to exercise in the event of an emergency.[35]

Heads of legislation were circulated to the cabinet on 14 September 1938.[36] Of very serious concern at this early stage was whether article

30 R. Fanning, *The Irish department of Finance: 1922–1958* (1978), pp 308–9. 31 On the development and use of British emergency legislation see B. Simpson, *In the highest degree odious: detention in wartime Britain* (1992), pp 42–50 and C. Townshend, *Making the peace: public order and security in modern Britain* (1993), pp 112–31. 32 D/T S.10834B, explanatory memorandum, 6 Oct. 1938. 33 R.J. Sharpe, *The law of habeas corpus* (1989), p. 95. 34 D/T S.10834B, 6 Oct. 1938. 35 Ibid., note by Ó hÓgáin, 4 Jan. 1939 and explanatory memorandum, 6 Oct. 1938. 36 D/T S.10834A.

28.3.3 of the constitution could be satisfactorily relied upon if European war erupted but Ireland remained neutral. The 21 September 1938 draft heads continued:

> Having regard to the difficulties of interpretation involved by the words 'in time of war' contained in Article 28(3)3 of the Constitution it is proposed to preface the operative clauses of the Bill by a declaration to the following effect: 'Whereas war has broken out between certain European Powers which involves a threat to the State and whereas it is necessary and expedient that extraordinary powers should be conferred on the Government forthwith for the purpose of securing the public safety and the preservation of the State'.

But this question could not be explored adequately until drafting had progressed further.

On 20 September 1938, the cabinet authorized the drafting of a Defence of the State (Emergency Powers) Bill. The following day the attorney general was given revised heads and asked to draft the proposed bill. 'The matter is one of extreme urgency', explained Muiris Ó Muimhneacháin.[37]

The assistant parliamentary draftsman prepared a preliminary draft by 23 September 1938. The bill was divided into four parts: part 1 covered 'defence orders' (subordinate legislation) and dealt with the general and specific powers the government could exercise in the event of an emergency; part 2 provided for a special criminal court; part 3 dealt with treason and cognate offences; part 4 covered miscellaneous matters. P.P. O'Donoghue had opposed the inclusion of treason legislation in a temporary statute,[38] but the Committee on Emergency Measures overruled him in view of 'the rapid development of the crisis'.[39] Further indicating the anticipated scale and the rapid development of the crisis, were discussions on including provisions in the bill covering 'unlawful organisations' and permitting the searching and the closing of buildings, and the examination of records and bank accounts. The department of Justice wondered, though, if such provisions should be included in this legislation at all, and if it might be better to wait until a genuine need arose.[40]

The bill was quickly redrafted and ready for re-examination on 30 September 1938.[41] Section 1(1) gave the government a general power to

37 Ibid., Ó Muimhneacháin to the attorney general, 21 Sept. 1938. 38 D/T S.10834B, O'Donoghue to Ó hÓgáin, 24 Sept. 1938. 39 Ibid., meeting of the Committee on Emergency Measures, 26 Sept. 1938; explanatory memorandum, 6 Oct. 1938. 40 Ibid., note prepared by Roche, attached to Ó hÓgáin's memorandum of 7 Oct. 1938. See also D/T S.10845/1, 29 Sept. 1938, Roche to Ó Muimhneacháin. 41 G.C.2/14. 27 Sept.

make 'such provisions as are, in the opinion of the Government, necessary or expedient for securing the public safety, or for the preservation of the State or the provision of supplies and services essential to the life of the community.' The question of the judiciary determining if an emergency did genuinely endanger the safety of the state had been abandoned. As de Valera later explained: 'Would it be better to leave it to a court to decide that or to the representatives of the people? I am not sure that we would be able to express it in such particular terms that a court could be permitted to decide it. After all, conditions of this sort are conditions which are best known by the Government and best appreciated, perhaps, by the representatives of the people than by any court.'[42]

'Without prejudice to the generality' of section 1(1), section 1(2) also contained a more specific recitation of the powers the government could exercise by means of defence order:

> *(a)* provide that any person who contravenes or fails to comply with a defence order or an order, regulation, rule, bye-law, or instrument made or issued under a power conferred by a defence order shall be guilty of an offence triable summarily or on indictment;
>
> *(b)* authorise and provide for the apprehension of persons charged with or suspected of having committed any such offence as aforesaid;
>
> *(c)* authorise the infliction on persons convicted of any such offence as aforesaid of the following punishment, that is to say:–
>
> (i) in the case of a court of summary jurisdiction, a fine not exceeding one hundred pounds or, at the discretion of the Court, imprisonment for a term not exceeding six months or both such fine and such imprisonment, or
>
> (ii) in the case of conviction on indictment, a fine not exceeding five hundred pounds or, at the discretion of the Court, penal servitude for a term not exceeding ten years or imprisonment for a term not exceeding two years or both such fine and such penal servitude or imprisonment, and
>
> (iii) in any case, in addition to or in lieu of the punishment aforesaid, such forfeitures, disqualifications, and restrictions as may be authorised by a defence order;
>
> *(d)* authorise and provide for the detention of persons where such detention is, in the opinion of a Minister of State, necessary

1938, D/J D.42/37, Ó Muimhneacháin to Ruttledge, 30 Sept. 1938. 42 Dáil Debates vol. 77 col. 17, 2 Sept. 1939.

or expedient in the interests of the public safety or the preservation of the State;

(e) authorise and provide for the entering into and searching of any lands or premises in circumstances and by persons specified or indicated in such defence order;

(f) authorise and provide for the acquisition, taking possession, or control (either compulsorily or by agreement) by or on behalf of the State of any land or other property whatsoever and the payment in proper cases of compensation therefor;

(g) authorise and provide for the searching of persons in circumstances and by persons specified or indicated in such defence order

(h) authorise and provide for the censorship, restriction, control, or partial or complete suspension of communication by means of all or one or more of the services maintained or controlled by the Minister for Posts and Telegraphs or by any other means, whether public or private, specified or indicated in such defence order;

(i) make provision for preserving and safeguarding the secrecy of official documents and information and for controlling the publication of official information and for prohibiting the publication or spreading of subversive statements and propaganda;

(j) authorise and provide for the prohibition, restriction, or control of the entry or departure of persons into or out of the State and the movements of persons within the State;

(k) authorise and provide for the control, regulation, restriction, or prohibition of the import or of the export of particular kinds or classes of goods;

(l) authorise a Minister of State to buy and sell goods of a particular kind or class or to engage in any other form of trade in relation to goods of a particular kind or class, and make such provisions as may be requisite in relation to such buying, selling, or trading;

(m) authorise and provide for the regulation and control by or on behalf of the State of all or any essential supplies or services and, where the Government so thinks proper, the maintenance and provision of essential supplies by or on behalf of the State and the provision and operation of essential services by or on behalf of the State;

(n) authorise the Government or a Minister of State, whenever and so far as appears to them or him to be necessary for the purposes of such defence order, to suspend the operation of

> or to amend or apply (with or without modification) any enactment for the time being in force.

Emphasizing the overriding nature of these powers, the draft provided that 'Every order … shall have the force of law, and shall have effect, notwithstanding anything inconsistent therewith contained in any enactment other than this Act or in any instrument having effect by virtue of any enactment other than this Act.' A resolution passed within 21 days by either House of the Oireachtas could annul any order, 'but without prejudice to the validity of anything previously done under such order'. The legislation would operate retrospectively.

Part 2 covered special criminal courts, which could be established 'whenever and so often' as the government thought fit. The proposed courts would deal with treason and offences under acts specified in the schedule,[43] and any offence declared by government order to be a scheduled offence. Each court was to consist of an uneven number of members, not fewer than three, who would 'be appointed and be removable at will by the President acting on the advice of the Government'. The draft stipulated that each member be 'by reason of his training and experience … a fit and proper person' in the opinion of the President acting on the advice of the government and that at least one member of each court be a barrister or solicitor of not less than seven years' standing and qualified to practise in Ireland. Decisions were to be determined by simple majority, with only the majority decision being disclosed.[44] The rules of evidence and 'so far as practicable' and subject to the provisions of the bill, the practice and procedure applicable to the trial of a person on indictment in the central criminal court would apply to every trial by a special criminal court. Sentences and orders were to be carried out in a like manner to those of the central criminal court. There was also provision for appeal to the court of criminal appeal.

Persons charged with scheduled offences were to be sent or sent forward for trial by a special criminal court by district justices 'if the Attorney-General so requests'. In the case of a non-scheduled offence, 'a certificate by the Attorney-General in writing that he is of the opinion that the ordinary Courts are inadequate to secure the effective administration of justice' in relation to a particular trial, would be required before a special criminal court could try the offence.

43 The Explosive Substances Act, 1883; The Official Secrets Acts, 1911 and 1920; The Firearms Act, 1925; sections 4 to 10 of the Treasonable Offences Act, 1925; part 3 of this act. In addition, 'attempting or conspiring or inciting to commit any such scheduled offence shall itself be a scheduled offence for the said purposes.' 44 Additional technical matters covered sittings, procedure, authentication, punishments, oaths and recognisance.

Part 3 covered treason and treasonable offences and provided that treason would be tried in the same manner as murder, with the maximum punishment being death. It also dealt with the offences of encouraging, harbouring, or comforting persons engaged in committing or who have committed treason and of misprision of treason. Largely based on section 3 of the Treasonable Offences Act, 1925, offences against the state of a treasonable nature, though not amounting to treason, were also defined. These included attempting 'by force of arms or other violent means to overawe or intimidate in any way' the President, the government or any government minister, the Oireachtas or any Oireachtas member in relation to his functions as such member, or any lawful court or any judge or member of any such court with a view to influencing their or his actions. It also prohibited the establishment of pretended courts or courts martial, inciting members of the Garda or the army to desert or mutiny, or interfering with court witnesses.

Miscellaneous matters provided that any court could exclude the public from any portion of its proceedings and prohibit the publication or disclosure of any information regarding them when trying offences under the bill if satisfied 'that it is expedient in the interests of the public safety or the preservation of the State.'

P.P. O'Donoghue was more or less satisfied with the draft of 30 September 1938, though he had serious reservations about particular aspects of it. Rather significantly, he noted the special criminal courts would be an integral part of the Defence of the State (Emergency Provisions) Bill, drawing validity from article 28.3. Although he felt that a good case could be made in favour of deriving all powers in the bill from one article of the constitution, this was not necessarily the best course:

> Article 38(3) recognises as a normal constitutional organisation the establishment of special criminal courts in certain contingencies and, in my opinion, it would be most advisable to utilise the formula contained in Article 38(3) as a preface for the establishment of the Special Courts without any express mention of that Article.[45]

He believed it would be 'safer' if the bill provided that the government could establish special criminal courts whenever it was satisfied that the ordinary courts were inadequate to secure the effective administration of justice and the preservation of public peace, to better reflect the words of article 38.3.

The parliamentary draftsman disagreed: 'it is better to rely exclusively on the "time of war" proviso which justifies Part I of the Bill … as oth-

45 D/J D.42/37, P.P. O'Donoghue to M. Ó Muimhneacháin, 30 Sept. 1938.

erwise the Courts might become suspicious that the [government] were not sure of their ground in relying on "time of war" for the Bill as a whole.' He also believed that the treason and treasonable offences provisions would be best included in a permanent Treason and Treasonable Offences Bill, submitting that three separate bills should be drafted:

- An Emergency Powers Bill relating to a 'time of war'
- A Special Criminal Court Bill to operate whenever the government was satisfied that the ordinary courts were inadequate
- A Treason and Treasonable Offences Bill.

The first two would be temporary measures, to be activated in times of emergency, the third would be permanent.[46]

In light of these proposals, on 18 October 1938, the cabinet decided to detach parts 2 and 3 from the bill and ordered the drafting of a separate Special Criminal Court Bill as contemplated by article 38.3, in addition to separate Treasonable Offences and Unlawful Associations Bills.[47] Parts 1 and 4 of the Defence of the State (Emergency Powers) Bill would be redrafted.

Far more worrying for ministers and senior civil servants was that article 28.3.3 of the constitution, which provided that 'Nothing in this Constitution shall be invoked to invalidate any law enacted by the Oireachtas which is expressed to be for the purpose of securing the public safety and the preservation of the State in time of war or armed rebellion, or to nullify any act done or purporting to be done in the pursuance of any such law,' and thus permitted the most wide-ranging powers if Ireland became involved in a war, made no definite provision for the outbreak of war that affected but did not directly involve Ireland. A number of preambles to the Emergency Bill had been drawn up, but none satisfactorily resolved the issue. Eventually, de Valera requested that

> the question should now be examined further and that a suggestion should be made as to the most appropriate manner in which Article 28 (3,3°) of the Constitution could be amended for the purpose of removing any doubt that, notwithstanding the Constitution, the widest possible powers could be taken in the public interest during a war in which this country was not a belligerent but in which the nearness and character of the conflict necessitated emergency measures.[48]

46 D/T S.10834, 'Points on draft Bill', Arthur Matheson, no date, between 8 and 13 Oct. 1938. 47 G.C 2/17, 18 Oct. 1938. 48 D/T S.10834B, 20 Oct. 1938, referred to in a note by Ó Muimhneacháin to the attorney general.

The parliamentary draftsman wrote that the weakest aspect of article 28.3.3 was the presence of the term 'armed rebellion' after 'time of war', which, he believed, connoted something happening within the state and thus strongly suggested that the words 'time of war' 'refer only to a war in which our State is engaged as a belligerent, whether the actual fighting does or does not occur within our State.'[49] P.P. O'Donoghue and J.J. Hearne (of the department of Foreign Affairs) added that article 28.3.3, as it stood, conferred the widest powers in the case of Ireland becoming involved, as a belligerent, in a war, but warned, 'Article 28 3 3° cannot be relied upon ... with any degree of confidence to support extra-constitutional legislation, or action based on such legislation, during a national emergency arising out of a war ... in which Ireland is neutral.'[50] Alterations were immediately mooted. The attorney general had suggested amending the article by including a reference to war in a neighbouring state,[51] but the parliamentary draftsman cautioned:

> On a strict construction, Northern Ireland is the only territory neighbouring to ours; if a wider construction is adopted, difficulties arise at once – for instance, is France a neighbouring state, and would a Franco-Italian war be a war in a neighbouring State? It might even be argued that events at present taking place in Spain constitute an armed rebellion in a neighbouring State.[52]

He preferred Muiris Ó Muimhneacháin's suggestion of 20 October 1938 that would expand the term 'time of war' to include 'not only a war in which this State was a participant but also circumstances in which the vital interests and security of this country were threatened by an outbreak of war between other European Powers, including Great Britain.'[53]

At this early stage, it appeared to P.P. O'Donoghue and J.J. Hearne that the constitution could be amended in four ways:

- by the insertion of a new article in the same general terms as article 28.3.3° supporting legislation expressed to be for the purpose of the preservation of the state in a neutrality emergency
- by the insertion of a new subsection to that effect in article 28 itself

49 D/T S.11039, Matheson to the attorney general, 25 Oct. 1938. 50 Ibid., 'Form of amendment of the Constitution', memorandum by O'Donoghue and Hearne, 16 Nov. 1938. 51 Ibid., note by the attorney general, 21 Oct. 1938. 52 Matheson to the attorney general, 25 Oct. 1938. 53 D/T S.10834, Muiris Ó Muimhneacháin to the attorney general, 20 Oct. 1938.

- by the insertion of appropriate additional words in article 28.3.3°
- by a definition in a new subsection 4° of the expression 'time of war' now contained in article 28.3.3°.[54]

Manager of the emergency law drafting project, Sarsfield Ó hÓgáin,[55] preferred the third and fourth suggestions, believing the first two to be 'undesirable as creating the impression that the government were attempting to undermine Constitutional safeguards' and would require new and independent provisions in the constitution. He added it would be easier to justify an amendment if it related directly to the existing provisions of article 28.3.3. He had initially preferred the idea of further defining 'time of war' by the creation of article 28.3.4 and not grafting additional words to article 28.3.3.

Of particular concern was section 1 (1) of the draft emergency bill. While the need to rely on its general powers could not be gauged until an emergency had arisen, it could not be used unless article 28.3.3° applied. Additionally, the provision in section 1(2) permitting the 'acquisition, taking possession, or use (either compulsorily or by agreement) by or on behalf of the State of any land or other property whatsoever and the payment in proper cases of compensation therefor' would be in conflict with article 43. The section 1(2) provision permitting the government to suspend 'the operation of or amend or apply (with or without modification) any enactment for the time being in force or any instrument made under such enactment' would also be highly problematic as it would be in conflict with article 15.2.1°. The remainder of the subsection, though, could be employed without constitutional difficulties. A further source of anxiety was the retrospective nature of the bill, bringing it into conflict with article 15.5.

These constitutional concerns had to be balanced with the dangers that might confront the state. Ó hÓgáin argued that government inability to take any necessary action in an emergency would definitely cause embarrassment. The powers of section 1(1) of the Defence of the State (Emergency Powers) Bill were vital he believed, even if the state attempted to remain neutral in some future conflict:

54 Their suggested draft was: 'A national emergency arising out of a war in Europe in which Ireland is not engaged as a belligerent but which emergency is declared by Dáil Éireann (*or, alternatively*, both Houses of the Oireachtas) to threaten the vital interests of the Community.' Memorandum, 16 Nov. 1938. 55 Sarsfield Ó hÓgáin (1901–1989) BA and MA from UCD, he entered the civil service in 1923, beginning as an administrative officer in the department of Finance. He was an early private secretary to Ernest Blythe, later involved in emergency planning before and during the War, exchange control, and afterwards in administering Marshall Aid; he was also a director with Irish Steel. After retirement, he was appointed chairman of Irish Steel.

> It is impossible to foresee all the detailed powers which the Government might need to exercise in such an emergency, and even if it were possible to recite all such necessary powers there would be the danger that the statutory clauses might not give full effect to the Government's intentions to protect them sufficiently against attack in the Courts, and, consequently, a general overriding provision is a necessary safeguard.[56]

He admitted, though, 'there may be political considerations which would be directed against a proposal to amend the Constitution for such a purpose.'

There were other fundamental questions: who should determine whether a war genuinely threatened the 'vital interests and security' of the state. Matheson had argued that it was impracticable to leave such a decision to the courts and empowering the government was tantamount to allowing the executive suspend the constitution. He proposed that the Oireachtas should decide.[57]

When the constitution should be amended was also at issue. Article 51 provided that:

56 S. Ó hÓgáin to M. Ó Muimhneacháin 22 Nov. 1938. 57 The parliamentary draftsman to the attorney general, 25 Oct. 1938. Matheson suggested the deletion of the words 'and armed rebellion' from Article 28.3.3 and the addition of an extra paragraph as follows:

> '40. For the purpose of this section of this Article, a time of war shall be deemed to exist during the occurrence of any of the following events:–
> i. an armed rebellion against the organs of government established by this Constitution;
> ii. a war in which Ireland is involved as a belligerent (whether alone or with an ally or allies) against another State or other States;
> iii. a war between other States in which Ireland is not involved as a belligerent but which is declared by the Oireachtas so to affect the normal administration of government and the normal life of the community within the State that it is expedient that extra-constitutional measures should be adopted for the preservation of law and order and the continuance of essential supplies and services;
> iv. a civil war or armed rebellion in another State in respect of which such declaration as aforesaid is made by the Oireachtas.'

This proposal was regarded as 'verbose and complicated', and the Taoiseach later agreed in principle with Ó hÓgáin's recommendation of 22 Nov. 1938 (based on the earlier suggestion of O'Donoghue and Hearne). Ó hÓgáin to Ó Muimhneacháin, 29 Dec. 1938. Ó hÓgáin's proposal of 22 Nov. 1938: 'For the purpose of the foregoing subsection of this Article and for that purpose only, the expression 'time of war' shall be deemed to include a national emergency which (a) arises out of a war waged between European Powers in which this State is not a belligerent, (b) is declared by Dáil Éireann to threaten the vital interests of the State.

> Notwithstanding anything contained in Article 46 hereof any of the provisions of this Constitution, except the provisions of the said Article 46 and this Article, may, subject as hereinafter provided, be amended by the Oireachtas, whether by way of variation, addition or appeal, within a period of 3 years after the date on which the first President shall have entered upon his office.

It appeared, therefore, that the constitution could be altered without recourse to a referendum before 25 June 1941; afterwards, an amendment would have to be submitted to the people under articles 46 and 47. If no emergency was likely before 25 June 1941, Ó hÓgáin urged that the Dáil amend the constitution prior to then because 'a referendum would involve delay'. The rapid passage of an amendment and the enactment of emergency legislation were vital, he believed, in legalizing the Defence of the State (Emergency Powers) Order: 'Any material time lag would cause embarrassment to the Government. There is particularly the danger of Court action during the period between the issue of the Order and the passage of the covering legislation.' De Valera supported these arguments, but felt that the amendment should be introduced before a crisis developed, suggesting sometime during the first six months of 1939.[58]

On 7 December 1938 the attorney general was informed on behalf of the Taoiseach that the proposed amendment was to make 'it clear that nothing in the Constitution should be invoked to invalidate any law enacted by the Oireachtas for the purpose of securing the public safety and the preservation of the State in time of national emergency arising from a war in which the state is not a belligerent.'[59] The parliamentary draftsman took this as the Taoiseach's final view on the subject.[60] The 7 December draft proposed the addition of a new subsection to article 28.3:

> 4°.– For the purpose of the forgoing sub-section of this Article and for that purpose only, the expression 'time of war' shall be deemed to include a national emergency which (a) arises out of a war waged by or between European powers in which the State is not a belligerent, and (b) is declared by Dáil Éireann to threaten the vital interests of the State.

Of a more technical concern, Matheson was unsure how to appropriately title a bill amending the constitution.[61] Reliance on the old format –

58 D/T S.11039, Ó Muimhneacháin to Ó hÓgáin, 3 Dec. 1938. 59 Ibid., Ó Muimhneacháin to the attorney general, 7 Dec. 1938. 60 Ibid., Ó hÓgáin to Ó Muimhneacháin, 29 Dec. 1938. 61 Ibid., parliamentary draftsman to the attorney

Constitution (Amendment No. xx) Act – would lead to confusion; he suggested that numbering be abandoned altogether. Instead, he proposed specifically naming the article to be amended. This could be further distinguished by year, and where an article was amended twice in the same year '(No.2)' could be added. These bills would therefore be introduced as an 'Amendment of the Constitution (Article xx) Bill' – essentially the old format reversed.

Regarding the long title of a bill to amend the constitution, article 46.3 required that it state that it was 'An Act to amend the Constitution', but article 51 gave no such directions. Therefore, Matheson argued that the instructions provided in article 46 should be extended to article 51 and that these instructions should only be regarded as necessitating at a minimum the inclusion of these words – they did not prevent the inclusion of further appropriate indicative and informative words concerning the nature of the amendment.

Ó hÓgáin felt the legal-like lettered sub-paragraphing of the 7 December 1938 draft was not in harmony with the general scheme of the phraseology and layout of the constitution.[62] Given the constitution's permanent nature, he argued that to mention European powers or any geographical limitation was unwise. More substantially, he argued that the draft did not adequately define what constituted a national emergency, though, that could be tackled by further redrafting.[63]

M. Ó Muimhneacháin, S. Ó hÓgáin, P.P. O'Donoghue, J.J. Hearne and P. Ó Cinnéide of the Taoiseach's department met on 11 January 1939 to consider the extent to which article 28 should be amended to cover national emergencies, other than those arising out of an armed conflict involving the state.[64] Two possible amendments were considered. One, the wide amendment,[65] would allow for the declaration of a state of emer-

---

general, 22 Dec. 1938 (no reference was made to any proposed alternative wording). **62** Ibid., Ó hÓgáin to Ó Muimhneacháin, 29 Dec. 1928. **63** Ó hÓgáin suggested the following:

> 4. For the purpose of the next preceding sub-section in this section (and for no other purpose) the expression "time of war" shall be deemed to include a national emergency which arises out of a war in which the State is not a belligerent and threatens the vital interests of the State, provided that Dáil Éireann shall have first declared that such a national emergency exists.

64 Memorandum prepared following the conference, 15 Jan. 1939. **65** Draft A (redrafted following the 11 Jan. 1939 conference): Delete existing Article 28.3.30 and insert a new subsection as follows:

> 3. Nothing in this Constitution shall be invoked to invalidate, or to nullify any act done or purporting to be done in pursuance of, any law enacted by the Oireachtas which is expressed to be for the purpose of securing the public safety and the preservation of the State in time of national emergency, provided that the President shall have signified by a message addressed to Dáil

gency on the outbreak of war (whether or not Ireland was involved) or in the event of a social or economic crisis not related to actual warfare; the other, the narrow amendment,[66] would permit the declaration of a state of emergency only when war was being waged (whether or not Ireland was involved) in Europe, though the geographical limitation might be dropped.

The conference concluded that the wide amendment would cause political difficulties, particularly in light of the democratic principles of the constitution, though it considered a number of supporting arguments:[68]

(1) Salus populi suprema lex. If this maxim is accepted, the Government should be in a position to ask the legislature for the widest possible powers to protect the Community in time of national emergency.

(2) The recent international crisis showed that by reason of the limiting expression 'time of war' and 'armed rebellion' Article 28.3.3°. could not be relied upon for the purposes of a neutrality emergency. Even if additional words or definitions are now inserted it may subsequently be found that in some future crisis the Government and the Legislature are hampered in taking necessary measures for the protection of the State, because the particular emergency does not fall strictly within the phraseology used in the Article.

(3) A national emergency may arise from a cause not connected with a war or with armed rebellion inside the State. A Civil War or even wide social upheaval in Great Britain might cause conditions of great insecurity in this country. Internal disorder not amounting to armed rebellion or some great economic disaster might create a state of affairs amounting to a national

---

Éireann and Dáil Éireann shall thereupon have declared by resolution, that a national emergency exists which threatens the vital interests of the State.

66 Draft B (redrafted following the 11 Jan. 1939 conference): '40. For the purpose of the next preceding subsection of this section the expression "time of war" shall be deemed to include a national emergency arising from an armed conflict in which the State is not a participant provided that the President shall have signified by a message addressed to Dáil Éireann and Dáil Éireann shall thereupon have declared by resolution, that such armed conflict threatens the vital interests of the State'. 67 Hearne to Ó hÓgáin, 19 Jan. 1939. J.J. Hearne suggested that safeguards might be inserted into the wide amendment ensuring that no legislation could be enacted for the purposes of 'altering or purporting to alter the organic structure of the State as at present constituted' or destroying the existing Governmental and Constitutional make-up without being put to the people. 68 D/T S.11039, memorandum prepared by the department of the Taoiseach, 15 Jan. 1939.

emergency which the Government of the day might find it necessary to deal with by extra-Constitutional action.

(4) The declaration of a state of national emergency could, under the suggested amendment, be effected only by a resolution of Dáil Éireann and it must be assumed that the majority in the Dáil would not take that drastic step without due reason such as would be manifest to the community as a whole.

(5) The restricted form of amendment which deals with a situation in which Ireland is neutral while other Powers are at war cannot be introduced without provoking declarations and discussions as to our relations with Great Britain and the British Commonwealth in present-day international affairs. The wider amendment, therefore, holds an advantage in that it need not be related to the requirements of an existing situation but to general considerations and to the long view as to the special powers which the Government should ask from the legislature in any time of national emergency.

Arguments against it were also advanced:

(1) Power should not be given to Dáil Éireann or in effect to the majority party in Dáil Éireann to suspend the Constitution for an undefined national emergency.

(2) It is difficult to give convincing illustrations of the type of national emergency for which such drastic powers would be necessary, other than those which arise form a state of war (whether Ireland is or is not a participant) or from armed rebellion.

(3) Even if hypothetical examples could be cited, it is difficult to state with certainty that these hypothetical dangers could not be met by the exercise of executive powers within the framework of the present Constitution.

(4) A Government introducing an amendment of the kind suggested will certainly be faced with the criticism that it is seeking to obtain these extraordinary powers, not for the reasons indicated but for the purpose of weakening the democratic basis of the Constitution and for removing the protection which the Constitution gives to all citizens to organise peaceful resistance to unpopular or tyrannical Government.

(5) It will also be urged by opponents of the amendment that if there is such a radical defect in the existing Constitution as is represented by the proposers of the amendment it should have been foreseen and provided for when the original Constitution was being drafted.

Only Hearne favoured retaining the geographical qualification, while P.P. O'Donoghue believed that the use of either amendment depended on its 'legislative navigability' through the Dáil,[69] though the conference as a whole opposed the wider amendment.[70]

Although this issue was not resolved immediately, agreement was reached on other points. The conference favoured Dáil Éireann deciding whether a crisis threatened the vital interests of the state. It further agreed that 'armed conflict' be substituted for 'war' and 'participant' for 'belligerent' in sub-section (a) of the 7 December draft, being in line with internationally recognized usage, and allowing the government to deal with the effects of civil war or revolution in Britain. In the interests of giving a state of emergency 'greater solemnity', the conference suggested that the declaration of an emergency should be preceded by a message from the president. It also recommended that bills to amend the constitution should be given distinctive short titles, in this case 'The First Amendment of the Constitution'.

The principal outstanding question was that of defining what constituted an emergency and hence how article 28 should be amended. Three further alternative amendments (A,[71] B,[72] and C[73]) were drafted between 19 and 24 January.

---

69 Ibid., O'Donoghue to Ó hÓgáin, 17 Jan. 1939. 70 Ibid., Hearne to Ó hÓgáin, 19 Jan. 1939.

71 '28.3. Nothing in this Constitution shall be invoked to invalidate, or to nullify any act done or purporting to be done in pursuance of any law enacted by the Oireachtas which is expressed to be for the purpose of protecting and preserving the vital interests of the State and the public welfare in time of war or armed rebellion, or during a national emergency arising from an armed conflict in which the State is not a participant, or from any other cause whatsoever; provided that this sub-section of this Article shall not apply to laws enacted for the purposes of such national emergency unless the President shall have signified by a Message addressed to Dáil Éireann, and Dáil Éireann shall thereupon have declared by resolution, that a national emergency exists which involves a threat to the vital interests of the State.'

72 '28.4. Nothing in this Constitution shall be invoked to invalidate, or to nullify any act done or purporting to be done in pursuance of, any law enacted by the Oireachtas which is expressed to be for the purpose of protecting and preserving the vital interests of the State and the public welfare during a national emergency arising from an armed conflict in which the State is not a participant or from any other cause whatsoever, provided that the President shall have signified by a Message addressed to Dáil Éireann and Dáil Éireann shall thereupon have declared by resolution that a national emergency exists which involves a threat to the vital interests of the State'.

73 '28.4 For the purpose of the next preceding sub-section of this section the expression "time of war" shall be deemed to include a national emergency arising from an armed conflict in which the State is not a participant, provided that the President shall have signified by a Message addressed to Dáil Éireann, and

On 24 January 1939, the government provisionally accepted the amendment allowing for emergency powers to be taken when the vital interests of the state were threatened because of the existence of an armed conflict in which the state was not a participant. Therefore, an amendment along the lines of draft 'C' would be presented to the government. It further agreed that, following a message from the President, both Houses of the Oireachtas should make a resolution declaring that an outbreak of war threatened the state.[74]

Further redrafting was undertaken by Ó hÓgáin, Hearne and Ó Muimhneacháin between 31 January and 2 February 1939, and the parliamentary draftsman prepared two alternative drafts ('A'[75] and 'B'[76]) following a conference on 3 February 1939. The main decision reached was that any new words would be added to article 28.3.3 (there would be no paragraph 28.3.4) and consideration was to be given (as is seen in draft 'B') to whether the provision for a message from the President should be dropped. Both those points, it was hoped, would strengthen the argument that the amendment was a minor one, thus justifying an amendment under article 51 as opposed to article 46.[77] The parliamentary draftsman admitted that the latest drafts might not be wholly satisfactory, though by drawing on both alternatives, he believed that an acceptable draft could be delivered.[78]

Debate continued as to how, from a technical point of view, the amendment should be made and how much reliance should be placed on either

---

Dáil Éireann shall thereupon have declared by resolution, that a national emergency exists which involves a threat to the vital interests of the State.'

74 Memorandum by M. Ó Muimhneacháin for the attention of P. Ó Cinnéide and Ó hÓgáin, 25 Jan. 1939.

75 '1. The Constitution shall be and is hereby amended by inserting the following words at the end of, and as part of, subsection 30 of section 3 of Article 28, that is to say:–

In this subsection "war" includes an armed conflict in which the State is not a participant, but in respect of which –

(i) the President shall have signified, in a message under his hand and seal addressed to the Chairman of each House of the Oireachtas, and

(ii) each such House shall, after receipt of such message by its Chairman, have resolved, that such armed conflict creates a national emergency which threatens the vital interests of the State.'

76 '1. The Constitution shall be and is hereby amended by inserting the following words at the end of and as part of subsection 30 of section 3 of Article 28, that is to say:–

In this subsection "war" includes an armed conflict in which the State is not a participant and in respect of which each House of the Oireachtas has resolved that such armed conflict creates a national emergency affecting the vital interests of the State.'

77 Note by Ó hÓgáin, 6 Apr. 1939. 78 Matheson to Ó hÓgáin, 21 Mar. 1939.

article 46 or article 51. The parliamentary draftsman summarized his understanding of the situation thus:

- The experience of amendments to the constitution of Saorstát Éireann could not be relied on as a guide as neither article 46 nor 51 expressly permitted amendments to Bunreacht na hÉireann by means of 'ordinary legislation'.
- The provisions of article 46 were to be assumed to apply to amendments under article 51 except that a referendum was obligatory under article 46, but under article 51, the President decided whether the amendment should be submitted to the people.
- A reading of article 46 indicated that there had to be a 'proposal' for an amendment and that had to be embodied in a 'Bill', requiring the normal formalities when enacting a bill. It would have to be confirmed by referendum and would then signed into law by the President.
- Bills amending the constitution would have to adhere to normal legislative procedure and could differ only slightly from ordinary bills in matters of form and by not numbering them.
- Compliance with article 46 required that the bill be entitled 'An Act to Amend the Constitution', which would necessitate a long title, though there was no reason to prevent the inclusion of a recital in the 'proposal', followed by an enacting clause.
- The operative part of the bill could be divided into numbered sections, with the wordings of the main sections approximating those used in amendments of the constitution of the United States.
- The numbering of acts was not obligatory;[79] in keeping with the dignity of a constitutional amendment it should not be given a particular number (for instance No. 7 of 1939) but would be inserted at the beginning of the annual bound volume of Acts of the Oireachtas of the year in which it was enacted.[80]

Ó hÓgáin conceded this proposed amendment might be regarded as more than 'a mere drafting amendment', but argued that if the position were adopted that the constitution could be relied on to deal with a neutrality emergency, then the amendment was 'for the purpose of removing doubts and for safeguarding the legal position'.[81] He contended that for

79 See section 7(1) Interpretation Act, 1937. Acts of the Oireachtas may be cited 'by calendar year in which the Act so cited was passed and the consecutive number of such Act in such year.' 80 Matheson to Ó hÓgáin, 22 Mar. 1939. 81 Ó hÓgáin to Ó

three years, minor, verbal amendments could be made under article 51 by means of ordinary legislation, without any reference to article 46. He made this point in view of what de Valera had said to the Dáil in 1937 regarding minor amendments that would simply remove doubts or minor oversights and major amendments – ones of principle – that would be dealt with under article 46:

> There is a period of three years in which an opportunity will be given, if they are small matters of drafting and not Constitutional principles, to change them, if the President agrees.[82]

> Once the Constitution is adopted by the people as a whole it ought to be changed only by their direct and immediate will.[83]

> If some minor, some verbal, amendments reveal themselves as necessary during the period laid down, I think it is only right that it should be possible to make them easily … [The next Dáil] will be charged with … seeing that any minor amendments that are necessary to fill up any gaps that may not have been averted to, will be made.[84]

> I think that, once we have settled [the Constitution], it ought to be the people alone who would change it, and I think that the provision for a three year period ought not to be availed of lightly. I do not know what views would be taken of it under the powers to be given to the President under the Constitution but my own view would be that matters of principle certainly should go to the people, and that any other changes should be only changes of a minor character which were necessary in order to deal with some oversight.[85]

Regarding what position the courts might adopt, Ó hÓgáin wrote

> The amount of risk that exists in relation to an adverse Court decision on the question of national emergency arising from a war in which we are neutral is a matter of speculation. I doubt very much whether any court would hold that a European war in which Great Britain was engaged did not in fact create a national emergency for this country, whether or not we are participants.[86]

Muimhneacháin, 23 Mar. 1939. **82** Dáil Debates vol. 67 col. 47–8, 11 May 1937. **83** Dáil Debates col. 67 col. 1902, 4 June 1937. **84** Dáil Debates vol. 68 col. 285, 10 June 1937. **85** Dáil Debates vol. 68 col. 288–9. Deputy McDermot had proposed an eight year limit to Article 51 during the report stage. **86** Note by Ó hÓgáin to Ó Muimhneacháin, 23 Mar. 1939; Ó Muimhneacháin to the attorney general, Ó hÓgáin to the parliamentary draftsman, 25 Mar. 1939.

He proposed entitling the bill the 'Constitution (Amendment under Article 51) Bill, 1939' and giving it a long title of: 'A Bill entitled an Act to amend, by way of addition, the provisions of subsection 3° of section 3 of Article 28 of the Constitution.'

Matheson disagreed, 'I read Article 51 as a proviso qualifying Article 46; to my mind Article 46 is in force all the time, but during the three years it is qualified by Article 51 and must be read with that qualification. To my mind Article 51 cannot stand by itself.'[87]

Following an examination of these questions by P.P. O'Donoghue,[88] the government decided that the bill should be drafted in such a way to make it suitable for submission to referendum, as directed by article 46, but that the Oireachtas would pass the amendment only. Previous discussions on what form the bill should take were reappraised in view of three final questions to be settled by de Valera. Specifically, would the message from the president be retained or deleted, would the message from the Dáil and the Seanad be retained or deleted, and would 'armed conflict' be qualified by 'in Europe'.[89] A further draft was now prepared.[90]

---

87 D/T S.11039, To Ó hÓgáin, 23 Mar. 1939. 88 P.P. O'Donoghue to the attorney general, 31 Mar. 1939. 89 Note by Ó hÓgáin, 6 Apr. 1939, in light of the views of the attorney general's office, he suggested that the preamble should clearly explain which provision was being amended, as it stood, the bill was not be self explanatory and therefore unsuitable for submission to the people. 90 Draft (6 Apr. 1939) of a

BILL

entitled

AN ACT TO AMEND THE CONSTITUTION.

WHEREAS by virtue of Article 46 of the Constitution any provision of the Constitution may be amended in the manner provided by that Article:

AND WHEREAS it is provided by Article 51 of the Constitution that any of the provisions of the Constitution may, subject as thereinafter provided, be amended by the Oireachtas within a period of three years after the date on which the first President shall have entered upon his office:

AND WHEREAS the first President entered upon his office on the 25th day of June, 1938:

AND WHEREAS subsection 3o of Article 28 of the Constitution is as follows:–

'3o. Nothing in this Constitution shall be invoked to invalidate any law enacted by the Oireachtas which is expressed to be for the purpose of securing the public safety and the preservation of the State in time of war or armed rebellion, or to nullify any act done or purporting to be done in the pursuance of any such law.'

AND WHEREAS it is proposed that the Constitution be amended by inserting the following words at the end of and as part of subsection 3o of section 3 of Article 28, that is to say:–

'In this subsection war includes an armed conflict in which the State is not a participant but in respect of which each House of the Oireachtas shall have resolved

The wording of the 6 April 1939 draft differed somewhat from previous drafts but was deemed to include all matters agreed to.[91] The government finally felt that the work had almost reached a conclusion and asked that the draft be circulated for final consideration.[92] The Taoiseach approved the proposed amendment, though he requested that the term 'war' be replaced by 'time of war',[93] with the addition of the words 'time of war includes a time of armed conflict' though the precise wording would be left to Matheson.[94] P.P. O'Donoghue cautioned that only 'war' should be extended, posing the following question: 'would an outbreak in the Six Counties constitute a "time of war" or a "time of armed rebellion".'[95] Similarly, Matheson expressed concern at the difficulties involved in extending 'time of war' and not simply 'war', arguing that the word 'time' in the phrase 'in time of war or armed rebellion' governed both 'war' and 'armed rebellion', 'time of war' was part of a larger expression and it was wrong to define them as if they stood alone.[96] These concerns were ignored. The finalized amendment was an addition of words to article 28.3.3:

> In this subsection 'time of war' includes a time when there is taking place an armed conflict in which the State is not a participant but in respect of which each House of the Oireachtas shall have resolved that, arising out of such armed conflict, a national emergency exists affecting the vital interests of the State.

---

that, arising out of such armed conflict, a national emergency exists affecting the vital interests of the State.'

BE IT THEREFORE ENACTED by the Oireachtas as follows:–

1.– Upon the due promulgation of this Act as law the said proposed amendment of the Constitution shall forthwith become and be effective and the following words, that is to say:–

'In this subsection war includes an armed conflict in which the State is not a participant but in respect of which each House of the Oireachtas shall have resolved that, arising out of such armed conflict, a national emergency exists affecting the vital interests of the State.'

shall be inserted at the end of and as part of subsection 30 of section 3 of Article 28 of the Constitution.

2.– (1) The amendment of the Constitution effected by this Act shall be known as and may for all purposes be referred to as the First Amendment to the Constitution.

(2) This Act may be cited as the First Amendment of the Constitution Act, 1939.

91 Ó hÓgáin to P.P. O'Donoghue, 17 Apr. 1939. **92** Cabinet Minutes G.C.2/63, 14 Apr. 1939. **93** Note by Ó Muimhneacháin, 4 May 1939. **94** Memorandum by Ó Muimhneacháin, 10 May 1939. **95** P.P. O'Donoghue to the attorney general, 8 May 1939. **96** Matheson to the attorney general, 8 May 1939.

The Taoiseach gave final approval of the draft bill on 10 May 1939, and the amendment was filed away until an emergency arose.

The Defence of the State (Emergency Powers) Bill was redrafted in November[97] and again in December,[98] its provisions drawn from parts 1 and 4 of the 30 September 1938 draft. Although it had not been possible to finalize the recital or the long title until the constitution amendment had been settled, Ó hÓgáin, Matheson and Gerald McCarthy[99] favoured re-titling the bill the Emergency Powers Bill and replacing the term 'Defence Order' by 'Emergency Powers Order', thus dispensing with references to the defence or preservation of the state.[1]

Section 1 now covered a number of definitions, though section 2(2) came verbatim from the September draft. The latest draft provided for the devolution of powers in emergency orders to specified persons, subject to various conditions. Arthur Matheson added the words 'to make provision for the maintenance of law and order' to the bill's long title, contending that they were necessary to cover situations not directly related to public safety or the preservation of the state but which should be included to deal with civil commotion or disturbance.[2]

The list of specific powers in section 2(2) was also shortly rearranged, with the addition of provisions covering the compulsory acquisition, control and restriction of currency (though not Irish currency), bills, gold, securities, etc.; control of and restriction in dealings in these, and the control and restriction of capital issues; the regulation and control of air and sea navigation; restrictions on the transfer, mortgaging and registration of ships and aircraft.[3] Further, the powers of search in section 2(2) were extended to include vehicles, ships and aircraft, and the powers to arrest without warrant were increased to include persons suspected of being about to commit an offence.

Section 5 defined offences, the mode of prosecution and appropriate punishments. Initially, these had been included in section 2(2), but it was felt more appropriate to place them elsewhere in the bill. The date on which the Emergency Powers Order would be promulgated had been left

97 The Defence of the State Bill was redrafted by 4 Nov. 1938. D/T S.10834B, The parliamentary draftsman to the attorney general, 4 Nov. 1938, Memorandum by Ó hÓgáin, 8 Apr. 1939. 98 D/T S.10834B, Matheson to Ó hÓgáin, 31 Dec. 1938. 99 Gerald McCarthy, called to the Bar 1910, served with the British army 1914–8, the Irish army 1922–3 (judge advocate general's office), became assistant parliamentary draftsman in 1925, parliamentary draftsman in 1943, and director of the Statute Law Reform Commission in 1951. He retired in 1958 and died in 1961. 1 Note by Ó hÓgáin, 22 Dec. 1938. 2 D/T S.10834B, Ó hÓgáin to Ó Muimhneacháin, 4 Jan. 1939, though this was shortly amended to 'maintenance of public order'. 3 Section 2(2)(d), (e) and (f) respectively in the enacted bill.

blank – the date of the crisis could not be predicted. The legislation would be temporary, lasting 12 months.[4]

By now, though, drafting work was more or less complete, and Ó hÓgáin concluded that the recital in section 2(2) was comprehensive in so far as it covered the most important provisions made in the Emergency Powers Order, though in no way would it preclude the government from undertaking measures not specifically mentioned. Ó hÓgáin recommended that the draft be circulated to government departments and their views sought.

Most critical of the bill was the department of Justice. Stephen Roche believed that the provision permitting Emergency Powers Orders to amend or to suspend legislation was too wide, giving the government power, in effect, to 'over-ride statute law at its pleasure.' He counselled that the offending subsection be closely re-examined: 'if it *can* safely be cut down then it should be cut down – there is no sense in cutting it down *after* a public debate if it can be cut down now.'[5] This was not a new concern, having been previously raised by the Committee on Emergency Measures, which had suggested that the paragraph be prefaced with the words 'for the purpose of an Emergency'. But both Matheson and Ó hÓgáin felt that such a proposition could only have 'an unduly hampering effect'. Ó hÓgáin cautioned that if the provision were restricted 'its value in time of crisis would be greatly reduced. The Government must, it is submitted, be relied upon to administer the provision in a due and proper manner, only using the power to amend etc. when the public safety or the preservation of the State is clearly involved in time of national emergency.'[6]

The department of Foreign Affairs suggested the government should state clearly its position on Irish citizens enlisting in foreign armies, in view of the proposed policy of neutrality. It also felt consideration could be given to how espionage and anarchistic activities might be dealt with.[7] Other matters such as compensation for land or property compulsorily acquired or commandeered, abrogation of contracts made impossible by the emergency, and industrial conscription might be considered later.[8]

By 8 April 1939, the drafting work was largely completed, though the long title and preamble would remain incomplete until the nature of the emergency was known, and the drafting committee was clear about how the constitution would be amended.[9] The Committee on Emergency Measures was satisfied that the draft bill would suffice in all eventualities,

4 D/T S.10834B, mentioned by Ó hÓgáin in correspondence with Ó Muimhneacháin, 20 Jan. 1939. 5 D/T S.10834, Roche to Ó Muimhneacháin, 24 Feb. 1939, Roche's emphasis. 6 D/T S.10834, Ó hÓgáin to Ó Muimhneacháin, 8 Apr. 1939. 7 Ibid., J.P. Walshe to Ó Muimhneacháin, 31 Jan. 1939. 8 Ibid., memorandum by Ó hÓgáin, 8 Apr. 1939. 9 Ibid., Ó hÓgáin to Ó Muimhneacháin, 8 Apr. 1939.

at least in the initial stages of an emergency.[10] The government accepted the final draft bill on 24 April 1939.

In tandem with the drafting of emergency legislation was the preparation of the Defence of the State (Emergency Powers) Order (later the Emergency Powers Order). It was to be promulgated on the outbreak of war and would give specific effect to the Emergency Powers Act. Additional orders would be made after the legislation came into force and as circumstances dictated. Although being laid before the Oireachtas, TDs and Senators could not scrutinize or seek amendments to orders as they would legislation, and unless a majority in either the Dáil or Seanad voted to annul an order, it became effective without a vote. Very few were even debated and none was annulled. Speaking generally, de Valera later explained:

> there is no intention on the part of the Government to use those powers in such an arbitrary way. If at any time I get from responsible leaders of Parties any representations that such Orders should be considered by the Dáil—that the Dáil should be summoned in order to give an opportunity for the Dáil to discuss them— in so far as that is at all possible it will be done. The Government is prepared to meet any reasonable demands that may be made by any members of the House, but, as you will all understand, we have a very heavy burden of responsibility placed upon us. Problems of all types will have to be solved, and solved without delay.[11]

A preliminary draft order[12] was prepared by 18 September 1938 and communicated to departments on 20 September. Their views and suggestions *vis à vis* amendments, additions, deletions, etc. were sought by 24 September in view of the 'utmost urgency' of the situation.[13] In anticipation of further orders and subsidiary regulations, departments were asked to examine matters directly pertaining to their areas of responsibility. As Muiris Ó Muimhneacháin later explained to the secretary of the department of Local Government and Public Health, J. Hurson, 'the present draft order may not cover all contingencies likely to arise if an acute emergency situation was prolonged [... though] we do not want to include powers that appear to be unnecessary for immediate emergency purposes.'[14]

The department of Justice suggested that specific attention be paid to the form that future orders might take, proposing that:

10 Ibid., note by the department of the Taoiseach, 11 Apr. 1939. 11 Dáil Debates vol. 77 col. 6–7, 2 Sept. 1939. 12 Based on the Committee of Imperial Defence draft 1324/b. 13 D/T S.10845/1, note by Muiris Ó Muimhneacháin. 14 D/T S.10834B, 19 Dec. 1938.

- all orders be identical in form, and that that form be as simple as possible, with a standard clause to the effect that the order was made pursuant to the Defence of the State (Emergency Powers) Act and that the words in the order had the same meaning as those in the act
- orders be given consecutive identification numbers to facilitate the creation of a separate series of orders (as distinct from ordinary peace time orders) to be published immediately in the *Iris Oifigiúil*
- that a regular system be instituted giving the government (or a committee thereof) an opportunity to examine at least the most important orders before being published.

Roche maintained that those steps could be easily and quickly implemented, believing that the government should make the most important orders, securing 'uniformity, consultation … and a greater sense of authority.' He added that the 'whole arrangement and phraseology of the Order' should be revised with a view 'not so much to its improvement as a piece of drafting, but to making its source of origin less obvious.'[15] Work on the order was finalized between 14 and 21 April 1939.[16]

The Emergency Powers Order, 1939 was divided into 11 parts covering definitions; restricting movements and activities (including internment under article 6); sabotage, interference, misrepresentation and obstruction; control of communications; safeguarding information; essential supplies and services (compulsory cultivation of land under article 33, carrying on of trade by a minister under article 36, compulsory acquisition of land under article 38); public safety (curfew under article 47, censorship of films under article 52, and a temporary police force under article 54); ships and aircraft (detaining ships and aircraft under article 55); transport; special powers (arrest and search under article 74, power to obtain information under article 78), miscellaneous (power to dissolve local authorities under article 81).

As war became an ever-greater prospect, certain elements in the IRA again began to consider the possibility of renewed action. Throughout 1920s and 1930s the IRA had, as the historian J. Bowyer Bell argued, 'drifted along in the wake of events, pulling small stunts and talking of a future Armageddon'.[17] As the 1940s approached, pessimism pervaded the organization's ranks. By April 1938, the IRA leadership faced an organization eager for action. In an ambitious and essentially desperate move,

15 D/T S.10845/1, 29 Sept. 1938, Roche to Ó Muimhneacháin. 16 G.C.2/65, 21 Apr. 1939. 17 Bell, *The secret army*, p. 152.

Seán Russell proposed using a plan devised during the Civil War to bomb key British industries and essential services, in addition to attacking symbols of imperialism. He believed that the British government could be forced to sue for peace and leave Northern Ireland. Although leading to another split in the organization, Russell became chief of staff and the IRA was on a war footing by November 1938. On 15 January 1939, the organization posted proclamations throughout the country calling for public support for its campaign to remove the British from the North.[18]

Although IRA units in Britain were isolated, poorly prepared and ill-equipped,[19] the bombing campaign began on 16 January 1939 with explosions on electrical lines and at power stations.[20] There were further explosions on 4 February 1939 at underground railway-stations. That pattern continued for several months. In April, Russell went to America seeking material and moral support for a revolution 'to take over the whole of Ireland by force', once a European war provided the necessary opportunity.[21]

The campaign was not without civilian casualties. The most serious incident occurred on 25 August 1939 when a bomb in Coventry killed five people. Two IRA members were later hanged for the attack. The British responded to the campaign with the Prevention of Violence (Temporary Provisions) Act, 1939, which empowered the authorities to expel or restrict persons from the United Kingdom.[22] Heavy police pressure on easily identifiable IRA volunteers saw the campaign fail by the autumn of 1939.

Against the background of IRA preparations for a campaign in England and the growing likelihood of European war, draft legislation covering treasonable offences, special criminal courts, and anti-social organizations was completed by 4 November 1938.[23]

The draft Treasonable Offences Bill was taken almost verbatim from Part 3 of the 30 September 1938 draft of the Defence of the State Bill and would repeal sections 1 to 3 of the Treasonable Offences Act, 1925.

The draft Special Criminal Court Bill differed somewhat from part 2 of the Defence of the State Bill. It provided that a special criminal court would come into operation as soon as the bill was enacted and that additional courts could be established and abolished as the government saw fit. Additionally, whenever the government was 'satisfied that the ordi-

18 Ibid., pp 145–63. 19 Cronin, *The McGarrity papers*, p. 167. 20 *The Times*, 18 Jan. 1939. 21 *New York Times*, 16 Aug. 1939, Bell, *The secret army*, p. 159. In Russell's absence, Stephen Hayes took over as chief of staff. 22 See O. Lomas, 'The executive and the anti-terrorist law of 1939', [1980] Public Law, pp 16–33. 23 D/T S.10454A. A bill regulating the constitutional right of public meetings had been contemplated, but as many of its provisions were covered by section 11 of the Anti-Social Organizations Bill there was little urgency in completing it. The Street Collections Bill had not been completely drafted at this stage. Draft general observations, December 1938.

nary courts are inadequate to secure the effective administration of justice and the preservation of public peace and order' regarding offences of 'any particular class or kind or under any particular enactment', it could, by order, declare them to be scheduled offences. Otherwise, as regards member qualifications, removing members, rules of evidence, procedure, punishments and appeal, both bills were essentially the same. Similar requirements regarding the transfer of trials of scheduled and non-scheduled offences to the special criminal court were also proposed.

The Anti-Social Organisations Bill[24] defined an 'antisocial organisation' as one that

> (a) engages in, promotes, encourages, or advocates the commission of treason or any activity of a treasonable nature, or
> (b) advocates, encourages, or attempts the procuring by force, violence, or other unconstitutional means an alteration of the Constitution, or
> (c) raises or maintains or attempts to raise or maintain a military or armed force in contravention of the Constitution or without constitutional authority, or
> (d) engages in, promotes, encourages, or advocates the commission of any criminal offence or the obstruction of or interference with the administration of justice or the enforcement of the law, or
> (e) engages in, promotes, encourages, or advocates the attainment of any particular object, lawful or unlawful, by violent, criminal, or other unlawful means, or
> (f) engages in, promotes, or encourages the stirring up of political, religious, racial, or class hatred or antagonism, or
> (g) promotes, encourages, or advocates the non-payment of moneys payable to the Central Fund or any other public fund or the non-payment of local taxation.

The government could make a 'suppression order' 'if and whenever … of opinion that any particular organisation is an antisocial organisation.' The draft also provided that 'Whenever and so long as a suppression order is in force, it shall not be lawful for any person, after the publication of such

24 Section 1 defined the word 'organisation' to include 'associations, unions, and other organisations of whatsoever nature or kind', and 'incriminating document' to mean 'a document of whatsoever date, or bearing no date, issued by or emanating from an organisation in respect of which a suppression order is in force or appearing to be so issued or so to emanate or purporting to aid or abet any such organisation or purporting or appearing otherwise to relate to or be connected with any such organisation.'

order in the *Iris Oifigiúil*, to be a member of the organisation to which such order relates.' A suppressed organization's property was to be forfeited to the minister for Justice, to dispose of as he saw fit. Members of a suppressed organization were, however, entitled to apply to the high court for a 'declaration of legality' for their organization. If a final declaration of legality was obtained, all detainees were to be released and all property returned. While awaiting the outcome of such an application, however, persons charged with membership of a 'suppressed organisation' could be detained. Any Garda could arrest without warrant any person whom he believed or suspected was a member of a 'suppressed organisation'.

The possession of incriminating documents was prohibited. Proof to the 'satisfaction of the court' that an incriminating document issued by or emanating from a 'suppressed organisation' was found in the possession of a person 'shall, without more, be evidence until the contrary is proved that such person was a member of the said organisation at the time alleged in the said charge.'

The draft also prohibited printing, publishing or distributing documents by or on behalf of suppressed organizations. It also prohibited holding meetings by or on behalf of or in support of suppressed organizations. A district justice would be empowered to issue search warrants if satisfied by information given on oath by a Garda not below the rank of inspector that there was reasonable ground for believing that an offence under the bill was committed and that relevant evidence was to be found in any premises or place specified in such information. Search warrants would last for one month and would permit named Gardaí to seize anything believed to be evidence of the commission of an offence under the bill, and to demand the name and address of persons found on the premises.

Roche suggested that the attorney general's office and his department present separate lists of observations to the cabinet on the draft bills before fresh instructions were transmitted to the parliamentary draftsman. He explained in his draft 'General Observations' on the draft unlawful associations and special criminal court legislation that 'having regard to their nature, importance and difficulty, and the desirability of giving the Government a proper opportunity of deciding between the various possible points of view, it was though desirable to adopt a somewhat unusual procedure. The Parliamentary Draftsman agreed … to prepare preliminary drafts of these two Bills, without detailed instructions.' Although it would have been possible to resolve disagreements between both offices before submission, he wrote: 'there is a positive advantage in letting the Government see both sides of any really important point'.[25]

25 D/T S.10454B, 30 Dec. 1938, Roche to P.P. O'Donoghue.

Among the main differences between the proposed special criminal court and the constitution tribunal was that the latter had absolute discretion as regards penalties, the special criminal court would be restricted to imposing penalties available under the ordinary law. More importantly, convictions and sentences could be appealed to the court of criminal appeal, there was no attempt to prevent certiorari, and the normal rules of evidence would apply. Sentences of the new court would not carry disqualifications from public employment or lead to the forfeiture of state pensions. Both the attorney general's office and the department of Justice supported this last difference.

Further, the constitution tribunal had miscellaneous additional powers: it could close premises and declare periodicals to be seditious. Investing special criminal courts with powers other than that of trying offences would have been constitutionally impossible, though Roche had clearly given some time to this idea:

> The logical end of this line of thought [if constitutionally possible] would be to regard the Court as a permanent body of high authority charged generally with the duty of preserving the State from internal disruption – a Committee of Public Safety second in importance only to the Government itself. Under such a scheme emergency powers which have formerly been vested in Ministers, Courts, and police would be concentrated in the hands of the Special Court and it would perhaps be less difficult to induce the Oireachtas and the public to view the existence of such powers without apprehension if the body entrusted with such powers had the full status of a permanent Court, independent of the Executive.[26]

He felt that the additional powers exercised by the constitution tribunal could be transferred to the Gardaí.

While the constitution restricted the special criminal court to trying offences, its character was not yet determined. Roche sought a court with 'a high status and extensive powers' that 'should be respected and even feared'. 'Experience has shown', he argued, 'that there is no danger of giving the court the most extensive powers [or] to apprehend undue severity.' He believed that cases coming before the special criminal court (which in normal conditions might be rather trivial) would be viewed very seriously, persons would be more inclined to respect it, defend themselves or plead guilty in the hope of clemency 'if they feel that their fate is entirely in the hands of the Court.' In any case, the government would have powers of pardon and remission.[27]

26 Ibid., draft 'General Observations', December 1938. 27 D/J 93/2/8, observations by

Allied to this were the issues of court procedure and appeal. Roche believed these questions remained as they did in 1931: 'It was felt then as is felt now that to ask the Special Court to do its work effectively and at the same time to do it with the same attention to forms of procedure and the law of evidence as is required of an ordinary court is to ask an impossibility.' Essentially, the constitution tribunal was established in 1931 because the ordinary courts were unable to deal with the IRA, when the state handed matters over to 'a Commission chosen not as lawyers but as men of known courage, patriotism, and ability, who were not fettered by any legal rules, and who constituted in reality, not a Court but a Committee of Public Safety'. Any attempt to regulate such a court to ordinary rules of procedure or evidence would 'lessen its effectiveness'.[28]

A rather different view was taken by the attorney general's office. It believed that securing 'a large measure of respect' for the special criminal court was more important than overawing the public: 'The view has been largely shared in this office that very few, if any, of the late Tribunal's decisions on questions of fact would have been reversed by the court of criminal appeal. The absence, however, of such appeal was frequently urged as criticism of the late system.' It feared that the 'fiercer and more drastic' the legislation the greater the likelihood of an unfavourable review by the courts on constitutional grounds: 'The danger must never be lost sight of that the Supreme Court might be tempted to invoke principles of natural justice, as they would be called, as animating the judicial provisions in the Constitution.' The attorney general's office added that it could find no case where ordinary law punishments were exceeded by the constitution tribunal, the most serious offences were punished by long terms of penal servitude, though in practice two years' imprisonment was found to be the most practical and appropriate maximum punishment.[29]

Additionally, the department of Justice opposed scheduling offences: 'It is impossible to say in advance that *all* offences of a certain kind are unfit for trial by the ordinary courts.'[30] It proposed that each case be considered on 'its merits'. It also felt that provision for more than one special criminal court 'tends to give the … unduly pessimistic … impression of a great number of courts operating separately throughout the country', particularly as a single tribunal dealt with all matters occurring between 1931 and 1937.

The draft courts bill permitted the government to remove members 'at will', which gave 'an obvious incentive for criticism', the department of Justice argued. It proposed a number of possible safeguards, including

the office of the minister for Justice and comments by attorney general's office, 19 Jan. 1939. **28** Ibid. **29** Ibid. **30** Ibid.

provision for the appointment of members for a minimum of five years or if a high court judge were appointed, that dismissals would have to be approved by him. The department also suggested that all new appointees to the high court should be obliged to act as president of the special criminal court if the need arose.[31] The attorney general's office agreed that providing for a judge to sit on the court would greatly strengthen it.

Under this draft, normal sentencing regulations would apply, unless the government employed different general regulations. The department of Justice believed there should be provision for additional regulations in political cases, allowing for greater flexibility as regards special detention and treatment, conditional releases, etc. It also felt that the draft bill was 'unduly lenient' as regards a refusal to plead, particularly as this was a case of 'a State endeavouring to defend itself against grave internal dangers' arguing it was reasonable to compel the accused to answer any relevant questions that might be addressed to him.

The department of Justice made no recommendation for internment. Although Roche admitted there was a strong case for it, he cautioned:

> It is a very arbitrary power and apart from the question of principle there are practical difficulties in interning any large number of people without undue hardship to the individuals and at the same time without giving them opportunities as good as, or better than, they would have outside to make their plans for the future. Despite its advantages, internment has never been looked upon with favour by this department and it is not now proposed, although the Government may be forced to use it at a later stage if events take an unfavourable course.

The Public Safety (Emergency Powers) Act, 1926 remained on the statute book.

Also omitted were special police powers of interrogation: powers to compel detainees to divulge information regarding the commission of offences, and to account for their movements during a specific period. Roche explained that under article 2A these powers were regularly employed to detain suspects for up to three days, 'nominally for interrogation', from whom no information or cooperation would ever be gained, permitting Gardaí to check their activities at critical times. Doubtless, very strong arguments could be made in favour of retaining such powers, and while safeguards could be drawn up to protect those divulging information, Roche concluded:

31 There was a vacancy in the high court at that time and the department wondered if this proposal should be attempted even before the bill became law

> No such assurance can, however, be wholly satisfactory: the admission made by the person under interrogation may not be used, as such, against him in subsequent criminal proceedings, but the State knows the facts so admitted and that knowledge may, and very probably will, be brought to bear against the witness in some indirect manner.[32]

Additionally, in place of remanding suspected members of unlawful organizations before peace commissioners until the next convenient sitting of the district court, as would normally happen after an arrest, the department recommended holding them for a month, without recourse to legal aid, 'quite frankly, for the purpose of making things unpleasant for members of such organisations and as some sort of partial substitute for arbitrary internment', until cases could be evaluated by the attorney general, who would either order them released or charged and remanded for trial before the special criminal court.[33] Roche explained, 'The department of Justice would prefer to keep District Justices out of these matters as far as is reasonably possible and that remark applies even more forcibly to Peace Commissioners.'

Regarding the Anti-Social Organisations Bill, Roche described its short title as being rather 'mild and philosophical', in view of the 'violent and lawless nature of the associations concerned.' He also suggested that a person seeking a declaration of legality should be obliged to give oral testimony and to be open to cross-examination.[34]

The department of Justice believed that forfeiting IRA property was, from a practical point of view, not a viable option. The organization owned no property, but normally rented premises from members or sympathizers or by means of subscription. The process of seizing property, as proposed by the draft bill, would be awkward because of the difficulty involved in establishing ownership. Although the department believed the provision would do no genuine harm, it argued that it would add to the bulk of the bill and lead to 'useless debate', giving the Labour Party 'a pretence for feigning alarm'. Because of constitutional restrictions on the special criminal court, it proposed making the provision of premises for use by unlawful associations an offence, with punishment including the closing of the building. Alternatively, chief-superintendents could be empowered to close buildings where Gardaí found incriminating documents.

32 D/T S.10454B, draft 'General Observations', Dec. 1938. 33 This course of action was described as 'most practicable' by the attorney general's office, though it felt that seven days might be a more appropriate length of detention. 34 The attorney general agreed to this.

The department also suggested inserting a clause providing that any document that appeared to advocate, encourage or condone any of the offences that defined an unlawful organization (without naming the organization) would be deemed an 'incriminating document'. Regarding the IRA's printing of documents Roche felt that some form of prevention was vital: printed matter had to be seized before distribution, once offered for sale it caused damage. He sought continuing warrants permitting constant pressure on errant printers through repeated raiding and seizing of seditious material. Chief superintendents could exercise this, ensuring that district justices did not become involved in political cases and non-judicial matters. Similarly, the department of Justice believed that Garda officers only, and not district justices, should issue search warrants in political cases.[35]

The three draft bills, with department of Justice and the attorney general observations on the Anti-Social Organisations Bill and on the Special Criminal Court Bill were presented to the cabinet on 19 January 1939.[36] Following discussions between Roche and Ó Muimhneacháin on 24 January 1939,[37] it was clear that the department of the Taoiseach favoured combining as much controversial material as possible in a single bill as opposed to being spread over several,[38] with necessary modifications, though Roche insisted, 'the courts Bill must be a separate Bill.' Further, Ó Muimhneacháin noted divergences between Special Criminal Court Bill and the Defence of the State (Emergency Power) Bill. For instance, the Defence of the State Bill permitted the government 'whenever and so often they think fit to establish a special criminal court by order', while under the Special Criminal Court Bill, the court was to be established as soon as the bill became law. Roche responded: 'O'Donoghue and I agree that [the provision in the Special Criminal Court Bill] is the right method: don't bring in the Bill until it is essential and then act at once.' Ó Muimhneacháin noted other differences, but Roche wrote that little could be 'gained by comparison to the Emergency Power Bill which deals with a war situation and which so far as I am concerned was never really discussed thoroughly so far as the Special court … is concerned. It is better to consider the present Bill on its own merits and in relation to its own problem. It should be a model for war time legislation rather than *vice versa*.'[39] Ó Muimhneacháin also viewed the proposed one-month's detention as too long, wanting it reduced to seven days. On the side margin, Roche wrote, 'I don't agree at all. I consider the month's detention the

35 The attorney general's office suggested that power to grant search warrants be exercised concurrently by district justices. 36 D/J 93/2/8, observations by the office of the minister for Justice. 37 D/J 93/2/8, M. Ó Muimhneacháin to Roche, 25 Jan. 1939. 38 D/T S.10454B, Roche to Ruttledge, 25 Jan. 1939. 39 Roche's emphasis.

most useful thing in the Bill. Weekly remand by a Peace [Commissioner] or a [District Justice] would only be asking for trouble.'

The cabinet finally met to consider the draft legislation on 1 February 1939.[40] It decided that a new measure – the Treason Bill – would deal solely with treason as defined by article 39 of the constitution and certain related offences, and would also repeal the Treasonable Offences Act, 1925. Sections 4 to 10 of the 1925 Act would be re-enacted separately, with offences 'dealt with in comprehensive phraseology', covering attacks against the organs and servants of state, usurpation of the functions of government, etc., thus dispensing with an itemized list of offences.

Regarding the Anti-Social Organisations Bill, the cabinet was undecided if the measure should remain separate (in which case it would be retitled The Unlawful Organisations Bill) or if it should be incorporated with the other bills. It also requested that persons seeking declarations of legality would have the onus of proof shifted to them and that they would be required to submit themselves to cross-examination.

The cabinet met again on 3 February and agreed to implement Roche's one-month detention proposal but requested the retention of provisions covering the forfeiture of property belonging to an unlawful organization.[41] Additionally, it directed that the legislation empower chief superintendents to issue search warrants, warrants for the regular supervision of printing works, in addition to granting them powers to prohibit meetings in support of suppressed organizations or contentious meetings near the Oireachtas and to close certain buildings. It also requested provisions covering the regulation of printers (including the forfeiture of machinery), documents purportedly issued in support of unlawful organizations and the publication of seditions letters in the press.

In order to give effect to the Taoiseach's department's proposal to group as much controversial material into a single bill, in addition to the Treason Bill, an 'Offences Against the State' Bill would be produced. It would include a revision of the Treasonable Offences Act, 1925 excluding treason; provisions dealing with unlawful organizations; a special criminal court; and miscellaneous matters. Following department of Justice representations, the cabinet directed that there should be no appeal from the special criminal court and that it would begin operating as soon as the bill was enacted, but could be dissolved and re-activated later. The cabinet also removed the 'legal member' requirement and requested wide powers of internment, despite the view put forward by Roche earlier.[42]

40 G.C. 2/43. 41 G.C. 2/44. 42 D/J 93/2/8, department of Justice memorandum, 6 Feb. 1939, cabinet minutes, G.C. 2/45, 6 Feb. 1939.

Other proposals put forward by Roche drew serious comment from the Gardaí. The department of Justice reported that Gardaí described the omission of powers of interrogation or obliging suspects to answer questions as 'a most serious defect'.[43] Those powers were, the Gardaí declared, 'the most valuable and most effective means under Article 2A of combating the activities of illegal bodies', maintaining, 'The refusal to answer questions was in itself practically an admission of membership and failure to answer such questions being a chargeable offence was a very effective means of removing persons from the area of their activities.' The Gardaí contended, 'it must be remembered that this power was not abused, in so much as only those who were known to be active and dangerous members were charged with this offence (failing other possible charges) in order to remove them from their activities.' They added:

> It must be recognised that the police know in 90% of cases who are the real culprits in any outrage and who are the real organizers of trouble in any area. If these can be removed, peace will result. It must also be recognised that the technique of avoiding the furnishing of evidence is perfected in this country and if dependence is placed upon building up cases on such evidence then few cases will be brought to Court.

The Gardaí also criticized the omission of powers to search persons and vehicles as provided by sections 13 and 18, respectively, of article 2A and powers to record prisoner information (such as fingerprints and photographs) similar to section 15 of article 2A.

Although the legislation was taking definite shape, Roche felt that 'there are still some points about the Bill which are by no means satisfactory.' The chief fault he identified was the idea that an organization was 'not unlawful *for practical purposes* until it has been specifically "suppressed".'[44] In his opinion, formal suppression should be no more than an 'ancillary affair' – an organization was illegal, not because it had been formally outlawed, but because of its aims or methods. To this end, he wanted the term 'suppressed organisation' replaced by 'unlawful organisation' throughout the bill, except where 'suppressed' was preferable to 'unlawful'. He also proposed that proof of membership of an unlawful organization should be established if a Garda officer stated on oath that he believed that to be true, and could only be disproved if the accused denied the charge on oath.[45] This suggestion was not implemented, however.[46]

43 D/J 93/2/8, office of the minister for Justice memorandum, referring to Garda correspondence, 7 Feb. 1939, no signature. 44 Roche's emphasis. 45 D/T S.10454B, Roche to Ó Cinnéide, 14 Feb. 1939. 46 Ibid., Roche to Ó Muimhneacháin, 10 Feb. 1939,

The cabinet met again on 10 February 1939,[47] deciding that suspects would be obliged to answer questions posed by the Gardaí, though only when the special criminal court operated. Powers to search vehicles and to record prisoner information, as suggested by the Gardaí, would also be included. Following Roche's advice, the bill would declare that an organization was *ipso facto* unlawful if its aims fell within any of the definitions of an unlawful organization, and not simply because a suppression order had been made against it. Additionally, internment was to be given a separate part in the bill and would provide for the establishment of a commission to inquire into internments. Provision for forfeiture of pensions and disqualification from state employment of persons convicted of scheduled offences by the special criminal court were also inserted.

The first draft to combine the Special Criminal Court, the Anti-Social Organizations and the Treasonable Offences Bills, in addition to other matters, was completed by 10 February 1939. Part 1 covered unlawful organizations, part 2 the special criminal court, part 3 covered internment and permitted a minister for state to order the arrest and detention of persons he was satisfied were 'engaged in activities calculated to prejudice the preservation of the peace, order, or security of the State.' Part 4 covered miscellaneous and general matters, including chief superintendents' powers to close buildings. Following the adaptation of sections 4 to 10 of the Treasonable Offences Act, 1925, the draft also provided for offences including usurpation of the functions of government and obstruction of government by force, unlawful drilling, unlawful oaths, and secret societies in the army and Gardaí. Additionally, the draft prohibited the possession of seditious and treasonable documents, printing material designed to undermine the authority of the state and meetings that led to breaches of the peace or passed close to where the Oireachtas was sitting. The draft also contained various printing regulations.

Under the 10 February draft, a Garda could arrest without warrant any person whom he suspected 'of having committed or being about to commit or being or having been concerned in the commission of an offence under' the act or scheduled to it, or whom he suspected of 'carrying a document relating to the commission or intended commission of any such offence … or a document which is an incriminating document … or whom he suspects of being in possession of information relating to the commission or intended commission of any such offence.' In exercise of these powers, a Garda could stop 'any vehicle or any ship, boat, or other vessel which he suspects to contain a person whom he is empowered … to arrest without warrant.' Detainees would be obliged to give their name

Roche's emphasis. 47 Ibid., G.C. 2/47.

and address, and could be searched and fingerprinted. If there was at least one special criminal court in operation, a Garda could 'demand of such person a full account of his movements and actions during any specified period and all information in his possession in relation to the commission or intended commission by another person' of any offence under the bill. If a Garda officer so directed in writing within 24 hours of arrest, the prisoner could be detained for a further 28 days, though the prisoner would be entitled to apply to the high court for bail, immediate trial or release on condition that he declared on oath that he was not a member of an unlawful organization.

The various draft bills, additions, and amendments had been cobbled together, but Roche warned, 'The general plan or arrangement of this Bill is not good.'[48] Drawing heavily on the Treasonable Offences Act, 1925 and article 2A, the bill had been hastily drafted, and he believed the order of the parts and sections lacked 'the logical sequence which might have been observed if the task had been undertaken with more leisure.' It seemed to Roche that the bill contained 'everything that is required', and all that needed attention was reorganization.

The long title described it as

> An Act to make provision in relation to actions and conduct calculated to undermine public order and the authority of the state, and for that purpose to provide for the punishment of persons guilty of offences against the state, to regulate and control in the public interest the formation of associations, to establish special criminal courts in accordance with Article 38 of the Constitution and provide for the constitution, powers, jurisdiction, and procedure of such courts, and to make provision generally in relation to matters connected with the matters aforesaid

This, Roche argued, suggested that the part dealing with unlawful associations should follow the general idea of the bill, that is, 'actions and conduct calculated to undermine public order'. Nevertheless, the draft began by prohibiting the coming together of persons for certain aims and with the intention of carrying out certain actions, but did not specifically deal with those aims and actions until part 4. This oversight could be easily rectified: part 1 could cover 'Offences against the State' and would prohibit advocating the non-payment of taxes, the usurpation of the functions of government, secret societies in the army or Gardaí, etc. Part 2 would

48 D/T S.10454C, draft memorandum, signed the office of the minister for Justice, corrected by Roche, 18 Feb. 1939, draft bill circulated 18 Feb. 1939.

then cover 'Unlawful Associations', not in the detail proposed in the Anti-Social Organisations Bill, but in more general terms such as organizations that 'engage, advocate, promote, encourage, the doing of anything which is declared to be unlawful [under Part I of the Act]'. He also argued that the term 'association' was more suitable than 'organisation', being used in the bill's long title and in the constitution.

There were other issues. Roche wrote that proposals for the holding of suspects for up to 28 days and permitting them to apply to the high court for immediate trial, bail or release had mistakenly survived from an earlier draft following the insertion of special police powers and internment provisions. He described the provision as 'dangerous owing to its novelty, and on more detailed grounds, it is almost grotesque that a man who may be detained on suspicion of armed robbery or murder should claim to be released on bail on the grounds that he is not a member of an unlawful organisation.'[49] He recommended holding suspects for 14 days and permitting them to apply for bail only after they had been detained without charge for at least 7 days.

The bill was redrafted between 10 and 17 February and considered by the cabinet on 20 February 1939.[50] The cabinet directed that the special criminal court would operate by government proclamation which could be withdrawn or annulled at any time by the Dáil. Consideration was to be given to the reorganization of the bill, with permanent matters being placed at the beginning, and the special criminal court and internment provisions afterwards.[51] The cabinet also directed that an organization could not seek an application for legality until a suppression order had been made. Provision forbidding the unlawful exercise of a function of government was extended to cover acts of intimidation of members of the legislature, judiciary and the executive. It also decided to reduce the maximum period of detention – initial detention would be in a Garda station for up to 48 hours following arrest pending a decision to further detain for up to 8 days, or to charge. The right to apply to the high court for bail was also dropped.[52]

A few days later, Roche again wrote on the arrangement of the bill. After drawing up a table comparing the draft Offences Bill with article 2A and the Treasonable Offences Act, 1925, he was 'again struck, more forcibly than ever, by the bad arrangement of the Bill and by the ease with which it could be rectified'.[53] He declared, 'We have brought the Bill to the very edge of being an excellent Bill and I hate the idea of giving up

49 D/T S.10454B, Roche to Ó Cinnéide, 14 Feb. 1939. 50 G.C.2/49. 51 D/T S.10454C, Ó Cinnéide to Ó Muimhneacháin, 24 Feb. 1939. 52 Decided by 24 Feb. 1939. 53 D/T S.10454C, Roche to Ó Muimhneacháin, 22 Feb. 1939.

the task just at the point when a couple of hours of easy work would put the crown on our labours.'[54]

Clearly, only a small number of other matters remained outstanding.[55] On the obstruction of or interference with government, there was no mention of the president. While O'Donoghue regarded such a provision as unnecessary, being covered by reference to the legislature, it was felt that 'to fail to provide specifically for the President might be regarded as lack of courtesy or as disrespect.' Regarding court members, Roche noted the draft contained no minimum qualification requirements:

> There is nothing in the Bill to prevent the Government establishing courts consisting of members of their own party or of members of the detective branch of the police force and there is nothing to stop them, if they find the members of a particular court unsatisfactory, from dismissing these members and replacing them with a more complacent court, and generally from having particular cases disposed of by their own nominees appointed ad hoc.

He proposed that members be at least captains or barristers of five years' standing. Alternatively, he wanted a judge advocate with legal qualifications attached to the court and a judge advocate general to review and confirm sentences.[56]

The cabinet requested that the court members be drawn from the high court, circuit court, district court, and barristers and solicitors of seven years' standing, or army officers not below the rank of commandant.[58] Additionally, the offence of obstruction of the president was added as a separate section. The issue of rearrangement had also been finally attended to, though the itemized list of activities which defined unlawful organizations was retained. If other problems were identified with the bill or additional changes were proposed, the Dáil could consider them. The bill was ready for distribution to TDs.[59]

Part 1 was now devoted to definitions used throughout the bill, including 'organisation' and 'incriminating document'.[60] Part 2 dealt specifically

54 Ibid., note by Roche, 28 Feb. 1939. **55** Ibid., Ó Cinnéide to Ó Muimhneacháin, 24 Feb. 1939, Ó Cinnéide to the parliamentary draftsman, 25 Feb. 1939. **56** Ibid., undated, between 22 and 28 February 1939. **58** Ibid., Ó Cinnéide to Matheson, 25 Feb. 1939. **59** Ibid., note by department of Justice, 25 Feb. 1939. **60** 'the expression "incriminating document" means a document of whatsoever date, or bearing no date, issued by or emanating from an unlawful organisation or appearing to be so issued or so to emanate or purporting or appearing to aid or abet any such organisation or calculated to promote the formation of an unlawful organisation'.

with offences against the state, namely usurpation of the functions of government; obstruction of the branches of government and the president by violence or intimidation; illegal drilling; formation of secret societies in the army or the Gardaí; administering unlawful oaths. Additionally, it prohibited the printing, publishing and distribution of treasonable and seditious documents and those supporting unlawful organizations.

Part 3 sought to 'regulate and control in the public interest the exercise of the constitutional right of citizens to form associations' and dealt specifically with unlawful organizations. The definition of unlawful organizations was taken directly from the Anti-Social Organisations Bill, though the 'hatred' clause was dropped. Although the government could make suppression orders when it was 'of opinion that any particular organisation is an unlawful organisation', following Roche's earlier representations, 'Whenever and so long as a suppression order is in force', was replaced by 'It shall not be lawful for any person to be a member of an unlawful organisation'. Otherwise, the remainder of this part was taken almost verbatim from the Anti-Social Organisations Bill and provided for appeal from proscription, forfeiture of property, and defined how membership would be established. Further, chief superintendents could issue closing orders lasting three months whenever 'satisfied that a building is being used or has been used in any way for the purposes, direct or indirect, of an unlawful organisation'.

Part 4 covered miscellaneous matters including special police powers of arrest. Chief superintendents could issue search warrants for documents relating to offences under the bill. They could also prohibit meetings near the Oireachtas, those on behalf of unlawful organizations or those leading to a breach of the peace, though prohibitions could be appealed in the high court.

Part 5 was taken almost verbatim from the Special Criminal Court Bill, but provided that the court would come into force after the government made a proclamation declaring itself 'satisfied that the ordinary courts are inadequate to secure the effective administration of justice and the preservation of public peace and order'. The other significant difference was the absence of provision for appeal.

Part 6 dealt with internment, which would come in to force whenever the government made a proclamation that internment was 'necessary to secure the preservation of public peace and order'. Dáil Éireann could annul a proclamation at any time. Whenever a minister of state was 'satisfied that any particular person is engaged in activities calculated to prejudice the preservation of the peace, order, or security of the State', he could order the person's arrest and internment. Gardaí were permitted to arrest without other warrant a person whose internment had been ordered. The minister might 'by writing under his hand, if and whenever he so thinks proper', order the release of any internee. Part 6 also provided for an internment commission to investigate detentions when internees specifically requested.

Speaking on 2 March 1939, the minister for Justice, Patrick Ruttledge, told the Dáil that the sole object of the bill was 'the prevention of the display, the use, or the advocacy of force as a method to achieve political or social aims.'[61] Referring to the IRA proclamations posted around the country,[62] he warned that claims by a group to be the real government of Ireland should not be dismissed as some TDs had suggested.[63] Fine Gael, however, would do little to oppose the government on matters of security. Its position was expressed by W.T. Cosgrave: 'If the situation be as serious as the minister has described it, it is all the more necessary that there should be as widespread support for such steps as the Legislature considers necessary as is possible throughout the country.'[64] The leader of the opposition did express unease, though, at the fact that four of six parts of the bill would be permanent.

Fine Gael proposed a number of significant amendments, though, including a proposal that would make the whole bill subject to a proclamation, not simply the special criminal court and provisions for internment. The department of Justice remarked:

> that it should not be an offence to overthrow or undermine the public authority except during a period when the Government is satisfied that the ordinary Courts and the ordinary law are insufficient to secure the administration of justice – is so indefensible that it is difficult to anticipate what arguments will be adduced to support the amendment ... no State could accept the position that a person who kidnapped a member of the Government or seized a military post or forcibly occupied the seat of the Oireachtas was guilty of no more than common assault or trespass.

The amendment was withdrawn.

Fine Gael's Professor Marcus O'Sullivan had sought the insertion of a provision permitting appeals from special criminal court convictions and sentences. The minister for Justice initially opposed the amendment, 'When the special criminal courts would be in operation it would be in a

61 Dáil Debates vol. 74 col. 1283, 2 Mar. 1939. **62** Dáil Debates vol. 74 col. 91, 8 Feb. 1939, the minister declared, 'That is a position which the Government is not going to tolerate.' **63** Labour's Deputy Norton argued that there was 'no set of circumstances within the country which justifies the introduction of this unusual type of legislation and the exceptional type of court which the legislation foreshadows.' **64** Dáil Debates vol. 74 col. 1292–3, 2 Mar. 1939.

time of emergency, such a time as was visualized under article 2A. To deal with a situation like that you must act quickly and not be held up by appeals to the court of criminal appeal.' John A. Costello, attorney general in 1931, interjected:

> I think that the absence of the appeal to the court of criminal appeal will inevitably lead to efforts being made to get round the decisions of the special tribunals ... We found a way out to meet the injustices meted out to some of our supporters during the operation of Article 2A by the present Government. We found a way out for a considerable number of these injustices. We found gaps through which people could creep. Ingenuity will be exercised in the same way to get over the provisions of this Bill ... I think that the fact that there is an appeal to the court of criminal appeal will in no way operate to the detriment of the Government. I believe it will strengthen their hands in an emergency ... the public will feel that these special tribunals are not mere creatures of the Government, that everybody that comes before them will get a fair trial and a legal trial.

Ruttledge agreed and promised to examine the proposal.

Following Fine Gael representations, the government also agreed to reduce the period Gardaí could detain suspects without charge to 24 hours, which could be extended by an additional 24 hours.[65]

On 25 April 1939, the cabinet agreed to include provision for appeal from the special criminal court to the court of criminal appeal.[66] Final consideration to amending the legislation was given on 22 May 1939, following points raised in the Seanad.[67]

The Offences against the State Act, 1939 became law on 14 June 1939 and the IRA was declared unlawful under section 19 on 23 June 1939. Part 5 (covering the special criminal court) came into force on 22 August when the government made a proclamation under section 35 that it was 'satisfied that the ordinary courts are inadequate to secure the effective administration of justice and the preservation of public peace and order'. Although the act provided for the appointment of members of the high court, circuit court and district court to the special criminal court, the government appointed the former members of the constitution (special powers) tribunal to it on 22 August 1939 under section 39: Colonel Francis Bennett, Colonel (later General) Daniel McKenna,[68] Major (later Colonel)

65 Dáil Debates vol. 75 col. 728–731, 732, 716–20, 19 Apr. 1939. 66 G.C.2/66. 67 D/T S.10454. 68 Replaced 29 Jan. 1940 by Major (later Colonel) Felix Devlin, when

John Vincent Joyce, Major (later Lieutenant-Colonel) Cornelius Whelan, and Major (later Lieutenant-Colonel) Patrick Tuite. Commandant Richard Feely was appointed court registrar the same day.[69] The internment provisions (part 6) also became effective on 22 August following the issuing of a proclamation under section 54.

The Treason Bill, which had been detached from the Offences against the State legislation in early February 1939, posed fewer problems than the primary public safety measure. It was a short four section bill giving effect to the terms of article 39 of the constitution. It provided for the death penalty for persons convicted of treason within the state and of Irish citizens who were convicted of committing treason against Ireland outside of the state.[70] It also covered the ancillary crimes of encouraging, harbouring and comforting person guilty of treason,[71] and the offence of misprision of treason.[72]

Although treason legislation no longer represented the mainstay of the state's security legislation, de Valera spoke of the bill in symbolic terms, arguing that it gave further legitimacy to the Irish state:

> The moment the Constitution was enacted by the people, treason had a new meaning ... To make it clear that treason must no longer be understood in terms of allegiance to foreign powers ... treason was defined as an act of treachery against this State, and nothing else ... The penalty here, as in most countries, because of the character of the crime, is the greatest penalty that, in modern times, States can impose on an individual— the penalty of death.[73]

Although the constitution defined treason in very narrow terms, debate in the Dáil revealed a large degree of confusion regarding the offence. Responding to queries raised about the meaning of 'levying war', de Valera explained, 'the Irish judges interpreting the Constitution would be quite at liberty to decide what was the intention of the legislature, and what was the intention of the people and what was the intention in the Constitution in regard to levying war.'[74] Nonetheless, he admitted that greater clarification might be needed and promised to have the whole question re-examined. The former minister for Justice, James Fitzgerald-Kenny, had sought to introduce a distinction between 'actual' or 'direct' and 'constructive' levying of war in order to provide for punishments less than death.

McKenna was appointed army chief of staff. **69** D/T S.11387A, statement issued by the publicity bureau on 22 Aug. 1939, D/D S.106, 23 Aug. 1939, for a list of persons recommended by the minister for Defence to Ó Muimhneacháin. **70** Section 1. **71** Section 2. **72** Section 3. **73** Dáil Debates vol. 74 col. 966–8, 23 Feb. 1939. **74** Dáil Debates vol. 74 col. 999.

The attorney general's office explained that the 1937 constitution freed the term 'treason' of any complications that previous legislation and judicial decisions had created. The constitution defined treason in very narrow terms, and earlier cases, rulings and statutes would not bind the supreme court, if it were called on to determine what was precisely set out in article 39, though the court might use them to illustrate general aspects of the offence. Further, the Oireachtas could not alter article 39. As it made no mention of constructive levying of war, the term had no place in Irish law.[75] P.P. O'Donoghue felt that although there were probably an inordinate number of ways in which war might be levied, the purpose of levying war was to overthrow by violence the organs of government as established by the constitution and this, probably, was the simplest definition of treason. Anything of a treasonous nature that fell short of treason as defined by the constitution would be dealt with under the Offences against the State Act and not the Treason Act.

75 D/T S.11284, 27 Feb. 1939, note by P.P. O'Donoghue.

6

'The Emergency', 1939–1948

The day following Germany's invasion of Poland, de Valera addressed the Dáil to explain how the government intended dealing with the emerging crisis.[1] The Taoiseach admitted that the order paper for 2 September 1939 looked suspiciously like a list of guillotine motions, but he assured TDs that that was not the government's intention: 'we considered that it was more in accord with the general feeling of the House, probably, and more likely to be understood by our people, if we dispensed with such a motion, although there is extreme urgency for the passing of these measures.' The purpose of the proposed constitutional amendment was one of 'extending "time of war" or, if not extending it, we are making it clear that "time of war" should mean a crisis such as the present, provided, when there are hostilities and conflict about us, there is a resolution both by the Dáil and the Seanad indicating that such an emergency exists, that such a condition exists.'

Despite the extraordinary nature of the amendment, there was no genuine opposition to it or effort to impede its passage. Indeed, Fine Gael TD James Dillon argued the Dáil was obliged to give the government these powers it sought. The Labour Party leader, William Norton, sought assurances that the powers would not be abused or that some distant conflict would not be used as a pretext to invoke them, though de Valera could give none: 'The trouble is this, that when this amendment is passed if you had an unscrupulous majority, both in the Dáil and in the Seanad, it could by pretending to have an emergency and by pretending to submit to the rules of law and the Constitution, do that.'[2]

The constitutional amendment was speedily passed, permitting the introduction of the Emergency Powers Bill, 1939. The provisions of section 2(1) were clearly the widest possible and would allow the government to deal legally with any emergency. Although impossible to foresee all circumstances, the government decided to recite all potentially necessary powers in section 2(2). Seán Lemass explained that it 'sets out, by way of illustration and without prejudice to the generality of subsection (1), the various powers which the Government will secure when subsection (1) is enacted.' He added, 'It is obvious that many immediate difficulties will

1 Dún Mhuire, De Valera Papers 1198, *Irish Press*, 4 Sept. 1939, *Irish Times*, 3 and 4 Sept. 1939. 2 Dáil Debates vol.77 col. 2, 5, 13, 10, 19, 2 Sept. 1939

arise, some of them of considerable magnitude, but difficulties which are at present unforeseeable may also be experienced and it is necessary that the government should be equipped with powers to deal ... expeditiously with such difficulties should they occur.'[3] Fine Gael's Dr Thomas O'Higgins, who expressed disappointment at the case made for the bill, said he would support it unenthusiastically and uneasily, but added, 'I would stand at all times for giving any Irish Government any powers whatsoever that they asked for on any occasion when they were demanded and the Government itself said that those powers were necessary.'[4]

Nevertheless, government assurances that there would be no courts martial established to try civilians, military or industrial conscription, or tax imposed by emergency powers order proved inadequate to the Dáil, forcing it to add them as prohibited functions to section 2(5). John A Costello sought, but failed, to wholly remove internment powers, though the Dáil voted to restrict section 2(2)(k) to persons other than natural born Irish citizens.

The Emergency Powers Bill was quickly enacted, and the Emergency Powers Order was promulgated on 3 September 1939.[5] Between 3 September 1939 and 11 April 1946, 7,864 emergency powers orders were made, including 443 amendment orders and 95 revocation orders.[6] Of the first figure, 522 orders were made by the government, and 7,303 orders, 22 regulations, 3 rules and 14 schemes were made in exercise of powers conferred by emergency powers order. Of the 7,303 subsidiary orders, 5,330 were wages standstill orders.[7] Principal orders covered matters as diverse as street collections,[8] compulsory tillage,[9] the suspension of duty on horseshoes,[10] amendments to the Ministers and Secretaries Act, 1924,[11] and the remuneration of employees.[12]

On more specific security grounds, in September 1939, a temporary police force, *An Taca Síochána*, was established under article 54 of the Emergency Powers Order, 1939.[13] Initially, it numbered 228, but grew to 300 in February 1940. Its members were later assimilated in to the Garda Síochána.[14] A part-time auxiliary police force was also established in June 1940.[15] The wearing of foreign uniforms was prohibited by Emergency

3 Dáil Debates vol.77 col. 20–1. 4 Dáil Debates vol.77 col. 42. 5 Government minutes, G2/78. 6 These figures do not include orders made by local authorities acquiring land compulsorily. 7 100 Dáil Debates col. 1765–6, 11 Apr. 1946. See also index and list in D/T S.10845/3. 8 Emergency Powers (No. 8) Order, 1939 9 Emergency Powers (No. 12) Order, 1939. 10 Emergency Powers (No. 96) Order, 1941. 11 Emergency Powers (No. 111) Order, 1941. 12 Emergency Powers (No. 260) Order, 1943. 13 Emergency Powers (Temporary Special Police Force) Order, 1939, SRO 243/1939. See D/T S.11445/10, undated memorandum. 14 Dáil Debates vol.77 col. 247–50, 27 Sept. 1939 and 'Departmental Notes', p.73, 15 Emergency Powers (No.49) Order, 1940, replaced

Powers (No.17) Order, 1939 and the Official Secrets Acts, 1911 and 1920 were replaced by Emergency Powers (No.42) Order, 1940.

Derived from section 2(2)(j) of the principal act, article 3 of the Emergency Powers Order, 1939 empowered the minister for Justice to restrict passenger traffic into and out of the state. Article 4 removed the restrictions on deporting aliens (other than British citizens) created by section 5(5) of the Aliens Act, 1935. The Emergency Powers (Deportation) Order, 1939[16] empowered the minister for Justice to deport anyone (other than Irish citizens) if he considered it necessary for the public safety or for the preservation of the state, while Emergency Powers (No.11) Order, 1939 required British citizens who remained in Ireland for over 30 days to register with the Gardaí. Emergency Powers (Restrictions on Outward Travel) Order, 1942,[17] prohibited persons leaving the state (unless travelling to the North or to Britain) without a permit from the minister for External Affairs.

Under section 7 of the Emergency Powers Act, 1939, court hearings could be held in camera and the publication of information relating to proceedings restricted or prohibited if the court was satisfied, on representations by the attorney general, that it was expedient to do so in the interests of the public safety or the preservation of the state.[18] Emergency Powers (No.47) Order, 1940 permitted the minister for Justice to restrict the evidence that might be taken and the verdicts that might be given at coroners' inquests. Emergency Powers (No.74) Order, 1941 dispensed with the requirement that a coroner view a body before holding an inquest, provided that a Garda had seen the body beforehand.[19] District justices could alter their sittings where necessary under Emergency Powers (No.156) Order, 1942.[20] Additionally, the 'six month limitation' created under the Petty Sessions (Ireland) Act, 1851 was removed from all summary trials of offences under section 5 of the Emergency Powers Act, 1939.[21] Juries were dispensed with in civil actions in the circuit court, and reduced to seven in criminal cases. Further, juries could be called from smaller areas than stipulated by the Juries Acts.[22] The right of an accused to have his trial transferred from the circuit court to the central criminal court was restricted by Emergency Powers (No.250) Order, 1943.

Once the constitutional amendment and the Emergency Powers Bill were enacted, the government could turn its attention to the IRA. On 8

by Part III of the Emergency Powers (No. 61) Order, 1940 SRO 391/1940. **16** SRO 230/1939. **17** SRO 455/1942. **18** Emergency Powers (No.40) Order, 1940, amended by Emergency Powers (No.40) Order, 1940 (Amendment) Order, 1943. See D/T S.11997. **19** Introduced because of transport restrictions. **20** See D/T S.12290. **21** Emergency Powers (No.178) Order, 1942, D/T S.12822. **22** Emergency Powers (No.223) Order, 1942, later amended by Emergency Powers (No.346) Order, 1944, D/T S.12957.

September 1939, Gerald Boland was appointed minister for Justice,[23] immediately ordering the arrest of those believed to be the most important and active members of the organization. A Garda special branch raid in Dublin the following day netted most of the IRA's leadership and most of its liquid assets, though Stephen Hayes, IRA chief of staff, escaped.[24] Internment warrants were issued for about 70 IRA members on 15 September.[25]

The special powers available to Gardaí had obviously been remoulded since 1931. Section 30 empowered any Garda without warrant to stop, search, interrogate, and arrest any person whom he suspected of 'having committed or being about to commit or being or having been concerned in the commission of an offence' under the Offences Act, scheduled to it, 'or whom he suspects of carrying a document relating to the commission or intended commission of any such offence … or whom he suspects of being in possession of information relating to the commission or intended commission of any such offence.' Unlike the provisions of article 2A, a Garda's suspicion was not explicitly stated to be 'conclusive evidence, incapable of being rebutted or questioned by cross-examination, rebutting evidence or otherwise, that [the Garda] did at [the time of arrest] so suspect such person and was then entitled to stop and interrogate such person'. Further, there was no provision permitting Gardaí to use such 'force as may be necessary' when employing the powers of section 30.[26]

Once arrested, a suspect was to be removed to a Garda station or 'other convenient place' where he could be detained for 24 hours or for 48 hours at the direction of a chief superintendent. During detention, suspects were obliged to give their name and address, and could be searched, fingerprinted, and photographed. If a special criminal court was operating, section 52 empowered any Garda to demand from a detainee 'a full account of [his] movements and actions during any specified period and all information in his possession in relation to the commission or intended commission by another person of any offence under any section or sub-section of [the Offences against the State] Act or any scheduled offence.'

The absence of potentially unlimited punishments that had been a significant aspect of article 2A, and the reduced periods Gardaí could hold suspects without charge were the most obvious differences between the

23 See 'Departmental Notes', 71. Ruttledge became minister for Local Government and Public Health. 24 Bell, *The secret army*, pp 168–9; 'Departmental Notes', pp 71–3. By 27 Sept. 1939, 93 persons had been arrested under the Offences Act, 67 of whom were being held in Arbour Hill, and 15 were awaiting trial, see Dáil Debates vol.77 col. 247. By 8 Nov. 1939, 116 had been arrested under the Offences act, 62 were being held in Arbour Hill, and three in Mountjoy, see Dáil Debates vol. 77 col. 939. 25 'Departmental Notes', pp 73, 145–7, D/T S.11449 and D/T S.11829. See table 5a and 5b. An internment commission was established on 16 Sept. 1939 under section 59.

Offences against the State Act and the 1931 legislation. Indeed, as Gerald Boland explained to John A. Costello, the Offences against the State Act 'was not at all as drastic as the Act which it replaced. I am personally of the opinion that there were some powers given in the former Act which we replaced to which we should have held on.'[27]

Persons detained on suspicion under this legislation were not given access to legal advisers either before or during interrogation. As Gerry Boland later explained to John A. Costello:

> In the opinion of the Garda authorities, it is important, in the working of these provisions, that accomplices of a detained person shall not be in a position, during the period of detention, to communicate with the detained person or to know what, if any information the detained person has given or proposes to give.[28]

It had been suggested that a lawyer should advise detainees of their obligations under the act and to the questions they were bound to answer, but the Garda commissioner believed such a 'concession … would be troublesome in practice.'[29]

Prior to June 1940, at least, the procedure employed when sending persons for trial by the special criminal court was similar to that operating under article 2A, though the maximum length of detention permitted before a charge had to be made was reduced to 48 hours and persons were usually remanded before a district justice. For example, Gardaí arrested Thomas Wall on suspicion of possession of incriminating documents, but released him without charge after 48 hours. He was rearrested six weeks later on the same charge. When he enquired about his treatment, the *Irish Times* reported, 'the superintendent said that it had not been possible to comply with the regulation requiring the appearance of the accused man before a district justice within forty-eight hours of his arrest, and he was released. The police had to wait for a court, and for instructions from the Attorney General.'[30]

Under section 25, Garda chief superintendents could issue 'closing orders' lasting three months against buildings they were satisfied were being used or had been used in any way for the purposes, direct or indi-

26 Article 2A, section 13(1), 13(5). 27 Dáil Debates vol. 101 col. 1139–40, 29 May 1946. 28 Dáil Debates vol. 100 col. 947–8, 2 Apr. 1946. 29 D/T S.13921, no date, late March 1946, 1 Apr. at the latest, unsigned note from the department of Justice for the minister for Justice's information when answering the questions posed by Costello. These powers of interrogation were not used in cases of emergency powers offences unless specifically ordered by the commissioner. 30 *Irish Times*, 23 Dec. 1939.

rect, of an unlawful organization. Section 27 outlawed meetings by, on behalf of or in support of unlawful organizations and empowered Garda chief superintendents to prohibit such meetings on giving sufficient notice, though a prohibition could be challenged in the high court. Chief superintendents were also empowered to issue search warrants under section 29 for documents 'relating to the commission or intended commission of an offence' under the act, 'or any document relating directly or indirectly to the commission or intended commission of treason'.

Additionally, article 74 of the Emergency Powers Order, 1939[31] extended Gardaí's and soldiers' powers to arrest and search persons suspected of committing offences scheduled to the Emergency Powers Order, 1939. Article 75 empowered district justices, Gardaí or other authorized persons with reasonable grounds for suspecting that a 'scheduled offence has been or is being or is about to be committed, and that evidence of the commission of the offence is to be found at any premises' to issue search warrants.[32] Article 76 permitted Gardaí and soldiers to stop and search vehicles; article 77 permitted the photographing and fingerprinting of suspects. Article 78 provided that 'Without prejudice to any special provisions contained in [the Emergency Powers Order, 1939], any person shall, on being requested by or on behalf of a minister so to do, furnish or produce to such authority or person as may be specified in the request any such information or article in his possession as may be so specified, being information or an article which the authority or person making the request considers it necessary or expedient in the interests of the public safety, or the preservation of the State to obtain or examine.'[33]

As with the 1931 legislation, the attorney general remained central to determining who would be tried. Where a person was charged with scheduled offences before a district justice, a simple request from the attorney general would suffice to send or send forward the accused for trial by a special criminal court.[34] In the case of persons charged before district justices with non-scheduled offences, the attorney general would be required to certify that the 'ordinary courts are in his opinion inadequate to secure the effective administration of justice and the preservation of public peace and order in relation to the trial of such person on such charge' before the district justice could send or send forward persons for trial by a spe-

31 See D/T S.11522. 32 D/T S.12644A, 8 Nov. 1941. 33 See *The Attorney General v. M. Bruton* (ILT and SJ [1942] 56–9, and A/G 21/41) where it was held that article 78 of the Emergency Powers Order, 1939 was intra vires the constitution, but its validity in any particular case depended on the Garda officer requesting any information being of the opinion that the furnishing or production of the information sought was necessary in the interests of the public safety or the preservation of the state. 34 Section 45.

cial criminal court.[35] Additionally, the attorney general could, in place of having a person charged before a district justice, direct that a person be charged before a special criminal court.[36] The attorney general was also empowered, on application to the high court, to transfer trials sent forward to either the central criminal court or the circuit court to a special criminal court.[37]

On 16 October 1939, Myles Heffernan became the first person to be convicted by the special criminal court, receiving a three-month sentence for possessing incriminating documents and for membership of an unlawful organization. Of the 31 persons it convicted before January 1940, the special criminal court sentenced two persons to 3 years' imprisonment each for unlawful possession of firearms and conspiracy; one to 2 years and four others to 12 months for unlawful possession of explosives. Generally, sentences were in the range of three to six months, primarily for the possession of incriminating documents, membership of an unlawful organization and refusal to answer questions or to account for movements.[38]

On 17 November 1939, the government made the first scheduled order under section 36 of the Offences against the State Act, 1939, declaring that offences under the Offences against the State Act, 1939 were scheduled offences for the purposes of part 5 of the act.[39] This had two effects: first, the trials of persons charged with scheduled offences could be removed from the ordinary courts to the special criminal court without the issue of the attorney general's certificate; a simple 'direction' would suffice. Second, on conviction by the special criminal court of a scheduled offence, the forfeiture and disqualification provisions of section 34 would apply. The attorney general's certificate was still required in the case of non-scheduled offences.[40]

Regardless of the many precautions and measures adopted by the government, it was clear as the winter of 1939 approached that the IRA's English bombing campaign was a failure. As in the past, the focus of IRA activity in the Twenty-Six Counties now shifted to the prisons. Several internees began refusing food and demanded release – Charles McCarthy was freed on 12 October and Jeremiah Lynch and Richard McCarthy were released on 18 November.[41] Patrick McGrath, a veteran of the 1916 Rising, who had been charged under the Offences against the State Act, also began to refuse food on 23 October, seeking release. The American minister to Ireland, John Cudahy, reported de Valera's 'grim determination not to give way.[42] But as

35 Section 46. 36 Section 47. 37 Section 48. 38 See figures, table 6a, 'Departmental Notes', p.140. 39 D/T S.11522, Government minutes, G2/103, 17 Nov. 1939. 40 D/T S.11438. 41 'Departmental Notes', pp 145–7. 42 See S. Cronin, *Washington's Irish policy 1916–1986: Independence, partition, neutrality* (1987), p.77.

McGrath's health deteriorated, de Valera's resolve weakened and on 15 November 1939, McGrath was transferred to hospital. He left hospital on 4 December 1939 and a *nolle prosequi* was entered in his case before the special criminal court on 7 December 1939.[43] But with so little IRA activity in late 1939, J. Bowyer Bell argued that the government 'could appear to be magnanimous.'[44]

Comprehensive as the Offences against the State Act, 1939 was, it remained ineffectual in one respect. When the government made a suppression order under section 22, all property of the proscribed organization was forfeited and vested in the minister for Justice. In practice, however, it was usually impossible to prove that property belonged to a particular unlawful organization. Further, the department of Justice complained that it could not permanently confiscate or freeze the personal assets of members of unlawful organizations or of their sympathizers. Gardaí pointed to the seizure of about $2,000 in September 1939 from a known member of the IRA, in circumstances 'which put it beyond doubt ... that the money is "enemy property" '. Nonetheless, the Garda commissioner believed that the money would have to be returned to its owner eventually. There was also an internee in Arbour Hill who had won £1,000 in the Hospital Sweepstakes. Although the money could not be described as belonging to an unlawful organization, the department of Justice wanted to seize it, describing its owner as an 'active and determined member ... who has been, and continues to be, a source of danger and expense to the State and upon whose property the State seems to have legitimate claim by way of recoupment, punishment and deterrent.' It also sought 'wider and prompter' powers to stop the pensions of active members of unlawful organizations. There was one prisoner in particular in receipt of an army pension, who the department believed it might be 'impractical to punish ... by imprisonment' or even to try him 'due to the state of his health.' In addition, the department sought provisions permitting the imposition of fines on members of illegal organizations or sympathizers who might 'risk a short term of imprisonment' but would 'hesitate to risk financial embarrassment.'[45] Although not approving all the department's proposals, the cabinet ordered the drafting of the Offences against the State (Forfeiture) Bill on 10 November 1939.[46]

The act empowered the minister for Justice to order the forfeiture of seized property (whether seized before or after the passing of the act) when he was of the opinion that it 'was acquired ... as a result or in the course of, or was being or intended to be used in furtherance, of an activity prej-

43 'Departmental Notes', pp 143–144A. 44 Bell, *The secret army*, p.171. 45 D/T S.11516, memorandum by Roche for the government, 30 Oct. 1939. 46 G.C. 2/114.

udicial to the peace, order and security of the State.'[47] Seized property was disposed of for the benefit of the exchequer or destroyed, if necessary.[48] A right of appeal to the high court was provided under section 4.[49] To further expedite the passage of the bill through the Dáil, it would last for 12 months, and would have to be renewed each September.[50] It became law 14 August 1940 and continued in force until September 1943. By July 1941, eight cars had been seized. In addition, Gardaí recovered over $20,000, some Irish currency, several radios and transmitting equipment, typewriters, and various miscellaneous items.[51]

But not all security issues resulted from the ongoing activities of republicans. For instance, on 17 November 1939, the Milk Producers' Association (MPA) for Dublin began withholding milk supplies from Dublin, protesting at cost increases caused by the war and demanding an immediate increase in the minimum price of milk 'commensurate with the increase in feeding stuffs and milk production costs.' It claimed that the price of cattle had increased by 60%, and feedstuffs by 20–40%, while the price of milk had fallen by 1*s.* 4*d.* per gallon.[52] The government moved quickly to contain the protests and the minister for Agriculture, Dr James Ryan, asked the censor to stop two newspaper advertisements highlighting the MPA's case.[53] The Irish Farmers Federation, which represented farmers in Dublin and in adjacent counties, also began striking to 'focus public attention on the plight of our industry.' It called on the public to back the farmers' campaign and began issuing a 'War Bulletin'. In a few days, disruption was reported to several fairs, though it seems there was little public sympathy for the farmers' protests – Peadar O'Donnell dismissed the MPA as the 'resurrected Blueshirt organisation'.[54]

The government responded to these protests by revoking a number of sections of the Milk (Regulation of Supply and Price) Act, 1936, permitting farmers in the south of the country to supply Dublin with milk. Significantly, it was reported that the strike was not causing an acute shortage of other agricultural goods, though fairs were poorly attended and roadblocks were in place preventing delivery. Further, H.B. Ltd believed that

47 Section 2(1). The definition of property included chattel (especially motor vehicles), money, or documents of title to money (i.e. cheques, bank drafts, etc.) and securities, shares, certificates, bonds, etc. 48 Section 3(1), D/J S.22/59, C.S. Almond, department of Finance to the secretary of the department of Justice, 20 May 1941. 49 D/T S.11516, 30 Nov. 1939. 50 D/T S.13222. 51 D/J S.22/59, See also 'Departmental Notes', pp 86f, Dáil Debates, 23 July 1941. 52 D/T S.11543 and Dáil Debates vol. 78 col. 489–566, 29 Nov. 1939. Prices were set by the Milk (Regulation of Supply and Price) Act, 1936. 53 D/T S.11543, note from Aiken, minister for the Coordination of Defensive Measures, to de Valera, 20 Nov. 1939. 54 'Departmental Notes', pp 74–5, *Irish Press*, 2 Dec. 1939. 55 *Irish Press*, 21 Nov. 1939, 22 Nov. 1939.

milk shortages were not as serious as those of an earlier milk strike in 1936 because of government actions. The protests continued, however, and certain farmers involved began to spill large volumes of milk, which led to arrests. Revoking portions of the 1936 act allowed farmers to seek higher prices, but as Dr Ryan explained, 'the Government cannot tolerate interference by the strikers with producers who are willing to supply milk'.[55]

In order to deal with continuing protests, the government promulgated Offences against the State (Scheduled Offences) (No. 2) Order, 1939 on 24 November 1939.[56] It scheduled unlawful assembly, the Malicious Damages Act, 1861, section 7 of the Conspiracy and Protection of Property Act, 1875 and section 5 of the Emergency Powers Act, 1939 to the Offences Act. Seventeen farmers were charged before the district court on 29 November 1939. Simultaneously, four farmers were convicted by the special criminal court of intimidation and unlawful assembly, but each entered into recognisance. Thirteen farmers were convicted by the special criminal court in February of conspiracy and unlawful assembly, all entering into recognisance. A further 24 farmers were convicted in March of conspiracy, unlawful assembly and damage to property; they were bound to the peace and ordered to pay compensation.[57] The protests quickly collapsed. On 30 November, a deputation from the milk producers was received by the department of Agriculture and the strike ended the following day.[58]

But the government's focus immediately returned to republicans when the first legal challenge to the Offences against the State Act, 1939 was made on behalf of internee Seamus Burke.[59] Mr Justice George Gavan Duffy, who heard the habeas corpus application, began by observing that 'There is no provision enabling the Oireachtas or the Government to disregard the Constitution in any emergency short of war or armed rebellion. And the Constitution contains no express provision for any law endowing the Executive with powers of internment without trial.'[60]

He then considered the meaning of 'satisfied' in section 55, which provided that 'Whenever a Minister of State is satisfied that any particular person is engaged in activities calculated to prejudice the preservation of the peace, order, or security of the State, such Minister may by warrant under his hand order the arrest and detention of such person'. Gavan Duffy noted that before a minister could issue an internment warrant, firstly, he had to be satisfied that a particular person was engaged in spe-

56 D/T S.11543, government minutes G2/105. The third and final order scheduled the Firearms Act, 1925, see G2/215, D/T S.12170, 26 Nov. 1940. 57 'Departmental Notes', pp 142a, 142g, 142j–142l. 58 *Irish Times*, 1 Dec and 2 Dec. 1939. 59 *The State (Burke) v. Lennon and the Attorney General*, [1940] IR 136, the case was heard on 28 and 29 Nov. and 1 Dec, 1939. 60 [1940] IR 145.

cific activities – this he described as a jury question.[61] Second, the minister had to consider if those activities were 'calculated to prejudice the preservation of the peace, order, or security of the State' – 'it is essentially a matter of fact to be determined with due regard to the evidence … the Minister has to be satisfied, as a matter of fact, that the activities in question are calculated to prejudice the preservation of the peace, order, or security of the State … the Minister in this weighing of the evidence has been acting judicially.'[62] In this particular case, Seamus Burke had been arrested on 15 September 1939 following the discovery of a number of apparently seditious documents in his house. This fact was communicated to Dublin and an internment order was signed by the minister for Justice the following day.[63] The minister, Gavan Duffy concluded, 'having under the Act the right to prosecute for the alleged offence, elected to take the alternate course of directing indefinite imprisonment without trial for the "activity" of possessing seditious or incriminating documents.' Gavan Duffy ruled that a minister who signed a warrant under section 55(1) was acting judicially and purporting to administer justice, which was unconstitutional. He explained:

> The administration of justice is a peculiarly and distinctly judicial function, which from its essential nature does not fall within the executive power and is not properly incidental to the performance of the appropriate functions of the executive; consequently a law endowing these powers is an invasion of the judicial domain and as such is repugnant to the Constitution.[64]

O'Duffy also ruled that the internment warrant did not show proper jurisdiction – it lacked any reference to the government's proclamation under part 6 of the Offences act giving a minister power to intern, and contained no reference to section 54 which authorized the proclamation.[65] He also concluded that the 1924 O'Connell case had only a superficial resemblance to this case, because it was decided under a constitution which was radically different from the 1937 constitution.[66] Famously, Gavan Duffy held that the liberty of a citizen was not respected in cases of internment without charge or trial:[67]

> In my opinion, the saving words in the declaration that 'no citizen shall be deprived of his liberty save in accordance with law' cannot be used to validate an enactment conflicting with the constitutional

61 [1940] IR 149. **62** [1940] IR 150. **63** [1940] IR 152–3. **64** [1940] IR 152. **65** [1940] IR 156. **66** [1940] IR 146–7. **67** [1940] IR 154.

> guarantees ... The Constitution, with its impressive Preamble, is the Charter of the Irish People, and I will not whittle it away.[68]

The internment orders issued under the Offences against the State Act, 1939 were illegal. On 15 December 1939, the supreme court, relying on *Cox v. Hakes*,[69] and notwithstanding the provisions of article 34.4.3 of the constitution, declared that there was no appeal from Gavan Duffy's ruling.[70] As de Valera explained

> The Government, its advisers and all those interested in the passing of the Constitution and in the meaning of the Constitution, were taken by surprise when we found that the Act which was passed here was held to be unconstitutional. We were still more surprised when we found that the Supreme Court held that there was not a right of appeal even in a case in which the validity of an Act – in view of the Constitution – was in question.[71]

The government met to consider whether internees should or could be detained under the Emergency Powers Act or under new legislation, but having no other immediate legal choice, released the remaining 53 detainees on 2 December 1939.[72]

Despite this unexpected development, and rather than simply address its consequences, Stephen Roche believed the government had been given an opportunity to reassess the Offences against the State Act, 1939. He doubted if parts 5 and 6 of the 1939 act embodied the 'best effort that the Government and its advisers' could make 'towards the solution of one of the most important problems with which this country is faced, viz., the weakness of our judicial system in the face of outbursts of violence and disorder ... prompted by organisations such as the so-called "IRA".' Indeed, the department of Justice had opposed provision for internment during the drafting of the Offences against the State Bill. Fundamentally, Roche argued that the law in Ireland had evolved to deal with two forms of emergency – war emergencies and subversion:

> The fact is that trial by jury has no real roots in this country and is quite unsuited for dealing with our most serious form of crime, viz., political crime. Instead of recognising that fact frankly, we have put up the pretext that occasionally – once in ten years or so – we

68 [1940] IR 155. **69** [1890] 15 AC 506. **70** J. Kelly, *The Irish Constitution* (3rd ed.), pp 896–912, and Sharpe, *Habeas corpus*, pp 201–17. **71** Seanad Debates vol. 24 col. 511, 4 Jan. 1940. **72** 'Departmental Notes', p.75.

> may find to our surprise that juries will not convict in political cases, whereupon the Government makes proclamations under the Offences Against the State Act.

While this approach had political advantages, he believed, in reality, 'we are living in a permanent state of emergency as regards the administration of justice.'[73]

But this was certainly not the only aspect of the law he faulted. In Roche's view, many members of the high court were unable to deal with criminal cases 'in a sensible way', because they strained 'the law beyond all reason in favour of the accused.' When dealing with a 'plain criminal appeal', a judge was 'only too willing to direct his mind, as he is invited to do by the appellant's Counsel, from the realities of the case into a discussion on forms, precedents and theories.' He contended that a high court judge was usually selected 'with little or no reference to his capacity as an administrator or even as a criminal lawyer.' What was needed, therefore, was a 'more rational and much firmer administration of the criminal law, not as an emergency measure but as a permanent necessity.'

Roche envisaged repealing the special criminal court and internment provisions of the Offences against the State Act, and creating a permanent juryless high court which would deal with all criminal cases, irrespective of political motivation, and which would also order internments, 'the jurisdiction of which would be such as might be conferred upon it from time to time', equivalent in status to the existing high court which would thereafter deal solely with civil cases:

> we need a high court for criminal cases which will be a respectable and permanent feature of our judicial system and not a mere temporary expedient, a Court Martial thinly disguised which functions in a half-apologetic way under the jealous scrutiny of the 'ordinary' Courts.

The high court for criminal offences would consist of a president and four ordinary members, and would replace the central criminal court, 'to the great relief of the Dublin jurors'.

The secretary's proposals rested there, however. On 23 December 1939, the IRA raided the Irish army's poorly protected arsenal in the Phoenix Park, Dublin and seized over one million rounds of ammunition.[74] Boland remarked, 'if it had not been for the decision of the courts … that raid would not have occurred.'[75] Although exposing serious security deficien-

73 D/J 93/2/9, 8 Dec. 1939, Roche to Boland. 74 Bell, *Secret army*, pp 172–4, 'Departmental Notes', pp 77–8. 75 Dáil Debates vol. 78 col. 54, 3 Jan. 1940.

cies, by 1 January 1940, Gardaí and the army had recovered most of the ammunition.[76]

Roche's legislative ambitions no longer seemed appropriate in the wake of this latest incident. He believed that the issues raised by Gavan Duffy's ruling were irrelevant to the difficulties now confronting the state, adding, 'any unnecessary haste in that direction might not look well.'[77] Urging that the problems raised be temporarily ignored, Roche emphasized that 'the *urgent* thing (as we must admit if the point is put to us) is to have the power *now*.'[78] He suggested ignoring the Offences Act altogether and examining the powers available under Emergency Powers Act.

Inevitably, the government would take steps to intern persons under the Emergency Powers Act, as it was not be open to judicial scrutiny. The Emergency Powers (Amendment) Bill, 1940 became law on 4 January 1940, removing the prohibition on interning natural-born Irish citizens added in September 1939, and permitting 'the arrest without warrant of persons whose detention … is, in the opinion of a minister, necessary or expedient in the interests of the public safety or the preservation of the State'. These new internment powers became effective with the making of Emergency Powers (No. 20) Order, 1940, which de Valera signed on 6 January 1940. An internment commission was established on 3 February 1940.[79]

But the government was not content to leave the issues raised by George Gavan Duffy unresolved. A replacement for part 6 of the Offences against the State Act, 1939 was quickly drafted, and introduced into the Dáil on 4 January 1940.[80] Its sections corresponded almost exactly with part 6 of the original Act, except that a minister would no longer be required to be 'satisfied that any particular person is engaged in activities calculated to prejudice the preservation of the peace, order, or security of the State'[81] when he ordered an internment, but would have to have formed an 'opinion that any particular person is engaged in activities which, in his opinion, are prejudicial to the preservation of public peace and order or to the security of the State'.[82]

76 'Departmental Notes', p. 78. 77 D/J 93/2/9. Roche to P.P. O'Donoghue, 28 Dec. 1939. 78 Roche's emphasis. 79 D/T S.11552, government minutes, 3 Feb. 1940 G.2/125, and D/T S. 11618. 80 Cabinet Minutes, G.C.2/129, 2 Jan. 1940. 81 Section 55(1). 82 Section 4(1). The bill contained one additional provision, section 9: 'The Government shall once at least in every six months furnish to each House of the Oireachtas particulars of (*a*) persons detained under this Part of this Act, (*b*) persons in respect of whom the Commission has made a report to the Government, (*c*) persons in respect of whom the Commission has reported that no reasonable grounds exist for their continued detention, (*d*) persons who had been detained under this Part of this Act but who had been released on the report of the Commission, and (*e*) persons who had been detained under this Part of this Act but who had been released without a report of the Commission.'

There were serious and weighty reasons for the enactment of the Offences against the State (Amendment) Bill, 1940. Most importantly was the government's desire to definitely settle the question of whether or not it had the right to intern persons at times other than wartime. 'The Government believed that such powers were not contrary to the Constitution, and I suppose that this is such an important question that it must be resolved authoritatively', de Valera explained to the Council of State on 8 January 1940.[83] The president duly submitted the bill under article 26 of the constitution to the supreme court, which examined its constitutionality before it could be signed into law.[84] De Valera had earlier warned the Dáil, 'if the legislature and the judiciary are going to be at loggerheads we shall have to change that situation.'[85]

The supreme court upheld the validity of the bill, ruling that the power of internment as set out in the amended bill did not purport to give a minister power to administer justice;[86] it was not in the way of punishment but of preventative justice, and did not take away the right of habeas corpus. Relying on *R. (Zadig) v. Halliday*,[87] Chief Justice Sullivan declared 'the only essential preliminary to the exercise by the minister of the powers contained in section 4 is that he should have formed opinions on the matters specifically mentioned in the section. The validity of such opinions cannot be questioned in any court.'[88] Noting that the constitution did not specifically prohibit internment without trial, and with reference to the preamble, he said, 'It seems to us difficult to understand how the dignity and freedom of the individual member of the State can be attained unless social order is maintained in that State. There is nothing in this clause of the Preamble which could be invoked to necessitate the sacrifice of the common good in the interests of the individual.'

Initially, there were few internments, though Garda pressure on the IRA increased in the early months of 1940.[89]

There were 26 IRA members convicted by the special criminal court in January, primarily for failure to answer questions or to account for movements, 24 in February and 27 in March.[90] A further 23 were convicted in April of illegal drilling and membership of an unlawful organization. Myles Heffernan was convicted a second time by the special criminal court on 11 January 1940 for failure to answer questions under section

83 D/T S.11577, 8 Jan. 1940, and *Irish Press*, 9 Jan. 1940. 84 Mac Donnchadha, secretary to the president, to the secretary of the government, 12 Jan. 1940, also *Irish Press*, 9 Jan. 1940 and 10 Jan. 1940. 85 Dáil Debates vol. 78 col. 1353, 3 Jan. 1940. 86 [1940] IR 470, *In re Article 26 and the Offences against the State (Amendment) Act, 1940*; *Irish Press*, 10 Feb. 1940. 87 [1917] AC 260. 88 [1940] IR 479. 89 See tables 5a and 6b. 90 'Departmental Notes', pp 142a–d.

52 of the Offences against the State Act, 1939 and received a six month sentence. Further, the special criminal court began dealing with increasingly complicated charges: S. Byrne, J. Plunkett, S. Mongan and J. McNeela, for instance, were convicted of usurpation of government functions on 1 March 1940, each receiving between 18 months and two years.[91] While the longest sentence in 1939 was 3 years, J. Parnell, J. Lyons and J. McDermott each received 12 years for their involvement in the Phoenix Park raid.

As 1940 progressed, Gardaí increasingly sought to disrupt, if not to destroy, the IRA. On 17 February 1940, 16 senior IRA members were arrested in Dublin and remanded to Mountjoy.[92] Not content to accept prison conditions, however, several turned to the hunger strike, hoping to compel the government to grant political treatment and improved prison conditions. It was decided that six men would strike, and that when or if they died, they would be replaced by six others.[93] Unlike the situation of only six months earlier, however, government policy had unmistakably stiffened. Roche wrote, 'such a demand could not possibly be acceded to as it amounted to a demand that all prisoners belonging to the [IRA] should be held in military custody, the obvious object being that they should be recognised as members of a military force, entitled to be treated as prisoners of war.'[94] If de Valera had been 'indecisive' at times in his dealings with the IRA, Gerald Boland would not shirk his responsibilities. Within a year of being appointed minister for Justice, he claimed, 'Mr de Valera would not try to force me to do anything.'[95] Two of the hunger strikers died, Tony D'Arcy on 17 April, and Jack McNeela two days later. The strike ended soon after, once a note purportedly from Stephen Hayes was sent into the prison.[96]

While the IRA continued to sustain heavy Garda pressure after the collapse of the hungerstrike,[97] the security situation appeared to deteriorate rapidly in May 1940. Speaking in a national broadcast after two Gardaí carrying diplomatic mail were shot on 7 May 1940, de Valera warned:

> Our policy of patience has failed and is over … I warn those now planning new crimes against the nation that they will not be allowed to continue their policy of sabotage. They have set the law at defiance. The law will be enforced against them. If the present law is

91 *Irish Press*, 2 Mar. 1940 and 25 Apr. 1940. 92 'Departmental Notes', pp 82–4. 93 Bell, *The secret army*, p.178. 94 A/G 19/40, draft memorandum, approximately 20 Apr. 1940. 95 *Irish Times*, Gerry Boland's Story, 19 Oct. 1968. 96 Fisk, *In time of war*, pp 345–6. 97 See generally 'Departmental Notes', pp 78–860. For example, 20 men were arrested for illegal drilling in Clontarf, 31 Mar. 1940, and a bomb exploded in the Garda special branch headquarters in Dublin Castle, 25 Apr. 1940.

> not sufficient it will be strengthened; and in the last resort, if no other law will suffice, then the Government will invoke the ultimate law – the safety of the people.[98]

Much worse, on 23 May, only days after Germany invaded Belgium, Luxembourg and the Netherlands, Gardaí discovered the safe house of the German spy, Herman Goertz, in Dublin. Although Goertz evaded arrest for a further year, Gardaí seized documents of a military character concerning Irish harbours, aerodromes, roads, bridges, etc., and as to the disposition of the Irish army.[99] Linking the find to the IRA, de Valera said the organization was 'meditating treason'. He said there 'was no time for non-sense'.[1] Drastic steps would now be considered to deal with the organization. Indeed, the IRA had been trying to interest the Germans in invading Northern Ireland (with IRA assistance),[2] though Goertz regarded these plans as 'childish' and 'completely useless'.[3]

An all party 'Defence Conference' was established on 28 May 1940 to assist the government in dealing with the emergency and to keep opposition parties abreast of developments, though Richard Mulcahy later complained it was forced to search for information 'like scratching hens'.[4] The conference composed of the ministers for Justice, Defence and for the Coordination of Defensive Measures; Richard Mulcahy, James Dillon and Dr Thomas O'Higgins of Fine Gael; and William Norton and William Davin of the Labour Party, first met on 30 May 1940.[5] O'Higgins immediately called for the internment of all the known IRA members; Mulcahy proposed that a sufficient number should be detained to prevent the possibility of a rising, though Norton cautioned that the concentration of so many in an internment camp would only 'provide facilities for the perfection of their organisation'. Following consultations with Garda HQ to ascertain who, given the circumstances, might be regarded as a danger to the state,[6] Boland issued over 400 internment orders on 3 June 1940.[7]

On the day of the Goertz discovery, the department for the Coordination of Defensive Measures and the parliamentary draftsman's office drew up a proclamation under article 28.3.2 of the constitution and

98 Speaking on 8 May 1940, quoted in D/T S.11564A, 'Memorandum on the policy of the Government with regard to Offences against the State'. 99 Dáil Debates vol. 101 col. 1119, 29 May 1946; A/G 24/40; and 'Departmental Notes', p. 86b. 1 *Irish Press*, 27 May 1940, quoted in Bowman, *De Valera*, p. 220. 2 Bell, *The secret army*, pp 185–6, and *Irish Independent*, 15 Dec. 1945, and D/FA A.12, Col. Bryan (G2) to Walshe, secretary of the department of Foreign Affairs, 21 Dec. 1945. 3 Bowman, *De Valera*, p. 211. 4 D/T S.11896A. See also D/FA A.24, and *Irish Press*, 29 May 1940, 2 Dec. 1944, P7/C/113, 1 Feb. 1941, quoted in Fisk, *In time of war*, p. 161. 5 'Departmental Notes', p. 86b. 6 D/T S.11896A. 7 See tables 5a and 5b.

drafted a rough order, equivalent to a declaration of martial law, to be made in case of invasion:[8]

> Where a person is alleged to have committed any offence mentioned in the Schedule hereto–
> (a) any commanding officer may appoint three officers to investigate the matter and to report to him whether in their opinion such person has or has not committed such offence,
> (b) if such three officers or a majority of them report that such person has committed such offence, such commanding officer may, if he thinks fit, order that such person shall suffer the penalty of death or be detained, and any such order may be carried into execution.

The schedule included treason, murder, espionage, arson, sabotage, looting, unlawful possession of arms, ammunition, bombs, or explosives, or any acts calculated to seriously prejudice the public safety or to endanger the security of the state.

Originally, the government intended to group the Explosives Act, 1875, the Explosive Substances Act, 1883, and the Firearms Act, 1925 into the schedule of the Emergency Powers Order, 1939, but were omitted because the 1883 Act included terms such as 'her majesty's dominions', 'subject of her majesty', 'United Kingdom', etc, which had not been adapted for general use in the Twenty-Six Counties. As a result, the stopping and searching of vehicles for arms, ammunition or explosives under article 76 of the order was not permitted.[9] While Emergency Powers (No. 25) Order, 1940 remedied this omission for the 1875 and 1925 acts,[10] the provisions of the Explosive Substances Act, 1883 remained problematic. On 24 May, the department of Justice suggested that the act be repealed and re-enacted in a way more suitable to Irish needs, adding that it would be 'a salutary gesture to make provision for the imposition of the death penalty under the Act in certain circumstances'.[11] Three days later, it wrote that if the list of capital offences during the emergency were extended, it should be done:

8 D/T S.12067, 23 May 1940. Draft prepared by the parliamentary draftsman on instructions from the attorney general, after consultation with the minister for the Coordination of Defensive Measures and Major Hodnett, deputy judge advocate general. Ó Muimhneacháin to General Mac Mathghamhna, 22 June 1940. 9 D/J S.109/40, department of Defence memorandum, 22 Feb. 1940, D/T S.11649, department of Justice memorandums, 19 Feb. 1940. 10 Irish Independent, 13 Mar. 1940. 11 D/T S.11649, 24 May 1940, the subject was resurrected, the department of Justice explained, following a bomb attack on the Garda special branch headquarters, Dublin Castle, and arms offences in Cork. No mention of the Goertz discovery was made. Signed the office of the minister for Justice.

> in the manner best suited to impress and terrify possible offenders and in considering this aspect of the matter the speed and certainty of the punishment are most important factors. The effect of making sabotage a capital offence will be greatly diminished if the trial is postponed and prolonged by reason of legal formalities: the effect will be further diminished if it is felt that any conviction is liable to be closely scrutinised by the court of criminal appeal, with further delay, and lastly the interval of about three weeks which would normally elapse between confirmation of a sentence and the actual execution and the possible difficulties of carrying out the execution … in the usual manner would tend to diminish the wholesome sense of fear inspired by the capital sentence. In short, if death is threatened at all, immediate and certain death should be threatened subject only to the possibility of the exercise of the prerogative of mercy.

The department proposed that the death penalty should be imposed for the possession of firearms with intent to endanger life, acts of sabotage, espionage, and active membership of an unlawful organization. More importantly, it called for the creation of a special military court to try these offences that could only impose the death penalty on persons it convicted and from which there would be no appeal. The proposed court would have full control of procedure to prevent all but the most unavoidable of delays. The government would confirm its sentences, which would, if no reprieve were forthcoming, be executed 'in military fashion' within 24 hours. There would be no provision for a coroner's inquest. The department sought provisions 'which will ensure beyond doubt that the procedure of the Special Court, etc. in these matters is entirely outside the jurisdiction of the ordinary courts: the words will require to be so definite that no judge of the high court will have a shadow of an excuse for interfering.'[12]

The department of Justice later wrote, 'the special criminal court was not an entirely satisfactory solution of certain difficulties in disposing of persons charged with serious offences against the state.' It described its principle flaws thus:

> (a) The special criminal court can inflict the only *normal* penalties for an offence e.g. it cannot impose the death sentence for anything except murder or treason, whereas in certain circumstances the fear of the capital penalty may be the only adequate deterrent for such crimes as sabotage, shooting with intent to kill, etc.,
>
> (b) the hunger strike device, employed to delay trial, as by McGrath and MacCurtain, can be adequately met only by trying the

12 D/T S.11649, 27 May 1940.

accused in his absence or by a procedure so summary that the accused is tried before his health has suffered so much that he is not fit to stand trial,

(c) the normal method of executing the death sentence, viz, with the interval of several weeks after judgement – longer in cases of appeal – and then by a process (hanging) which requires the attendance of a skilled executioner, whose attendance might be prevented by accident or design, is not suitable for cases in which the speed and certainty of punishment are essential considerations.[13]

The government accepted the department's proposals, though the Emergency Powers Act 1939 would be amended in order to avoid ad hoc legislation.[14] Further, special Garda powers of search under sections 29 of the Offences against the State Act, 1939 were extended by replacing the word 'inspector' by the word 'sergeant' and special powers to detain suspects under section 30 were extended to an initial period of 48 hours, and to a further 8 days on direction by a chief superintendent.[15] Additionally, the internment commission was scrapped.[16]

The first draft of the Emergency Powers (Amendment) (No. 2) Bill, 1940 was prepared by 28 May 1940[17] and simply removed the prohibition on the trial of civilians by military tribunals contained in section 2(5) of the parent act. After cabinet discussions,[18] the following was added: 'The Government may, by an order under section 2 of the Principle Act, make provision for the trial, in a summary manner, by commissioned officers of the Defence Forces, of any person alleged to have committed any offence specified in such order, and, in case of the conviction of such person of such offence, for the imposition and the carrying out of the sentence of death, and no appeal shall lie in respect of such conviction or sentence.'

The draft bill was considered by the Defence Conference on 4 June 1940[19] and introduced into the Dáil the following day. It passed the Seanad on 26 June 1940, where Boland told Senators:

> The Government has decided to ask for these powers because they felt that they are absolutely necessary ... this Bill is intended for a

13 'Departmental Notes', p. xxx. 14 Cabinet Minutes, G.C. 2/172, 28 May 1940. 15 D/T S.11900, Emergency Powers (No.27) Order, 1940, signed 4 June 1940. 16 Article 6 of the Emergency Powers (No. 20) Order, 1940 was revoked on 7 June 1940; see Government Minutes G.2/155, D/T S.11552A, department of Justice memorandum, 3 June 1940, 'Departmental Notes', p. 82. 17 D/T S.11901, P.P. O'Donoghue had apparently received verbal instructions to proceed on this matter but the exact date is unclear. 18 CAB G.C.2/174, 31 May 1940. 19 D/T S.11901, Ó Cinnéide to private secretary, minister for Justice, 4 June 1940.

> state of affairs such as existed in the immediate past … In an emergency like the present, people who go around with guns or fire at officers of State in the execution of their duty, or try to take the law into their own hands, or to upset the Government, will have to be dealt with in a summary and drastic fashion.

He warned them, however, if the situation deteriorated, the government would adopt even more stringent measures: 'For some time past there has been no shooting or blowing up of public buildings, but if a state of war should come there will be a more drastic order … nothing short of drumhead courts-martial.'[20]

Debate in the Defence Conference during mid-June 1940 centred on whether a certificate should be produced before the proposed special military court would try an accused (in order to prevent possible abuses) and whether it should be under the hand of the minister for Justice or of the government collectively.[21] The Conference concluded that a collective decision would expose the minister to less danger[22] – Boland had indicated as much to the Seanad.[23] But Roche contended that the sole prerequisite that would determine if a person could be charged and tried by the proposed special military court was that an offence scheduled to the order had been committed. He believed that the minister did not have to regard his Seanad statement as a binding guarantee – if the government decided against the certificate Senators would not feel deceived because their readiness to accept the bill 'would not have been altered in the slightest if nothing had been said about the certificate.' Roche advocated a different approach:

> The objections to a certificate by the Government are the formalities and delay which it would involve. The reasons for passing the new Act are that speed and severity are now essential in dealing with grave anti-State offences. It will be rather paradoxical if the first step taken in the direction of speeding up trials is to provide that there cannot be any trial until the case against the accused had been formally considered by the Government.

Fearing governmental indecision ('there would have to be a meeting of the Government at which possibly different opinions might be expressed'), Roche suggested that no certificate be issued at all, instead:

20 Seanad Debates vol. 24 col. 1990–2, the proposed court-martial is discussed below. **21** D/T S.11905A, Roche to M. Ó Muimhneacháin, 28 June 1940. **22** D/T S.11896A, 19 June 1940. **23** Seanad Debates vol. 24 col. 1991.

> to ensure that only really grave cases go before the Military Court: that object will be sufficiently ensured by the sense of proportion and responsibility of the higher police and other officers who will have to handle the matter in the ordinary course and it is not conceivable that in practice any case will go before a Military Court without the knowledge and approval of the minister for Justice.

He recommended that the government simply make an order or direction along the lines that it was of the opinion 'that the said charges are of exceptional gravity in the present circumstances of the country and that they should be investigated with all possible speed, hereby directs.' In practice, subsidiary orders were made under Order 41 (e.g. Order 41b) directing that the special military court try suspects.[24]

Under the terms of the finalized order, the special military court was constituted by any three army officers 'who are for the time being members of any special criminal court',[25] with the most senior officer acting as president, though in case of doubt, the adjutant general would decide questions.[26] Where a person was 'alleged to have committed a specified offence, such person may be brought before a military court.'

Before the commencement of a trial, the special military court was to satisfy itself 'that a statement of the charge or charges against [the accused] has been delivered to such person and that he has been afforded any facilities (which he has requested and which such military court, having regard to the exigencies of the situation, considers reasonable) for preparing his defence, and if not so satisfied shall adjourn such trial for such time as such military court thinks proper.'[27] The court was to determine its own procedure, and every question arising before it was to be determined by majority vote. When it found a person guilty, the court was obliged to sentence a person to death by shooting.[28]

A record of the proceedings at each trial and the court's findings were to be forwarded to the government,[29] which might remit the sentence, commute it to one of penal servitude or imprisonment or decline to remit or commute the sentence.[30] If it declined to remit or commute the sentence, the adjutant general was to ensure that the sentence was executed within 48 hours of the government's decision.[31] There would be no coroner's inquest,[32]and the body was to be interred as the adjutant general directed.[33] If the government decided to commute the sentence to penal

24 D/T S.12067, Mac Mathghamhna to Roche, 31 July 1940, Roche to Mac Mathghamhna, 11 Dec. 1940. 25 Article 3(1). 26 Article 3(2). 27 Article 6. 28 Article 8. 29 Article 9. 30 Article 10(a). 31 Article 10(b). 32 Article 11(a). 33 Article 11(b).

servitude or imprisonment, it was to be carried out 'in all respects as if it were imposed by a special criminal court.'[34]

The schedule covered treason; recording communicating or possessing information prejudicial to the public safety or the state; acts or omissions by persons with a duty to the public; sabotage; murder; unlawfully wounding; shooting at with intent to maim or to resist arrest; assault and kidnap, causing explosions with intent to injure life or property; unlawful possession of explosives, possession of firearms or ammunition with intent to injure life or property; attempting, conspiring to commit a scheduled offence or aiding, abetting, counselling or procuring the commission of a scheduled offence. The relatively small number of scheduled but serious offences had been accepted by the government on the proviso that a death sentence would not be executed unless it had an opportunity of first commuting it to one of penal servitude or imprisonment.[35]

A large number of active IRA members were swiftly arrested by the Gardaí which, often backed by soldiers, pursued the organization more vigorously than at any time since the end of the Civil War.[36] There were 26 incidents between May and August 1940 involving the IRA and the Garda special branch,[37] part of what Bowyer Bell described as a pattern of 'provocation, retaliation and revenge.'[38] There were many afterwards. For example, Michael Conway and Patrick McNeela were shot and arrested as special branch pressure mounted after May 1940. Gardaí supported by soldiers arrested Denis Griffin on 5 June 1940, after a shoot out in Dunmanway, Co. Cork; J.J. Kavanagh was shot dead near an uncompleted tunnel as he attempted to escape from Cork prison on 3 August.[39]

In addition to a general toughening of arrest policy, the special criminal court's sentences became noticeably stiffer. For instance, it sentenced at least three IRA members to be flogged for armed robbery following conviction under the Larceny Act, 1916. Sentences were carried out in the cases of Paddy Murphy and Willie Stewart, both receiving twelve strokes of the cat'.[40]

Further indicating how seriously the government now viewed the situation was its clear desire to see Tomás MacCurtain, son of the assassinated lord mayor of Cork, put to death. MacCurtain had shot Garda John Roche dead in Cork on 3 January 1940 and was subsequently convicted of murder by the special criminal court.[41] Delivered on 13 June 1940, the

34 Article 5(2). 35 D/T S.12067, department of Justice memorandum, 18 Nov. 1940. 36 See 'Departmental Notes', pp 86–86n. 37 Coogan, *The IRA*, p. 193. 38 Bell, *The secret army*, p. 183, and generally pp 182–95. 39 'Departmental Notes', pp 86f–o. 40 U. Mac Eoin (ed.), *The IRA*, pp 526–31. In another case, the sentence was remitted on health grounds. 41 'Departmental Notes', pp 79–80.

death sentence was to be executed on 5 July 1940. But not every minister believed he should die and one, Seán T O'Kelly, intervened. Speaking of his assistance, MacCurtain's counsel, Seán McBride recalled:

> [O'Kelly] advised me to take any sort of delaying action I could in the courts, which I did. I planned the moves very carefully. I went seeking a conditional habeas corpus at 3.30 in the afternoon, the courts then rising at 4 pm. I knew that I would be thrown out. At 3.55 Gavan Duffy refused the order. I lodged my appeal just before the office closed. MacCurtain was due to be hanged in Mountjoy the next day, so it was a very close shave. They tried to bring the supreme court together that evening, but they were unable because [Mr Justice] Murnaghan … was out, diplomatically maybe, walking with his dog … Straight away they had to postpone the execution for a couple of days.[42]

More in the hope of buying time than of bringing a successful action, MacCurtain's counsel sought an order of habeas corpus before George Gavan Duffy, arguing that the special criminal court was unconstitutional as it was staffed solely by military personnel and was, in fact, a military tribunal as contemplated by article 38.4 of the constitution, which could only operate in time of war.[43] Gavan Duffy rejected this:

> The fact that special provision is made for the setting up of a military tribunal in another section of the Constitution (Article 38, clause 4) for military offences and to deal with offences in time of war or armed rebellion cannot fairly be used to cut down the express power which the Constitution gives the Oireachtas to create Special [Criminal] Courts … In my opinion the constitution of the Special [Criminal] Court has been 'prescribed by law' as required by Art.38 of the Constitution, and I find that the composition of the tribunal so constituted is within the words of s. 39, sub-s 3 of the Offences Against the State Act, being composed, as authorised by that enactment, of officers of the Defence Forces.[44]

He also rejected the contention that the government was acting judicially when it made a proclamation under section 35 that it was satisfied that the ordinary courts were 'inadequate to secure the effective administration of justice and the preservation of public peace and order' in order to activate part 5 of the Offences against the State Act:

42 Mac Eoin (ed.), *Survivors*, p. 124. 43 *In re MacCurtain*,[1941] IR 83 and 90. 44 [1941] IR 85–6.

> The Oireachtas clearly considered the Government to be the authority best situated, from its position and the information at its disposal, to determine whether or not Special Tribunals were necessary in the circumstances set out in the section. In my opinion … [it] is clearly meant to be an essentially executive decision of the highest executive authority in the State.

He added that the high court could not expect the executive to give reasons for its decisions because the act did not require that it give reasons.[45]

Counsel also claimed that the attorney general's powers under section 46 to order the transfer of trials of persons charged with indictable non-scheduled offences to the special criminal court was unconstitutional as it vested judicial and legislative powers in the attorney general. George Gavan Duffy also dismissed this assertion:

> I do not follow the contention that because an offence is not scheduled, the Attorney General is therefore required to act either in a judicial or legislative capacity. He is precisely the person to whom one would expect the Legislature to entrust consideration of such a question essentially within his domain, because he is the State authority in charge of prosecutions under an express provision of the Constitution.[46]

Indicating how poor counsel's arguments were, Gavan Duffy declared that the view that trial by the special criminal court was an abrogation of trial by jury and therefore unconstitutional 'requires all [counsel's] courage and learning'.[47] The conviction was upheld but while that decision was appealed to the supreme court, the government was forced to suspend the execution until 13 July 1940.[48] The appeal was also shortly rejected. Nevertheless, on 10 July 1940, the government announced that the sentence had been commuted and reduced to penal servitude for life.

Following MacCurtain's reprieve, the government began to transfer IRA members convicted of the most serious offences to Portlaoise Prison, subjecting them to a harsh regime. If other IRA members were found guilty of murdering Gardaí, there appeared to be little likelihood they could escape death.

On 16 August 1940, the Garda special branch raided a house in Dublin, seeking the arrest of a number of IRA members, including Patrick

45 [1941] IR 86. 46 [1941] IR 87. 47 Ibid. 48 On the technical consequences of this decision see D/T S.11973, Roche to Ó Muimhneacháin, 3 July 1940, government minutes, G.2/167, 4 July 1940; *Irish Times*, 9 July 1940.

McGrath and Francis Harte. Two Gardaí died as a result of the ensuing gun battle, though Harte and McGrath were arrested. Within hours, the government established the special military court to try both men. Three days later, it found both guilty of murdering Garda Richard Hyland and sentenced them to death. The government declined to commute the sentence on 23 August 1940.[49] Relief was sought before Mr Justice Gavan Duffy, who granted a conditional order of habeas corpus, requiring the government to make Emergency Powers (No. 45) Order, 1940 which enabled the adjutant general to suspend the executions, though they could be ordered at any subsequent time.[50]

Counsel for McGrath and Harte took a number of lines of attack. Before George Gavan Duffy, Seán McBride argued that the first amendment to the constitution was invalid because it was not within the powers of amendment or repeal conferred on the Oireachtas by article 51.[51] Gavan Duffy rejected this: '[it] is clearly within the powers given to the Oireachtas within the first three years of the Constitution.' To the contention that the President did not consult with the Council of State about holding a referendum before he signed the bill, Gavan Duffy replied, 'Article 51 imposes no obligation.'[52] McBride also argued that the bill was signed by the President earlier than five days after it had been presented to him, contrary to article 25.2.1, but Gavan Duffy ruled that 'it is quite clear that Art. 25 subs. 2 does not apply to this constitutional amendment.'[53]

The second line of attack was that the Emergency Powers Acts, 1939 to 1940 did not have the protection of article 28.3.3 because, McBride argued, they were not expressed to be for the purpose of securing the public safety and preserving the state in time of war, and because the statutes did not recite the required resolutions by both Houses of the Oireachtas as contemplated by the first amendment of the constitution. Gavan Duffy ruled that the acts' long titles 'very clearly expressed' their purpose. The supreme court took the view that this recital was unnecessary.[54]

Gavan Duffy responded to the argument that Order 41 and Order 41A failed to show sufficient jurisdiction by failing to recite that they were, in the government's opinion, necessary or expedient for the public safety or for the preservation of the state, ruling that 'the Government acted under a specific power given them by s.2 of the Emergency Powers Act, 1939, as amended.'[55] Gavan Duffy discharged the order.

49 Bell, *The secret army*, p. 187, 'Departmental Notes', pp 86f–h. 50 D/T S.12048 51 *In re McGrath and Harte* [1941] IR 68. 52 [1941] IR 72. The supreme court ruled that this was within the president's discretion, [1941] IR 75. 53 [1941] IR 72. 54 [1941] IR 76. 55 [1941] IR 73.

The supreme court gave some more consideration to two other points. McBride argued that Emergency Powers (No. 41) Order, 1940 did not provide a system allowing for the selection of members of the special military court, but the supreme court responded:

> In our opinion no such provisions were necessary. Any three persons having the qualifications specified in clause 3 of the Order would, in our opinion, constitute such a court, and would have jurisdiction to try an accused person charged with a specified offence and brought before them for trial.[56]

The contention that the retrospective nature of Emergency Powers (No. 41) Order, 1941 was illegal was also demolished:[57]

> Section 3 of the Act provides that the Government may, by such an Order, make provision for the trial in a summary manner of any person alleged to have committed any offence specified in such Order. In our opinion these words, taken in conjunction with the provisions of section 2(1) of the Principal Act are sufficiently wide to enable the Government by Order, made under these Acts, to provide for the trial and punishment of persons alleged to have committed offences whether before or after the making of such Order.[58]

Speaking more generally, the supreme court described the 'clear language of [article 28.3.3], which, in the times and circumstances contemplated, makes it impossible to invoke other Articles of the Constitution to invalidate Acts passed by the Oireachtas and expressed to be for the purpose of securing the public safety and the preservation of the State within the terms of the Article.' The supreme court unanimously rejected the appeal without hearing arguments by counsel for the state.[59] McGrath and Harte were shot by firing squad on 6 September 1940.

A third man, Thomas Hunt, had initially escaped the raid, but was quickly arrested and convicted by the special military court on 23 September.[60] His death sentence was commuted to penal servitude for life on 25 September, however, because, as Boland explained, 'I felt that the boy was more of a tool than anything else.'[61]

The minister for Justice later said:

56 [1941] IR 77–8. 57 See also Kelly, *The Irish Constitution* (3rd ed.), pp 197–8. 58 [1941] IR 77 59 'Departmental Notes', p. 86g. 60 D/T S.12065, Emergency Powers (No 41b), Order, 1940. Hunt was released in July 1945 61 Dáil Debates vol. 101 col. 1131–2, 29 May 1946.

> This court has been described outside as a terror court. I have no objection to its so being described. That is exactly what it was. It was a terror court – a court set up to meet terror in a drastic and summary manner in order to save this nation from perils which threatened it at the time.[62]

Recalling how his resolve had faltered in the face of McGrath's hunger-strike in 1939, de Valera admitted:

> I urged upon my colleagues – I take full blame for it, because in the event it was very blame worthy – to have the man concerned transferred to a civil hospital. He was transferred there, and got out of prison, and within a year he was engaged with others in an attack upon the Gardaí, in which two of the Gardaí were killed, and he and another party engaged in the shooting had to be executed. That meant four deaths. Later on we had two more: Two men who died on hungerstrike because we had at some stage to stand absolutely firm ... It was one of the biggest mistakes that I have made in my life ... I will regret it until my death, because, had it not been for my action, there would have been only one death, whereas, in the event, there were ... six in all.[63]

The special military court held six further trials:

- Oliver Nixon was found not guilty of conspiracy to murder John Quinn at Dundalk on 1 January 1941.[64]
- Richard Goss and Joseph O'Callaghan were charged with shooting at Gardaí and soldiers: Goss was found guilty on 1 August 1941, while O'Callaghan was discharged. The government declined to remit or commute Goss' sentence on 6 August 1941 – he was shot by firing squad at Portlaoise Prison on 9 August 1941.[65]
- Seán McCaughey was found guilty of unlawfully assaulting and imprisoning Stephen Hayes on 18 September 1941. His sentence was commuted to penal servitude for life on 25 September 1941.[66]
- Michael Walsh, Patrick Davern, George Plant and Joseph O'Connor were charged with the murder of Michael Devereux in Tipperary. Only Joseph O'Connor was found not guilty on 26 Feb. 1942. Walsh's and Davern's sentences were commuted to

62 Dáil Debates vol. 101 col. 1116. 63 Dáil Debates vol. 91 col. 604, 9 July 1943. 64 D/T S.12202, Emergency Powers (No 41c) Order, 1940, dated 9 Dec. 1940. 65 D/T S.12540, Emergency Powers (No 41d) Order, 1941, dated 22 July 1941. 66 D/T S.12590, Emergency Powers (No 41e) Order, 1941, dated 10 Sept. 1941.

penal servitude for life, but the government declined to remit or commute Plant's sentence. He was executed and interred in Portlaoise Prison on 5 March 1942.[67]

- Maurice O'Neill was convicted of shooting at Gardaí with intent to resist arrest on 5 November 1942. The government refused to remit or commute the sentence on 9 November 1942 and O'Neill was executed and interred in Mountjoy Prison on 12 November 1942.[68]
- Michael J. Quille was found not guilty on 20 January 1943 of the murder of Detective Sergeant Denis O'Brien in Dublin.[69]

The 'drum-head' tribunals that Gerald Boland had spoken of in June 1940 would operate if the country were invaded.[70] Although the attorney general believed the constitution prohibited martial law, he concluded it did not require amendment as article 28.3.2 allowed the government to take whatever steps it considered necessary to protect the state 'in the case of actual invasion' and thus to confer both specific and general powers on the army.[71] The drafting and issuing of an Army Emergency Powers Order (eventually Order No. 65) and instructions (as might be revised) rendered any action under article 28.3.2 unnecessary, however.[72]

Emergency Powers (No. 41) Order, 1940 presupposed the government being able to function relatively normally, to receive reports and to issue orders. In the event of an invasion, however, and the resultant restrictions 'it might be anticipated that the ordinary Courts of Justice would require to be supported or replaced by military courts to a greater extent than at present.'[73] Emergency Powers (No. 65) Order would come into force 'whenever and so often' as the Taoiseach saw fit, who would 'direct, in such manner as he thinks proper' that the Order should become operative.[74] If this order came into force, the court created under Order 41 would employ the second order's schedule.[75]

Following an invasion, military tribunals could be established whenever and so often as a commanding officer not below the rank of commandant, commanding a command, a district, or a brigade thought fit. Tribunals would consist of 'any three officers', one of whom could not be

67 D/T S.12682, Emergency Powers (No 41f) Order, 1941, dated 31 Dec. 1941. 68 D/T S.12996, Emergency Powers (No 41g) Order, 1942, dated 27 Oct. 1942. 69 D/T S.13075, Emergency Powers (No 41h) Order, 1942, dated 30 Dec. 1942 70 See also D/T S.11986, S.11992, S.12199, S.12156, S.12223, S.12273, and D/T S.12290, P. Berry, private secretary, minister for Justice, to the assistant secretary of the department of Justice, 4 Apr. 1941. 71 D/T S.12067, memorandum by the department of Defence, 4 Mar. 1941. 72 D/T S.12067, D/D S.205, Ó Muimhneacháin to Roche, 4 July 1940. 73 D/T S.12067, 18 Nov. 1940, minister for Justice memorandum to the Government, considered 29 Nov. 1940. 74 Article 2(2). 75 Article 3.

below the rank of commandant, with one acting as president.[76] A tribunal would have jurisdiction to try any person alleged to have committed a scheduled offence once a Garda not below the rank of inspector brought an accused before it, and if the tribunal found such person guilty of that scheduled offence to order them to be shot.[77] A record of its findings were to be forwarded to a confirming authority,[78] who would be the commanding officer who established the tribunal or any officer authorized in that behalf by him,[79] or in the case of any military court 'the Adjutant General ... [or] any officer authorised in that behalf by the Adjutant General.'[80] The confirming authority might confirm or remit the sentence, or might confirm the sentence but suspend its execution, or reduce the sentence to penal servitude, imprisonment, or a fine.[81] The list of offences triable by the court was much longer than that of Emergency Powers (No. 41) Order, 1940 and included arson, attacks on trains and railways, damage to farm property and crops, membership of unlawful organizations, usurpation of the functions of government, and armed robbery.

Further, the tribunals would have jurisdiction to try civilians of any nationality committing scheduled offences within Irish jurisdiction, persons subject to military law, and, in order to avoid a multiplicity of types of military tribunal, would also deal with war treason, espionage and violations of the rules of war. Instructions to the army made it clear, though, that the 'subordination of the military to the civil authority remains, and members of the defence forces must in their actions towards the civil population keep strictly within powers accorded [them by various] Emergency Orders'. It was also made clear that these tribunals were not courts-martial as they would be created by statutory order, but 'they will resemble martial law courts in so far as they are intended to give the military authorities in time of war a speedy and simply method of dealing with serious crime.'[82]

Otherwise, these tribunals would function much as the special military court created under Emergency Powers (No. 41) Order, 1940: they would be obliged, 'having regard to the exigencies of the situation', to provide the accused with reasonable facilities to prepare his defence;[83] each tribunal would determine its own procedure, and every decision would be determined by majority vote.

The government examined the draft emergency powers order on 29 November 1940 and redrafting, with amendments suggested by the government, the army and the attorney general, was completed by 27 December

76 Article 5. 77 Article 7. 78 Article 11. 79 Article 6(1)(a). 80 Article 6(1). 81 Article 12. 82 D/T S.12067, department of Defence memorandum, 'Instructions as to the powers of the military authorities in relation to the civil population on an invasion occurring', 4 Mar. 1941. 83 Article 8.

1940. The order was secretly printed in case of immediate crisis. It would come into force once the country was invaded, the presumption being that the necessary administrative arrangements had been attended to beforehand.[84] It was also intended that the order would not become operative until the court system of Order 41 had ceased to function adequately.

On 2 May 1941, the government approved instructions prepared by the department of Defence regarding the powers of the military in relation to the civilian population in the event of an invasion.[85] No further action on the part of the government would now be necessary. As P.P. O'Donoghue explained

> If, in the event of an invasion, the powers were exercised by the military, such exercise could and would be related back to the approval already given by the Government and no additional direction given by the Government in the event of an invasion could add anything to the approval already accorded. Furthermore, the fact that the approval had been given before invasion would not in any way clash with the provisions of Article 28.3.2. The Dáil would, of course, have to be informed when it met, of the fact that the Government had approved of the exercise of the powers.[86]

On 13 June 1941, the government approved additional instructions in addition to the military courts to be followed in case of invasion. These were circulated to the relevant government departments on 19 June 1941. How instructions might be communicated to local authorities, the civil service operating outside Dublin, etc., would be settled by departments individually in consultation with the department of Finance. If an invasion occurred, a series of orders would be immediately promulgated. These would cover, for instance, the functions of the Taoiseach, Tánaiste, and members of the government and would permit the elevation of TDs to the cabinet without reference to the president.[87] There were also plans to establish county and regional commissioners.[88] Departments were informed that this list of orders might be added to later.[89]

It had also been proposed that committees of 'suitable local persons' could be appointed to deal with offences not covered by Emergency

84 D/T S.12078, proposals presented by the department of Defence, 4 Mar. 1941. 85 Ibid., Madigan, department of Defence, to Ó Muimhneacháin, 17 June 1941, with reference to a minute by Ó Cinnéide, 26 May 1941. 86 Ibid., Madigan to Ó Muimhneacháin, 17 June 1941, reporting O'Donoghue's final opinion on matters once the instructions had been approved. 87 Note of 16 July 1940, A/G 29/40 and D/T S.11982, Emergency Powers (No. 38) Order, 1940. 88 A/G 26/40, 17 July 1940, D/T S. 12078, 19 Sept. 1940. 89 D/T S.12078, D/J 119/74, P. Ó Cinnéide to the private secretary, minister for Justice, 19 June 1941.

Powers (No. 65) Order, 1941, where district justices were unable or unwilling to act. But there was considerable opposition to the plan and 'general agreement that an emergency such as was contemplated could not possibly be of long duration.'

Although the government prepared for the worst, clearly, its handling of the IRA had been highly effective. The FBI noted that IRA setbacks between 1939 and 1941 had

> resulted in a marked deterioration in the quality and quantity of IRA personnel. As a result of this, allegedly considerable dissatisfaction developed, particularly among the northern members of the Irish Republican Army. Stephen Hayes was still Chief of Staff of the Irish Republican Army and allegedly had become a chronic alcoholic by this time. Hayes was successful in avoiding arrest during this entire period and according to some reports, some suspicion arose concerning him.[90]

By the summer of 1941, senior members of the Northern Ireland IRA concluded that Stephen Hayes, the IRA chief of staff, was a Garda agent.

Seán McCaughey and others abducted Hayes on 30 June 1941. They questioned him over a period of weeks, eventually extracting a detailed confession claiming that all the events in which the IRA was involved since 1935, the bombing campaign in England, the Magazine Fort raid etc. had been elements of an elaborate conspiracy designed by the Dublin government to discredit and destroy the organization. Before Hayes could be killed, however, McCaughey was arrested. Hayes shortly escaped and surrendered to Gardaí.[91]

The IRA continued to fare badly after this, though the organization did not disappear immediately. There were four attacks on witnesses during 1942, and a failed Northern campaign in September of that year. Sergeant Denny O'Brien, who had led the special branch raid that netted McGrath and Harte, was gunned down on 9 September 1942. Michael Quille was later charged with O'Brien's murder but the special military court found him not guilty. (Charlie Kerins, IRA chief of staff in 1944, was later convicted of the murder by the special criminal court and hanged in December 1944.) On 30 September 1942, the special branch attempted to arrest IRA member Patrick Dermody at a wedding in Co. Cavan, but in the ensuing gun battle both he and a special branch officer died. On 19 October, the special branch attempted to arrest Harry White and Maurice O'Neill. Although White managed to escape, O'Neill was captured. He was charged with shooting at Gardaí while attempting to resist arrest and sentenced to death by the mil-

90 FBI memorandum to the State Department, 30 Sept. 1943, quoted in Cronin, *Washington's Irish policy*, p. 85. 91 See Bell, *The secret army*, pp 199–212.

itary court; he was executed in November.[92] Although no IRA activities were reported after June 1943, Gardaí and the army maintained heavy pressure on the organization and continued to find arms and materials.[93]

The Hayes affair further weakened an already disorganized and dislocated IRA.[94] While the truth or accuracy of Hayes' confession remains debatable, it appears to have led Gardaí to the body of IRA member Michael Devereux who had been shot in September 1940 on suspicion of being an informer. Four were charged with his murder and brought before the special criminal court. Michael Walsh and Patrick Davern, apparently accomplices in the killing, made statements to Gardaí, but then refused to testify, claiming that they had been beaten into giving evidence. The case before the special criminal court now simply collapsed. The matter did not end there, though.

It was to Taylor's *Law of Evidence* that the attorney general's adviser, P.P. O'Donoghue, turned: 'The true question … in trials of fact is not, whether it is possible that the testimony may be false, but whether there is sufficient probability of its truth; whether the facts are proved by competent and satisfactory evidence.' Faced with a public that refused 'to behave normally in the way of giving evidence', O'Donoghue contended, 'it becomes the plain duty of the Executive and the Legislature to make the necessary effort to find a remedy for this defection'. In this case, where Gardaí believed the witnesses had been interfered with after they had made their statements, later giving inconsistent information and then refusing to testify on oath, it seemed to O'Donoghue that the special military court should be given a fair chance to arrive at the truth, particularly as this was a case of the state defending itself against its internal enemies during an emergency.[95]

The attorney general entered a *nolle prosequi* before the special criminal court on 11 December 1941, and the government promulgated Emergency Powers (No. 41f) Order, 1941, transferring the trial to the special military court. It also issued Emergency Powers (No. 139) Order 1941,[96] which permitted a statement 'relevant to such offence', made 'voluntarily or lawfully taken under any enactment, and was taken down in writing, and was acknowledged by the person who made it,' to be read as evidence at any stage of the trial, whenever the prosecution elected.[97] Such statements could be read into evidence 'notwithstanding that the person who made the statement is not present at the trial or is dead, and where the person who made the statement is present at the trial, whether he gives or does not give evidence',[98] and could be 'be acted upon by the court as

92 Ibid., pp 223–9, 234. 93 See D/T S.11564A. 94 Bell, *The secret army*, pp 209–12. 95 D/T S.12683, memorandum, 17 Jan. 1942. 96 On 30 Dec. 1941. 97 Article 3(1). 98 Article 3(2).

evidence against all the accused persons of the facts contained in such statement.'[99] The order also provided that 'if, on any occasion during the trial before a court to which this order applies, the court considers it proper that it should not be bound by any rule of evidence, whether statutory or at common law, the court shall not be bound by such rule.'[1] Thus Walsh and Davern's unsworn and unsigned statements became available to the prosecution. In O'Donoghue's words,

> What the present order proposes to do is to give the trial Court an opportunity of getting at the whole truth if possible. If a voluntary statement taken under conditions of comparative tranquillity and free from any suggestion of undue influence is made admissible before the Court, which is also confronted at the trial with a lying and garbled account though given under oath by the maker of the former statement whose demeanour as a witness will also have been observed it may be said to be a further attempt to satisfy the demands of justice to place that Court in a position of being able to act upon the first statement if they are satisfied in their minds and consciences that it is true.[2]

While awaiting trial before the military tribunal, the four accused sought orders of habeas corpus and prohibition from the high court and then appealed to the supreme court.[3] Their counsel argued that Emergency Powers (No. 139) Order, 1941 altered the normal laws of evidence to such an extent that it robbed the special military court of the attributes of a judicial tribunal, thus preventing a trial as contemplated by section 3 of the Emergency Powers (Amendment) (No. 2) Act, 1940.[4] Counsel also attempted to limit the scope of article 28.3.3, arguing that the phrase 'nothing in this Constitution' had to be given a limited and defined meaning: to apply it to the institutions established under the constitution was an 'absurdity'. Essentially, counsel contended that article 28.3.3 left intact rights 'over and above those conferred by the Constitution'. For example, habeas corpus was affirmed and not created by the constitution.[5] President of the high court, Mr Justice Maguire, disagreed that rights such as personal liberty, habeas corpus, and due process have 'their source in the common law … uncontrolled by Art. 28, s 3, sub-s 3 … In my view they cannot be found elsewhere than in the Constitution.'[6] Further, Gavan Duffy explained the situation had changed utterly since the 1930s: 'The sweeping language of

99 Article 4(1). 1 Article 5. 2 D/T S.12683, memorandum, 17 Jan. 1942. 3 *The State (Walsh and Others) v. Lennon*, [1942] IR 112. 4 Counsel also argued that trying all four together robbed the military court of discretion and of control over its proceedings. 5 See Kelly, *The Irish Constitution* (2nd ed.), pp 241–2. 6 [1942] IR 117.

[article 28.3.3] shows a firm determination in the light of judicial decisions not many years old to use a terminology that will avoid the embarrassing recoil in the Courts of clauses framed on the misleading "no certiorari" model.'[7] The high court, he said, was in no position to help:

> the applicants have come for relief to a Court which has no power to give them relief. Their right to escort to the high court springs from constitutional guarantees, entrusted to the protection of the high court, and that right is suspended ... So long as the jurisdiction of this Court to enforce those constitutional rights remains in abeyance in pursuance of an Article of the Constitution, persons in the position of the applicants cannot justify an application to this Court by reference to the guarantees in the Constitution.[8]

He added that

> In time of war or armed rebellion the apprehension of judicial intervention may at some delicate moment hamper the legislative or executive authority when Government needs all possible strength and freedom to steer the ship of State through the crisis, consequently the Constitution has placed in the hands of the Oireachtas, as law giver, special authority to suspend judicial control over the other organs of government during any such emergency, that is the simple explanation of Article 28.3.3 of the Constitution – a permanent provision, but available only in time of war or armed rebellion.[9]

The supreme court refused to accept that the changes in the rules of evidence denied the military court its jurisdiction:[10]

> If ... the Government had power to set up a special tribunal to try specified offences, and to invest it with special powers for this purpose, it is, in our opinion, quite impossible to hold that the tribunal is deprived of its jurisdiction and powers by reason of alterations in the laws of evidence to be recognised by such tribunals.[11]

Regarding arguments that the emergency powers orders were 'manifestly oppressive and unjust' to the accused, the chief justice, Mr Justice Sullivan, concluded

7 [1942] IR 119. 8 [1942] IR 121–2. 9 [1942] IR 118–19. 10 The chief justice, Mr Justice Sullivan, also ruled that the entering of a *nolle prosequi* did not constitute an acquittal. See also Kelly, *The Irish Constitution* (2nd ed.), p. 374. 11 Mr Justice Sullivan at 130.

> In our opinion this contention is based upon a misconception of the duties and functions of the Court. This emergency legislation is of a temporary character, passed for the purpose of securing the public safety and the preservation of the State during a time of national emergency. During such period the duty of determining what provisions are necessary for securing that object is vested in the Government, but every such provision must be laid before each House of the Oireachtas and may be annulled by a resolution passed by either House. Many of the arguments addressed to us would be more fittingly addressed to either House of the Oireachtas when considering the propriety of, and necessity for, the Order in question. They are not matters which can properly be relied upon in a Court of law.[12]

The trial before the military tribunal proceeded, and three of the four were convicted,[13] though only George Plant was executed.

John A. Costello, attorney general when article 2A was drafted, said the order 'shocked both lawyer and layman'. But Gerald Boland responded:

> I think that if there is one charge that can be made against the Government – and it has been made often – it is that we have been too lenient and have allowed things to go on with which we should, perhaps, have dealt far more seriously ... The order, as I say, is absolutely necessary if we are to put down organised crime and, particularly organised murder ... I say it is far more important for us to see that organised murder does not exist in this country than that we should have these laws of evidence as they have come down to us from Britain.[14]

The IRA appeared to have been neutralized. J. Bowyer Bell wrote, 'In the autumn of 1941, the IRA no longer seemed a clear and present danger to the men of Leinster House ... [the government] felt the worst was over, but the pressure was kept up to finish what the Hayes affair had begun – the elimination of the IRA from Irish politics ... the unrelenting process of attrition by arrest continued unabated.'[15]

While it seemed to most that the IRA had been well and truly destroyed by 1942, many members sentenced by the courts or interned by order of the minister for Justice faced the prospect of a long period of incarceration.[16] There would certainly be no amnesty for those detained, especially

12 [1942] IR 131. 13 Only Joseph O'Connor was found not guilty, 26 Feb. 1942. 14 Dáil Debates vol. 85 col. 1450, 1483–6, 28 Jan. 1942. 15 Bell, *The secret army*, p. 216. 16 On internment regulations see 81 Dáil Debates col. 512–4, 4 Nov. 1940, and D/T S.11438A. On the Curragh internment camp, see J.B. Bell, *The gun in politics: an analy-*

while the war continued. Indeed, persons convicted by the special criminal court were, more often than not, interned as soon as they completed their sentences. Nevertheless, a slow process of release continued throughout the Emergency, though the prisons were only finally cleared in 1948.

Until June 1940, the government released internees who were willing to sign a form of undertaking[17] or to appeal their detention to the internment commission. That system ended in June 1940, and as Gerry Boland later explained:

> The cases of persons under detention are constantly under review, and whenever I am satisfied that an individual can be released without prejudicing the safety of the State, I make an order for his release. I cannot allow any consideration other than the interests of the public safety to determine my decision.[18]

Strict government practice was eased somewhat by Emergency Powers (No.20) Order, 1940 (Second Amendment) Order, 1942 which provided for the release of internees who entered 'into a recognisance, in a specified amount and with two sureties in specified amounts, to keep the peace and be of good behaviour for a period of three years.'[19] Internees who refused to 'sign-out' or have conditions attached to their release were finally freed in late 1944 or during 1945, though the first indication they received that they were about to be freed was given to them on the morning of their release.[20]

The holding of internees at the Curragh was, evidently, straightforward, aided in no small way by the bitter enmity that developed between detainees. The incarceration of persons sentenced by the special criminal court created several problems, however. Difficulties were exacerbated by the substantial increase in the numbers of ordinary prisoners detained and by the increases in military offenders that accompanied the massive expansion of the defence forces during the war. Because the army's prison in Arbour Hill held IRA members convicted of less serious offences, the army was without a jail. In the Eastern Command, for example, convicted military defaulters were detained in unit guardrooms alongside untried detainees. The Eastern Command found it impossible to subject convicted offenders (particularly deserters) to a rigorous detention routine, and thus the deterrent aspect of the punishment was lost. Following lobbying by the department

sis of Irish political conflict (1991), pp 99–107, Bell, *The secret army*, pp 179–81; D/T S.12212; cabinet minutes G.C.2/226, 16 Dec. 1940, G.C.2/228, 20 Dec. 1940; *Irish Press* 16–19 Dec. 1939; 'Departmental Notes', pp 86 l–n. **17** D/T S.11564. **18** Dáil Debates vol. 92 col. 963, 16 Dec. 1943. **19** D/T S.11552A, order made 13 Nov. 1942. **20** Interview with Mick McCarthy.

of Defence, however, Arbour Hill was returned to the army before the summer of 1942 when its 45 IRA prisoners were transferred to the Curragh.[21]

By July 1942, 64 IRA prisoners convicted by the special criminal court were serving sentences of penal servitude in Mountjoy Prison.[22] The number of ordinary prisoners detained in that prison had increased from 193 in May 1941 to 371 a year later, and was expected to rise further. In such deteriorating circumstances, the department of Justice wanted prisoners convicted by the special criminal court transferred to military custody.[23] As there was no suitable alternative prison available to hold these IRA prisoners,[24] and the government was unwilling to transfer them to the Curragh,[25] it ordered them and a number of those held in Portlaoise transferred to Arbour Hill in July 1943. The department of Defence was again confronted with the same difficulties that it had resolved only a year earlier. It attempted to cope by holding certain categories of military defaulter at Spike Island, others at the Curragh Camp and those awaiting trial in their unit's guardroom.

By April 1944, 52 persons convicted by the special criminal court were detained in Arbour Hill. The department of Defence again suggested that they be moved to the Curragh, arguing that the transfer posed little danger as the Curragh internees had formed into four distinctive groupings, each more or less wholly opposed to the others, while two groups characterized by similar bitterness had also formed in Arbour Hill.[26] The transfer was agreed to in May 1944.[27]

Revealing how firm government policy towards the IRA had become was its treatment of members convicted of the most serious offences and incarcerated in Portlaoise prison.[28] Republican prisoners held there were classed as 'ordinary convicts' and ordered to wear prison uniforms. When Tomás MacCurtain was transferred on 29 July 1940, he immediately refused to obey the prison regime, arguing, as he and the other hunger-strikers had a few months earlier, that he was a prisoner of war and entitled to be treated accordingly. Rather than submit to the clothes-rule, he fashioned some blankets into a 'smock'. Other Republican inmates committed to the prison afterwards followed Tomás MacCurtain's example.

21 D/T S.12896, memorandum by the department of Defence, 23 Feb. 1942. 22 D/T S.12896, memorandum by the department of Justice, 3 July 1942. 23 Ibid., 3 July 1942. By December 1942 the problem remained unresolved, CAB G.C. 2/396, 8 Dec. 1942. 24 Ibid., department of Defence memorandum, 25 Mar. 1943. 25 Ibid., 15 Jan. 1943, cabinet minutes G.C. 2/404, 26 Jan. 1943. 26 Ibid., memorandum by the department of Defence, 26 Apr. 1944. See also D/J S.15/46. 27 Cabinet Minutes G.C.3/62, 4 May 1944. On remissions and releases, see for example Government minutes G2/215, 246, 247, and D/T S.12081, S.12197, S.12415, D/T S.12433A, S.2444, D/J D.51/36, D/J S.3/42. 28 The question of the treatment of inmates was raised for the first time in the Dáil, 4 Nov. 1943, see Dáil Debates vol. 91 col. 1569–70.

Prisoners refused letters because their prison numbers were written on the envelopes. Refusal to obey prison rules resulted in the denial of privileges: prisoners received no visitors, books or newspapers, and were not allowed to attend Mass. They were held in solitary confinement, were not permitted to speak to one another and were forbidden to exercise in the open air. Unsurprisingly, some of these 13 prisoners showed signs of strain.[29]

Only after Seán McCaughey's death on 11 May 1946, following a hunger and thirst strike, were these conditions revealed to the country.[30] With the ending of censorship and the rescinding of various Emergency Powers Orders, an inquest into McCaughey's death was held. Reports in the press led to public and Dáil outcry, though Gerald Boland dismissed the hungerstrike as a propaganda stunt, claiming that were it not for McCaughey's fast and another hunger strike in the North (where the prisoner was unconditionally released), the IRA would have been a 'flop'.[31] De Valera added, 'If we gave way on the matter of the clothes then it was going to be on another matter and another matter until the prisoner got exactly what he wanted – immunity.'[32]

Several IRA members convicted of the most serious offences remained imprisoned after the end of the war. The sentences of 24 prisoners (including Willie Stewart, Brendan Behan and Denis Griffin) were remitted under section 33 of the Offences against the State Act, 1939 in December 1946.[33] On 9 October 1947, 15 persons sentenced by the special criminal court remained in custody.[34] By 24 February 1948, that figure had fallen to five, when the government decided to release Éamonn Smullen and Liam Rice from Portlaoise, because both were in very poor health.[35] Finally, on 8 March 1948, the government announced it would free the remaining prisoners, Tomás MacCurtain, Harry White, and James Smith. The new Taoiseach, John A. Costello, explained that 'a continuance of the detention of these three men would only result in the perpetuation of resentment and unrest and that the public interest would be best served by releasing them also.'[36] On 22 March 1949, the government remitted all forfeitures and disqualifications imposed under the Offences against the State Act still in force.[37]

Although the government had effectively contained the IRA by 1941, the continuing world war began to take its toll on the general population, espe-

29 D/T S.11443, department of Justice memorandum, 28 Feb. 1945. 30 Bell, *The secret army*, p. 243. 31 Dáil Debates vol. 101 col. 1126, 29 May 1946. He added that following the D'Arcy and McNeela inquests and McBride's handling of the juries he decided to dispense with coroners' juries by means of Emergency Powers (No.47) Order, 1940. 32 Dáil Debates vol. 101 col. 1159. 33 See Government minutes, G4/188, 17 Dec. 1946, D/T S.12490. See also D/J S.15/46 and D/T S.13921. 34 Dáil Debates vol. 108 col. 262. 35 *Irish Press*, 27 Feb. 1948, D/T S.13921. 36 *Irish Independent*, 10 Mar. 1948. 37 D/J 119/157, memorandum, J.E. Duff, 5 Apr. 1949.

cially after 1941, creating more basic problems, such as procuring and controlling essential supplies. This had been anticipated when contingency planning began in earnest in 1938, and at the outbreak of the war two new government departments, the department of Supplies and the department for the Coordination of Defensive Measures, were created. The department of Supplies had a very wide remit, including the control of exports and imports of all kinds; regulating the keeping, treatment, storage, movement, distribution, sale, purchase, use, and consumption of articles of all kinds; control of all prices.[38] As the war began to adversely affect the Irish economy, it instigated a number of extraordinary steps to ensure the government maintained control of the economy, and that the people had enough to eat.

The supplies situation deteriorated rapidly after December 1940 when the British imposed strict controls on trade following Ireland's refusal to enter the war. By then, there were severe petrol restrictions. Coal imports dried-up by the end of 1941, and there were also acute shortages of tea, sugar, tobacco, bread, fruit, feeding-stuffs and fertilizer. Prices rose rapidly, while wages were kept low by wages standstill orders, and the Trade Unions Act, 1941 restricted trade union activities. Blackmarketeering and overcharging became rampant, though general rationing was not introduced until the summer of 1942.[39]

In order to enforce general rationing, the Dáil enacted the Emergency Powers (Amendment and Continuance) Act, 1942 in July 1942,[40] which provided for increased punishments of up to 10 years' penal servitude and for fines up to £5,000 in cases of conviction on indictment for offences against Emergency Powers Orders.[41] It also provided for the punishment of non-compliance with orders[42] and for minimum penalties.[43] Further, as de Valera explained, 'As certain doubts have arisen [regarding the meaning of section 2(1) of the Emergency Powers Act, 1939] it has been thought well to put the matter beyond doubt … to make it clear that the intention of the legislature was that the general powers [of section 2(1)] were to be unaffected by anything whatever in the second subsection.'[44]

It was only the following summer, when the emergency legislation was being renewed, that the opposition finally began to express dissatisfaction with these extraordinary powers. For instance, W.T. Cosgrave argued that more than half the emergency powers orders promulgated should have been enacted as ordinary legislation. Further, he pointed to wages standstill orders, noting that while wages had been kept constant, prices had risen by 50% or 60% since the beginning of the war. The Fine Gael

38 D/T S.11418A. 39 Dunphy, *Fianna Fáil*, p. 224. 40 See also D/T S.11977. 41 Section 8(a)(6)(b). 42 Section 9(1). 43 Section 8(a)(6a), Dáil Debates vol. 87 col. 2075–175, 1 July 1942. 44 Dáil Debates vol. 87 col. 2075–6, section 6.

leader argued that particularly contentious and controversial orders should be justified to the Dáil. He also criticized the revoking of several traders' licences and complained that the Emergency Powers (Amendment and Continuance) Act, 1942 enabled the government to impose penalties in addition to those levied by the courts. 'The Government knows well that we are going to support the principle of having a measure of this sort. The Government has been told that we object to its abuse', he said.[45]

The minister for Supplies, Seán Lemass, explained that the licensing of traders of certain goods was essential to ensure effective rationing – the government sought to control supplies by enforcing conformity in the sale of a large variety of goods.[46] For example, in July 1943 there were 41,727 traders licensed to sell tea and sugar. Of those, 1,290 had been prosecuted under price control and rationing orders; licences were withdrawn in 31 cases. Notice of withdrawal had been given in others, but not enforced because the department of Supplies believed that several traders did not appreciate the seriousness of their activities. Despite some initial leniency, the minister warned that henceforth any trader convicted of contravening emergency orders – by failing to keep records, by keeping false records, by failing to attach price tags, by overcharging etc. – would lose his licence. In answer to another specific issue, he explained that the government could not rely on the courts to determine whether or not a trader's licence should be revoked: 'it would be impossible for any Minister for Supplies to carry on the rationing scheme in operation and exercise proper supervision over the sale of goods, unless he had the power to require traders in particular lines to have licences and the power to withdraw them, if his regulations were not complied with.'[47]

As the war progressed, and the special criminal court tried fewer and fewer IRA members, it increasingly focussed on blackmarketeering and rationing offences.[48] While the ordinary courts disposed of most cases against emergency powers orders, some were tried by the special criminal court, reflecting the gravity of offences.[49] It began to impose heavy sentences where it found systematic defiance of Emergency Powers Orders, as in the cases of R. O'Toole and P. Follan.[50] In the Sigal case, for example, it set bail at £40,000.[51] It also dealt with a number of agrarian offences.[52] Indeed, by mid-1943 the *Irish Times* claimed that there was a 'mounting crime wave in Ireland'.[53]

45 Dáil Debates vol. 91 col. 539–42, 9 July 1943. 46 Dáil Debates vol. 91 col. 573. 47 Dáil Debates vol. 91 col. 576–8. 48 See tables 7e–i, and 8a–d. 49 See *Irish Times* 22 May 1946; *Irish Press* 23 May 1946. 50 *Irish Times*, 21 Sept. 1944, 51 *Irish Times*, 27 Mar. 1945 and 7 May 1946. 52 See *Irish Times*, 19 Mar. 1943, 30 Apr. 1943 and Dáil Debates vol. 89 col. 1212–17, 11 Mar. 1943. 53 *Irish Times*, 24 July 1943.

It was a further year before the press began to grumble about these powers. The *Irish Independent*, while accepting that few could have questioned the necessity of having vested such extraordinary powers in the executive at the beginning of the war, and that powers were generally used for the 'good of the community as a whole ... it cannot be denied that there have been many instances in which the emergency powers have been used harshly or excessively, or in spheres in which even the emergency conditions did not justify their application.'[54] It continued:

> We fear, too, that the inevitable tendency of officials is to gather more and more power into their own grasp. There is to be said for officials: they cannot hit back when attacked. And hence they naturally seek to make themselves immune from attack by presenting the public with orders which have immediate force of law. That is one of the dangers of office made law rather than Parliament made law. Hence too, the menacing growth in the tendency of officials to have their acts and deeds placed above the reach of the Courts of Justice, to make the officials their own final court of appeal.[55]

It proposed that a new system be introduced giving the Dáil a greater say in the development and use of emergency powers.[56]

When the war ended in Europe on 8 May 1945 the government found itself with continuing supply difficulties. Although article 28.3.3 had been amended a second time on 30 May 1941 allowing the Oireachtas to continue the state of emergency until it 'resolved that the national emergency occasioned by such war, armed conflict or armed rebellion has ceased to exist', continued reliance on emergency powers, notwithstanding persistent supply problems, became increasingly difficult to justify.

By May 1945, 78 internees remained.[57] This included six aliens, five Germans and one Dutch, who would be treated separately. Of the Republican internees, the department of Justice felt it safe to release 58, but the minister had 'doubts whether it would be wise to release the remaining fourteen at the present time'.[58] De Valera explained, 'the feeling was that even when the war was over it would be necessary in the interests of

54 28 June 1944. It cited, for example, 'the imposition of a new rent code on the public, a thing which should have been done by a regular Act of Parliament.' 55 See also the *Irish Times*, 28 June 1944, for a less critical appraisal of emergency powers. 56 By late 1945, the special criminal court was being described as 'a danger to liberty'; see *Irish Times*, *Irish Independent*, 4 Dec. 1945. 57 Members of the German armed forces were interned under Emergency Powers (No. 170) Order, 1942. 58 D/T S.11552B, department of Justice memorandum, 11 May 1945, see also D/T S.13667, S.11577. Initially, it was suggested that if Emergency Powers (No. 20) Order, 1940 were revoked the six aliens could be detained under the Aliens Act prior to deportation.

public safety to keep a number of these internees, the hard core of the organization, in custody indefinitely until such time as the Government was satisfied that it could, with safety to the community, release them.' But in the event, they were also released because 'the Government decided to give them a chance to get back to normal lives.'[59] It ordered all internees released by 20 June 1945.[60] Irrespective of department of Justice concerns, Gardaí reported 'no crime attributable to members of the [IRA]' since July 1943.[61]

It was soon clear, however, that efforts to revive the IRA were underway. Almost immediately, Gardaí were anxious to re-intern at least one individual.[62] The department of Justice proposed revoking Emergency Powers (No.20) Order, 1940, repealing the Emergency Powers (Amendment) Act, 1940 and issuing a proclamation bringing part 2 of the Offences against the State (Amendment) Act, 1940 in to operation before the Emergency Powers Continuance Bill was passed.[63] Because of the six aliens, the minister was unable to sanction a total repeal of the internment provisions of the Emergency Powers Acts, merely a reversion to the September 1939 situation.[64] It would not have been impossible to issue warrants for their continued detention under the Offences against the State (Amendment) Act, 1940 because, as Roche noted, that

> Act authorises a minister to order a detention only when he is of the opinion that the person to be detained *is engaged* in activities prejudicial to the preservation of public peace and order or to the security of the State. As all these men have been in custody for several years, it would be impossible for the minister to say that they are at present engaged in such activities.[65]

The provisions of the Offences against the State (Amendment) Act, 1940 were activated by proclamation on 24 July 1945.[66]

As the government realized by the summer of 1945, reports of the disintegration of the IRA were inaccurate. A long process of reorganization began after June 1945.[67] A new army council was created in a Dublin pub on 10 March 1946, though Gardaí raided the meeting and arrested ten IRA members, seizing documents relating to the 1938 declaration of war on

59 Dáil Debates vol. 97 col. 1881, 4 July 1945. 60 See D/T S.13706A, following a Government meeting, 11 May 1945. 61 Ibid., 15 May 1947. 62 Ibid., 20 July 1945. 63 D/T S.11552B, J.J. McCarthy (Boland's private secretary) to Ó Muimhneacháin, 2 July 1945. 64 Ibid., extract of a department of Justice minute, 9 June 1945. 65 D/T S.11552A, 4 July 1945, Roche's emphasis, see also S.13706, 20 July 1945, a formal request concerning these matters was made on 20 July 1945. 66 D/T S.13706, 15 May 1947. An internment commission as required by section 8 was established, staffed by Mr Justice William Black, Colonel John V. Joyce, and Colonel George Hodnett, barrister-at-law. 67 See generally Bell, *The secret army*, pp 239–336.

England, and others addressed to the British foreign secretary and the British Labour Party regarding the evacuation by the British from Ireland, the release of republican prisoners in British jails, and a ceasefire.[68]

Despite efforts to resurrect the IRA, by 15 July 1947 the department of Justice reported, 'the situation has materially altered since the making of the proclamation [of 24 July 1945]. The IRA has disintegrated ... it can no longer be regarded as a serious menace to peace and good order.'[69] The government quietly issued a proclamation declaring that Part 2 of the Offences Against the State (Amendment) Act, 1940 was no longer in force. It would be nine years before the IRA had any noticeable impact on Irish politics and society.

The issue of internment was essentially resolved by July 1945, but the problem of essential supplies continued for some time.[70] Although several portions of the Emergency Powers Acts, 1939–1944 were abandoned in mid-1945, and a large number of Emergency Powers Orders were repealed, many orders would have to remain in place for several months after September 1945. The cabinet decided to repeal the Emergency Powers (Amendment) (No. 2) Act, 1940 and the portions of the Emergency Powers (Continuance and Amendment) Act, 1942 dealing with minimum fines on 5 June 1945.[71] It was clear, however, that some departments could not adapt all important emergency powers orders into the ordinary law within a proposed three to six month deadline. For instance, while the department of Supplies believed necessary enabling legislation could be easily prepared, more time was needed to consider the minimum powers it required to continue, for consultation with other departments and then for drafting and enactment.[72] The department of Agriculture expressed a similar position. Approximately 60 emergency powers orders were made on its behalf,[73] classed into three general groupings:

- orders introduced during the emergency, but whose importance made them indefinite necessities – orders dealing with the production of seed, the manufacture and sale of fertilizers and compound feeding stuffs, etc, which would have to be incorporated into the permanent law;
- orders of a temporary nature which could be revoked once normality returned, for example, pigs and bacon orders, matters relat-

68 See 'Departmental Notes' (2), p. 88, *Irish Times*, 5 Apr. 1946. See also D/FA A12, minute by Colonel Dan Bryan (G2), 14 Mar. 1946. 69 See D/T S.13706, 15 May 1947, and D/T S.13710. 70 See generally D/T S.13667. 71 Ibid., memorandum by the department of the Taoiseach, 2 June 1945, cabinet minutes, G.C.4/83, 5 June 1945. 72 Ibid., R. Mac Aonghusa, minister's private secretary, department of Supplies, 8 June 1945. 73 These were in addition to those made by the department of Supplies which were particularly relevant to the department of Agriculture.

ing to the export of animal offal, flax, poultry, rabbits, eggs etc, made following arrangements with the British ministry of Food;
- orders concerning questions of long-term policy – relating to the Dublin Milk Board, compulsory tillage etc. which would have to be considered at a later date.

Proposed legislation would, in certain instances, only require amendments to existing statutes, but in other cases, entirely new statutes were necessary. Given the volume of work, it felt that emergency legislation should not be repealed even after the proposed six-month deadline.[74]

The department of Justice was primarily concerned with paragraphs 'j' to 'o' of section 2(2) of the 1939 Act.[75] By May 1945, the only orders in force under paragraph 'j' were the Emergency Powers (Deportation) Order, 1939, which authorized the deportation of British citizens, and the Emergency Powers (Passenger Traffic Restrictions) Orders,[76] which required British citizens coming into Ireland from places other than Britain or Northern Ireland to have visas. No order was made restricting the movements of persons within the state.[77] By war's end, on internal security grounds, paragraph 'j' was no longer needed, eventhough the British authorities maintained similar powers over Irish citizens. The department of Justice added that articles 3 (restrictions on entering and leaving the state), 4 (control of aliens) of the Emergency Powers Order, 1939 could also be dropped. Further, paragraphs 'm', 'n' and 'o' of section 2(2) of the Emergency Powers Act, 1939, which permitted articles 74, 75 and 76 of the Emergency Powers Order, 1939, could be deleted because they were vague and largely unnecessary as emergency powers orders were scheduled to the Offences against the State Act, 1939.

The department of Justice also proposed dropping Emergency Powers (No. 17) Order, 1939 (wearing uniforms), in addition to several orders dealing with the functioning of the courts. The minister for Justice was expected to submit plans to incorporate Emergency Powers (No. 313) Order, 1944 into the proposed Rents Restrictions Bill.[78] Emergency Powers (No. 42) Order, 1940, which temporarily replaced the Official Secrets Acts, 1911 and 1920, had been adopted because of flaws in the ordinary law, and the department expected that the order would be adopted into the ordinary law.

The department of Local Government and Public Health was concerned with the continuation of only a few specific orders relating to the outbreak of disease, particularly Emergency Powers (No 46) Order, 1940

74 D/T S.13667, assistant secretary of the department of Agriculture, Seán Ó Broin to Ó Muimhneacháin, 9 June 1945. 75 Ibid., Seán Mac Cárthaigh to Ó Muimhneacháin, 9 June 1945. 76 This only operated at Shannon Airport. 77 D/T S.13667, 9 June 1945, memorandum by S. Mac Cárthaigh. 78 See D/T S.13168.

which permitted the detention of persons who were a source of infection. It believed the need for such powers would increase because of greater freedom of movement afforded by the end of hostilities. It hoped to adapt Order 46 into the proposed Public Health Bill but that legislation was unlikely to be ready before 1946. It also anticipated on-going supply problems for 12 months. Additionally, the continuation of article 38 of the Emergency Powers Order, 1939, which allowed a minister of state either to acquire land or to authorize a specific person (a local authority, for instance) to do so for the maintenance of supplies essential to the life of the community (such as the acquisition of land for cultivation as allotments) was under consideration.[79]

J.P. Walshe of the department of External Affairs expressed a somewhat different view:

> Although hostilities in Europe have ceased, people in Great Britain and the United States do not regard the war as being over. The war psychosis remains and it is a question for consideration whether, as long as this is the case, the Government can safely divest itself of the powers necessary to enable it to deal with a certain type of activity here (public demonstrations, propaganda, Fascist or other subversive organisation, etc.) capable, if it takes certain forms or is pursued to provocative lengths, of creating tension in our relations with other countries and, even, of exposing the State to danger.[80]

Those points related to paragraphs (h) to (o) of section 2(2) of the Emergency Powers Act, 1939. If legislation were enacted adapting Emergency Powers Orders, the department of External Affairs felt that the government should clearly declare that these enactments would not in any way prejudice the exercise or continuance of emergency legislation.

Because of the variety and volume of legislation required, the government decided that the parent act should be kept in force for a further 12 months.[81] Provisions relating to postal and telegraphic censorship, and the censorship of newspapers, periodicals and films were revoked, however. Therefore, paragraphs (h) and (i) of section 2(2) could be deleted, and the list of exempted powers in section 2(5) added to. Further paragraphs 'j' to 'o' were restricted to persons other than natural born Irish citizens, and the restriction on the trial of persons not subject to military law was reinstated. Emergency Powers (Amendment) Act, 1940, Emergency Powers (Amendment)(No.2) Act, 1940 and the Emergency Powers (Continuance)

79 D/T S.13667, Barrington, minister's private secretary, to the secretary of the department of the Taoiseach, 11 June 1945. 80 Ibid., 11 June 1945. 81 Ibid., draft memorandum by the department of an Taoiseach, 11 June 1945.

Act, 1944 would be repealed, and the provisions regarding minimum fines in Emergency Powers (Continuance and Amendment) Act, 1942 dropped.[82]

The Dáil greeted the news that the Emergency Powers Act would be continued for one more year with dismay. De Valera's assurances that 'it was not the desire of the Government to retain the Emergency Powers Acts in operation for a moment longer than the public interest required,'[83] left TDs unimpressed. Deputy Michael Donnellan expressed the views of many saying 'it was a mistake ever to give such powers to the Government. No Government, whether Fianna Fáil, Fine Gael, or any other should have such powers.'[84] Dr Thomas O'Higgins now described the legislation as undemocratic, and claimed there was discrimination and abuse involved in the application of the emergency powers.[85] Emergency powers would continue until 1946 and then lapse. Planning for future emergencies, which began in 1944, continued for several years to come, however.

In September 1944, the cabinet decided that a 'War Book' should be prepared

> in light of the experience gained during the present emergency, the legislative and other steps which should be taken, with a view to securing the public safety and the preservation of the State, at the outset of any similar emergency in the future and at the various stages in the course of such emergency, and drawing attention to the dangers and difficulties which should be guarded against.[86]

In addition, it was proposed that copies of all the important legislation, orders and memoranda should be assembled, either in a separate manual, or in a 'War Book' which might be of value to future governments.

Notwithstanding government preparations for future emergencies, one must acknowledge its competent performance during the years 1939 to 1946. Its effective stewardship of the state during 'the Emergency' had, in part, been facilitated by the Emergency Powers Act, 1939–1945 and by the Offences against the State Act, 1939. Those measures assisted the government in ensuring the state's survival in the face of two simultaneous emergencies. Though the country remained poor and somewhat isolated, Ireland emerged from World War II essentially unscarred. Without doubt, it was a most impressive achievement, especially in view of the great hazards faced.

82 Note from P. Ó Cinnéide to the private secretary of the attorney general, 13 June 1945. See D/T S.10845/3 for a list of orders revoked. 83 Dáil Debates vol. 97 col. 1879, 4 July 1945. 84 Dáil Debates vol. 97 col. 1899. 85 Dáil Debates vol. 97 col. 1952–60. 86 Cabinet minutes G.C. 4/1, 22 Sept. 1944, D/T S. 11445/10. See also D/T S.15911 for later proposals. For later preparations see, for the 1950s, D/T S.14880, S.14885C, S.14889, S.15906–15 and S.15991, and for the 1960s see D/D S.205.

7

Conclusion

In 1948, the government released the last IRA prisoners convicted by the special criminal court during 'the Emergency'. Tomás MacCurtain, for example, had to wait for the emergence of the inter-party government of Fine Gael, Labour and Clann na Poblachta to be freed. Once released, however, he and others began rebuilding the IRA, and in late 1956 the organization launched a campaign of limited violence along the border in Northern Ireland. Although some IRA members were arrested and charged under the Offences against the State Act, 1939 in December 1956 and in January 1957, large-scale measures to contain the IRA did not occur until Fianna Fáil's return to power later in 1957.[1] That summer, the government began interning active IRA members, while others were arrested and charged under the Offences against the State Act.[2] Later, in November 1961, the government re-established the special criminal court. Unlike earlier responses to IRA resurgences, it did not introduce new legislation. Similarly, the government reactivated the Offences against the State Act, 1939 in 1972 because of 'the Troubles' in Northern Ireland.

Between 1922 and 1948, civil servants drafted 29 public safety statutes. Each year of the 1920s after independence saw the passage of at least one public safety measure, and the 1930s were notable for article 2A and the Offences against the State Act, the two most important statutes devised to counter recurring difficulties of administering the criminal law in Ireland.

Doubtless, the nature of legislation altered radically between 1922 and 1948, moving from a system similar to martial law that legalized the execution or internment of persons captured in arms against the state in 1922 to a statutory, almost parallel legal system in 1931, and eventually to a well-defined supplement to the state's legal and judicial machinery that operated under the constitution. A great deal of time and effort was expended drafting public safety legislation, which witnessed repeated trial and error before ministers and civil servants correctly identified the bounds of effective public safety legislation, and the Offences against the State Act, 1939 came into being.

1 Bell, *The secret army*, pp 299–300. 2 Dáil Debates vol. 165 col. 36–8, 12 Feb. 1958. During 1957, 122 persons were charged under the Offences against the State Act, 1939 of which 116 were convicted and 13 were acquitted. Between 8 July 1957 and 12 Feb. 1958, 146 persons were interned, 20 of whom were released during that period.

Legislation drafted between 1922 and 1948 sought to deal with two different forms of emergency, however. First, there was the permanent difficulty involved in the administration of the criminal law and, second, the state faced two major crises, the Civil War and World War II which immediately threatened its survival. Without doubt, fundamental differences existed between the government's legislative responses to these.

Born out of war in 1921, independent Ireland was almost instantly cast back into serious crisis after the signing of the Treaty. Although a majority in southern Ireland accepted the agreement, there remained a sizeable minority opposed to it. The provisional government's most urgent task during its first months was the unquestionable achievement of the Free State's sovereignty throughout the Twenty-Six Counties. This finally led to the outbreak of hostilities between the National Army and the anti-Treaty IRA on 28 June 1922. Although quickly becoming a guerrilla conflict, as the Civil War began to drag on the provisional government came to believe that sovereignty could only be achieved by employing 'utterly drastic action' against persons who had taken up arms against the new state. Martial law was introduced under the Army (Special Powers) Resolution in September 1922, drawn up within the provisional government's unusual administrative and constitutional boundaries, but was supported by the Dáil.

Admittedly, the numbers executed and interned by the Irish government during the Civil War were significantly higher than the corresponding figures for the War of Independence.[3] Moreover, there was a large number of unofficial executions carried out by the National Army between 1922 and 1923.[4] But because the land question had been largely resolved, and the south of Ireland achieved a central government under the Treaty, a majority of voters supported the new state. This was despite the imposition of several distasteful conditions in the Treaty. The provisional government's use of extraordinary measures hastened victory and did not de-legitimize its authority, unlike the British experience of 1916 to 1921.[5] In any case, anti-Treaty leaders presented no concrete war aims or viable alternative to the Treaty. In short, a sufficient proportion of the population had a stake in the new state that they were unwilling to risk or lose.

The government's position in victory in 1923 was unequivocal. Kevin O'Higgins declared that 'this is not going to be a draw with a replay in the autumn'.[6] Clearly, the IRA had not the capacity nor did the bulk of its members have the desire to resume fighting. Revealing how decisive the Free State's victory was, the government was able to clear the prison camps within a year of the end of the conflict. Indeed, as it took only four years

3 Campbell, *Emergency law*, pp 108, 241. 4 Fanning, *Independent Ireland*, p. 21. 5 Campbell, *Emergency law*, p. 348. 6 Quoted in de Vere White, *Kevin O'Higgins*, pp 150–1.

from the end of the war for the vast majority of anti-Treatyites to openly accept the authority of the Free State (when Fianna Fáil entered the Dáil), it was clear that the independent Irish state would be extremely stable.

There had been some doubt as to the government's power to legally continue internments once the Civil War formally ended and wide-scale problems with juries were anticipated. The secretary of the department of Home Affairs, Éinrí Ó Frighil argued that the Free State's constitution did not afford the legislature the 'freedom and elasticity' needed to contend with emergencies such as the post-Civil War situation, particularly as it stipulated that juries had to try serious offences.[7] Once a number of legal doubts were dispelled, though, the government decided that the district courts should dispose of certain public safety offences, including agrarian agitation, armed robbery and poitín-making; internment was also temporarily continued, and provision was made permitting changes to trial venues, for flogging in certain cases and for special Garda and army powers of arrest and detention.

Military victory did not end the Free State's reliance on emergency law because the IRA shortly re-emerged. The government's first permanent attempt to deal with the organization, the Treasonable Offences Act, 1925, proved largely ineffectual, though. Introduced to a very hostile Dáil in early 1925, the measure's problems stemmed partly from poor drafting, from the inclusion of cumbersome procedures, and from the provision of inappropriate offences. More fundamentally, it failed to address the problem of juries regularly refusing to convict IRA members.

Although the Oireachtas passed the Public Safety Act, 1927 in the wake of Kevin O'Higgins' assassination, that act was never seriously enforced. But it was the increasing confrontation between the state and the IRA that followed the minister for Justice's death that finally and conclusively exposed the defects of the ordinary criminal law when employed against the IRA.[8] The courts would not tolerate the Gardaí's repeated illegal arrests and detentions of IRA members, while provisions for secret jury selection, majority jury verdicts and the clearing of courthouses under the Juries (Protection) Act, 1929 failed to overcome jury unwillingness to convict.

Only after three killings in 1931, did the government resolve to act decisively. Article 2A represented a comprehensive response to every difficulty that the state had experienced with the IRA: members' refusal to recognize the courts, their refusal to cooperate with the Gardaí, among other problems. The measure also created a range of special Garda pow-

7 See D/J H171/17, memorandum prepared by Éinrí Ó Frighil for the executive council, May 1923. 8 See speech by Ernest Blythe, Dáil Debates vol. 20 col. 856–9, 26 July 1927 and by James Fitzgerald-Kenney, Dáil Debates vol. 30 col. 79, 22 May 1929.

ers (including power to detain suspects without charge for up to 72 hours) and several new offences that evolved from the illegal police tactics of the late 1920s.[9] These included obliging suspects to account for movements, to give their name, address, and information regarding the commission of offences when demanded. Further, the creation of the offence of membership of an 'unlawful association' discarding the loaded terminology of the past, and permitted the prosecution of IRA members on simple grounds. In short, the legislation enabled Gardaí to bring some charge when previously none would have been possible.

Most importantly, article 2A created the constitution tribunal which removed a great deal of the uncertainty involved in trying members of illegal organizations because it ended reliance on juries for convictions. Further, in a concerted attempt to prevent any court interference with the tribunal – to 'judge proof' it[10] – its convictions and sentences were not open to appeal and certiorari was explicitly prohibited. The assistant secretary of the department of Justice proposed developing a tribunal with the power of life and death, which was prepared 'to exercise those freely'. Stephen Roche wanted to drive IRA leaders into the 'certainty that if they persist in their activities they will suffer death'. In order to ensure that tribunal had 'ample powers to preserve its dignity',[11] it did not have to adopt fixed procedures and was not bound by the normal rules of evidence. It could, in addition, inflict any greater punishment, including death, than the ordinary law normally permitted.

Irrespective of the widespread criticism, article 2A was undeniably effective. Convictions rates of 36% and 34% were recorded for offences under the Treasonable Offences Act, 1925 in 1925 and 1926 respectively, but fell to 7% and 10% in 1928 and 1929; the tribunal recorded 89% convictions under the act in 1931. Indeed, it convicted 91% of IRA members it tried between 1931 and 1937. In operation, Article 2A appeared to make conviction almost inevitable.[12] In fact, once the government applied defi-

9 See table 3h. In the period 1931–7, 105 of 464 (23%) IRA members were convicted of membership of an unlawful association; 69 of 464 (15%) for failure to account for movements and/or to give name and address, etc. Firearms: 96 of 464 (21%); riot/ unlawful assembly: 41 of 464 (9%); illegal drilling: 26 of 464 (6%). Figures available for the period of 'the Emergency' (table 6i) are somewhat distorted because the data available is incomplete, and additionally only 68% of those tried were IRA members. However, figures are comparable: firearms: 131 of 808 (16%); unlawful association: 106 of 808 (13%); failure to account for movements, etc.: 111 of 808 (14%); riot, etc.: 30 of 808 (4%). **10** See Campbell, *Emergency law*, pp 353–5. **11** D/T S.4469/17, 7 Sept. 1931, Ó Cuinneóin (assistant secretary, department of Justice) to the parliamentary draftsman. **12** Tables 3a–h. The figures for the Blueshirts, 1933–1935, 434 convicted of 480 tried, represent a rate of 90%.

nite pressure, the IRA quickly retreated. Once these powers were in place and proved so effective, no government would lose them.

When employed against the Blueshirts in 1933 and 1934, these powers proved more problematic. Firstly, Gardaí experienced difficulties when prosecuting on charges of membership of an unlawful association.[13] Unlike the IRA, the Blueshirt leadership maintained that the organization was lawful, despite its military-like attire and the violence that their rallies witnessed. Few statements it made prior to the summer of 1934 brought the Blueshirts within article 2A's definition of unlawful associations. A total of 38 Blueshirts were charged with membership of an unlawful association after August 1933, in 13 cases a *nolle prosequi* were entered, 7 were found 'not guilty'; of the 18 found guilty, 13 received non-custodial sentences.

Further, several Blueshirts successfully challenged particular provisions of article 2A in the courts. The higher courts ruled that they could exercise limited control over the tribunal, despite the best efforts of civil servants in 1931. In the short term, the Blueshirts forced the government to draft the Wearing of Uniforms (Restrictions) Bill, 1934, and indirectly led to the abolition of the Seanad, as well as to the drafting of a new constitution. Despite these initial problems, the adoption of illegal and desperate measures by hundreds of farmers and Blueshirts after the summer of 1934 finally enabled the government to effectively suppress the organization.[14]

Fianna Fáil took a rather different approach to the IRA. Relying on various schemes and inducements, its political and economic programme and constitutional change, the government sought to draw as many members as possible away from militant republicanism and into accepting the legitimacy of the state, while gradually increasing coercion until it formally outlawed the IRA in 1936.

Naturally, civil servants in the department of Justice and the attorney general's office learned a great deal during the 1930s. By mid-1934 Stephen Roche conceded that article 2A was 'grotesque' and was 'not proper for retention in the Constitution'.[15] While the essential elements of article 2A and the Treasonable Offences Act were re-enacted in 1939, a number of important changes were implemented. Nonetheless, the department of Justice pressed for a court that would terrify those brought before it, a court which 'should be respected and even feared.' The attorney general's office sought a different approach, believing that inspiring public confidence in the court was more important. It pressed for provision for appeal,

13 Table 3l. 14 See table 3l: 228 of 480 convicted (47.5%) were charged of road/rail interference, 100 of 480 (21%) charged with cutting telegraph wires, and 22 of 480 (5%) charged with riot/unlawful assembly. 15 D/T S.2979, draft note, prior to 14 June 1934, and the Constitution Committee's final report, 3 July 1934, D/T S.8211.

believing that few of the constitution tribunal's decisions would have been overturned by the court of criminal appeal,[16] though only Fine Gael pressure finally swayed the government to support this view. Additionally, the legislation provided for the appointment of ordinary judges (in addition to army officers) to the special criminal court,[17] for the normal rules of evidence, and contained no unlimited punishments.[18] The power to extract confessions from suspects was also less severe than existed under article 2A. The department of Justice had sought extended Garda detention powers but these were also reduced following Dáil debate. Provisions permitting persons to challenge suppression orders in the high court and for the Dáil to annul proclamations establishing special criminal courts and permitting internment appeared to provide some safeguards against abuse.

The Offences against the State Act consolidated and rationalized public safety legislation into one statute. But the differences between it and article 2A appear to have had no impact on conviction rates.[19] Between 1939 and 1946, the special criminal court convicted 914 of 1,013 persons it tried – 90%. That those changes could be implemented indicated that the government simply 'over-compensated' for the difficulties it faced in 1931.

Unaffected by jury problems, special courts achieved remarkable conviction rates. This was partly due to the attention paid by the Gardaí, the department of Justice and the attorney general when selecting suspects for trial, who ensured that evidence gathered was likely to lead to conviction. The creation of special offences that the IRA continually committed or which could be easily proved further increased the likelihood of conviction. Heavy Garda surveillance on what was a small organization ensured that the authorities knew most IRA members and could closely monitor its activities.

Although this system appeared to almost ensure conviction, when persons admitted guilt, denied membership of an unlawful association, recognized the courts, etc and were willing to make undertakings to sever their links with an unlawful organization, sentences were often deferred or prisoners released on recognisance. In more serious cases, sentences were reduced as cooperative attitudes were taken into account.[20] The government believed that if less committed members could be compelled to openly

16 See D/J 93/2/8, General Observations. 17 During the periods 1939 to 1946 and 1961 to 1962 the special criminal court remained staffed by the officers who had sat on the constitution tribunal. 18 Garda powers were reactivated in a less extreme manner, though initially Stephen Roche proposed empowering members of the force to detain suspects for up to one month. See also G. Hogan and C. Walker, *Political violence and the law in Ireland* (1989), pp 202–5. 19 See tables 6a–i. 20 See D/J D.20/35 and by the register in the Military Archives, Cathal Brugha Barracks, and Hogan and Walker, *Political violence*, p. 260 (note 18).

disavow membership of the IRA, for example, they would be dismissed from the organization. Again, that policy evolved from Garda tactics of the late 1920s. In March 1929, the Garda Commissioner noted, 'All [the IRA] documents that I have read in six years show me that [successfully inducing persons to sign an undertaking] is a sound move. Their leaders have an absolute horror of form signers.'[21] This may appear rather quaint today, but in the 1920s and 1930s it was clearly a matter of some importance.

Further, the sentences imposed by the constitution tribunal, for example, were not severe. Between 1931 and 1937, 34% of IRA members convicted received 6 months or less, 38% 12 months or less, 8% 18 months or less, 5% 2 years or less, 2% 3 years or less, 1% 5 years or less, 1% greater (11% other). While sentences became noticeably stiffer after 1935, of the 13 persons sentenced to more than three years detention during the tribunal's last 3 years, none served his full sentence.

There was a public opinion factor that made the use of emergency powers unpopular, especially after Ireland's experience of English coercion and so soon after the Civil War. The Cumann na nGaedheal and subsequent Fianna Fáil governments must have been conscious that extreme punishments in post Civil War Ireland could have generated sympathy for anti-state organizations. Clearly, there was another aspect to this: W.T. Cosgrave wrote in June 1931, 'generally speaking there is public order'.[22] Similarly, Patrick Ruttledge concluded that 'the history of these six years [1931–6] is not discreditable to the people of this country: that in spite of a lot of strong talk and a good deal of violence here and there, there was, on the whole, little bloodshed.'[23] Ruttledge's comments were despite the department of Justice's observation of late 1940 that many of the most serious offences committed during the political disturbances of 1931–6 went unpunished;[24] only Michael Conway was convicted of murder. However unacceptable the violence of the 1930s was, the IRA and the Blueshirts were not perceived as constituting fundamental threats to the Irish state. Essentially, their capacity to attack the state was limited to desultory incidents – the government could always contain such organizations before the situation became dangerous.

Under a looming threat of European war in 1938 and 1939, civil servants realized that a greater range of problems lay ahead than simply the IRA's activities. Consequently, a new type of legislation was required, which would empower the government to control a wide range of economic and financial activities and essential supplies and services, in addition to secu-

21 P80/856/7. 22 De Valera Papers 1147/10, W.T. Cosgrave to Seán Ó Muirthile, 6 June 1931. 23 D/T S.9472, Ruttledge to de Valera, 23 Oct. 1936. 24 'Departmental Notes', pp xxii–xxiii.

rity issues. It is a testament to the civil servants involved that the doubts surrounding article 28.3.3 were exhaustively examined and removed before the Emergency Powers Bill was enacted. Although the scope of this book prevents a thorough analysis of the extent to which delegated legislation took the place of ordinary legislation or the extent to which the government took control of the economy and restricted the courts during 'the Emergency', clearly these were significant.

The coming of World War II witnessed prompt government action against the IRA. Initial government repression was limited, though. In the months prior to January 1940, 76 persons were interned and fewer than 40 were tried by the special criminal court. But as the security situation deteriorated after Christmas 1939, the special criminal court began imposing increasingly heavy sentences on IRA members, and legal questions relating to internment and other matters were rapidly settled. Most serious of all, Gardaí discovered IRA contacts with Germany and the government became aware of the real prospect of invasion, by far the greatest danger to confront the state since 1922. The government responded ruthlessly. To a point, circumstances resembled those of the Civil War as special military tribunals were devised and operated in an almost wholly summary manner – six persons were executed. Indeed, the language used by government ministers and civil servants also mirrored the Civil War period. In 1946 the minister for Justice, Gerald Boland, described the tribunal established under Emergency Powers (No.41) Order, 1940 as a 'terror court'.[25] When that order was being first considered in May 1940 the department of Justice called for a special court 'best suited to impress and terrify possible offenders', adding that the threat of death should be 'immediate and certain'.[26]

During World War II, the government sought to deny all active IRA members liberty. Although the numbers of IRA members convicted by the special criminal court in either 1940 or 1941 exceeded the figures for any single year when the constitution tribunal operated, ultimately, the government contained the organization by indefinite internment, detaining over 1,100. When convictions were achieved, but releases occurred before the authorities felt it appropriate, prisoners were more often than not interned as soon as they completed their sentences. The uncompromising nature of the government's position was further illustrated by how it dealt with persons charged with serious offences who attempted to evade the law, as the Walsh case demonstrated, when the government made significant temporary changes to the laws of evidence.[27] In addition, two IRA members were

25 Dáil Debates vol. 101 col. 1116, 29 May 1946. 26 D/T S.11649, 27 May 1940, department of Justice minute. 27 *The State (Walsh and Others) v. Lennon* [1942] IR 112.

flogged following conviction for armed robbery.[28] Revealing the effectiveness of government's measures, within three years of the beginning of 'the Emergency', the IRA appeared to have been totally neutralised.

What marked 'the Emergency' and the public safety legislation used between 1939 and 1945 apart from earlier periods was the Dáil's almost complete silence on questions of security, particularly regarding the IRA. While the 'Defence Conference' clearly helped to keep opposition parties abreast of developments, and the Offences against the State contained a range of apparently less severe powers than article 2A, by 1939, it was clear that political opposition to emergency measures had largely waned, indicating that the Offences against the State Act was accepted, if somewhat reluctantly, as a permanent necessity in Ireland. Nevertheless, the use of the Emergency Powers Acts, 1939–1945 in non-security areas was occasionally questioned in the Dáil, and continued reliance on them after May 1945 was severely criticized.

The courts were called on to consider several public safety measures between 1922 and 1942. Undeniably, during war-emergencies the courts could only examine emergency measures in a very restricted way. Although hearing a number of cases concerning the Army (Special Powers) Resolution, the courts took no steps to hinder the state defending itself during the Civil War. While the constitutional situation was radically different, the courts adopted a similar stance when hearing cases under the Emergency Powers Act between 1940 and 1945.

At other, less serious times, the courts showed no reluctance to examine public safety measures. One of the most noteworthy judicial inquiries of the state's security measures in post-Civil War Ireland did not examine public safety legislation per se, but the use of extra-legal methods by the Gardaí in the late 1920s. Unwilling to tolerate illegal Garda arrests and detentions of IRA members, Judge Shannon quickly blocked police activities.

The issues of special powers of arrest and detention were contentious matters in the struggle between the king and parliament before the English civil war of the 1640s. Prior to then, the petition of right obliged the courts to take on good faith that the king had substantial legal grounds for imprisoning persons. For instance, the courts supported his right to arrest and detain 'per speciale mandatum domini Regis' in Darnell's case in 1627. But as the king weakened, the English parliament eventually demanded that special powers of arrest and detention could not be employed unless first granted by an act of parliament. Legal historian R.J. Sharpe noted that the effect of those developments was that the review of emergency detention, for example, 'becomes an exercise in statutory interpretation. Claims for

28 The sentence was not carried out in another case.

wide executive power to detain in the name of public safety continued to be made, but thereafter always under the guise of Parliamentary sanction.'[29]

While the unusual powers and procedures permitted by emergency legislation might appear to have prevented an accused receiving wholly fair treatment, the courts' responsibilities were not to hinder or block the Oireachtas. As Mr Justice Willes explained, 'I utterly repudiate the notion that it is competent to a judge to modify the language of an Act in order to bring it in accordance with his views of what is right or reasonable.'[30] In *The State (McCarthy) v. Lennon and Others*,[31] Mr Justice Fitzgibbon said

> When the legislature has enacted a law, no court has power to disregard the plain provisions of that law because it thinks them unreasonable or unjust. If the language used be reasonably capable of two constructions, one of which would give rise to manifest injustice, the Court is free to, and will in most cases, adopt the other, but when the language or intent is plain, the Court must give effect to it, however unreasonable or unjust the result may appear to the Court to be. It is the right of the legislature to make laws, and the duty of the courts to enforce them.[32]

In *R. (O'Connell) v. the Military Governor of Hare Park Camp*,[33] Mr Justice Mahony explained that the courts were 'a place where justice is judicially administered'. Quoting Lord Justice O'Brien in *R. (Martin) v Mahony*, he explained the courts achieved that by having to observe:

> In all matters of procedure the essentials of justice … [i]t is one of the essential requirements of justice that a charge shall be duly formulated, that an accused person shall have notice of it, and that he should be given an adequate opportunity of defending himself. Such matters are not mere formalities; they are the essential requirements of justice.[34]

Undoubtedly, discounting the four wartime cases of Childers,[35] Johnstone,[36] McGrath,[37] and Walsh,[38] in most of the cases examined in this book (O'Brien,[39] O'Duffy,[40] Bennett,[41] Hughes,[42] Burke[43] and Bruton[44]) the higher courts found for the individual against the state.

29 Sharpe, *Habeas corpus*, pp 93–4. 30 LR 6CP 371. 31 [1936] IR 485. 32 [1936] IR 502. 33 [1924] 2IR 104. 34 [1910] 2IR 695. 35 [1923] 1IR 5. 36 [1923] 2IR 13. 37 *In Re McGrath and Harte*, [1941] IR 68. 38 *The State (Walsh and Others) v. Lennon* [1942] IR 112. 39 *R. (O'Brien) v. Military Governor* NDU, [1924] 1IR 32. 40 *In Re O'Duffy*, [1933] IR 550. 41 *The State (O'Duffy) v. Bennett*, [1935] IR 70. 42 *The State (Hughes) v. Lennon*, [1935] IR 128. 43 *The State (Burke) v. Lennon*, [1940] IR 136. 44 *The Attorney-General v. Bruton*, [1942] ILTSJ 56.

Further, if one considers article 2A, despite government efforts to 'judge-proof' the measure,[45] to place the constitution tribunal outside the higher courts' ambit, to prevent appeal and certiorari, the higher courts made several searching examinations of the measure and insisted they were entitled to exercise limited control over the tribunal. Without doubt several court actions dented the tribunal's awesome reputation and, undeniably, had a significant impact on the government and civil servants when drafting new public safety legislation between 1937 and 1939. The Ryan and McCarthy cases of 1934 and 1935, respectively, revealed the limitations of how far the courts were willing to examine the extraordinary powers of Article 2A, however.[46]

Granted, the courts subjected several public safety measures to rigorous scrutiny. In the O'Brien case, the court insisted that the government fulfil an obligation under article 47 of the Free State constitution. In the Bennett and Hughes cases, the high court ruled that the constitution tribunal was an inferior court and, therefore, demanded that its warrants, orders and sentences show clear jurisdiction. In the final analysis, however, public safety measures were only scrutinised on technical grounds. Except for the Burke case in 1939, there was occasional criticism, but no fundamental confrontation between the judiciary and the legislature. Indeed, Gavan Duffy's December 1939 ruling on internment was essentially overturned by the supreme court within a matter of weeks.

Irrespective of how one appraises these court rulings, their effects were easily rectified by the speedy re-enactment or amendment of offending legislation, or by more careful preparation of summonses, orders, warrants, etc. Indeed, if laws were carefully drafted, were free of ambiguity, and once in operation, the powers permitted were executed clearly and correctly, court challenges to the government's use of public safety measures appeared foredoomed to fail. Surely, civil servants and Gardaí could not have found such basic requirements taxing.

The inclusion of provision for appeal from the convictions and sentences of the special criminal court to the court of criminal appeal in 1939 removed a great deal of criticism of emergency laws and, perhaps, made the higher courts less eager to hostilely inquire into the workings of the special criminal court. It was very much a question, as the criminologist Austin Turk argued, of the government seeking to legitimize special powers by channelling them 'through at least the formal machinery of due process and public accountability'.[47] He further argued, 'That political repression must be justified ... by authoritative declarations to the effect that whatever was

45 See D/T S.4469/17, 28 Sept. 1931, memorandum by Roche. 46 The Ryan and McCarthy cases. 47 A. Turk, *Political criminality: the defiance and defense of authority* (1982), p. 118.

done was "legal" … is usually better understood by higher levels of enforces, especially the judiciary, than by the police, whose tendency is to perceive the "lawyers' talk" as irrelevant nitpicking and obfuscation.'[48]

Although the years 1923 to 1931 marked a period of heavy Oireachtas criticism of emergency laws, by 1939 public safety legislation drew little comment. Given the Irish Free State's victory in 1923, the effective administration of the state by successive governments and the overwhelming democratic support the state enjoyed, especially after Fianna Fáil entered the Dáil in 1927, could the Oireachtas genuinely oppose the use of such powers against the IRA or other groups opposed to the state? The English jurist, A.V. Dicey, wrote 'a law is merely a rule which men are compelled to obey by the power of the State, and coercion is but another name for compulsory obedience to the law, to object to Coercion is to object to law itself, or in effect to the existence of political society.'[49] But that statement will be contrasted with the question posed by the German legal philosopher Carl Friedrich: 'How can one, how must one deal with declared enemies … yet as citizens are entitled to the protection of the Constitution, and more specifically are beneficiaries of its guarantees of basic human rights or civil liberties.'[50] Who can deny that IRA members have been denied a range of constitutional rights, such as the right of trial by jury, the right to silence, etc since 1922? How can a modern democratic state justify treating particular citizens or groups of citizens differently from others when it claims all are equal?

While constitutions may claim all citizens are equal, in practice only those who submit to the constitution, and accept the social, political and economic realities of the state and do not seek to radically alter these through violence will be treated as equals under the law and the constitution. As Eoin O'Duffy argued in July 1931, members of the IRA 'should be [placed] outside the protection of the Constitution, which at the same time they are attacking and sheltering behind … There is no good reason why an organisation making war on the State should be afforded the protection which the State affords its loyal citizens.'[51] In the words of the German jurist Carl Schmitt, 'A democracy demonstrates its political power by knowing how to refuse or keep at bay something foreign and unequal that threatens its [constitutional and political] homogeneity.'[52] He argued, 'Every actual democracy rests on the principle that not only are equals equal but unequals will not be treated equally.' This was true of both

48 Ibid. pp 156–7. 49 A.V. Dicey, *England's case against home rule* (1886), p. 111. 50 C. Friedrich, *The constitutional reason of state* (1957), p. 109. 51 P80/857, 27 July 1931. A similar position was echoed by W.T. Cosgrave in 1924, Dáil Debates vol. 6 col. 46, 10 Jan. 1924. 52 C. Schmitt, *The crisis of parliamentary democracy*, p. 9.

external as well as internal enemies. Indeed, he noted that 'Every state provides … some kind of formula for the declaration of an internal enemy.' In Schmitt's view, 'The endeavour of a normal state consists above all in assuring total peace within the state and its territory. To create tranquillity, security and order and thereby establish the normal situation is a prerequisite for legal norms to be valid.'[53] Those who threaten this are the enemies that states are compelled to neutralize.

Twenty-Six County Ireland, for the most part, was a politically homogenous state. The great majority of citizens deferred to the state, accepted its legitimacy and lived within its legal and constitutional parameters. The only real source of opposition were anti-Treatyites and the IRA, in particular, was the constitutional 'enemy' that Schmitt had described.[54] Anti-Treaty opposition was quickly and effectively contained, however. Within 15 years of the establishment of the Irish Free State, the vast majority of anti-Treatyites had accommodated themselves to the state. Although the Offences against the State Act, 1939 had taken cognisance of a number of criticisms levelled at public safety legislation in Ireland, it seemed that as opposition to the state became ever more insignificant, the use of public safety legislation against the state's enemies attracted less and less criticism. J. Bowyer-Bell argued that

> One of the primary reasons that such gross invasions of civil liberties have been tolerated by the general public is that as long as coercion is directed at the known Republicans, the restrictions are not seen as relevant to Irish society in general, not unfair for use against those dedicated to dismantling the state.[55]

Does this mean that the modern Irish state is any less a democracy? The answer is, invariably, 'no'.

But what of a state that faces well-organised, militarily strong, undefeatable opponents? Questions about the justification of using extraordinary measures become far more complicated. Simply, what should a state do when faced with a violent uprising that has a good chance of overthrowing the government? When is repression simply defence of sovereignty, democracy and the constitution, and when does it become oppression and tyranny or simply the use of extraordinary measures by one political faction within a state attempting to control and suppress another faction? Fortunately for the modern Irish state, these were questions it did not have to confront.

53 C. Schmitt, *The concept of the political* (1996), p. 46. 54 Ibid., p. 26. 55 Bell, *The gun in politics*, p. 228. See also O. Kirchheimer, *The use of legal procedure for political ends* (1961).

Although opposition to the state was minimal, largely ineffectual, and could be speedily contained when the government chose to act, the Irish state was unable to resolve the issue that perpetuated republicanism. As Stephen Roche noted in late 1939, the Irish government had to expect a resurgence of republican activities and violence approximately every ten years.[56]

56 D/J 93/2/9, Roche to the minister for Justice, 8 Dec. 1939.

Tables

Table 1[1]
Number of persons in custody (interned or sentenced by a military tribunal or committee), number released, June 1923 to May 1924

Date	*Number in custody in previous month*	*Number released*
1 June	10,884	n/a
1 July	11,480	284
1 Aug	n/a	427
1 Sep	n/a	521
1 Oct	9,697	944
1 Nov	8,023	1,780
1 Dec	5,494[2]	2,304
1 Jan	1,852	3,574
1 Feb	1,306	539
1 Mar	1,076[3]	248
1 Apr	941[4]	138
1 May	772	143
21 May	618	165

1 D/T S.1369/4. 2 See Dáil Debates vol. 5 col. 1274, by 4 Dec. 1923, number interned 4,955, with 2,647 released since 1 Nov. 1923 (including 714 since the end of the Hunger Strike). 3 Dáil Debates vol. 6 col. 2114, 19 Mar. 1924, breakdown 658 interned, 317 serving sentences imposed by military tribunals. 4 Dáil Debates vol. 6 col. 2736, 2 Apr. 1924. Of which 627 interned; 314 sentenced by Tribunals, this broke down to: sentenced to penal servitude for life: 2; lesser sentences of penal servitude: 262; Imprisonment with hard labour: 36, 2 years' imprisonment: 14.

Table 2
Prosecutions instituted under the Treasonable Offence Act,
1925 – 1925–37.[1]

Year	*No. of prosecutions instituted*	*No. of persons prosecuted*	*Section*	*No. indicted*	*No. convicted*
1925	22	39	1(d)	1	1
			3(d)	2	2
			6	19	10
			7	13	1
			9(1)	4	0
1926	15	32	1(d), 6	17	5
			4	1	1
			6	14	5
1927	6	7	4	1	1
			6	2	0
			7(3)	4	0
1928	4	15	6	3	1
			7	12	0
1929	4	10	6	10	1
1930	Nil	0	Nil	Nil	Nil
1931	3	9	6	2	0
			7(1)	4	3
			7(3)	3	0
1932	1	1	6, 7(3), 9	1	1
1933	Nil	Nil	Nil	Nil	Nil
1934	1	4	3(1)(d)	4	4
1935	1	3	6	3	3
1936	2	22	7(1)	22	21
1937	Nil	Nil	Nil	Nil	Nil

1 74 Dáil Debates col. 1265, 2 Mar. 1939, 74 Dáil Debates col. 1778, 9 Mar. 1939. 2 D/J D.20/35, as far as possible the most serious offence charged (or what appeared to be) is given.

STATISTICS RELATING TO ARTICLE 2a, 1931–37
Persons tried by the constitution (special powers) tribunal.[2]

Table 3a
The IRA – 1931

Offence	*Nolle prosequi*	*Not guilty*	*Defer. no sent. recogn. fine.*[1]	*6 mths or less*	*12 mths or less*	*18 mths or less*	*2 yrs or less*	*3 yrs or less*	*5 yrs or less*	*Greater*	*Total*
Illegal drilling			3								3
Firearms/ammunition			2				1			2	5[2]
Robbery				2							2
Unlawful association		2	3	6			1				12
Account[3]			4	3	1						8
Perjury		2	5								7
No charge	1										1
TOTAL	1	4	17	11	1	0	2	0	0	2	38

Table 3b
The IRA – 1932[4]

Offence	*Nolle prosequi*	*Not guilty*	*Defer. no sent. recogn. fine.*	*6 mths or less*	*12 mths or less*	*18 mths or less*	*2 yrs or less*	*3 yrs or less*	*5 yrs or less*	*Greater*	*Total*
Sedition			1[5]								1
Unlawful association		1	5	3			1				10
Account			1								1
Firearms		1	7								8
No charge	1										1
TOTAL	1	2	14	3	0	0	1	0	0	0	21

1 That is deferment, no sentence, recognisance or a fine. 2 Includes three men who entered the house of Michael Kelly, Caherbriseaun, Galway 16 Nov. 1931, dressed as detectives and claiming to be searching for firearms. Kelly, a farmer, had withdrawn £200 from the bank the previous day, was held up along with the other occupants of the house by the men who fired shots to intimidate the household. Charged with illegal possession of firearms, not robbery. 3 Includes failure to give name and/ or address, failure to account for movements, or failure to disclose information relating to the commission of an offence. 4 Includes two cases adjourned from 1931 i.e. P. Mooney and Caffery. Figures include three members of Cumann na mBan tried, of which two were convicted and one acquitted. 5 Fine.

Table 3c
The IRA – 1933

Offence	*Nolle prosequi*	*Not guilty*	*Defer. no sent. recogn. fine.*	*6 mths or less*	*12 mths or less*	*18 mths or less*	*2 yrs or less*	*3 yrs or less*	*5 yrs or less*	*Greater*	*Total*
Robbery				6							6
Riot/unlawful assembly			2[6]	12							14
Assault					1						1
Firearms			4[7]	8	1						13
TOTAL	0	0	6	26	2	0	0	0	0	0	34

Table 3d
The IRA – 1934

Offence	*Nolle prosequi*	*Not guilty*	*Defer. no sent. recogn. fine.*	*6 mths or less*	*12 mths or less*	*18 mths or less*	*2 yrs or less*	*3 yrs or less*	*5 yrs or less*	*Greater*	*Total*
Firearms/ammunition		3		7	10	1		1	1		23
Explosives		1						1	1		3
Account				16							16
Obstruction of Gardaí		7		4	1						12
Assault		2		1	8	1					12
Riot/unlawful assembly				15	2						17
Shooting/intent						4					4
Contempt				1							1
Robbery		1		2	4	4	2				13
Attempted murder					1	1		1			3
Malicious damage					3						3
Illegal court martial				2	4						6
TOTAL	0	14	0	48	33	11	2	3	2	0	113

6 Released on account of their youth. 7 Two released on account of their youth.

Table 3e
The IRA – 1935

Offence	*Nolle prosequi*	*Not guilty*	*Defer. no sent. recogn. fine.*	*6 mths or less*	*12 mths or less*	*18 mths or less*	*2 yrs or less*	*3 yrs or less*	*5 yrs or less*	*Greater*	*Total*
Firearms/ammunition		4	2	3	12	9	9				39
Unlawful association	4	4	1	3	18						30
Account				23	3						26
Riot/unlawful assembly		2			4		3				9
Sedition	3				1	1					5
Arson							1				1
Contempt				1	1						2
Assault on a Garda								6	1		7
False imprisonment					2	1					3
Murder		5									5
Attempted murder									1	1	2
Conspiracy to assault		1			1						2
Larceny					2		1				3
No charge	5										5
TOTAL	12	16	3	30	44	11	14	6	2	1	139

Table 3f
The IRA – 1936

Offence	*Nolle prosequi*	*Not guilty*	*Defer. no sent. recogn. fine.*	*6 mths or less*	*12 mths or less*	*18 mths or less*	*2 yrs or less*	*3 yrs or less*	*5 yrs or less*	*Greater*	*Total*
Unlawful association	3	4	3	7	48	4	1	1			71
Firearms/ammunition					4	3	2				9
Account		2		19							21
Drilling					23						23
Threatening to murder								1			1
Murder										1	1
No charge	1										1
TOTAL	4	6	3	26	75	7	3	2	0	1	127

Table 3g
The IRA – 1937

Offence	*Nolle prosequi*	*Not guilty*	*Defer. no sent. recogn. fine.*	*6 mths or less*	*12 mths or less*	*18 mths or less*	*2 yrs or less*	*3 yrs or less*	*5 yrs or less*	*Greater*	*Total*
Firearms			3			3			1		7
Unlawful association	1										1
Riot/unlawful assembly					3						3
TOTAL	1	0	3	0	3	3	0	0	1	0	11[8]

Table 3h
The IRA – Total, 1931–7

Offence	*Nolle prosequi*	*Not guilty*	*Defer. no sent. recogn. fine.*	*6 mths or less*	*12 mths or less*	*18 mths or less*	*2 yrs or less*	*3 yrs or less*	*5 yrs or less*	*Greater*	*Total*
Firearms		8	18	18	27	16	12	1	2	2	104
Explosives		1						1	1		3
Unlawful association	8	11	12	19	66	4	3	1			124
Riot/unlawful assembly		2	2	27	9		3				43
Account		2	5	61	4						71
Contempt				2	1						3
Murder		5								1	6
Illegal drilling			3		23						26
Perjury		2	5								7
Robbery		1		10	6	4	3				24
Sedition	3		1		1	1					6
Assault[9]		3		1	10	1					15
Obstruction of the Gardaí		7		4	1						12
Shooting/intent						4					4
Attempted murder					1	1		1	1	1	5
Malicious damage					3						3
Illegal court-martial				2	4						6
Arson							1				1
Assault on Garda								6	1		7
False imprisonment					2	1					3
Threatening to murder								1			1
No charges	8										8
TOTAL	19	42	46	144	158	32	22	11	5	4	483

8 John Harnett was charged on 31 Dec. 1936 and convicted on 1 Jan. 1937. 9 Includes conspiracy to commit assault.

The Blueshirts

Table 3i
The Blueshirts – 1933[10]

Offence	*Nolle prosequi*	*Not guilty*	*Defer. no sent. recogn. fine.*	*6 mths or less*	*12 mths or less*	*18 mths or less*	*2 yrs or less*	*3 yrs or less*	*5 yrs or less*	*Greater*	*Total*
Unlawful assembly	1	3									4
Unlawful association	9		1								10
Firearms/ammunition		3	3								6
TOTAL	10	6	4	0	0	0	0	0	0	0	20

Table 3j
The Blueshirts – 1934

Offence	*Nolle prosequi*	*Not guilty*	*Defer. no sent. recogn. fine.*	*6 mths or less*	*12 mths or less*	*18 mths or less*	*2 yrs or less*	*3 yrs or less*	*5 yrs or less*	*Greater*	*Total*
Unlawful association		1	3								4
Riot/unlawful assembly		5	20		1						26
Firearms			1	6	3						10
Account			1	5							6
Wires[11]			60	3	8	1					72
Road[12]		22	159[13]	21	42	1					245
Robbery[14]				1	1	1	3				6
Shooting/intent			1		1	1					3
Attempted murder		1		1	2						4
Unlawful imprisonment		1									1
Suborning of Garda							1				1
TOTAL	0	30	245	37	58	4	4	0	0	0	378

10 Consisting of the National Guard, Young Ireland Association and League of Youth. R.J. Cronin was convicted twice. 11 Cutting of telegraph wires as part of sabotage campaign in 1934. 12 Includes the blocking of roads and railway lines. 13 Includes two released on account of their youth. 14 Includes armed assault.

Table 3k
The Blueshirts – 1935[15]

Offence	*Nolle prosequi*	*Not guilty*	*Defer. no sent. recogn. fine.*	*6 mths or less*	*12 mths or less*	*18 mths or less*	*2 yrs or less*	*3 yrs or less*	*5 yrs or less*	*Greater*	*Total*
Firearms/ammunition		3		6	3	1	1	1	5		20
Wires		3	1	3	14	4	2	4			31
Road				1		1	3				5
Unlawful association	4	6	11[16]	1	2						24
Account		1		1							2
Contempt			2	10							12
Arson									1		1
Escape				1							1
TOTAL	4	13	14	23	19	6	6	5	6	0	96

Table 3l
The Blueshirts – Total, 1933–5

Offence	*Nolle prosequi*	*Not guilty*	*Defer. no sent. recogn. fine.*	*6 mths or less*	*12 mths or less*	*18 mths or less*	*2 yrs or less*	*3 yrs or less*	*5 yrs or less*	*Greater*	*Total*
Unlawful association	13	7	15	1	2						38
Firearms/ammunition		6	4	12	6	1	1	1	5		36
Riot/unlawful assembly	1	8	20		1						30
Account		1	1	6							8
Wires		3	61	6	22	5	2	4			103
Road/rail		22	159	22	42	2	3				250
Robbery[17]				1	1	1	3				6
Shooting/intent			1		1	1					3
Attempted murder		1		1	2						4
Unlawful imprisonment		1									1
Suborning of Garda							1				1
Contempt			2	10							12
Arson									1		1
Escape from custody				1							1
TOTAL	14	49	263	60	77	10	10	5	6	0	494

15 Includes 11 persons belonging to L.A.D.A. 16 Fines. 17 Includes assault with intent to rob.

UNATTACHED

Table 3m
Unattached – 1934–7

Offence	*Nolle prosequi*	*Not guilty*	*Defer. no sent. recogn. fine.*	*6 mths or less*	*12 mths or less*	*18 mths or less*	*2 yrs or less*	*3 yrs or less*	*5 yrs or less*	*Greater*	*Total*
Firearms ammunition		6	5	5		3	5				24
Unlawful association	5	2			1	1					9
Unlawful assembly			1								1
Contempt				1							1
Wires						1					1
House-breaking			1	1	1						3
Shooting/intent							1				1
Assault of a Garda							1				1
Account				4							4
No charge	1										1
TOTAL	6	8	7	11	2	5	7	0	0	0	46

STATISTICS RELATING TO BLUESHIRT DISTURBANCES, 1934–5

Table 4a
Outrages: malicious damage to property: cutting of telegraph and telephone wires; blocking of roads; felling of trees

Division	*No. outrages reported*		*No. detections made*		*No. persons arrested*		*Convictions*	
Period	*1*	*2*	*1*	*2*	*1*	*2*	*1*	*2*
Cork[1]	197	87	63	14	192	24	143	10
Limerick	109	8	33	4	100	5	84	2
Tipperary	36	4	14	–	19	–	18	–
Waterford & Kilkenny	145	3	41	1	168	2	155	2
Kerry	–	10	–	2	–	3	–	2
Carlow & Kildare	8	1	1	–	1	–	1	–
Wexford	19	1	5	–	15	–	15	–
Louth & Meath	49	–	26	–	39	–	35	–
Longford & Westmeath	38	–	1	–	2	–	2	–
Clare	1	–	–	–	–	–	–	–
Leix & Offaly	2	–	–	–	–	–	–	–
TOTALS	604	114	184	21	536	34	453	16

Period '1' covers the period 1 July 1934 to 16 January 1935. Period '2' covers the period 16 January 1935 to 31 May 1935. These figures include persons tried by both the district court and the constitution (special powers) tribunal.[2]

1 Gardaí believed that four of the cases committed in the Kanturk area were attributable to the IRA and not Blueshirts. 2 D/J D.28/34, G. Brennan to Stephen Roche, 1 June 1935.

Table 4b
Obstruction of persons collecting rates, land annuities, and other public monies, 1 January 1934–31 December 1934[3]

County or county borough	*No. occasions at scene*	*No. occasions: otherwise*	*No. of occasions persons charged*	*No. persons charged*	*No. persons convicted*	*Remarks*
Louth	1	1	1	1	1	–
Meath	–	17	11	57	48	3 cases pending
Westmeath	–	27	6	9	2	3 cases pending
Longford	–	3	–	–	–	–
Kildare	1	3	1	24	–	1 case pending
Carlow	–	6	1	1	1	–
Offaly	–	3	1	2	–	–
Wexford	1	17	1	7	7	–
Cavan	–	1	–	–	–	–
Waterford Co.	5	18	7	46	4	1 case pending
Waterford City	–	2	–	–	–	–
Kilkenny	–	82	30	160	145	1 case pending
Tipperary	1	29	11	26	21	1 case pending
Cork Co.	2	114	28	174	116	2 cases pending
Cork City	3	3	3	38	18	–
Clare	–	1	–	–	–	–
Limerick	5	78	32	161	129	–
TOTAL	19	405	133	706	492	

Table 4c
Unlawful interference by force with public meetings:
1 January 1934–31 December 1934[4]

County or county borough	*No. of incidents*	*No. of cases where conviction secured*	*No. of persons convicted*	*Remarks*
Louth	1	–	–	–
Meath	1	1	1	–
Wicklow	1	1	5	–
Dublin County	2	2	18	–
Wexford	1	–	–	–
Cork	2	1	3	–
Kerry	1	1	20	–
Clare	3	2	18	–
Waterford City	1	–	–	–
Tipperary	2	1	11	–
Leitrim	1	1	14	–
Mayo	1	–	–	Case pending
TOTALS	17	10	90	

3 Dáil Debates vol. 54 col. 2081–2, 20 Feb. 1935. 4 Dáil Debates vol. 54 col. 2081–2, 20 Feb. 1935.

THE EMERGENCY, 1939–1946

Table 5a
Number of members of an unlawful organization interned in each of the years 1939 to 1945

	1939	*1940*	*1941*	*1942*	*1943*	*1944*	*1945*
January	–	–	6	24	13	2	1
February	–	7	20	7	4	2	–
March	–	7	13	27	18	–	1
April	–	20	16	8	7	1	1
May	–	66	10	7	4	1	–
June	–	427	3	8[a]	9	1	1
July	–	23[b]	19	7	6	3	–
August	–	26[c]	7	15[d]	4	–	–
September	69	15	6	18	1	–	–
October	7	15	13	16[e]	5	1	–
November	–	1	21[f]	21	2	2	–
December	–	27	16	13	3	1	–
Total	76	641	150	171	76	14	4

a Also interned that month Wilhelm Pretz, Werner Martin Unland, Jan Van Loon. b Also interned Edward Byas, Belfast, British Crown Forces. c Prisoners interned in Cork Prison were transferred to the Curragh on 9 and 10 August 1940. d Also interned 14/8/1942, Ernst Weber-Drohl. e Also interned 7/10/1942, Carl Andersen. f Also interned that month Hermann Goertz.

Figures on:	31 Mar 1944	31 Mar 1945
No. 1 Internment Camp	229	104
No. 3 Internment Camp	7	7
Arbour Hill	1	1
St Moibhí's Hospital	1	0
Mountjoy prison	2	3
Total	240	115

All the men in No. 1 internment Camp were members of the IRA; those in No. 3 were aliens i.e. Goertz, Marschner, Unland, Preetz, Van Loon, Anderson and Weber-Drohl; Arbour Hill held O'Reilly, the parachutist; St Móibhí's Hospital held Kenny, a second parachutist who was injured (later transferred to Mountjoy); Mountjoy held Andrews and Eastwood who had been interned for suspected espionage activities. On 30 Mar. 1943 there were 66 internees on parole (i.e. bereavement, illness, tilling of crops etc.), on 30 Mar. 1944 – 27 on parole; on 30 Mar. 1945 – 8 on parole. D/J S.15/46.

Figures do not include females interned, of whom 16 were interned and one released in 1940. Discrepancies occur in these figures, which is probably due to persons being interned on more than one occasion, or being imprisoned and then reinterned, though there is always the possibility of error, administrative or otherwise. List draws on D/T S.10981, 'Departmental Notes', pp 148–199, and a Military Archives Register for 1939. D/J S.15/46 gives these figures (which may include female internees) as 1939: 75; 1940: 669; 1941: 152; 1942: 191; 1943: 86; 1944: 19: 1945: 4.

Table 5b
Number of interned members of an unlawful organization released between 1939 and 1945.

	1939	*1940*	*1941*	*1942*	*1943*	*1944*	*1945*
January	–	–	36	4	3[a]	27	2
February	–	–	35[b]	10[c]	4[d]	34	1
March	–	–	24[e]	13[f]	2	25	1
April	–	2	6	7[g]	8	26	3
May	–	8	12[h]	3	8[i]	18	89
June	–	32	17[j]	9[k]	16[l]	21	12
July	–	64	11	8	34	7	2
August	–	20	9	6	10	3	–
September	4	23	16	2[m]	24[n]	34	–
October	2	7	3[o]	5[p]	113	2	–
November	15	24	4[q]	3	39[28]	4	–
December	55	23[r]	7[s]	4[t]	24	7[u]	–
Total	76	195	180	74	285	208	110

a Michael Quille released for trial by the military court. b Of these, 24 were convicted by the special criminal court (following the burning of prison huts in the Curragh in Dec. 1940). c 6 transferred for trial by the special criminal court (all convicted). d 2 released for trial by the special criminal court (both convicted). e 13 transferred for trial by the special criminal court (all convicted). f 6 transferred to Gárda Custody. g Does not include William Fitzpatrick, died in a bicycle accident, 7 Apr. 1942 while on parole. h 1 convicted by the special criminal court. i 1 convicted by the special criminal court. j 7 convicted by the special criminal court. k 1 convicted by the special criminal court. l 1 convicted by the special criminal court. m 1 transferred to Gárda custody for trial by special criminal court. n 1 convicted by the special criminal court. o 1 released into Gárda custody. p 1 transferred to Gárda custody. q 1 released for trial by the special criminal court. r Does not include B. Casey killed 16 Dec. 1940. s 1 transferred to civil custody. t 1 does not include S. Kilroy died on parole. u 1 transferred to civil custody.

1 Dáil Debates vol. 91 col. 1956, 11 Nov. 1943, reported between 1 June 1943 and 9 Nov. 1943 249 internees had applied for parole, which was granted in 188 cases.

Table 6
Number of members of an unlawful organization convicted of offence against the state and sentenced to imprisonment in each of the years 1939 to 1946.[1]

Year	*Number tried*[2]	*Number charged whose cases involved violence, intimida-tion, membership of an unlawful organization, etc.*[3]	*Number found guilty*	*Members of IRA*[4]	*Numbers convicted but not members of the IRA*	*Transferred to Military custody*	*Number discharged before completion of sentence*
1939	37	33	31	N/A	N/A	N/A	N/A
1940	289	255	268	195	73	161	8
1941	207	168	184	134	50	90	9
1942	145	107	139	61	78	33	23
1943	106	72	97	33	64	76	13
1944	86	16	74	2	72	2	4
1945	94	21	78	4	74	1	21
1946[5]	49	18	43	N/A	N/A	N/A	N/A
TOTAL	1013	690	914	N/A	N/A	N/A	N/A

1 As an indication of the difficulty involved in compiling accurate figures, table 6 shows that even the department of Justice could give three sets of differing numbers over a three month period to the Dáil. The tables below were compiled using what information was available, though do not include information on those acquitted and do not deal with appeals of sentences or convictions; on occasion there are a large proportion of 'unknowns'.

Members of the IRA, sentenced and in detention in Ireland, 1940–45.

UNDER SENTENCE ON 31 MARCH:	S.C.C.	MILITARY COURT	TOTAL
1940	8	0	8
1941	134	1	135
1942	129	1	130
1943	95	4	99
1944	76	4	80
1945	55	4	59

NOTE: PERIOD ENDED 31 Mar. 1944: 9 prisoners convicted of subversive activities were released by order of the government before the expiration of their sentences, 4 were on parole; corresponding number for period ending 31 Mar 1944. was 3 prisoners, 4 were on parole. See 'Department Notes'(2) p. 73, D/J S.15/46, Dáil Debates vol. 91 col. 1699, 9 Nov. 1943. By 2 Apr. 1946, there were 8 held in Portlaoise, and 24 in the Curragh. By 1 June 1948, there were 22 remissions of forfeiture, 18 of these involved IRA members, see department of Justice memorandum, 1 June 1948, D/T S.12433. 2 Figures given by Boland, 11 July 1946, see D/T S.13921. 3 Figures given to Mr McGilligan, Dáil Debates vol. 101 col. 1458–60, 6 June 1946, for the period ended 31 May 1946. This information gives numbers convicted as: 1939: 33; 1940: 257; 1941: 184; 1942: 128; 1943: 97; 1944: 85; 1945: 78; 1946: 43. 4 Figures given by Boland to Deputy Larkin jnr, Dáil Debates vol. 101 col. 1612, 12 June 1946. Compare with figures given in D/J S.15/46, members of the IRA convicted and imprisoned given as 1939: 25; 1940: 198; 1941: 136; 1942: 65; 1943: 33; 1944: 2; 1945: 4. 5 To 31 May 1946.

Table 6a[6]
1939

	6 mths or less	*12 mths or less*	*18 mths or less*	*2 yrs or less*	*3 yrs or less*	*5 yrs or less*	*10 yrs or less*	*14 yrs or less*	*Greater*	*Fine or recogn.*	*Fine and impris.*	*Total*
Unlawful organization	11											11
Firearms/ammunition		1	3	1	3					1		9
Explosives	1	4								1		6
Unlawful assembly										4		4
Incitement of a state officer	1											1
TOTAL	13	5	3	1	3	0	0	0	0	6	0	31

Table 6b
1940

	6 mths or less	*12 mths or less*	*18 mths or less*	*2 yrs or less*	*3 yrs or less*	*5 yrs or less*	*10 yrs or less*	*14 yrs or less*	*Greater*	*Fine or recogn.*	*Fine and impris.*	*Total*
Section 30/52	78									4		82
Documents	3									3		6
Firearms/ammunition	3	1	2	12		13	5	4		6		46
Explosives					1		4					5
Unlawful organization	9	14	7	1						3		34
EP					1	3						4
Unlawful assembly										14		14
Usurpation of a function of government			2	2								4
Common law conspiracy										24		24
Illegal drilling	1	20		1						7		29
Printing documents										1[7]		1
Assault of Garda	1											1
Murder									1[8]			1

6 Source: 'Department Notes' pp 140–142xx, Military Archives Register for period 1939–1945, D/T S.12433, *Irish Times*, and *Irish Press*, 1939–1946. Note 'Firearms' includes prosecutions under section 2 and 15 of the Firearms Act, 1925. 'Explosives' includes possession and placing of explosives. 'Documents' includes Treasonable, seditious and incriminating documents for lesser sentences, and larger sentences deal with the possession of documents prejudicial to the security of the State. 'EPO' deals with offence against the Emergency Powers Orders, and includes such matters as passport violations, wireless telegraphy offence, illegal communication of information, etc. Section 30/52 includes offences under section 30 or section 52 of the Offences against the State Act, 1939. 7 Fine. 8 Penal servitude for life.

	6 mths or less	*12 mths or less*	*18 mths or less*	*2 yrs or less*	*3 yrs or less*	*5 yrs or less*	*10 yrs or less*	*14 yrs or less*	*Greater*	*Fine or recogn.*	*Fine and impris.*	*Total*
Malicious damage	1											1
Obstruction of Gardaí	1		1	1								3
Obstruction of government				2		1						3
Attempted murder							1	3				4
Contempt	1											1
Conspiracy to rob	1			2								3
TOTAL	99	35	12	21	2	17	10	7	1	62	0	266

Table 6c
1941

	6 mths or less	*12 mths or less*	*18 mths or less*	*2 yrs or less*	*3 yrs or less*	*5 yrs or less*	*10 yrs or less*	*14 yrs or less*	*Greater*	*Fine or recogn.*	*Fine and impris.*	*Total*
Unlawful organization	2	25	7	2						3		39
Illegal drilling			1							9		10
Documents	1		2	3			1			1		8
Section 30/52	14											14
Robbery/aggravation				1		1		5				7
Harbouring a fugitive		1	1									2
Firearms/ammunition			5	5	4	6	1	1		4		26
Explosives			1		2	7						10
Shooting/intent								1				1
EPO			1			1						2
Arson		6	8	10	3	6	4					37
Aiding and abetting desertion	1											1
Blackmarket	1		1		1						5	8[9]
Assault[10]	1	1	2									4
Inciting a soldier to sell his arms	1											1
Unknown												13
TOTAL	21	33	29	21	10	21	6	7	0	30	5	183

9 All petrol offences. 10 Includes assaults on Gardaí.

Table 6d
1942

	6 mths or less	*12 mths or less*	*18 mths or less*	*2 yrs or less*	*3 yrs or less*	*5 yrs or less*	*10 yrs or less*	*14 yrs or less*	*Greater*	*Fine or recogn.*	*Fine and impris.*	*Total*
Firearms/ammunition		1	9	1	5	4	5			5		30
Explosives					1							1
Section 30/52	10											10
Documents		8		2						1		11
Usurpation of a function of government						1						1
Wireless							1					1
Unlawful organization	4	1										5
Intimidation										1		1
Malicious damage				2	1							3
EPO				1								1
Armed assault				3		2						5
Demanding with menaces			1									1
Larceny					2	1						3
Attempted murder									2			2
Assisting an internee evade arrest											1	1
Blackmarket	4									4	3	11[11]
Permit violations	1									5		6[12]
Overcharging		1		1								2
Breaking and entering			1	1								2
Assault on a Garda	1											1
Receiving stolen goods				1								1
Unknown												39
TOTAL	20	11	11	12	9	8	6	0	2	16	4	138

11 Includes 6 petrol offences. **12** 6 offences of exporting without permit: six months or less: 1, fine: 1; 4 motorcar offences: four fines.

Table 6e
1943

	6 mths or less	*12 mths or less*	*18 mths or less*	*2 yrs or less*	*3 yrs or less*	*5 yrs or less*	*10 yrs or less*	*14 yrs or less*	*Greater*	*Fine or recogn.*	*Fine and impris.*	*Total*
Firearms/ammunition	2	1	6		3	3	3			2		20
Explosives			1		2							3
Unlawful organization	3		1									4
Unlawful assembly		1								2		3
Documents	3											3
Overcharging	1				1						1	3
Blackmarket		2	1							13		16[13]
Wholesale										3		3
Larceny			2	1			1					4
Section 30/52	2									1		3
Contempt	1											1
Agrarian	16				1							17[14]
Attempted murder									1			1
Unknown												18
TOTAL	28	4	11	1	7	3	4	0	1	21	1	99

Table 6f
1944

	6 mths or less	*12 mths or less*	*18 mths or less*	*2 yrs or less*	*3 yrs or less*	*5 yrs or less*	*10 yrs or less*	*14 yrs or less*	*Greater*	*Fine or recogn.*	*Fine and impris.*	*Total*
Blackmarket	6	1			1					30	8	46[15]
Armed assault		2	3									5
Wholesale			1									1

13 Sugar – 11 fined; petrol – 2: twelve months or less, 1: 18 months or less; clothes – 2 fined.

14 12 illegal ploughing, 4 felling of a wall, 1 shooting cattle.

15

Offence	*Fine*	*Fine and imprisonment*	*6 months or less*	*Greater*	*Recognisance*	*Total*
Clothing	16	1	2			19
Petrol	6			2	1	9
Tea			1			1
Sugar		1	1		4	6
Butter	3	1	2		5	11
TOTAL	25	3	6	2	10	46

	6 mths or less	*12 mths or less*	*18 mths or less*	*2 yrs or less*	*3 yrs or less*	*5 yrs or less*	*10 yrs or less*	*14 yrs or less*	*Greater*	*Fine or recogn.*	*Fine and impris.*	*Total*
Overcharging	1									3	1	5
Explosives								2				2
Kidnap					1	2						3
Section 30/52	1											1
Armed robbery								1				1
Obstruction of justice		1										1
Murder									1			1
Unknown												5
TOTAL	8	4	4	0	2	2	0	3	1	38	9	71

Table 6g
1945

	6 mths or less	*12 mths or less*	*18 mths or less*	*2 yrs or less*	*3 yrs or less*	*5 yrs or less*	*10 yrs or less*	*14 yrs or less*	*Greater*	*Fine or recogn.*	*Fine and impris.*	*Total*
Blackmarket										12	3	15[16]
Overcharging	1	1								1	2	5
Wholesale	1									2		3
Arson			1									1
Riot	3	1	1		1	3						9
Permit violations	1									1		2
Escape from custody					1							1
Larceny		2	1		1							4
Contempt		4										4
Unknown												18
TOTAL	6	8	3	0	3	3	0	0	0	21	5	62

16 Watches: 7 fines; Tea: 1 recognisance, 2 fined; clothing: 1 recognisance, 1 fined; Sugar: 2 fined and imprisoned; Tyres: 1 fined and imprisoned.

Table 6h
1946

	6 mths or less	*12 mths or less*	*18 mths or less*	*2 yrs or less*	*3 yrs or less*	*5 yrs or less*	*10 yrs or less*	*14 yrs or less*	*Greater*	*Fine or recogn.*	*Fine and impris.*	*Total*
Blackmarket	1									12	14	27[17]
Refusal to recognise the court	3											3
Shooting/intent	1											1
Section 30/52	1											1
Sedition	3											3
Murder								1				1
Unlawful organization	4	9										13
Damage to property		1										1
Ammunition		1										1
Unknown												2
TOTAL	13	11	0	0	0	0	0	1	0	12	14	53

Table 6i
Total 1939–1946

	6 mths or less	*12 mths or less*	*18 mths or less*	*2 yrs or less*	*3 yrs or less*	*5 yrs or less*	*10 yrs or less*	*14 yrs or less*	*Greater*	*Fine or recogn.*	*Fine and impris.*	*Total*
Firearms/ammunition	5	5	25	18	15	26	14	5		18		131
Explosives	1	4	2		6	7	4	2		1		27
Unlawful assembly/riot	3	2	1		1	3				20		30
Unlawful organization	33	50	14	3						6		106
Section 30/52	106									5		111
Documents	7	8	2	5			1			6		29
EPO			1	1	1	4	1					8
Illegal drilling	1	20	1	1						16		39
Incitement of state official	2											2
Usurping a function of government			2	2		1						5
Common law conspiracy										24		24
Intimidation/assault of a Garda	5	3	6	3		2				1		20
Murder								1	2			3

17 Gold: recognisance 4, 6 months or less 1, 8 fined, 13 fined and imprisoned; Sugar: 1 fined and imprisoned.

	6 mths or less	*12 mths or less*	*18 mths or less*	*2 yrs or less*	*3 yrs or less*	*5 yrs or less*	*10 yrs or less*	*14 yrs or less*	*Greater*	*Fine or recogn.*	*Fine and impris.*	*Total*
Attempted murder							1	6	1			8
Malicious damage	1	1		2	1							5
Obstruction of Gardaí		1	1	1								3
Obstruction of government				2		1						3
Contempt	5	4										9
Robbery, etc.	1	2	3	5	3	2		7				23
Harbouring a fugitive, or aiding escape		2	1		1					1		5
Arson		6	9	10	3	6	4					38
Blackmarket offence	12	3	2		2					71	33	123
Permit violations	2									6		8
Over-charging	3	1	1		2					4	4	15
Breaking and entering			1	1								2
Agrarian	16				1							17
Wholesaling	1		1							5		7
Kidnap					1	2						3
Obstruction of justice		1										1
Sedition	3											3
Unknown												95
TOTAL	207	113	73	54	37	54	25	21	3	279	37	903

PERSONS CONVICTED BY THE SPECIAL CRIMINAL COURT OF OFFENCE AGAINST THE EMERGENCY POWERS ACTS

Table 7a[1]
Number of persons proceeded against, classification of offence and results of proceedings

Classification of offence	*A*	*B*	*C*	*Total*
Number of persons:				
Proceeded against	42	158	42	242
Convicted	34	141	39	214[2]
Sentence:				
Imprisonment only	31	35	1	67
Imprisonment and fine	1	28	23	52
Fine only	–	57	10	67
Probation	–	12	–	12
Recognizance	2	6	5	13

1 D/T S.13921. 2 In three cases no penalty was imposed.

Table 7b
Length of sentences

Classification of offence	*A*	*B*	*C*	*Total*
Sentence:				
Three months	2	12	13	27
Four months	–	2	8	10
Six months	1	23	–	24
Nine months	1	7	1	9
Twelve months	3	10	–	13
Eighteen months	2	6	–	8
Two years	6	–	1	7
Three years	8	3	1	12
Four years	2	–	–	2
Five years	4	–	–	4
Seven years	3	–	–	3

Table 7c
Amount of fines

Classification of offence	*A*	*B*	*C*	*Total*
Fine:				
£50 and under	–	20	10	30
Over £50 and up to £200	1	30	10	41
Over £200 and up to £500	–	22	8	30
Over £500 and up to £1,000	–	8	2	10
Over £1,000 and up to £4,500	–	5	3	8

Table 7d
Remission of penalties

Class A	*Original sentence*	*Remission granted*
	7 years	2 years 3 months
	5 years	2 years 9 months
	3 years	6 months
	3 years	9 months
	2 years	7 months
	18 months	8 months
	12 months	3 months
	12 months	3 months

Class B	*Original sentence*	*Remission granted*
	3 years	10 months
	18 month	4 months
	9 months and £300 fine.	3 months remitted on payment of additional £300.
	6 months and £500 fine (or a further 6 months in default)	term of imprisonment in default reduced to 3 months on payment of £50
	6 months and £300 fine (or 3 further months in default).	term of imprisonment in default reduced by 6 weeks
	6 months and £200 fine (or 2 months extra in default)	term of imprisonment on default reduced by 5 weeks.
	3 months	6 weeks
	£700	£450
	£400	£200
	£200	£50
	£100	£50
	£20	£10

Class C	*Original sentence and or fine*	*Remission granted*
	3 months and £500 fine	2 months and £450 of fine
	£250	fine wholly remitted
	£200	fine wholly remitted
	£200	fine wholly remitted

Note on the nature of these offence.
Class A consisted of security offence (e.g. possession of wireless transmitting apparatus, landing or disembarking at a place other than an approved seaport or airport, interference with the military or police, unauthorised possession of military information, etc.).

Class B covered cases of contraventions of orders relating to the maintenance of essential supplies and services i.e. price controls and rationing.[3]

Class C covered matters such as unlawful dealings in gold, foreign currency, watches, etc.

3 As the Minister's memorandum on the matter explained, 'Very frequently – particularly as regard Class B – a large number of individual offence of the same kind (e.g., overcharging) were brought against the same person on the same occasion. In these cases all the charges are dealt with as one charge: if the result on every charge was an acquittal the case is treated as an acquittal then the case is treated as an acquittal: if there was one conviction the case is included as one conviction with the penalty imposed, the acquittals being ignored: if there were several convictions the case is included as one conviction and the cumulative penalties are added together (ignoring concurrent sentences of imprisonment) and included as one penalty. A couple of examples of actual cases will serve to illustrate the method that has been followed. Thus, where a person was charged on fourteen separate counts, acquitted on one count, convicted on the other thirteen and sentenced to nine months' imprisonment on each of three counts, six months' imprisonment on each of five counts, and three months' imprisonment on each of two counts, all sentences of imprisonment to run concurrently, and fined £100 on each of the remaining three counts, the case is included as one conviction with a sentence of imprisonment and a fine in Table 1 of the return, as one sentence of nine months' in Table 2 and as one fine of £300 in Table 3.'

Bibliography

PRIMARY SOURCES

National Archives, Bishop Street, Dublin
Department of an Taoiseach: 'S' series.[1]
Department of Justice: 'A', 'B', 'C', 'D', 'H', 'S', '119' series, miscellaneous material from the Security Division, and 93/2 files dealing with individual pieces of legislation.[2]
Office of the Attorney General.[3]
Department of Finance: 'E' and 'F' series.[4]
Department of Foreign Affairs: 'A' and 'S' series.[5]
Minutes of the Provisional Government (1922), executive council (1922–1937), cabinet (1937 onwards), and government (1937 onwards).

Archives Department, University College, Dublin
P4: Papers of Hugh Kennedy.
P7: Papers of Richard Mulcahy.
P24: Papers of Ernest Blythe.
P67: Papers of Seán McEntee.
P80: Papers of Desmond Fitzgerald.

Dún Mhuire, Killiney, Co. Dublin
Papers of Éamon de Valera.

National Library Of Ireland, Dublin
Papers of Desmond Fitzgerald, Thomas Johnson, and Joseph McGarrity.

Military Archives, Cathal Brugha Barracks, Dublin
Department of Defence: 'A', 'S', '2' series, and miscellaneous material relating to the special criminal court and internments in 1939.

Cahir Davitt Papers
Memoir of his time as judge advocate general, 1922–3.[6]

Dáil and Seanad Debates, 1922–1948

1 Department of the Chairman of the Provisional Government, 1922; President of the executive council, 1922–1937; department of an Taoiseach, 1937 onwards. 2 Department of Home Affairs, 1922 to 1924; department of Justice, 1924 onwards. 3 Office of the attorney general, 1922 onwards. 4 Department of Finance, 1922 onwards. 5 Department of External Affairs, 1922 onwards. 6 In the possession of his son.

Newspapers and Periodicals

Irish Times
Irish Press
Irish Independent
Evening Herald
Cork Examiner
Freeman's Journal
The Times
New York Times
San Francisco News
An Phoblacht (1925–1936)
Wolfe Tone Weekly (1937–1939)
The Nation.

SECONDARY SOURCES

Akenson, D.H. and Fallin, J.F., 'The Irish Civil War and the drafting of the Free State Constitution', in *Éire/Ireland* (1970): spring pp 10–26, summer pp 42–93, winter pp 28–70.

Barber, Sotorious A., *On what the constitution means*, Johns Hopkins University Press, Baltimore, MD, 1984.

Blackstone, William, *Commentaries on the laws of England*, Professional Books, Oxford, 1982.

Bonner, D., *Emergency powers in peacetime*, Sweet and Maxwell, London, 1985.

Bowman, John, *De Valera and the Ulster question, 1917–73*, Clarendon, Oxford, 1982.

Bowyer Bell, J., *The secret army: the IRA, 1916–1979*, Poolbeg, Dublin, 1990.

Bowyer Bell, J., *The gun in politics: an analysis of Irish political conflict, 1916–1986*, Transaction, Piscataway, NJ, 1991.

Boyce, G., *Nationalism in Ireland*, Croom Helm, London, 1982.

Brady, Connor, *Guardians of the peace*, Gill and Macmillan, Dublin, 1974.

Brady, Connor, 'Police and government in the Irish Free State, 1922–1933', MA thesis, UCD, 1977.

Campbell, Colm, *Emergency law in Ireland, 1918–1925*, Clarendon, Oxford, 1994.

Casey, J.P., *The office of the attorney general in Ireland*, Institute of Public Administration, Dublin, 1980.

Coogan, Tim Pat, *The IRA*, HarperCollins, London, 1993.

Coogan, Tim Pat, *De Valera: long fellow, long shadow*, Hutchinson, London, 1993.

Cotter, C.P., 'Constitutional democracy and emergency powers legislation', DPhil, Harvard, 1953.

Cronin, M.J., 'The Blueshirts in Ireland: the movement and its members, 1932–5', DPhil, Oxford, 1993.

Cronin, Seán, *The McGarrity papers*, Anvil, Tralee, 1972.

Cronin, Seán, *Irish nationalism: a history of its roots and ideology*, Academy Press, Dublin, 1980.

Cronin, Seán, *Washington's Irish policy, 1916–1986: independence, partition, neutrality*, Anvil, Dublin, 1987.

Curran, J., *The birth of the Irish Free State, 1921–23*, University of Alabama, University, AL, 1980.

Dangerfield, George, *The damnable question: a study in Anglo-Irish relations*, Quartet Books, London, 1976.

De Vere White, T., *Kevin O'Higgins*, Anvil, Tralee, 1986.

Diamond, Stanley, 'The rule of law versus the rule of custom', in Wolff, Robert Paul (ed.), *The rule of law*, Simon and Schuster, New York, 1971.

Dicey, A.V., *England's case against home rule*, John Murray, London, 1886.
Dicey, A.V., *Introduction to the study of the law of the constitution* (10th ed.), Macmillan, London, 1973.
Duker, William F., *A constitutional history of habeas corpus*, Greenwood Press, Westport, CN, 1980.
Dunphy, Richard, *The making of Fianna Fáil power in Ireland, 1923–1948*, Clarendon, Oxford, 1995.
English, Richard, *Radicals and the republic: socialist republicanism in the Irish Free State, 1925–1937*, Clarendon, Oxford, 1994.
Fanning, Ronan, 'The rule of order: Éamon de Valera and the IRA, 1923–1940', in J.P. Carroll and J.A. Murphy (eds), *De Valera and his times*, Cork University Press, Cork, 1983.
Fanning, Ronan, *The Irish department of Finance, 1922–1958*, Institute of Public Administration, Dublin, 1978.
Fanning, Ronan, *Independent Ireland*, Helicon, Dublin, 1983.
Farrell, B., 'A note on the Dáil constitution, 1919', [1969] *Irish Jurist*, 4, pp 127–38.
Farrell, B., 'Legislation of a "revolutionary" assembly: Dáil decrees, 1919–1922', [1975] *Irish Jurist*, p. 120.
Farrell, B., 'The drafting of the Irish Free State constitution', [1970] *Irish Jurist*, pp 115–40 and 343–56, [1971] *Irish Jurist*, pp 111–35 and 345–59.
Farrell, B., *The founding of Dáil Éireann: parliament and nation building*, Gill and Macmillan, Dublin, 1971.
Farrell, B. (ed.), *De Valera's constitution and ours*, Gill and Macmillan, Dublin, 1988.
Farrell, B. (ed.), *The creation of the Dáil* (A volume of essays in the Thomas Davis Lecture Series), Blackwater, Dublin, 1994.
Farrell, M., *The apparatus of repression*, Field Day Pamphlet 11, Derry, 1986.
Finn, John E., *Constitutions in crisis: political violence and the rule of law*, Oxford University Press, New York, 1990.
Fisk, Robert, *In time of war: Ireland, Ulster and the price of neutrality*, Paladin, London, 1985.
Foley, Conor, *Legion of the rearguard: the IRA and the modern Irish state*, Pluto Press, London, 1992.
Forde, M., *Constitutional law of Ireland*, Mercier, Dublin, 1987.
Friedrich, Carl J., *Constitutional reason of state*, Brown University Press, Providence, RI, 1957.
Garvin, Tom, *1922: The birth of Irish democracy*, Gill and Macmillan, Dublin, 1996.
Gaughan, A., *Thomas Johnson, 1872–1963: the first leader of the Labour party in Dáil Éireann*, Kingdom Books, Dublin, 1980.
Gumplowicz, Ludwig, *The outlines of sociology* (translated from German by Frederick W. Moore), American Academy of Political and Social Science, Philadelphia, 1899.
Gurr, T.R., *Rogues, rebels and reformers: a political history of urban crime and conflict*, Sage, Thousand Oaks, CA, 1976.
Hale, Matthew, *The history of the common law of England*, ed. Charles Gray, University of Chicago Press, Chicago, 1971.
Hale, Matthew, *The history of the pleas of the crown*, 2 vols, Professional Books, London, 1972.
Heuston, R.F.V., *Essays in constitutional law*, Stevens, London, 1967.
Hogan, G. and Walker, C., *Political violence and the law in Ireland*, Manchester University Press, Manchester, 1989.

Holdsworth, William, *A history of English Law*, 16 volumes, Sweet and Maxwell, London, 1966.
Hopkinson, Michael, *Green against green: the Irish Civil War*, Gill and MacMillan, Dublin, 1988.
Hurst, James Willard, *The law of treason in the United States: collected essays*, Greenwood Publishing, Westport, CT, 1971.
Kelly, John, *Fundamental rights in the Irish law and constitution* (2nd ed.), Allen Figgis, Dublin, 1967.
Kelly, John, *Constitution of Ireland* (2nd ed.), Jurist Publishing, Dublin, 1984.
Kelly, John, *A short history of western legal theory*, Clarendon, Oxford, 1992.
Kelly, John, *Constitution of Ireland* (3rd ed.), ed. G. Hogan and G. White, Butterworths, Dublin, 1994.
Keogh, Dermot, 'De Valera, the Catholic Church and the "Red Scare", 1931–2', in J. O'Carroll, and J.A. Murphy (eds), *De Valera and his times*, Cork University Press, Cork, 1983.
Keogh, Dermot, 'The Irish constitutional revolution: an analysis of the making of the constitution', in Litton, Frank (ed.), *The constitution of Ireland, 1937–1987*, Institute of Public Administration, Dublin, 1988.
Keogh, Dermot, *20th century Ireland: nation and state*, Gill and Macmillan, Dublin, 1994.
Kirchheimer, Otto, and Neumann, Franz, *Social democracy and the rule of law* (translated from German by K. Tribe and L. Tanner), Allen and Unwin, London, 1987.
Kohn, Leo, *The constitution of the Irish Free State*, Allen and Unwin, London, 1932.
Kotsonouris, Mary, *Retreat from revolution: the Dáil courts, 1920–24*, Irish Academic Press, Dublin, 1994.
Lee, J.J., *Ireland, 1912–1985: politics and society*, Cambridge University Press, Cambridge, 1988.
Lee, J.J., 'The significance of the First Dáil', in B. Farrell (ed.), *The creation of the Dáil* (A volume of essays in the Thomas Davis Lecture Series), Blackwater, Dublin, 1994.
Lomas, O., 'The executive and the anti-terrorist law of 1939,' [1980] *Public Law*, pp 16–33.
MacArdle, D., *The Irish Republic*, Corgi, London, 1968.
McEldowney, John F., 'The Case of *The Queen v. McKenna (1869)* and jury packing in Ireland', [1977] *Irish Jurist*, pp 339–54.
MacEoin, Uinseann (ed.), *Survivors*, Argenta, Dublin, 1980.
MacEoin, Uinseann (ed.), *The IRA in the twilight years, 1923–1948*, Argenta, Dublin, 1997.
McMahon, D., *Republicans and imperialists: Anglo-Irish relations in the 1930s*, Yale University Press, New Haven, 1984.
Manning, M., *The Blueshirts* (2nd ed.), Gill and Macmillan, Dublin, 1987.
Mitchell, Arthur, *Revolutionary government in Ireland: Dáil Éireann, 1919–22*, Gill and Macmillan, Dublin, 1995.
Milotte, M., *Communism in Ireland: the pursuit of the workers' republic since 1916*, Gill and Macmillan, Dublin, 1984.
Moynihan, M. (ed.), *Speeches and statements by Éamon de Valera, 1917–73*, Gill and Macmillan, Dublin, 1980.
Mulloy, E., *Dynasties of coercion*, Field Day Pamphlet 10, Derry, 1986.
Ó Broin, Leon, *Revolutionary underground: the story of the Irish Republican Brotherhood, 1858–1924*, Gill and Macmillan, Dublin, 1976.
O'Donnell, Peadar, *The gates flew open*, Jonathan Cape, London, 1932.
O'Donnell, Peadar, *There will be another day*, Dolmen, Dublin, 1963.

Ó Drisceoil, Dónal, *Censorship in Ireland, 1939–45: neutrality, politics and society*, Cork University Press, Cork, 1996.

O'Halpin, Eunan, 'Intelligence and security in Ireland, 1922–45', in *Intelligence and National Security*, 5:1, 1990, pp 50–83.

O'Halpin, Eunan, 'Army, politics and society in independent Ireland, 1923–1945', in T.G. Fraser and Keith Jeffrey (eds), *Men, women and the war*, Lilliput Press, Dublin, 1993.

O'Halpin, Eunan, 'Aspects of intelligence', in *Irish Sword*, [1993–5], pp 56–65.

Ó Síocháin, P.A., *The criminal law of Ireland (outlined)* (3rd ed.), Thom, Dublin, 1952.

O'Sullivan, Dónal, *The Irish Free State and its Senate*, Faber and Faber, London, 1940.

Prager, G., *Building democracy in Ireland: political order and cultural integration in a newly independent nation*, Cambridge University Press, Cambridge, 1986.

Rossiter, Clinton, *Constitutional dictatorship*, Greenwood Press, Wesport, CT, 1979.

Rubin, G.R., 'The royal prerogative or a statutory code? The war office and contingency legal planning, 1885–1914', in R. Eales and D. Sullivan (eds), *The political context of law*, Hambledon Press, London, 1986.

Sandes, R.L., *Criminal practice, procedure and evidence in the Irish Free State*, Thom, Dublin, 1930.

Salmon, Trevor C., *Unneutral Ireland: an ambivalent and unique security policy*, Clarendon, Oxford, 1989.

Schmitt, Carl, *The crisis of parliamentary democracy*, MIT Press, Cambridge, Massachusetts, 1985.

Schmitt, Carl, *The concept of the political*, University of Chicago Press, Chicago, 1996.

Sharpe, R.J., *The law of habeas corpus*, Oxford University Press, Oxford, 1989.

Simpson, Brian, *In the highest degree odious: detention without trial in wartime Britain*, Oxford University Press, Oxford, 1992.

Skinner, Quentin, *The foundation of modern political thought*, two volumes, Cambridge University Press, Cambridge, 1978.

Sommerville, Johann P., *Thomas Hobbes: political ideas in historical context*, Macmillan Press, Basingstoke, Hants., 1992.

Tarpey, Marie Veronica, *The role of Joseph McGarrity in the struggle for Irish independence*, Arno Press, New York, 1976.

Thornley, David, 'The Blueshirts', in F. MacManus (ed.), *The years of the great test, 1929–39*, Mercier, Cork, 1967.

Tierney, Mark, *Modern Ireland, 1850–1950*, Gill and Macmillan, Dublin, 1972.

Townshend, Charles, *The British campaign in Ireland, 1919–1921: the development of political and military policies*, Oxford University Press, Oxford, 1975.

Townshend, Charles, *Political violence in Ireland: government and resistance since 1848*, Clarendon, Oxford, 1983.

Townshend, Charles, *Making the peace: public order and public security in modern Britain*, Oxford University Press, Oxford, 1993.

Turk, Austin, *Political criminality: the defiance and defense of authority*, Sage, Thousand Oaks, CA, 1982.

Valiulis, M., *Portrait of a revolutionary: General Richard Mulcahy and the foundation of the Irish state*, Irish Academic Press, Dublin, 1992.

Watkins, F.W., *The failure of constitutional emergency powers under the German republic*, Harvard University Press, Cambridge, Massachusetts, 1939.

Index

Table of cases